MYSTICISM AND SACRED SCRIPTURE

Mysticism and Sacred Scripture

Edited by
Steven T. Katz

OXFORD
UNIVERSITY PRESS
2000

OXFORD
UNIVERSITY PRESS

Oxford New York
Athens Auckland Bangkok Bogotá Buenos Aires Calcutta
Cape Town Chennai Dar es Salaam Delhi Florence Hong Kong Istanbul
Karachi Kuala Lumpur Madrid Melbourne Mexico City Mumbai
Nairobi Paris São Paulo Shanghai Singapore Taipei Tokyo Toronto Warsaw

and associated companies in
Berlin Ibadan

Published by Oxford University Press, Inc.
198 Madison Avenue, New York, New York 10016

Library of Congress Cataloging-in-Publication Data
Katz, Steven T., 1944–
Mysticism and sacred scripture / edited by Steven T. Katz.
p. cm.
Includes bibliographical references and index.
ISBN 0-19-509703-3
1. Mysticism. 2. Sacred books. I. Title.
BL625.K37 2000
291.4'22—dc21 99-28187

9 8 7 6 5 4 3 2 1

Printed in the United States of America
on acid-free paper

Contents

Contributors

Peter Awn is dean of the School of General Studies (GS) and professor of Islamic religion and comparative religion in the department of religion at Columbia University. He received his Ph.D. in Islamic religion and comparative religion from Harvard University in 1978. Previously, he earned degrees in philosophy, classical languages, and Christian theology. In addition to his work at Columbia, he has been visiting professor of religion at Princeton University. His *Satan's Tragedy and Redemption: Iblīs in Sufi Psychology* received a book award from the American Council of Learned Societies. In 1995, Awn received the Great Teacher Award from the Society of Columbia Graduates. He has also received numerous grants, including a Fulbright, and several grants from the National Endowment for the Humanities.

Shlomo Biderman received his B.A., M.A., and Ph.D. degrees from Tel Aviv University. Between 1992 and 1996 he was head of the Porter School of Cultural Studies at Tel Aviv University and since 1995 chairman of its philosophy department. Among his many publications are three books in Hebrew—*Indian Philosophy* (1980), *Early Buddhism* (1995), and *Mahayana Buddhism* (1998). He has also published *Knowledge and Scripture: An Essay in Religious Epistemology* in English (1995) and edits a yearbook published by E. J. Brill entitled *Philosophy and Religion.*

William C. Chittick teaches religious studies in the department of comparative studies at the State University of New York at Stony Brook. He has published numerous articles on Islamic thought and Sufism. His books include *A Shi'ite Anthology* (1981); *The Sufi Path of Love: The Spiritual Teachings of Rumi* (1983); *al-Sahīfat al-sajjādiyya: The Psalms of Islam* (1988); *Faith and Practice of Islam: Three Thirteenth-Century Sufi Texts* (1992); *The Self-Disclosure of God: Principles of Ibn al-ʿArabī's Cosmology* (1988); and, with his wife, Sachiko Murata, *The Vision of Islam* (1994).

Ewert Cousins is a specialist in early Franciscan mysticism and theology. He has written *Bonaventure and the Coincidence of Opposites* (1978) and *Christ of the 21st Century* (1992). He is chief editorial consultant for the sixty-volume series *The Classics of Western Spirituality*, and the translator and editor of the Bonaventure volume in the series *Bonaventure: The Soul's Journey into God, The Tree of Life, The Life of St. Francis* (1978). Involved in the dialogue of world religions, he is a consultant to the Vatican Secretariat for Non-Christians. In contemporary religious thought, he has specialized in Teilhard de Chardin and process theology and edited *Process Theology* and *Hope and the Future of Man*. He is the director of the graduate program in spirituality at Fordham University and a visiting professor at Columbia University.

Michael Fishbane is the Nathan Cummings Professor of Jewish Studies and chair of the committee of Jewish studies at the University of Chicago. He is the author or editor of many books. Among these, his *Biblical Interpretation in Ancient Israel* (1985) and *The Kiss of God: Death and Dying in Jewish Spirituality* (1994) won the National Jewish Book Award, among other prizes. His most recent book is *The Exegetical Imagination: On Jewish Thought and Theology* (1998). He has been a Guggenheim Fellow and twice a Fellow of the Institute for Advanced Studies at the Hebrew University of Jerusalem. Fishbane is a Fellow of the Academy of Jewish Research.

Daniel Gold is professor of South Asian religions at Cornell University. A specialist in North Indian popular traditions, he has published *The Lord as Guru: Hindi Sants in North Indian Tradition* (1987) and *Comprehending the Guru: Towards a Grammar of Religious Perception* (1988). His more recent work includes articles and book chapters on popular yogic traditions, Hindu nationalism, and problems involved in the study of religion.

Barbara A. Holdrege is associate professor of the comparative history of religions at the University of California, Santa Barbara. Her research has focused on historical and textual studies of Hindu and Jewish traditions, as well as cross-cultural analyses of categories such as scripture, mysticism, myth, and ritual. She is the author of *Veda and Torah: Transcending the Textuality of Scripture* (1996); the editor of a collection of essays, *Ritual and Power* (1990); and author of numerous articles on representations of scripture in the brahmanical tradition and the rabbinic and kabbalistic traditions. She is currently completing *The Mythic Dimensions of Religious Life* and an edited collection, *Purity, Hierarchies, and Boundaries: Case Studies in Hinduisms and Judaisms.*

Moshe Idel is the author of numerous publications on Jewish mysticism, among which the most important are *Kabbalah: New Perspectives* (1988); *The Mystical Experience in Abraham Abulafia* (1988); *Language, Torah, and Hermeneutics in Abraham Abulafia* (1989); *Hasidism: Between Ecstasy and Magic* (1995); and *Messianic Mystics* (1998). He has also edited, with Bernard McGinn, *Mystical Union and Monotheistic Faith, An Ecumenical Dialogue* (1989). He has published several dozen articles in Hebrew, French, and English. He is professor of Jewish mysticism at the Hebrew University, Jerusalem, and has been a visiting professor at Harvard University and at the Jewish Theological Seminary of America.

Steven T. Katz, in addition to editing this volume, has edited *Mysticism and Philosophical Analysis* (1978), *Mysticism and Religious Traditions* (1983), and *Mysticism* *and Language* (1992). He is also the author of *Post-Holocaust Dialogues: Studies in Modern Jewish Thought* (1983); *Historicism, the Holocaust, and Zionism* (1992); and the multivolume *Holocaust in Historical Context*, volume 1 of which appeared in 1994; volume 2 is in press. He is a member of the editorial team for the *Cambridge History of Judaism* and the *History of Nineteenth Century Religious Thought* and is the editor of the journal *Modern Judaism*. He has been awarded the Lucas Prize by the University of Tübingen for 1999. At present, he is director of the Center for Judaic Studies at Boston University.

Livia Kohn is professor of religion and East Asian studies at Boston University; adjunct professor of Chinese Studies at Eotvos Lorand University in Budapest; and visiting professor of Japanese religion at the Stanford Center for Technology and Innovation in Kyoto, Japan. Her main area of specialization is medieval Chinese Taoism, on which she has published widely. Her major works include *Taoist Meditation and Longevity Techniques* (1989), *Early Chinese Mysticism* (1992), *The Taoist Experience* (1993), *Laughing at the Tao* (1995), and *Lao-tzu and the Tao-te-ching* (1998).

Arvind Sharma received his early education in India, where he also served in Gujarat as an I.A.S. officer. He subsequently resumed higher studies in the United States and turned to religious studies after graduating with a degree in economics. He obtained his Ph.D. in Sanskrit and Indian studies, specializing in Hinduism. He began his regular teaching career in Australia at the University of Queensland in Brisbane; he also taught at the University of Sydney before moving to McGill University in Montreal, Canada, where he is currently Birks Professor of Comparative Religion in the faculty of religious studies. He is the author of several books, including *The Hindu Gita: Ancient and Classical Interpretations of the Bhagavadgītā* (1986), *Essays on the Mahābhārata* (1991), *The Experiential Dimension of Advaita Vedānta* (1993), *Hinduism for Our Times* (1996), *The Philosophy of Religion: A Buddhist Perspective* (1996), and the editor of *Our Religions* (1993).

Ninian Smart is the author of numerous books, among which the most important are *Reasons and Faiths* (1958), *Philosophers and Religious Truth* (1964), *Doctrine and Argument in Indian Philosophy* (1964), *The Religious Experience of Mankind* (1976), *The Concept of Worship* (1972), *The Phenomenon of Religion* (1973), *Dimensions of the Sacred* (1996), *Reflections in the Mirror of Religion* (1997), and *World Philosophies* (1998). He has also published several dozen articles and reviews in such leading philosophical and religious journals as *Mind, Philosophical Quarterly, Religion, Religious Studies*, and *Philosophy*. In 1979 and 1980, he gave the Gifford Lectures. He was professor of theology at the University of Birmingham, in England, from 1961 to 1967 and then became the first professor and chairman of the department of religious studies at the University of Lancaster, in England, a post he held from 1967 to 1975. He has also been a visiting professor at Yale University, Harvard University, Princeton University, the University of Wisconsin, and Benares Hindu University. He has recently retired from the J. F. Rowney Professorship of Comparative Religions at the University of California at Santa Barbara. He is presently vice president of the American Academy of Religion and president-elect for the year 2000.

MYSTICISM AND SACRED SCRIPTURE

Editor's Introduction

This volume, dealing with the essential, though often neglected, link between mysticism, mystical experience, and sacred scripture, is the latest result of an ongoing reconsideration of the nature of mysticism and mystical experience in its generality and totality. In 1978, with the collected essays published under the title *Mysticism and Philosophical Analysis*,[1] a basic reevaluation of the nature of mysticism was started, and a new paradigm for its decipherment was proposed. This paradigm, which is most simply described as "contextualist," repudiated the older "essentialist" model, which argued that (a) mystical experience was essentially independent of the sociocultural, historical, and religious context in which it occurred and (b) all mystical experience, at its highest and purest level, was essentially the same. In its methodological and epistemological emphasis on context, this alternative model was intended, as I described it in 1978, to indicate that

> in order to understand mysticism it is *not* just a question of studying the reports of the mystic after the experiential event but of acknowledging that the experience itself as well as the form in which it is reported is shaped by concepts which the mystic brings to, and which shape, his experience. To flesh this out, straightforwardly, what is being argued is that, for example, the Hindu mystic does not have an experience of X which he then describes in the, to him, familiar language and symbols of Hinduism, but rather he has a Hindu experience, i.e., his experience is not an unmediated experience of X but is itself the, at least partially, pre-formed anticipated Hindu experience of Brahman. Again, the Christian mystic does not experience some unidentified reality, which he then conveniently labels God, but rather has the at least partially prefigured Christian experiences of God, or Jesus, or the like. Moreover, as one might have anticipated, it is my view based on what evidence there is, that the Hindu experience of Brahman and the Christian experience of God are not the same. We shall support this contention below. The significance of these considerations is that the forms of consciousness which the mystic brings to

> experience set structured and limiting parameters on what the experience will be, i.e., on what will be experienced, and rule out in advance what is "inexperienceable" in the particular given, concrete, context.[2]

To begin to develop and extend the myriad implications of this epistemological argument, a second group of original essays was collected and published in 1983 under the title *Mysticism and Religious Traditions*.[3] There the emphasis was primarily on the way in which mystics emerge out of the larger religious community of which they are a part and how, in turn, they relate to this original community—that is, how they influence it and, in turn, are influenced by it in a fluid and ongoing dialectic. The following issues were considered: the role of teachers and gurus; the nature of discipleship; the character of religious and, in a more narrow sense, mystical communities; questions related to the passing on and reworking of oral and textual traditions; the nature and functions of meditation; the influence of personal "models" in religious and mystical communities; the role of worldviews and ontologies in mystical teachings and experiences; the investigation of the relationship between mysticism and morality; and the relationship of religious dogma to mystical teaching and experience, among other subjects. Given the general neglect of the historical and sociological dimensions of mystical data and instruction—a neglect due largely to the mistaken epistemological paradigm that asserts that mystics transcend their cultures, social settings, and historical contexts—this second set of essays made an important contribution, the impact of which is becoming clear in the scholarship that has appeared since 1983.

From the outset of this larger project of reconceptualization it was compellingly evident that the unavoidable issues of religious language, of how language works or fails to work in mystical contexts and experience, needed to be reexamined. In fact, this central topic had already received extensive attention in the essays published in *Mysticism and Philosophical Analysis* and in *Mysticism and Religious Traditions*. Yet the analysis of the diverse roles of language in mystical contexts, and the ramifications as studied in these first two collections, only reinforced an awareness that this subject was so crucial to the entire conversation that it required a deeper, closer, more extended consideration. In consequence, a third collection of new essays was commissioned and published in 1992 under the title *Mysticism and Language*.[4] The contributors to this set of essays, a number of whom had participated in the first two collections, provided valuable and learned reflections on a very wide range of matters that bear upon the analysis of the roles of language in mystical settings. These included the role of canonical texts as linguistic creations in mystical education and experience; the transformational character of language in mystical contexts, as is intended, for example, in a Zen koan or in a Hindu mantra; the propositional and referential employment of words in mystical teachings and writings; the nature and function of *dhikr* ("recollection" of the Divine names) in Sufism; the role of alphabets and lexicons based on a belief in the special sacredness of specific languages, for example, Hebrew for kabbalists, Arabic for Muslims, Sanskrit for Hindus; the idea of language as power; the magical and theurgical use of words; the talismanic conception of language—for example, letters as vessels that could capture the divine influx into the world; the language of prayer and the use of prayer as the vehicle of mystical ascent;

philosophical reflections on the literal and nonliteral nature of mystical reports; the role of language in phenomenological cross-cultural comparisons; and many different sorts of reflections on and analyses of what the notion of "ineffability" means in diverse mystical contexts. Indeed, in their richness and diversity the contributions to this volume more than confirm its initiating premise: the study of mysticism and the study of language cannot be separated.

These investigations of mystical language also made it still more evident that not only did mystics inescapably employ language in a host of remarkable and essential ways but also their language and the ways in which they used it were inseparably related to the world's major religious scriptures and their interpretation. The teachings of Jewish mysticism and of individual kabbalists were unintelligible outside of the Tanach and later rabbinical commentaries thereon;[5] Christian mystics drew deeply from and were fundamentally shaped by the new Testament story and its many forms of reading and rereading; Sufism was a Qur'ān-intoxicated mystical form; Hindu teachers and teachings were incomprehensible apart from the Vedas and Bhagavad Gītā; and even in Buddhism scripture played an important role. This being so, that is, given the richness of this internal dialogue among mystics, mystical traditions, and canonical scriptures—and recognizing that these repercussive connections had been little studied—it was felt that a symposium dedicated to this subject would be both timely and appropriate. Hence the present collection of essays.

Here I should repeat, in a slightly emended form, what I wrote in my editor's introduction to one of the earlier collections: in the essays prepared for this collection, the issues have been analyzed with a particularly acute methodological acumen. All the contributors have recognized and helped us recognize that to approach these substantive and theoretical matters properly, one must know a good deal about specific religious traditions and communities, as well as about particular mystical authors and groups. Without such knowledge one might generate theories that are ingenious, but scarcely related to the evidence and therefore flimsy when subjected to serious technical analysis. Many of the best-known accounts of mysticism are indeed the product of a priori metaphysical and theological requirements, and not the result of any close encounter with the mystical sources of the world's religions. Such presentations, whatever their appearance, are independent of the data and brook no contradiction. They are proclaimed to be "true" no matter what the details of scholarly research reveal. Rejecting this dogmatic approach as out of place in the serious academic study of mysticism, the contributors to this volume have attempted, on the contrary, to fully engage the texts and traditions of the world's religious and mystical communities. Moreover, and especially, our contributors offer the results of their work as, at least in theory, possibly discomfirmable—that is, they are open to scrutiny and scholarly discussion: they argue from the texts and traditions and allow others to consider these same materials and to respond. There is no wish to offer new dogmas in place of the old.[6]

It is my special pleasure, as editor, to thank those who have helped produce this work. First, I would like to thank the contributors for their essays. Each was a pleasure to work with, and together we have produced a distinguished volume. Second, I would once again like to thank Cynthia Read, my longtime editor at Oxford University Press. Her personal concern, intelligent advice, and enormous patience have made this book possible, and better than it would otherwise have been. Finally, and as always, I would like to thank my children and my wife, Rebecca, for allowing me the time and space that serious scholarship requires.

Steven T. Katz

NOTES

1. Steven T. Katz (ed.), *Mysticism and Philosophical Analysis* (New York, 1978).
2. Steven T. Katz "Language, Epistemology and Mysticism," in Katz, *Mysticism and Philosophical Analysis*, pp. 26–27.
3. Steven T. Katz (ed.), *Mysticism and Religious Traditions* (New York, 1983).
4. Steven T. Katz (ed.), *Mysticism and Language* (New York, 1992).
5. Tanach is an acronym formed from the first letters of the three parts of the Hebrew Bible—Torah (the five books of Moses), Neviim (the prophets), and Ketuvim (writings such as the Song of Songs).
6. "Editor's Introduction," in *Mysticism and Religious Traditions*, p. ix.

1

Mysticism and the Interpretation of Sacred Scripture

STEVEN T. KATZ

A Review of the Extant Literature

A review of the extant scholarly literature on mysticism—which ranges from William James's classic, pioneering work at the beginning of the twentieth century, through the studies of Evelyn Underhill, Rufus Jones, Baron Von Hugel, and Rufus Jones, to the near-contemporary and contemporary investigations of Walter T. Stace, R. C. Zaehner, Frits Staal, Ninian Smart, Nelson Pike, William Wainwright, Huston Smith, and Wayne Proudfoot (to name only the more prominent figures)—would reveal a nearly uniform neglect of the significance of sacred scriptures in the descriptive studies and the analytic discussions of these works. This neglect is in no way surprising, given the general conceptual and interpretive tendencies that have governed the study of this subject. That is, mysticism—and, more especially, mystical experience—has been, and in many quarters still is, presented as an essentially individualistic, acultural, ahistorical, asocial, acontextual, anomian (if not primarily antinomian) phenomenon. As such, its decisive characteristics are said to be its individuality, its spontaneity, and its transcending of prevailing cultural, intellectual, social, and theological norms and influences, whatever they happen to be. Accordingly, Hindu mystics are said to transcend the Hindu context, just as Jewish, Christian, Muslim, and Buddhist adepts, and those emerging from still other religious traditions and communities, are said to transcend theirs. Among the normative cultural and religious realia that are disregarded in the scholarly analysis of the mystical experience is the prevailing scriptural tradition out of which the mystical personality has emerged. In consequence, Eckhart's, Tauler's, and Suso's thoughts and experiences are understood as being intelligible apart from the New Testament. Shankara's nondualism is dissociated from the Vedas; Abraham Abulafia's and Isaac Luria's teachings are disconnected from the Torah; Ibn

ʿArabī's and Rūmī's theosophical reflections are analyzed independently of the saturating influence of the Qurʾān, with additional "examples" of dissociation being putatively provided by all the major mystical traditions. Of course, many scholars continue to fall back on simplistic explanations of the postexperiential usage by mystics of the particularistic languages of Christianity, Hinduism, Judaism, and Islam, respectively, but this relationship is seen as relevant only in terms of the postexperiential need to find a usable language in which to report their experience.

But this widely held explanatory paradigm, this highly influential and broadly repercussive decipherment, is, at its worst, misleading and conceptually crude, and, at best, deficient, defective, and misrepresentative. The role of scripture, contrary to much scholarly opinion, is essential to the major mystical traditions and to the teachings and experience(s) of their leading representatives. And because it is, I attempt to explain in this essay, consistent with my previously developed contextualist reading of mystical experience and mystical sources,[1] how this seminal connection has functioned during the history of mysticism across traditions and why the failure to appreciate its correct value and inescapable significance leads to a mistaken morphological and phenomenological deconstruction of the relevant literary and experiential data.

The most direct evidence of this deep mystical connection to and inextricable engagement with scripture is the literature produced by the major mystical traditions themselves. This literature is not, as one might infer from scholarly studies on the subject of mysticism, primarily about an independent and individual religious experience but is, rather, more often than not, composed of esoteric commentaries on canonical texts. Without much effort one can identify, in supporting this essential claim, the following major works that have been created by the Jewish, Christian, Muslim, Hindu, and Buddhist mystical traditions.

Jewish Mystical Sources

The mystical compositions of the rabbinic era are based primarily on the elusive passages in the Bible that are connected with the creation of the world (that is, in the book of Genesis), Moses' various theophanies, the vision(s) of Isaiah, the Song of Songs, and the extraordinary vision of the chariot (*merkavah*) in chapter 1 of Ezekiel. Commenting on these passages, the sages of the Mishnah and the Talmud produced the sources on the so-called *heikalot* (palaces) and the *merkavah*, and related material. Included here are the *Heichalot Rabbati*, the *Heichalot Zutarti*, and the *Sefer Heichalot*, all of which contain material on the ascent to the heavenly palaces; the *Shiur Komah*, which develops themes first articulated in the Song of Songs; and the widely influential *Sefer Yezirah*, which is best understood as a commentary on the mechanics of creation (stated all too skimpily in Genesis 1), as is the less well known *Seder Rabba de-Bereshit*. Medieval Kabbalah, beginning with the *Sefer ha-Bahir* and the *Iyyun* circle of Rabbi Isaac the Blind (c. 1160–1235), produced a now lost commentary on the "taamei ha-mitzvot" (the reasons for the commandments of the Torah) and a commentary on *Sefer Yezirah* that was in effect a supercommentary on Genesis. Ezra ben Shlomo of Gerona (d.c. 1245) composed a kabbalistic commentary on the Song of Songs (it was erroneously attributed, in most sources, to Nahmanides); Azriel ben Menachem of Gerona (early thirteenth century), authored *Commentary on the*

Aggadot—that is, in effect, an esoteric commentary on the Torah; and Jacob ben Sheshet (mid-thirteenth century), intended his *Ha-Emunah ve-ha Bitachon* and his *Meshiv Devarim Nekhochim* as kabbalistic exegeses of the Torah. The diverse compositions of Isaac of Acre—especially his *Me'irot Eynayim*; Menachem Recanati's *Ta'amei ha-Mitzvot* and *Commentary on the Torah*; Joseph Gikatilla's *Sha'arei Orah* (and other works); and Joseph of Hamadan's *Sefer Ta'amei ha-Mitzvot*—all belong to the genre of commentary, understood broadly. The greatest of all medieval Jewish centers, in Spain, produced Nahmanides' *Commentary on the Torah*, which, next to Rashi's commentary, was the most influential of all medieval Jewish exegetical works. And above all, the Zohar, the preeminent Jewish mystical work, presented itself in the form of a commentary on the Torah. In turn, a large number of supercommentaries on the Zohar appeared, the most famous and influential of which was written by Moses Cordovero, the great sixteenth-century Kabbalist from Safed. But enough—the quality and quantity of the sources already cited here are such that one need not continue to list major and minor additions to this inventory from the late medieval period, from the school of Lurianic Kabbalah in the sixteenth century, and from the Hasidic community that emerged in the late eighteenth century, in order to conclude that the history of Kabbalah is, in a fundamental and dynamic way, a history of esoteric biblical exegesis.

Christian Mystical Sources

The Christian mystical tradition, developed primarily but not exclusively out of the Pauline corpus—including Paul's own mystical ascent to the "third heaven" (2 Cor. 12:2–4)—the Gospel of John, and the same set of biblical passages that were so influential among the talmudic sages, drawn from Genesis, Exodus, Isaiah, the Song of Songs, and Ezekiel. The patristic era had already seen such seminal and influential works as Basil of Caesarea's (fourth century) *Hexaëmeron*, on the story of creation in Genesis; Gregory of Nyssa's (fourth century) *De Vita Moysis* and his *Homilies on the Song of Songs*; John Chrysostom's (fourth century and early fifth century) *Homilies on Paul's Epistles*; Hilary of Poitiers's (fourth century) *Homilies on Psalms*; Ambrose's (fourth century) *De Abraham* and his *Hexaëmeron*; Origen's vast corpus of biblical commentaries; the Pseudo-Dionysius's (late fifth–early sixth century) comments on the names of God in his *The Divine Names*, and on Moses' ascent in *The Mystical Theology*; and Gregory the Great's (540–604) *Moralia on Job*, *Commentary on 1 Kings*, *Homilies on* Ezekiel, and *Commentary on the Song of Songs*. This commentarial tradition then vigorously continued into the medieval era. The major works that serve simultaneously as the biblical commentaries and building blocks of the great medieval Christian mystical tradition include John Scotus Erigena's two commentaries on John, his *Periphyseon*, and his *Commentary on Genesis*; Bernard of Clairvaux's twelfth-century *Commentary on the Song of Songs* and his *Exposition of Romans*; William of St. Thierry's (twelfth century) *Exposition of the Song of Songs*; John of Ford's (late twelfth–early thirteenth century) *Commentary on the Song of Songs*; Rupert of Duetz's (twelfth century) commentary on Matthew, called *The Glory and Honor of the Son of Man*; and Hugh of St. Victor's (twelfth century) many biblical commentaries, especially those on Noah's ark—*De archa Noe morali* and *De archa Noe mystica*. Other major works include Richard of St. Victor's (twelfth century) *The Mystical Ark*, which deals with various themes in Genesis and other biblical books; Gilbert of Hoyland's (twelfth century) *Commentary on the Song of Songs*; Eckhart's (late twelfth century and early thirteenth century) *Commentaries on Genesis* (as well as on other biblical texts), and his German sermons on biblical themes; many of Johannes Tauler's (fourteenth century) sermons on biblical topics and verses; and Jacob Boehme's early-seventeenth-century *Mysterium Magnum*, which is a commentary on Genesis. Here I do not cite the many lives of Jesus and related works—for example, Julian of Norwich's (fourteenth century) *Showings*; Thomas a. Kempis's *The Imitation of Christ* (fifteenth century); the highly influential sermons of Bernardine of Siena (fifteenth century); the anonymous fifteenth-century *Meditations on the Life of Christ*; or those many treatises that concentrate on the life of Mary. Nor do I introduce the role of the mystical interpretation of the Bible in the religious reform movements and the controversies that occupied so central a place in the history of the late medieval church from the time of Wycliffe to the Reformation.

Sufi Mystical Sources

Among Sufis, the Qur'ān is the work around which all speculation, teaching, and experience revolve, and the experience of the Prophet is the paradigmatic "mystical" moment. Indeed, as Sahl ibn-Adullāh al-Tustarī announced, "All ecstacy is vain if it is not witnessed by the Qur'ān and the Prophetic example."[2] At the same time, Sarrāj emphasized, "Allah most high taught us that Allah's love for the believers, and the believer's love for Allah, lies in following His messenger."[3] In consequence, Sufis, over the centuries, were continuously and consistently preoccupied with the production of commentaries on the Qur'ān. Among the most important writers included in this genre are the following, along with the titles of their classic works: Ja'far al-Ṣādiq (d. 765), *Tafsīr al-*Qur'ān; Muhammed Sahl ibn 'Abdullāh at-Tustarī (d. 896), *Tafsīr al-*Qur'ān; Abu al-Qasim al-Junayd (825–910), *Rasā'il*; Husayn ibn Manṣūr al-Ḥallāj (d. 922), *Kitab al-fawāsīn*, a mystical commentary on sura 27, dealing with Allah's power and majesty; Abū Naṣr Abdullāh bin Ali al-Sarrāj al Ṭusī (d. 988), *Kitāb al-Luma fi't Taṣawwuf*; 'Abdu'r Raḥmān al-Sulamī (d. 1021), *Haqa'iq al-Tafsīr*, an allegorical reading of the Qur'ān; and Ali ibn 'Uthmān al Hujwīrī (d. 1076), *Kashf al-maḥjūb*. Other Sufi writings include Abdullah-i Ansari's (1006–1089) highly influential but uncompleted *Tafsīr*, which eventually led to a significant Persian commentary on the Qur'ān, written by his student Rashīd al-Dīn Maybudī (d. 1126) and known as "The Unveiling of Secrets" (*Kashf al-asrār*); Shihāb al-Dīn Yaḥyā Suhrawardī's (1153–1191) more than fifty works, many of which are allegorical commentaries on the Qur'ān, the most famous of which, *Ḥikmāt al-ishrāq*, provides a critique of Aristotelian philosophy and a plea for unitive mystical experience (based again on sura 24:35); Abu al-Qushayrī' (d. 1072), *al Rasā'ul al Qushayriyya* (explains Qur'ānic terminology and Sufi expressions predicated on this foundation); *Ar-risāla fi ilm al-tassawuf* and *Kitab al mi'rāj* (on Muhammed's mystical ascent, cited in sura 17:1), and a running Sufi commentary on the Qur'ān, entitled *Laṭā' if al-ishārāt* (The subtle Quranic allusions); Abū Ḥāmid Al Ghazzālī (d. 1111), *Mishkāt al Anwār* (The niche of lights), a commentary based largely on sura 24:35, the so-called light verse: "Allah is the light of Heaven and the earth. . . . It is light upon light. Allah guides by His light those whom He wishes; Allah speaks to humanity in similitudes; Allah is knowing with all things"; Ibn ʿArabī's (d. 1240) vast corpus that is continually engaged in commentary and almost always relates itself to the Qur'ān; Ruzbihān Baqlī's (d. 1209) annotated collections of Ḥallāj's teachings, including, especially, his *Shar-i shaṭḥiyāt*, which seeks to gather together and explain the paradoxical comments on Hallaj on the Qur'ān and on other matters and to explain his own gnostic commentary *'Arā'is al-bayān* (The brides of elucidation); 'Abd ar Razzāq al-Kāshānī's (d. 1330) *Tafsīr* (mistakenly attributed to Ibn 'Arabī, al-Kāshānī's teacher, and therefore usually known as *Tafsīr al-Shaykh al-Akbar*); the work of Shādhilī shaykh, Ibn 'Ata' Allah al-Iskandari (d. 1309), *Laṭā'f al-minan*; the gnostic theosophical work of Mullā Ṣadrā (d. 1640); Ismā'il Haqqi's (d. 1715) *Ruḥ al-bayan fi tafsīr al-Qur'ān*; and Shihab al-Din al-Alusi's (d. 1854) *Ruḥ al ma'ani fi tafsīr al-Qur'ān al-'azim wa'l-sab 'al-mathāni*. All of these sources can and should be identified as belonging to a central and unbroken esoteric exegetical tradition.

In addition, the many works that praise Muhammad represent a complementary form of Qur'ānic teaching. Like Christian mystical narratives based on the life of Jesus, and later those on the life and person of Mary, Muhammad's external acts and inherent personal qualities, as revealed in the Qur'ān and hadith, become models for subsequent Sufi hopes and aspirations. So, for example, Bāyazīd Basṭami (d. 874), Rūzbihān Baqli, and Ibn ʿArabī's diverse teachings on the ascent to heaven—as well as their own experiences of ascent—are, in effect, commentaries on Muhammad's *miraj* (sura 17:1).

Hindu Mystical Sources

In the Hindu tradition—with its powerful sense of rootedness in the Vedas, and then the Upaniṣads that are traditionally held to be the concluding section of Vedas, and its authentic manifestation of *Vāk*, the eternal word—commentarial activity, the exegesis of the canonical texts, is an ancient and fundamental endeavor broadly categorized as Mīmāṃṣa and Pūrva Mīmāṃṣa. In turn, Pūrva Mīmāṃṣa is integrally related to the study of grammar (*vyākarana*),[4] and of logic (*nyāya*), two additional disciplines required for the serious study of scripture. Understood as constituting a spiritual discipline, exegetical effort and Vedic study (*svādhyāya*) are means of gaining insight into and ways of accessing the gnostic truths at the core of the original revelation(s). As such, they are intellectual-spiritual procedures of estimable weight that, not surprisingly, have spawned an enormous corpus. One could, and should, count the Rāmāyaṇa, Mahābhārata, and Purāṇas as commentaries on the Vedas and Upaniṣads, in a way that is somewhat analogous to seeing the later books of the Bible as inner-biblical commentaries on the Torah. Beyond these canonical documents one may well begin the summary of the explicitly commentarial literature with the following: Jaimini's work on the Vedas, especially his (Pūrva) Mīmāmsā Sūtras; the shadowy Upavarsa's (circa 100 B.C.E. to 200 B.C.E.) lost Mīmāṃṣa and Brahma Sūtra commentaries; and the commentaries of Sabara, Kumarila, and Prabhakara. Then there is the massive exegetical literature of the Advaitans that began with Gauḍapāda's Kārikās on the Māṇḍūkya Upaniṣad (late seventh century to early eighth century C.E.), and that reached its apotheosis in the many towering works of

Śaṅkara[5] (eighth century C.E.), on nearly all the major canonical texts of the Hindu tradition. Śaṅkara's works came to have authoritative value for the entire later Advaitan (as well as larger Indian) tradition, and this continued in the substantive studies of his four main disciples—Mandana Misra (eighth century), author of the *Brahṁasiddhī*; Padmapāda (eighth century), author of the *Pañcapādika*; Sureśvara (eighth century), author of such commentaries as the *Brahadāraṇyakopaniṣadbhāsya-vārttika* and the *Taittirīyopaniṣadbhāsyavārttika*; and Toṭaka (eighth century), author of the *'Srutisārasamud-dharma*.[6]

As a complement to this consequential Advaitan creativity, the vast tradition of bhakti Vaiṣṇavite commentaries began flowing, in the first instance, from the work of Rāmānuja (eleventh and twelfth centuries C.E.). Rāmānuja was the author of several commentaries on the Vedānta Sūtra, including his well-known *Sribhāṣya*, his *Vedāntadīpa*, and his *Vedāntasāra*, as well as commentaries on the Bhagavad Gītā, and on the Vedas, including his celebrated *Vedārthasamgraha*. Following Rāmānuja's lead, one should recognize the important work of his disciple, Tirukkuruhai Piḷḷān (Kurukeśa), author of a commentary on Nammālvar's Tiruvāymoli, and Viṣṇu Citta's commentary on the Viṣṇu Purāṇa.[7] Two generations after Rāmānuja, and emerging from within the Śri Vaiṣṇava camp, we note Parā'sara Bhaṭṭar's *Visnusahasranāma*.[8] And from this point on, the Vaiṣṇavite tradition continued to produce significant works of basic commentary. Note also the different, but material, perspective represented by Srikantha's eighth-century *Śaiva* commentary on the Brama Sūtra; Madhva's thirteenth-century commentaries on the Vedas, Upaniṣads, Gītā, and the Vaiṣnava-Āgamas, such as his *Brahmasūtrabhāsya*, his *Bṛhadāraṇyaka Upaniṣad Bhāsya*, his *Chāndogya Upaniṣad Bhāsya*, his *Gītābhāsya*, and his *Gītātat Paryanirnaya*; and the commentaries of Sāyana on the Vedas. This listing of significant Hindu mystical commentaries from the medieval era to our own could be extended almost indefinitely, for the exegetical and reflective achievements mentioned are, in fact, a very small segment of the major mystical commentaries produced within this tradition.

Buddhist Mystical Sources

Buddhism, too, has a rich, internally important exegetical tradition. Moving away from the Suttapiṭaka, which is probably the earliest record of the Buddha's teaching and was compiled by the First Buddhist Council at Rājagrha[9] (following the Buddha's death on the testimony of the Buddha's closest disciples), the dharma has continued to grow and to be lived through the channels of commentary and explanation. The different schools of Buddhist interpretation that arose after the Buddha gained *pari-nirvāṇa*—Mahāyāna, Theravāda, Hīnayāna—and the arguments about doctrine that divided them, required theological and logical defenses that were based on construals of the first, unimpeachable layers of accepted teaching. This meant settling on certain understandings, and not others, of the Abhidharmapiṭaka, and then of the Mahāvibhāṣā. Like early Christian debates about the person of Christ, or the meaning of the crucifixion, or the mystery of the Mass, Buddhists argued over, and gave competing explications to, doctrines like dependent origination (*pratitya samutpada*), the denial of selfhood (*anātman*), the nature of the dharma, the character of emptiness (*śūnyatā*), and the meaning of *nirvāṇa*. Given the nature of these disputes, they could be settled only by arguments based in large measure on the exegesis—or what was claimed to be the exegesis—of the accepted canonical writings of the community. In consequence, we have 2,500 years of Buddhist midrash, which began with the sutta, the scriptures that comprise the Pāli canon, and to which were added the documents that comprise the Chinese Tripiṭaka (*Shinsu Daizokyo*) and the Tibetan Tripiṭaka.

On this foundation the *Sarvāstivāda Jñanaprasthāna* and the *Mahāvibhāṣā* were constructed, the latter a commentary on the former, which in turn was a commentary on the *Sutrapiṭaka*. This progressive unfolding continued first with the *Abhidharma-hṛdaya*, and then with the *Abhidharma-kośa*, of the Vasubandhu. Simultaneously, the Theravāda school produced the *Petakopadesa*, the *Nettippakaraṇa*, and the highly influential *Milindapañha*. And these works were followed by the major fifth-century commentaries of Buddhaghosa, which themselves achieved a near-canonical status as *Buddhavacanam* (Buddha works), in certain parts of the Buddhist world—for example, in Sri Lanka. These were followed by the smaller, more manageable works of Buddhadatta—for example, his *Abhidharmāvatāra*—and Anuruddha's *Abhidammatthasaṅgaha*.[10]

Internal, ongoing theological debates and the spread of Buddhism throughout southeast Asia meant the further production of commentaries reflecting, in part, local customs and religious mores. So, for example, in thirteenth-century Japan, both Nichiren and Shinran gave Buddhism original, "local," formulations that subsequently grew into two separate Japanese schools of Buddhism. Earlier, before 100 C.E., the Indian Mahāyāna school had developed a new and repercussive literature on the matter of emptiness. Kajiyama Yūichi describes its development in four stages over a period of roughly one thousand years, as follows:

> (1) the period of formation of the *Sūtra of Perfect Wisdom in 8,000 lines* (*Astasāhasrikā-prajñapāramitā-sūtra*), which is the basic Perfection of Wisdom sūtra (before 100 CE), itself having older and newer layers; (2) the period of enlargement (100–300), during which the basic sūtra was enlarged to form the *Sūtras on Perfect Wisdom in 18,000 lines, 25,000 lines, and 100,000 lines*, prose compositions named after the number of thirty-two-syllable śloka (stanzas) they contain; (3) the period of condensed scriptures in prose and verse (300–500), such as the *Diamond Sūtra* (*Vajracchedikā*) and the *Heart Sūtra* (*Prajñāpāramita-hṛdaya*); (4) the Tantric period (600–1200), in which scriptures were composed under the influence of Tantrism. The most important of these sūtras was translated into Chinese several times, and Hsuan-tsang compiled a six-hundred-volume collection of almost all the Perfection of Wisdom sūtras.[11]

Of course, these strata of comments produced still further responses, and novel initiatives like the Pure Land construal(s). But we need follow this chain no further, except that we should emphasize that Buddhism, like the other major religious-mystical communities, is a community in which sacred scripture and its continuing exploration play an essential role.

This brief review of the extant commentary literature produced within the world's great mystical traditions offers strong evidence that such interpretive activity has been central to these traditions as well as to the larger religious communities of which they are an integral part. I now progress to more intricate hermeneutical matters that help us to comprehend the contents of these esoteric sources.

First Hermeneutical Issues

Before further inquiry—for example, before examining specific examples of how the relationship between sacred scripture and mystical experience (and teaching) has been instantiated, and before considering the many epistemological, methodological, and hermeneutical issues that the analysis of such examples will raise—we should explicitly state one essential precondition of all such relationships: mystics across traditions and cultures have always assumed that the sacred texts of their traditions are authentic centers of divine, transcendental, ultimate truth.[12] As Hugh of Saint Victor describes it, the study of scripture seeks "an understanding of the secrets of God,"[13] nothing less than the "secrets of God," while Hallaj announces, in reflecting on the centrality of the Qur'ān, especially verses 7:1 and 47:19: "fi'l Qur'ān ilm kull shay" (In the Qur'ān is the knowledge of all created things). The sacred texts—that is, the texts taken as sacred—are not just literary compositions but also revelations, the opening up of God's will, or, in nontheistic language, the source, the ground, for the disclosure of what is Ultimate. These texts are not merely human accounts, the product of human imagination, no matter how lofty and sublime they may be. They, and their interpretation—a subject to which we return again and again—are authoritative, the very *Urgrund* for all subsequent theological insights and aspirations. For this reason the definition of the Vedas as *śruti* is "truths that were heard" by *ṛṣi*s (seers) at the beginning of the cycle of creation. And, complementarily, *ṛṣi*s are defined as seers because they "see the truth." In like manner, the mystical quest is, quite literally, the discovery or rediscovery of the mysteries encoded in scripture, the recovery of the superabundant truth and meanings hidden in these primal documents.

Consistent with this, another premise conceives of these specially valued documents—or at least some of them—as being ontologically primitive, that is, as part of the very fabric of reality itself. So the sages of the rabbinic era referred to the Torah as the blueprint of all creation:

> R. Hoshaiah opined: "Then I was beside Him as an *'āmôn*, and I was His delight day after day" (Prov. 8.30). . . . *'Āmôn* is an artisan ("*ûmān*). The Torah declares, "I was the working instrument (*kelî*) of the Holy One, blessed be He." In the normal course of affairs, when a mortal king builds a palace he does not build it by his own skill but by the skill of an architect. Moreover, the architect does not build it out of his head but makes use of plans and tablets in order to know how to make the rooms and the doors. Thus, the Holy One, blessed be He, looked (*hibbît*) into the Torah and created the world. And the Torah declares, "with *re'sîṯ* [E. V. 'In the beginning'] God created" (Gen. 1.1) and re'sîṯ means nothing other than the Torah, as it is said, "The Lord made me *re'sîṯ* [E. V. 'as the beginning'] of His way" (Prov. 8.22).[14]

The text of the Torah was the design by which god "created" the angels "and all the worlds and through which they all subsist." Every word, name, or genealogical list, if properly deciphered, reveals the guiding wisdom by which the Almighty organizes creation. As the *Zohar Chadash* describes it, "There is no difference [in the spiritual significance] between [the list] of captains of Esau and the Ten Commandments for it's all one entity and one structure."[15]

In a different idiom, and as part of an alternative theological Weltanschauung, the *Jaimīnya Upaniṣad Brāhmaṇa* describes the threefold creation of the world from the Vedas as follows:

> Prajāpati indeed conquered this [universe] by means of the threefold Veda (*traya veda*). . . . He reflected, "If the other gods sacrifice thus by means of this Veda they will certainly conquer this conquest that is mine. Well then let me extract the essence (*rasa*) of the threefold Veda." [Saying] "*bhūḥ*," he extracted the essence of the Ṛg-Veda. That became this earth. The essence of it that streamed forth became Agni, fire, the essence of the essence. [Saying] "*bhuvah*," he extracted the essence of the Yajur-Veda. That became the midregions. The essence of it that streamed forth became Vāyu, wind, the essence of the essence. [Saying] "*svaḥ*," he extracted the essence of the Sāma-Veda. That became yonder heaven. The essence of it that streamed forth became Āditya, the sun, the essence of the essence. Now of one syllable (*akṣara*) alone he was not able to extract the essence: Om, of this alone. That became this Vāc.[16]

Compare with this Śaṅkara's description of the Vedas that parallels, in many ways, the midrashic and zoharic notion of the Torah as the blueprint of creation:

> How then is it known that the world arises from the word (*śabda*)? "From direct perception (*pratyakṣa*) and inference (*anumana*)." "Direct perception" denotes *śruti*, the authoritativeness (*pramanya*) of which is due to its independence. "Inference" denotes *smirti*, the authoritativeness of which is due to its dependence on [*śruti*]. These two prove that the creation was preceded by the word. Thus, *śruti* says, "[Saying] *'ete'* ('these') Prajapati brought forth the gods; [saying] *'arsgram'* ('have been poured out') he brought forth human beings; [saying] *'indavah'* ('Soma drops') he brought forth the ancestors; [saying] *'tirah pavitram'* ('through the filter') he brought forth the [Soma] libations; [saying] *'asavah'* ('swift') he brought forth the *stotra*; [saying] *'visivani'* ('all') he brought forth the *śastra*; [saying] *'abhi saubhaga'* ('for the sake of blessings') he brought forth the other beings." And, moreover, elsewhere it says, "with his mind he entered into union with Vac." By these and other [*śruti* texts] it is declared in various places that the creation was preceded by the word. *Smṛti* also says, "In the beginning, divine speech, eternal, without beginning or end, consisting of the Vedas, from which all manifestations are derived, was sent forth by Svayambhu [Brahma]." The "sending forth" of speech is to be understood in the sense of initiating the tradition [of Vedic recitation and learning], since any other kind of "sending forth" [of speech] that is without beginning or end is impossible. Again [*smṛti*] says, "In the beginning Maheśvara formed from the words of the Vedas alone the particular names, activities, and conditions of all [beings]."[17]

The effort to understand scripture is, therefore, not merely a literary or intellectual exercise, but also a highly charged spiritual encounter. For to discern the meaning of the sacred text is to come to know something of God—or Brahman, or Being, or the Ultimate—who reveals Himself or Itself in the text. It is in this sense that Pseudo-Dionysius, despite his radical apophatic theology, acknowledges: "With regard to the secret Deity beyond Being, it is necessary to avoid all speech, that is, every incautious thought beyond what Holy Scriptures divinely reveal to us. For in these sacred texts, the Deity itself manifested that which suited its goodness."[18] And Philo, referring to his own mystical creativity, which he experienced while writing his allegorical commentaries on the Bible, reminisced:

> I feel no shame in describing my own experience, a thing I know from its having occurred numberless times. On occasion, after deciding to follow the standard procedure of writing on philosophical doctrines and knowing precisely the elements of my composition, I have found my understanding sterile and barren and have abandoned my project without result. . . . At other times I have come empty and have suddenly become full, the ideas descending like snow, so that under the impact of divine possession I had been filled with corybantic frenzy and become ignorant of everything, place, people present, myself, what was said, and what was written. For I acquired expression, ideas, an enjoyment of light, sharp-sighted vision, exceedingly distinct clarity of objects, such as might occur through the eyes as the result of the clearest display.[19]

Going still further, a medieval Christian spiritual master describes the "pious probing into the profundities of scripture" as an act of "retrieving Christ the Lord from the depths of the Scriptures."[20] Likewise, Eckhart refers to the central concern of his investigation of scripture—a highly ramified enterprise in which he was irresistibly and continuously engaged—as the experience of "Christ, the truth" in the text.[21] It was in this broad experiential sense that Catholic mystics looked to scripture as "magistra fidei nostrae" (the mistress of our faith). And it is with reference to this same experiential mode that Louis Massignon describes Qur'ānic recitation as an event during which "the heart is called upon to experience a particular creative inference, *taf'il*, [that is], one of those adorable modalizations of the uncreated will, the multiform during realization."[22]

It should also be remembered, given the enormous importance of Neoplatonism for subsequent Jewish, Christian, and Muslim mystical traditions, that the pagan, Neoplatonic doctrine attests to a similar reverence for texts, but now the apposite texts comprise the Platonic corpus. Speusippus (c. 407–339 B.C.E.) already appears to believe Plato was the son of Apollo, and by the beginning of the fourth century B.C.E., Plato's works had achieved a canonical status in the Academy. The philosophical tradition that spans the centuries from Speusippus and Xenocrates (396–314 B.C.E.), to Antiochus of Ascalon (c. 130 B.C.E.–67 B.C.E.) and Philo of Alexandria—and that culminates in Plotinus—treats the Platonic dialogues as scripture. They are assigned the transcendental status of "wisdom" (*sophia*) and are likened to theological (i.e., not only philosophical) sources of authority. On the basis of this normative assumption, for example, Philo is able to make Plato a distinguished student of Moses (through the mediation of Pythagoras[23] and Jeremiah), while Moses is seen as the supreme teacher of middle Platonic doctrine. This assumption also allows the Torah to be read as a Platonic allegory, while Plato can be read as a mystical Jewish midrash. And in a related way, this belief permitted the middle Platonists to define philosophical inquiry as "a striving after wisdom" that produces the religious experience of "the release and turning away of the soul from the body."[24]

In India, too, the exploration of, and involvement with, scripture is a foundational religious experience—so, for example, the recitation of the Vedic mantras constitutes the doorway to ultimate religious experience. In the Hindu metaphysical environment, the essential mystical practice of Vedic recitation depends on the assumed status of the mantras as a form of *śruti*—that is, the mantra is derived from the Vedas, which have the absolute status of transcendental word/truth. For this reason the recitation of the mantra, in effect, repeats the original act of "speaking" and "hearing" that occurred at the beginning of the cosmic cycle, when the *ṛṣis* "heard" the Vedas for the first time. The repetition of the mantra provides a contemporary moment of *śruti*, of revelation and religious experience. Concentration on the sound/syllable *Om* is given primacy due to its status as the "essence" of the Vedas and the sound-form of the Brahman.[25]

If the Qur'ān, the Torah, and the Vedas were not the source of truth, wisdom, and grace, as well as the portals through which one goes to meet the Divine, the Absolute, then the mystics of the great religions of the world would have had no interest in them. Their deep and abiding concern with—their extraordinary immersion in—these texts is rooted precisely in the belief that the texts are transcendental ontic markers of absolute significance. Ibn ʿArabi's Muslim credo states: "The Qur'ān unveils all the knowledges sent down in the scriptures and contains that which is not contained by them. He who has been given the Qur'ān has been given the perfect luminosity (*diya*') which comprises every knowledge."[26] This exalted sentiment can be paralleled in the respective teachings of nearly every major mystical tradition vis-à-vis its particular canonical source. In other words, only if the Qur'ān "unveils all the knowledges" there ever were and will be, and if the Torah is "min ha-shamayim" (from heaven),[27] and if the Vedas "are unlimited and without end"[28] can the great mystical communities built on these scriptural foundations function. To reverse the argument, if these authoritative texts were denied their transcendental status or otherwise rejected, these traditions would collapse. In turn, this argument can and should be broadened and applied to other mystical traditions and to their reliance on, and engagement with, scripture as appropriate. Even in the Zen tradition we find this rebuke: "A bigoted believer in nihilism blasphemes against the sūtras on the ground that literature . . . is unnecessary. . . . You [disciples] should know that it is a serious offense to speak ill of the sūtras, for the consequence is grave indeed."[29] The Zen master knew, relative to the structure of Buddhist teaching and belief, whereof he spoke.

The Pluralism of Scriptural Interpretation

Given these shared presuppositions regarding scripture that are held by mystical practitioners, it now becomes possible—since the governing preconditions and a priori assumptions have been adequately conceptualized and properly contextualized—to take up some of the salient issues that arise from the diverse and fascinating techniques of scriptural exegesis and interpretation that spiritual masters employ. In fact, this becomes immediately necessary for the study of mysticism because mystics, almost always, are not only learned students of scripture but also teachers and seekers who understand their discrete teaching and goal as *an*, if not *the*, authentic reading of (a particular) scripture. Even, or perhaps especially, when they offer apparently radical doctrinal views, they most usually do so in terms that relate their doctrines, no matter how novel,[30] to the canonical source of their tradition. They do this both for purposes of legitimation—that is, in order to justify their seemingly idiosyncratic claims—and because they sincerely believe that the master text that is appealed to has inexhaustible levels of meaning, the innermost layers of which they alone, rather than the "ordinary" believer or rational exegete, are able to plumb. Precisely because the text is God's Word (Logos, *aql*, *śruti*, or Torah), it carries the inherent possibility, even the necessity, of multiple meanings.

This open-endedness, this prospect of interpretive possibilities, engenders such hermeneutical schema as the threefold method of understanding favored by a long and distinguished line of Christian exegetes, one that runs from Jerome and Origen to Eckhart and beyond, and that divides the meanings in scripture into three categories: the theological, the natural, and the moral. As Eckhart described this method in his *Commentary on Exodus*: "Sacred scripture frequently tells a story in such a way that it also contains and suggests mysteries, teaches the natures of things, furnishes and sets in order moral actions."[31] Again, this presumed hermeneutical openness encourages the construction of the "fourfold" method of scriptural interpretation that was employed by patristic and medieval Christian mystics; the similar (though not exactly) kabbalistic theory of the four types of exegesis of the Torah, known by the acronym *PaRDeS*; the traditions of *ta'wil* and *tafsir* among Sufis; and the threefold method of Vedic interpretation that deciphers the text as referring to the *adhiyajña* (sacrificial acts), to the *adhidaiva* (gods), and to the *adhyatma* (self).

This type of conceptual paradigm, this allowance for polysemous readings, also makes room for many schools of mystical (and nonmystical) interpretation. Thus, in the Middle Ages, there were not only differences between Jewish rationalists and kabbalists, but even among kabbalists themselves; there were Neoplatonic, Aristotelian, and other types of interpretation among patristic and medieval Christian mystical (and nonmystical) exegetes; there were not only Sunni and Shia ways, but also distinctively, and diverse, Sufi ways of reading the Qur'ān; there were six *Darsána*s—the competing schools of Vedic teaching—within Hinduism; and the traditionally counted eighteen early schools of Buddhist doctrine. Ibn ʿArabī interestingly explains the grounds of this diversity of meaning within the totality of divine revelation:

> As far as the Word of God is concerned, when it is revealed in the language of a certain people, and when those who speak this language differ as to what God meant by a certain word or group of words, due to the variety of possible meanings of the words, each of them—however differing their interpretations may be—effectively comprises what God meant, provided that the interpretation does not deviate from the accepted meanings of the language in question. God knows all these meanings, and there is none that is not the expression of what he meant to say to this specific person. But if the individual in question deviates from the accepted meanings in the language, then neither understanding nor knowledge has been received. . . . As for him to whom understanding of all the faces of the divine Word has been given, he has received *wisdom and decisive judgment* [Qur'ān 38:20], that is, the faculty of distinguishing among these faces.[32]

Ibn ʿArabī's assumptions about the Qur'ān that justify this interpretational pluralism have parallels in other, non-Sufi, mystical communities that share the premise that because God—or the Ultimate, whatever the Ultimate is—is the author of scripture, every true interpretation of scripture was already intended by Him/It.

At the same time, however, this openness has to be understood correctly: the suggestive flexibility of these mystical interpretive systems is not to be confused with the absence of all limits. And this is true in at least two senses. First, each tradition holds that there are things that the canonical texts do not (and could not) claim and do not (and could not) teach. So, for example, for Jewish kabbalists the Torah cannot have Christological meanings, though it does possess such meanings for the Christian tradition in general and for Christian kabbalists like Pico della Mirandola and

Johannes Reuchlin in particular. Conversely, for Christian kabbalists the Jewish reading of scripture, particularly of the *mitzvot*, is not, and cannot be, correct. This should not be surprising insofar as Judaism and Christianity (mystical and nonmystical) are rooted in alternative systems of legitimation and plausibility. Similarly, Śaṅkara rejects the cardinal teachings of the Buddhists while the Buddhists reject his insistence on the reality of Ātman and Brahman. Second, each mystical tradition recognizes specific texts as canonical, and not others. Jewish mystics authorize the Torah, not the New Testament or the Qur'ān or the Vedas or the works of the Pāli Canon; Christian mystics authorize the Torah and the New Testament, not the Qur'ān or the Vedas or the Pāli Canon. Sufis, following the teachings of the Qur'ān,[33] authorize the Torah, the New Testament, the *Zend Avesta*, and indeed the Qur'ān but give absolute priority and ultimacy to the Qur'ān, while at the same time denying the Vedas and the Pali Canon. Hindus deny the Western scriptural tradition and the Pāli Canon, and they authorize the Vedas and other subordinate Sanskrit texts like the *Brāhmaṇas*. Buddhists reject the various Western scriptures, as well as those of Hinduism. Indeed, insofar as all of these—and other religious communities—are defined by the texts they hold sacred, this process of textual affirmation and negation is one of the essential activities of any such community.

I introduce this recognition of constraints not only to support the notion that mystical interpretation knows limits, but also to reinforce the claim that these limits are connected to orthodox and prescriptive religious axioms and rules that operate within the traditions from which they emerge. Hence while the *Bahir*, the Zohar, and Lurianic texts do creative things with the inherited Torah text, it is only with the Torah text that they do marvelous things. Conversely, Hindus do not pursue their fundamental meditative techniques through the recitation of the Hebrew texts of Genesis or Deuteronomy, because these texts lack, in their view, the gnostic, cosmic power of the Sanskrit scriptures. *Om* cannot be replaced by the Tetragrammaton or by the Greek Jesus Prayer or by the *tahlil* formula "La ilāha illā'llāh'." Likewise, the vast Sufi exegetical tradition that is based on the Arabic of the Qur'ān cannot, for the Sufi, be replicated in any other language. Only the divine speech to the Prophet provides the secure grounds for comprehending Allah's self-disclosure (*tajalli*) and the hermeneutical truths derivative from this ontic origin. Moreover, mystical interpretation must at least generally conform to accepted moral rules—and often mystics set far higher standards. As the Venerable Bede described this relationship, "Tropologice, id est, juxtra moralis intelligentiae regulas"[34] (tropology, which is to say, in accordance with the rules of moral understanding).[35] Then, too, when one provides a reading of a canonical text, despite the legitimate interpretational multiformity recognized above, the original context of the relevant scriptural verses has to be taken into account and "respected" (this is a very broadly interpreted rule). This latter requirement has arisen because scripture was revealed by God and is, therefore, to be assessed as an "ordo divinae dispensationis" (an order based on divine dispensation). In the language of the rabbinic tradition, it is held to be "min ha-shamayim" ([unchanging] teaching from heaven). In the idiom of Hinduism, it is regarded as "the eternal eye of the ancestors, gods, and human beings" (*Manu-Smṛti* 12:94). In the formula of the Qur'ān, it is considered in these terms: "lā tabdīla fī kalimāti Ilah" (the words of Allah do not change) (sura 10:64). Now, even though one immediately recognizes that this requirement is inherently ambiguous, it is not meaningless, and mystics were not, and did not feel themselves, altogether free to treat their sacred scripture as a Rorschach test. And history affirms that they did not.

One further issue must be introduced into this already overly complex, dialectical, hermeneutical circumstance. Contrary to the misunderstanding of the mystical principles of exegesis that, because they claim to center on the "deeper," "spiritual" purport of the text, are usually portrayed as denigrating the literal meaning of the scripture, it is essential to recognize that the mystical interpreter, while searching out the underlying purposes and truths encoded in the canonical sources, generally acknowledges both the objective correctness and the value of the exoteric doctrine entailed in the literal meaning of the authoritative text. Indeed, it is essential that the literal text be given normative value as the direct revelation of God or, à la the Vedas, categorized as *śruti*, so that it can serve as the indubitable basis for all further investigation and interpretation, that is, if other (mystical) hermeneutical possibilities are to exist. Alternatively, to deny the verbatim account is to diminish God's or Being's power of expression—on the original assumption that the text is God's own speech, or *śruti*—and to suggest that He/It does not mean what He/It reveals. Therefore, the literal level, while not the only or final level—and with the full awareness that the term *literal* is in need of much further analysis and that it even, at times, undergoes redefinition, as, for example, in the twelfth book of Augustine's *Confessions* and in Eckhart's "Prologue" to his *Book of the Parables of Genesis*—is always appreciated as a necessarily true level. I note, in addition, that all of the symbolical equivalencies, mathematical letter permutations—as, for example, in *notrakon* and *gematria* and their parallels in Arabic, Chinese, Sanskrit, and Pāli texts—analogical arguments, gnostic and theosophical modes of textual fusion and fission, and other mystical methods of reading and analytic deconstruction and reconstruction depend on the authenticity, integrity, and authority of the literal construction of scripture. All these imaginative forms of mystical interpretation enrich the signification of the literal sources, but they never cancel or alter them.

Most important, though this is not its only material implication, this entails that at least in the main Western mystical traditions and in Buddhism—especially relative to the Buddha's sermons and enlightenment—the historicity of the events reported in the scriptural documents, the historical narrative they tell, is affirmed as having occurred as narrated. Whatever further secrets the historic story alludes to, the historic story is, and must be, accurate as history. So while Rumi and Ibn ʿArabī read the Qur'ān gnostically, they never deny the historicity of Muhammad, his *miraj*, and his revelation. While Abulafia and Moses de Leon read the Torah theosophically, they never question the historicity of the Exodus, the giving of the law to Moses at Sinai, or the wandering in the desert. Neither does Bonaventure or Eckhart, who both adhere to the approach of negative theology initiated by Pseudo-Dionysus, cast a shadow of doubt on the "biographical" tale of Jesus' birth, ministry, death, and resurrection as it is retold in the Gospels. Commenting on John 1:6, Eckhart affirms his belief in the report concerning the relationship of John the Baptist and Jesus—what he refers to as the historical *veritas*—even though his primary interest in this material, as in other New Testament sources, lies in exposing "serum naturalium et earum proprietas" (truths of natural things and their properties). Eckhart may, eventually, take us far into the recesses of his medieval Neoplatonic, scholastic ontology but the whole of his message depends, in the first instance, on the historical validity of John the Baptist and Jesus, and the dialogue said to have occurred between them. Though the object of his exceptional discourse may be to uncover the riches beneath the literal text—"latentia sub figura et superficie sensus litteralis"—to know just where to dig, to explain this specific story and not another, to comment on a given word and not a different one, is inextricably tied to the tale told in John 1:6 and throughout the Gospels, whose authority, sanctity, and legitimacy is the sine qua non for the Meister's entire contemplative project of *Abgeschiedenheit* (detachment from things) and of *Gelassenheit* (abandonment of oneself in God).[36]

Ibn ʿArabī, one of the most radical theosophical reinterpreters in the whole of the Sufi tradition, speaks of Muhammad's prophetic role and the status of the Qurʾān and insists on the following principle:

> He was told: transmit that which has been revealed to you! And he did not stray from the very form of that which had been revealed to him, but rather transmitted to us exactly what had been told to him; for the meanings that descended upon his heart descended in the form of a certain combination of letters, of a certain arrangement of words, of a certain order of verses, of a certain composition of those suras whose totality comprises the Qurʾān. From that moment on God gave the Qurʾān a form. It is that form that the Prophet has shown, such as he himself had contemplated it. . . . If he had changed something, what he brought to us would have been the form of his own understanding, and not the revelation that he had received. It would not be the Qurʾān, as it came to him, that he transmitted to us.[37]

This is a principle we, too, would do well to remember if we wish to comprehend the thought of such towering figures as Ibn ʿArabī, Eckhart, and DeLeon.

A Detailed Analysis of the Forms of Interpretation

I now analyze, in more detail, some of the concrete forms and methods of interpretation that are employed by various mystics and mystical schools across esoteric traditions.

PaRDeS—Four Levels of Scriptural Meaning

I begin with the widely employed technique that is called, by the medieval Jewish mystics, PaRDeS (orchard), an acronym derived from four Hebrew words used to describe four different levels of textual reading: *Peshat* = literal (or "plain"); *Remez* = allegorical; *Derash* = homiletical; *Sod* = mystical. This method has a close, though not an exact, parallel among Christian mystics, who, as characterized in one well-known Latin couplet, held, "Littera gesta docet, quid credas allegoria, moralis quid agas, quo tendas anagogia" (The letter [of scripture] teaches events; allegory, what you should believe; morality teaches what you should do; anagogy, what mark you should be aiming for).[38] In this comparative context, the *littera gesta docet* is comparable to the Jewish understanding of *peshat*; *allegoria* is related to the Jewish sense of *remez*, but has a more distinctively typological character—that is, in comparison to the freer allegorical style favored by the earlier rabbinic sages or to the more philosophical allegory of the medieval philosophers; *moralis* is not simply *derash* (homily) but a more narrowly defined moral reading of scripture;[39] and *anagogia* overlaps with the category of *sod* but is not simply equivalent to it because *anagogia* narrowly concentrates on the fate of the soul after death, while *sod*, *yesodei ha-Torah* (the "secrets" of the Torah), involves much more than this otherworldly concern.[40] At the same time, however, transcending the relevant parallels, overlaps, and distinctions is the consequential claim, shared by both of these fourfold "systems," that scripture is polysemous. So Augustine had already argued: "What harm does it do to me that different meanings can be taken from the same words as long as they are true?"[41]

Despite their hierarchical arrangement, the four tiers of the PaRDeS do not work in such a way that the "superior" levels, *remez*, *derash*, and *sod*, cancel out the meaning of *peshat*, or that *sod* invalidates the significance of the homiletical (*derash*) or allegorical (*remez*) strata. Rather, each level has its own integrity and, in its special way, confirms and supports the other levels of meaning. In the words of Gregory the Great's *Commentary on 1 Kings*: "Be strengthened by the plain as well as the profound meanings of scripture."[42]

The method of PaRDeS, and its Christian parallel, is so well known as not require further general description at this juncture.[43] However, a few amplifying notes on specific aspects of this technique will add to our understanding and appreciation of it.

First, and most fundamental, the polysemous understanding of the Hebrew Bible and the New Testament—and later the Qur'ān—created the possibility of perceiving the enterprise of mystical theology as coincident with mystical exegesis. (And it created, at the same time, the fertile interconnection between theology, exegesis, and mystical experience.) Bonaventure, whose Neoplatonic interpretations of scripture are masterpieces of the medieval Christian mystical and exegetical traditions, makes this unbreakable symbiosis of scripture and theology eminently clear when he speaks of "sacra scriptura quae theologia dicitur" (sacred scripture that is called theology), a position, an understanding, he shared with Aquinas as well as with Eckhart.[44] All theology is a version—a vision—of scripture. Consider, for example, Ibn ʿArabī's theosophical comment on the Qur'ānic verse: "Have we not appointed for him [man] two eyes . . . and guided him on two highways?" (90:8–10):

> The Real is sheer Light, while the impossible (*al-muḥāl*) is sheer darkness (*zuema*). Darkness never turns into light, nor does light turn into darkness. Creation is the Barzakh between Light and darkness. In its essence it is qualified neither by darkness nor by light, since it is the Barzakh and the Middle (*al-wasaṭ*), which has a property from each of its two sides. That is why He appointed for man two eyes and guided him on the two paths. Through one eye and one path he accepts light and looks upon it in the measure of his preparedness. Through the other eye and the other path he looks upon darkness and turns toward it.
>
> In himself, man is neither light nor darkness, since he is neither existent nor nonexistent. He is the firm impediment which prevents sheer light from dispelling darkness, and he prevents sheer darkness from taking away sheer light. He receives the two sides through his own essence, and he acquires, through this reception, that light whereby he is described as "existent" and that darkness whereby he is described as "nonexistent." So he shares in both sides and protects both sides.

> Everything manifest in the cosmos is an imaginal, engendered form that conforms to a divine form. For He discloses Himself to the cosmos only in accordance with that which corresponds (*munāsaba*) to the cosmos—in the entity of an immutable substance, just as man is immutable in respect of his substance. Thus you see the immutable through the immutable, and that is "unseen" in respect to you and Him. You see the manifest through the manifest, and that is the "witnessed, the witnesser, and the witnessing" in respect to you and Him.
>
> Just as you perceive Him, you perceive your own essence. However, in every form you are known to be you, not other than you. Exactly in the same way, you know that Zayd is Zayd and no one else, even though he undergoes variation in his qualities, such as shame and fear, illness and health, satisfaction and wrath, and every state through which he fluctuates. Hence we say that so-and-so has changed from state to state and from form to form. Were it not for the fact that this is the situation, we would not know him once his state changed and we would say that he no longer exists.
>
> Hence, we come to know that there are two eyes, as God said: "Have We not appointed for him two eyes?" (90:8). One eye is that through which he who undergoes transmutation is perceived. These are two different paths which God has made clear to the Possessor of Two Eyes, as He said, "And guided him on the two highways" (90:10), that is, made clear for him the two paths. . . .
>
> Each eye has a path. So know whom you see and what you see. For this reason it is correct that, "You did not throw when you threw, but God threw" (8:17). The eye through which you perceive that the throwing belongs to God is different from the eye through which you perceive that the throwing belongs to Muhammad. So know that you have two eyes, if you possess the knowledge. Then you will know for certain that the thrower is God in the corporeal form of Muhammad. Imaginalization and assuming imaginal forms is nothing but this. . . .
>
> This is the station of "God created Adam upon His own form." When someone makes something upon his own form, that thing is identical to the form, so it is it/not it. Hence it is correct to say, "You did not throw when you threw," for the root of everything which became manifest from that form derives from Him upon whose form it is.[45]

This deeply gnostic reading that finds Allah everywhere and nowhere; that connects man and his Creator and distinguishes completely between man and his Creator; that is witness to Allah's disclosure in all things and denies His disclosure in anything; that insists that Allah's ultimate revelation, the Qurʾān, is both qurʾān (a reality that acts to bring things together) and *furqān* (that which differentiates things from one another)—this reading is, for Ibn ʿArabī, the truest type of exegesis. Now, one might well question this assertion, this theosophical form of explication, but a reader will never understand Ibn ʿArabī's work if he does not take totally seriously the claim that what is transpiring—however much it looks like eisegetical theology—is exegesis. To even begin to comprehend Ibn ʿArabī, one must take as a given that Ibn ʿArabī believed that, through all of his theosophical instruction, he was doing nothing other than teaching scripture.

To further support the present argument for the symbiosis of mystical theology and mystical exegesis, I recall an esoteric observation in the zoharic *Midrash ha-Ne-elam*: In commenting on a verse in Genesis, "Let there be light," the kabbalistic author makes a *theological* point on the basis of its numerological *exegesis*. He teaches that the "light" that is here indicated by the Hebrew word *or* (which has a numerical value of 207) refers "secretly" to *raz* (mystery), which also has the numerical value of 207—that is, the light of the Torah is found in the mysteries it reveals.[46] Is this the real intention behind—the authentic meaning of—the words of Genesis? The a priori assumptions with which the medieval author of the *Midrash ha-Ne-elam* was working allowed him to answer this query affirmatively. The linkage between letters and numbers is just as fixed and just as relevant a part of scriptural hermeneutics as the relationship between letters and words. As a consequence, the words *or* and *raz*, revealed in the text by divine design, bear mystical possibilities, equivalencies, and correlations that can be appropriately identified as nothing other than exegesis. This zoharic midrash deciphers the Torah from the perspective of the totalizing character of God's revelation—that is, the fullness of its being and, therefore, its inherent possession of all theological truth, not matter how novel that may be. The belief in the plenitude of scripture, of its multivalent reading, legitimates this construal, at least as a tempting possibility, and, in so doing, binds together mystical teaching—understood as midrashic work—and biblical authority, the revelation at Sinai.

Comparable methods of reading scripture that produce theology out of exegesis can also be found among Advaitans, those who follow the principles of Mīmāṃṣa, and among adherents to the four additional classical orthodox Hindu philosophical schools of thought. Śaṅkara conceives his entire undertaking as exegesis and derives it from his absolute fidelity to the authority of the Vedas, however he reads them. Similarly, the Mīmāṃṣa school is defined by its distinctive manner of interpretation of Hindu scriptures. For the latter, the central issue is the establishing of a judicious reading of the Vedas as uncreated (*apauruṣeya*) and eternal (*nitya*). The school's unique line of argumentation concerning creation and eternity is actually a particular form of Vedic exegesis that is framed in opposition to the exegesis of the Nyāya, Vaiśeṣika, Sāṃkhya, and Yoga schools that favor some understanding, some permutation, of the Vedas as created (*pauruṣeya*) and noneternal (*anitya*).

Likewise, the centrality of the Hindu scriptures and of their interpretation in the Weltanschauung of the Advaitan school has been wisely described in these terms:

> For Advaita, the success of any theory of meaning arises from its relative success in explaining, consonantly with Advaita teachings, the meaning of the great sentences of the Upaniṣads. Sometimes there are said to be four of these great sentences, one from each Veda: "Brahman is wisdom" (*prajñānam brahma*) [*Aitareya Upaniṣad* 3.5.3]); "I am Brahman" (*aham brahmaśmi*) [*Bṛhadāranyaka Upaniṣad* 1.4.10]); "That art thou" (*tat tvam asi*) [*Chāndogya Upaniṣad* 6.8.7]); and "this Self is Brahman" (*ayam ātmā brahma*) [*Māṇḍūkya Upaniṣad* 4.2].

This is not just a general statement of basic theological principles. For Śaṅkara and his disciples it carries concrete metaphysical implications:

> Let us consider "that art thou." Uttered by Uddālaka Āruṇi to his son Śvetaketu, the context suggests that by "that" the sentence refers to Brahman; by "thou" it refers to Śvetaketu's self; and by "art" it is indicated that these two referents are identical. However, this straightforward explanation presents several problems for the Advaitin. For one thing, Śaṃkara explains in several places that Brahman is ineffable in the sense that words (even "Brahman") cannot denote It directly. It would seem to follow that if "that" means Brahman, it must mean it indirectly, consistently with Śaṃkara's thesis.
>
> Is "that art thou" metaphorical, then, a figurative identification—one's self is like Brahman, or Brahman is like one's true Self? No, Śaṃkara replies: figurative language

presupposes the speaker's knowledge that the things identified are really different, whereas "That art thou," insofar as it provides Self-knowledge, presupposes that the speaker knows that things are really identical. If one says, "Devadatta is a lion" figuratively, he knows Devadatta is not a lion.[47]

In this instance we see Śaṅkara using as his premise the famous scriptural pronouncement "tat tvam asi," and propounding his central doctrines of "self" and of Brahman as direct exposition of the *Chāndogya Upaniṣad.* In so doing he follows a long and central tradition of Advaitan interpretation that began in the writings of Gauḍapādacarya[48] and that functions through the commentarial mode. In Śaṅkara's case, beginning with a commentary on the *Māṇḍūkyakārikās* and on the *Taittirīyabhāṣya*, and culminating in his mature works, such as the *Brahmasutrabhasya*, the entire theological enterprise is sustained by a desire to interpret and defend a particular conception of the creative and eternal nature of the Vedas and of related canonical literature. Because these sources derive from Brahman, because, indeed, "Brahman is their source,"[49] they are eternal, essential, unchanging, and containing all wisdom—Brahman's wisdom. In sum, Śaṅkara's entire vast Advaitan project is encouraged and defended by a titanic effort at comprehending what he calls the "great *śāstra*," the hymn of praise, which is the *Ṛg-Veda*. For it is the *Ṛg-Veda* and related texts that together constitute *śabdapramāṇa*, the totality of revelation and authoritative testimony that alone provides certain knowledge.

Second—relative to the methodology of the PaRDeS—these complicated forms of exegesis, and this collaboration of exegesis and theology, are grounded, in the first instance, in a highly traditional piety. While these esoteric modes of interpretation are made to yield many exotic theological fruits, speculative flights of metaphysical and transcendental reconstruction, and even, on occasion, deviant and revolutionary religious teachings, the inner drive, that which generates and compels their applications, is a profound desire to maintain the authoritative, original revelation of the (diverse) traditions. This is to recognize that the move to allegorical, typological, moral, anagogical, and mystical interpretations of scripture is grounded in, among other causes, a desire to defend these *Ur*-texts against various forms of criticism, trivialization, and reductionism. When those who believe in the authenticity and authority of (a particular) scripture encounter criticism of their holy text, they need to defend it, and one way to do this is to find "higher" meanings in the text, and in its accompanying tradition, than a cursory or literal reading would reveal. This apologetic inspiration had already been evidenced in the Greek defenses of the Homeric texts that, by the time of Socrates and Plato, if not considerably earlier, were being decoded allegorically in order to save them from a blistering attack on their mythological and (im)moral content. Ancient reports tell us that Anaxagoras expounded Homer in a specifically ethical way, as Dante would later read various biblical tales à la the category of *moralis*; that his student, Metrodorus of Lampsacus, exposited Homer symbolically—for example, Hector was the moon and Achilles the sun;[50] and that Democritus of Abdera saved the Homeric text by explaining it allegorically.[51] Plato explicitly criticizes this defensive strategy and lampoons those "great Homer experts" who interpret Homer allegorically.[52] But such methodological maneuvers were required by lovers of the *Odyssey* and the *Iliad* if the Homeric tales were not to be discredited by the new rationalism of the Periclean era.

In the history of Jewish exegesis, this method of revaluation begins to find significant employment in the Hellenistic era, and for good reason: the Torah, and Jewish tradition, seemed less rational and persuasive to many intellectuals (and others) than the philosophical tradition of the Greeks, especially as the latter was incarnated in Plato and Platonism. As a consequence, Jews began to reinterpret scripture either to deflect such criticism or to foster the belief in the fundamental compatability of the teachings of the Torah and Greek philosophy, however different they appeared in form and content. Philo of Alexandria ranks first among those who labored in this apologetic vineyard, but he was by no means a lone voice.[53] What was required in this context was the repudiation of Greek skepticism or mockery and the shielding of biblical teaching. The allegorical method made such a defense possible.[54] Philo consistently cautions that readers should not construe the biblical text in a simplistic and unsophisticated manner. It should always be interrogated through μ̔πόνοια (hidden meaning) and ἀλληγορία (allegory) to reveal its true meaning. Philo was true to this declared position. His entire corpus on the *Allegorizing of the Laws* speaks to this conern.[55]

The church fathers likewise found the allegorical method appealing when they were required to defend their Christological beliefs. It provided defensive hermeneutical assistance for, among others, Justin Martyr, Irenaeus, Clement of Alexandria, Hippolytus, and, above all, Origen. Alternatively, it was rightly and soundly attacked by, for example, Celsus and Porphyry, two major pagan opponents of the early church. The main concern of these early Christian allegorists was the championing of the Christian explication of scripture that entailed finding Christ anticipated and promised throughout the Hebrew Bible. Whether in Justin, Melito of Sardis, Irenaeus, or Origen, no matter how far-fetched this sort of construal appears—for example, the murdered Abel is Christ; Joseph, sold into slavery, is Christ; Moses, exiled to the desert, is Christ; the Passover sacrifice represents Christ—the object of this tendentiousness was to protect and conserve the New Testament message that Jesus was the ultimate fulfillment of God's providential plan that began to unfold at Creation and that reached its climax at Calvary. It intended to show that the Catholic Christian reading of the Torah was the correct one; that the Jewish (or pagan or gnostic or heretical Christian) reading was false;[56] and that everywhere in the Torah the Christian truth, especially its soteriological and eschatological aspects, was embedded in such a way that it was only to be finally revealed clearly and fully in the Gospels.

Given the prominence of the allegorical reading among the church fathers, and recognizing, in particular, Origen's influence on later Christian scriptural exegesis and study, it is not surprising to find that mystical allegorical interpretations became central arguments in support of the Christian faith in the Middle Ages. Repeatedly, like Origen and Augustine before them, medieval mystics expressed their most cherished Christian beliefs through a particular Christian allegorical explication of scripture. Consider as exemplary the esoteric treatment—that is, the transvaluation—of the enormously threatening subject of sexuality as this is represented by the "pious" renderings given to the Song of Songs.[57] Following the lead of the rabbis, especially Rabbi Akiba, who insisted on an allegorical reading that understood the text as a love poem about God's relation to Israel: "The whole world is not worth the day on which the Song of Songs was given to Israel, for all the Scriptures are holy, but the Song of Songs is the Holy of Holies"[58]—churchmen from the time of Origen, and afterward,[59] have interpreted the Song as representing the romance of Christ and His church or Christ's love for the individual soul. Origen expresses both these possibilities in his *Commentary on the Song of Songs*: "This little book is an epithalamium, that is, a nuptial song, which it seems to me that Solomon wrote in a dramatic form, and sang after the fashion of a bride to her bridegroom, who is the word of God, burning with celestial love. Indeed, he loves her deeply, whether she is the soul, made in his own image, or the church."[60]

Developing this line of understanding, Honorius Augustodunesis's *Exposito in Cantica Canticorum* beautifully describes Christ's love of and for the church. Relating the Song to the Virgin Mary, while seeing Mary as the symbol of the church, he writes:

> Therefore, this book is read on the feast of Blessed Mary, for it shows the type of the church, which is virgin and mother. Virgin, because uncorrupted by all heresy; mother because through grace it always bears spiritual children. And therefore everything which is said about the church can also be said about the Virgin, understood by both bride and mother of the bridegroom. There is a little book published by us, called *Sigillum S. Mariae*, in which all of the Song of Songs is specially adapted to her person.[61]

As such, overdetermined by theological assumptions about the inspired origin of the Song—"the author of the book is the Holy Spirit"[62]—its absolute religious virtuosity vouchsafed by its inclusion in the biblical canon, the physical sensuality of the Song is transformed into the spiritual intimacy of Christ and human beings (Christian mystics of both sexes will read the Song in this manner).

The classical medieval exposition is that given by Bernard of Clairvaux in a series of "Sermones" that were originally presented to his Cistercian community. Interpreting the Song as a tale of mystical ascent, Bernard, commenting on the verse "Let him kiss me with kisses of his mouth" (Song of Songs, 1:1), guides the faithful from "kisses of the feet" to "kisses of the hand" "then, at last . . . to that mouth of Glory (I speak fearfully and trembling), not only to catch sight of it, but even to be kissed." In this rereading awe, reverence, fear, and finally nonphysical love replace the passionate, sexual language of the original. No longer a worldly eroticism, the Song becomes the apotheosis of sanctity, purity, and spirituality. Moreover, through the imaginative power of an allegorical rendering: "Now, according to the three states of love, there are three kisses of the lover. First, atonement or reconciliation; second, merit; third, contemplation. The first is of the feet; the second, of the hand; the third, of the mouth."[63] The actual human bodies of the male lover and the female beloved have passed away; they have been turned into a series of metaphors. The language of sexual union in the Song refers not to gross, carnal intercourse, but rather to the inflow of the divine into the human, and the raising up of the human to the transcendental: "By a special privilege, she receives him flowing from heaven into her intimate affections, and even into the innermost part of her heart, and she has present the one she desires, not in a shape (*non figuratum*) but in an infusion (*sed infusum*), not in appearance, but in affect; and without doubt it is more delightful because it is inward, not outward."[64] This is a metaphysical, nonbodily ecstasy, a union untainted by lust or degeneracy. In contrast to the negative view of the body, or of sexuality, that was held by the medieval church, this embrace is a perfect union, unsullied by sin, improper desire, or indecency. Bernard teaches:

> Be careful, however, not to conclude that I see something corporeal or perceptible to the senses in this union between the Word and the soul. My opinion is that of the Apostle, who said that "he who is united to the Lord becomes one spirit with him." I try to express, with the most suitable words I can muster, the ecstatic ascent of the purified mind to God, and the loving descent of God into the soul, submitting spiritual truths to spiritual men. Therefore, let this union be in the spirit, because "God is a spirit," who is lovingly drawn by the beauty of that soul whom he perceives to be guided by the Spirit, and devoid of any desire to submit to the ways of the flesh, especially if he sees that it burns with love for himself.[65]

Famously summarizing the quality of this mystical love affair of which Bernard writes, Hugh of St. Victor notes:

> But, you ask, who is this bridegroom, who is his bride? The bridegroom is God, the bride is the soul. The bridegroom is at home when he fills the mind with inward joy; he goes away when he takes away the sweetness of contemplation. But by what similitude is the soul said to be the bride of God? She is the bride because she is joined to him by a chaste love. She is the bride, since by the breath of the Holy Spirit she is made fertile with the offspring of the virtues.[66]

Piety and mystical dogma have combined, through an allegorical unfolding, to subvert the sexual content of, and to domesticate, the Song of Songs, making it, in the process, the preferred book of the mystical soul.[67] In effect, esotericism, mediated through cycles of scriptural exegesis, is the handmaiden of piety in this long Christian tradition. (Parenthetically, it should also be emphasized in this connection that what one has in all of these lofty decipherments of the love poetry of the Song is not a personal description of ecstatic experience—whatever the personal experience of the mystical author may be—but, rather, the repeated application of a literary-philosophical convention, according to which such renderings of the Song have essentially become standardized.)

Third—relative to the PaRDeS—and without elaboration, I should note that all these allegorical readings are, like all other allegorical readings, *necessarily* contextual. Noncontextual allegory is in fact inconceivable. Moreover, it is contextual in at least two senses: (1) the original text has a context in which it is read—for example, the synagogue or the rabbinical academy, the church or the monastic community, the mosque or among the Sufi brethren; and (2) it is contextual in that these socioreligious environments themselves evolve and reflect historical and historicized contexts. This means that not only is a Jewish reading not a Christian reading or a Muslim reading but also that a first-century Jewish or Christian reading is not a medieval Neoplatonic reading—as, for example, in Bernard of Clairvaux—or a modern existentialist, kabbalistic, or scholarly reading.[68]

Fourth, the PaRDeS, the theory that there can be and are multiple levels of exegesis of scripture, makes possible radical theological innovation within the ruling normative frame of reference. Because of the larger presumptive theological context in which PaRDeS operates, radical notions can be entertained and utilized without becoming heterodox or heretical. This freedom is made possible by mystical deconstructions of the authoritative texts—that is, analyses that operate at the level of *yesodei ha Torah* (secrets of the Torah), of anagogy, and of *batin* (secrets). At this exalted level, which is made known through the special exegetical techniques utilized by the mystic, even the most extraordinary doctrines now taught as a mystical commentary could be justified as "secrets" belonging to the *mira profunditis* (the "wondrous profundity") of scripture, their exceptionality reflecting their transcendental or divine origin.

Examples of this important type of extreme exegesis are found in nearly all the great mystical traditions. One immediately recalls the sexual interpretations fo the medieval kabbalists that employ an extraordinary explicitness, even attributing to the Almighty—"as if one could say this"[69]—a penis. As a result, the imagery of the Song of Songs becomes the locus for a highly erotic transcendental vision that includes the "coupling" of divine male and female elements (the Shekhinah) in the world above. Yet, despite these truly striking, excessively odd notions, so apparently at variance with the largely asexual idea of God in the Bible, particularly as represented by the Creation account in Genesis (which is distinguished from other Creation accounts found in the world's religions by the absence of sexuality or relations between a male deity and a female deity or consort) this esoteric teaching—admittedly held closely and taught only to the "elite"—became widely accepted, especially after the spread of Lurianic Kabbalah in the sixteenth century, even among the most conservative rabbinic elites (for example, by the Vilna Gaon, Rabbi Elijah of Vilna). This became possible because these doctrines were taken as "secrets" that did not cancel out the other levels of scriptural meaning and, in particular, did not lead to antinomian consequences. Indeed, through a rich mythic theology, these emanationist and sexual notions were employed to provide a theurgical explanation of the *mitzvot* that raised—rather than threatened—their ontic status. In effect, through the possibilities created by the hermeneutics of the PaRDeS, this most uncommon kabbalistic universe was wedded, was able to be wedded, to a most traditional religious practice, thereby producing a kabbalistic Weltanschauung that was simultaneously novel, erotic—"as if one could say this"—and orthodox.

The material collected in Abu 'Abd al-Raḥmān al-Shulamī's *Haqā'iq al tafsīr* (happily meaning "the truths of interpretation") in the early eleventh century contains almost wholly allegorical interpretations of the Qur'ān. Many of these constructions reveal Neoplatonic and other influences that derive from a conceptual schema far removed from the obvious meanings of the "clear verses" (*muhkamat*), which, according to sura 3:5–6, are "the essence of the book (Qur'ān)." Comparable to Philo's interpretation of Abraham's journeys and Bonaventure's mystical rendering of aspects of the life of Jesus, al-Sulami, for example, interprets Muhammad's *miraj* ("night journey to heaven" [sura 17:1]) as a hidden description of the mystical ascent of consciousness. Like Muhammad, the *'arif* (the mystical knower) gains, through this ascent, that supreme knowledge, gnosis (*ma'arifa*) that alone provides a knowledge of the unhidden Allah, in whom the self is "obliterated" in the ecstatic moments of *fana* and *baqa*. Now, this is strong theological stuff, pointing to, and deriving from, a gnostic vision not obviously present in the narrative content and legal theology of the Qur'ān. Yet, as an allegorical rendering of the *miraj*, given its link to the Prophet and his experience, it is legitimated as one, perhaps the most valuable, rendering of the Qur'ānic passage according to a theory of scriptures' multiple meanings and accepted as such by the faithful.

One has a second remarkable and profound exegetical example of this hermeneutical phenomenon in Fakhr al-Dīn al-Rāzī's commentary on the Qur'ān. In commenting on the Qur'ānic verse "Likewise we show Abraham the power of the heavens and the earth, that he might be one of those who are certain" (6:85), Rāzī explains the term *likewise* (*kadhalika*) as being reminiscent of the *daqiqa aqliyya* (subtle intellective realism) and interprets the passage as meaning that Allah's light shines eternally and continually connects itself to the human soul, except when separated by a veil (*hijab*). This veil is anything that draws humankind away from Allah, as, for example, idolatry does. In consequence, Abraham, in denying idolatry and rejecting his father's way, was making it possible to receive the flow of divine insight and power. As such, the term *kadhalika* in this verse means "in this manner" or "by these means"—that is, by rejecting idolatry. Still further, for Rāzī the knowledge that Abraham gains from these labors is not ordinary knowledge but a form of transcendental wisdom: "It is as if . . . he (Abraham) scanned the *malakut* (heavenly kingdom; angelic realm) with the eye of the intellect and heard with the ear of his intellect its witness as to its essential being-in-need."[70] In this brief commentary on a single verse in the Qur'ān, we find an entire complex theology of Allah's creative role; the mystical symbolism of light and the eternal light from above, to which humankind has continual access because of Allah's grace; and an understanding of knowledge (*ilm*) as a special form of mystical contemplation that eventuates in "radiance and splendor" (*ishraq wa lama'an*), and then finally in *ma'arifa* and *tawhid* (the learned confession of unity). It is not difficult to judge this Neoplatonic type of ascent in Sufi garb—in all likelihood due to the influence of Avicenna—as being far distant from the original Qur'ānic narrative. Yet the piety of its author, its passionate reverence for Allah, its love and elevation of Abraham, and its commitment to the Qur'ān as the source of ultimate wisdom—as well as Rāzī's profound knowledge of Arabic grammar, lexicography, and traditional Islamic exegesis—allow it, despite its untraditional juxtapositions, correspondences, and content, to become part of the standard retinue of Qur'ānic exegesis. The Muslim faithful—and the more intimate Sufi community—have both been persuaded to accept Rāzī's essential claim that all this material, all these luminous affirmations and allusions, are present in the text "by ways of symbols" (*ala sabil al-ramz*).

Throughout Sufi (and more generally Shi'a and Isma'ili) literature, one finds the continual invocation of the seminal claim that the Qur'ānic text has multiple interpretations. The external sense is known as the *zahr* and the internal sense is known as the *batin*, with the *batin* containing a further seven possible levels of meaning. The ultimate level of meaning, the *ta'wil*, is known only to Allah but He shares this knowledge with the mystical elite, "those who are purified." From these hermeneutical premises develops an entire elaborate theory of mystical reading, including an approach to Qur'ānic verses held to be *mutashabih* (ambiguous and capable of more than a single explanation). It was the Sufi, par excellence, who knew how to decipher these uncertain texts through the method of allegorical rendering. According to their own exegesis of the Qur'ānic verse (3:7) regarding the decipherment of the Qur'ān—"and none knows its interpretation (*ta'wil*), save only Allah and those firmly rooted in knowledge"—it is the Sufi alone who is fully rooted in the required esoteric knowledge. This rootage, this special knowledge, allowed the Sufi to perceive, and represent, all of their mystical activity as exegetical theology.

Eckhart—in an argument that closely parallels in meaning a position already introduced in the name of Ibn 'Arabī—makes this profound exegetical point: "The Holy

Spirit teaches all truth (1 John 16:13). Since the literal sense is that which the author of the writing intends, and God is the author of Holy Scripture, as has been said, then every true sense is a literal sense."[71] Now, if every true sense is a literal sense, then it is perfectly reasonable, consistent with Eckhart's Neoplatonic emanationism—*esse est Deus*[72]—to contend that the first verse in Genesis, "In the Beginning God created heaven and earth," teaches

> first the production or emanation of the Son and the Holy Spirit from the Father in eternity, then the production or general creation of the whole universe from the one God in time, and many of the properties of both Creator and creature.
>
> 9. You should know that in every natural action or production that is directed to what is outside the one who produces it and which implies a passage from something that is not an existing being to something that is, the principle of such production has the nature of a cause and that which is produced has the name and nature of an external effect. The first point is clear from Aristotle, who says: "A cause is that to which or from which something follows." The second point stands from the name itself. "Effect" is derived from *extra factus*, or "made outside the maker." From this it follows that what is produced in that way has the nature of something that is not an existing being to become some existing being, for example, a horse from what was not a horse, something white from what was not white. From this first conclusion regarding natural productions it is clear that in the Godhead, since every production or emanation is not directed to what is outside the producer, and is not from something that is not an existing being or from nothing, and in the third place is not directed to particular existence, what is procreated does not have the nature of something made or created and is not an effect. It is also clear that the producer does not have the nature of a creator or a cause, and that what is produced is not outside the producer and is not different from it, but is one with it. "I am in the Father, and the Father is in me" (Jn. 14:11); "The Father and I are one" (Jn. 10:30). In the Godhead the Son and the Holy Spirit are not from nothing, but are "God from God, light from light, one light, one God" with the Father. "These three are one: (1 Jn. 5:7). This is why it says here, "God created heaven and earth." Creation is a production from nothing; heaven and earth are particular beings. As we said, the Son and the Holy Spirit are not particular beings, but are simple, total, and full of existence. They are not from nothing.[73]

In this elaborate metaphysical explication we find the ground for Eckhart's theology of the unity of Being. "Whatever is outside of God . . . is nothing and does not exist." The elemental rhythm of Being is its going out and coming home. Ultimately the "spark" in the human soul "rejects all created things" and seeks "the source of this [its] essence; it wants to go into the simple ground, into the quiet desert, into which distinction never gazed."[74] Reflecting on this ontological claim, one might fairly question if such a Plotinean decoding of Genesis and John is, finally, reasonable,[75] but there can be no doubt that for Eckhart—and his many disciples over the centuries—this is the authentic meaning of the Christian faith, made available by the anagogical elucidation of the biblical accounts of the world's origin. Given his mental universe and his principles of exegetical reasoning—not least his belief in the interconnectedness of scripture and philosophy—he was able to justify the finding of a capacious doctrine of emanation and return in scripture—that is, in the exegesis of scripture.

One further aspect of these considerations of PaRDeS, and of related techniques, requires separate clarification. This concerns what the medievals called parabolic meaning. The most famous description of this mode of expression, as related to biblical literature, is provided by Maimonides in the "Introduction" to his *Guide for the Perplexed.*[76] In his observations on the nature of parables, he makes the telling comment that there are some passages whose literal meaning *is* their parabolic meaning—that is, there is no nonparabolic meaning. The "hidden" sense of the text is the meaning of the text *simpliciter*. So, for example, it is argued that Solomon, the traditional author of Proverbs, never meant his remarks about a harlot, in chapter 7, verses 6–21, to be taken at face value. He is not at all concerned in this context with an actual prostitute. Form the outset he is interested in describing the temptations that plague the flesh as a consequence of its material nature. To understand this passage otherwise is not to understand it at all.

One final observation: in the employment of all of these mystical hermeneutical gambits, in the exercise of all these forms of creative reading, one notes the continual striving to uncover an inner meaning, an essential verity, that can only be revealed by strenuous and unusual intellectual and religious exertion. The PaRDeS, and its parallels, do not constitute an easy way to paradise but an extremely strenuous form of conceptual-spiritual activity, of constructive and deconstructive interpretive explication of canonical texts, which one must work through if one is to open the transcendent gates, remove the veils of ignorance and illusion, and begin to reveal the secret of secrets.

Symbols and Symbolic Interpretation

Our extended analysis of PaRDeS, and especially of allegorical forms of interpretation, requires a complementary, but distinct, analysis of the related but separate notions of "symbol" and "symbolic interpretation." Though many exegetes and students of exegesis use the two terms—*allegory* and *symbol*—synonymously, it is to be recognized that at least for certain authors and schools the two terms (and the two ideas) are not equivalent and are not simply interchangeable. The source of the difference between them lies primarily in the necessary distinction between "allegory" when it is understood as a literary technique or device—one almost wants to say an *arbitrary* literary technique or device, in which one "says one thing and means another"[77]—and "symbol" when it is understood as a nonexchangeable, nontranslatable, ontic marker.[78] Given this differentiation, an allegorical reading of, for example, the Qurʾān or the New Testament tends, even when their literal truth is insisted upon, to diminish their literal signficance—*superficie sensus litteralis*, as the medieval Catholic mystics described it—in favor of claimed, more profound, nonliteral meanings. Such a subversive employment is notable, for example, in the Christian exegesis—beginning with Paul and the New Testament authors—of the legal sections of the Torah.[79] The Jewish reading of the Law, of the individual *mitzvot* (commandments), is likened by Christian commentators to Isaac's blindness, which did not allow him "to recognize the spiritual understanding [of the Law] under the veiling cloak of the letter."[80] By the twelfth century, we find that Rupert of Deutz has gone so far as to talk of the "cheap and shoddy letters [of the Law]";[81] and Pseudo-Hugh talks of "the hidden grain beneath the pile of straw."[82] What is called "keeping the law according to the flesh"—drawing upon Paul's view that the "letter of the Law kills"—is now, in consequence of the coming of Christ and the creation of His spiritual community, transcended. "Fleshly observance has been changed to a spiritual understanding."[83] At its very best, Jewish ritual law is an obscure, shadowy anticipation of Christian rites and ceremonies that are the signs of the "New Covenant." In consequence, the so-called ritual law of the Torah becomes simultaneously fulfilled and abrogated—it no longer binds the Christian nor dictates his or her behavior. The allegorical reading eliminates the deed biblically required.

Alternatively, the commandments of the Torah, the *mitzvot*, understood as symbols—as occurs, for example, among the medieval kabbalists—make such dissolution impossible. For, on their metaphysical rendering, the *mitzvot*, God's very own commandments, cannot be taken in any way but, at a minimum, literally—which requires their actual performance, because the commandments possess, as God's own creations, an ontological power, a supreme revelatory force, and their performance creates a moment of ultimate and irreplaceable human–divine interaction. That is, spiritual or moral values cannot substitute for obligatory physical acts insofar as these acts are understood to have been created by and revealed by the Almighty. The *mitzvot* can, of course, have additional spiritual or mystical meanings—in actuality, one would be hard-pressed to find a more extreme and elaborate theory of the supernal nature and implications of the Torah and the *mitzvot* than that proposed by the *mekubbalim* (Jewish mystics)—but its observance can never be less than obligatory. As the *Midrash ha-Ne'elam* puts it: "The words of the Torah may be likened to a nut. How? Just as a nut has a shell outside and a kernel inside, so the words of Torah contain *ma'aseh*, *midrash*, *agadah*, and *sod*, one inside the other."[84] The kabbalists are most interested in the content of the fourth level, *sod* (secrets), but insist that the level of *ma'aseh* (actual deeds) is nonnegotiable and binding. In the words of the *Tikkunei ha-Zohar*: "Without the *mitzvot*, the Torah is not the Torah of God."[85]

The *mitzvot*, valued as originating in God's will, are God's way to Him. They are divine channels of revealed wisdom, God's own wisdom, and the means that God Himself has established for communication between the world above and the world below. As such, they are not reducible to moral, allegorical, or other nonliteral meanings. Still further, according to the theosophical cosmic blueprint maintained by the kabbalists, each *mitzvah* was necessarily linked to one (or more) of the *sefirot* (divine attributes) and therefore directly influenced the heavenly realm. "The *mitzvot* of the Torah are all connected with the supernal, holy king."[86] What Jews do below in the keeping of the *mitzvot* directly affects what occurs in the sefirothic world above. Nothing else has, or can have, this theurgic power. The beneficial flow of the *shefa* (divine bounty) is regulated by the performance of the *mitzvot*. The immanent and transcendent struggle between good and evil both above and below is influenced by the proper, actual performance of the *mitzvot*. The upper world is united or kept divided by the performance or the nonperformance of the *mitzvot*. "The deed above is aroused by the deed below. If a man performs a deed below correctly, a power is aroused correctly in the world above."[87] Allegorical or anagogical interpretation, and mystical intention alone, is insufficient. As the Zohar describes it: "Blessing does not appear at an empty [that is, spiritualized or allegorized] place."[88] Even more striking is the Zohar's commentary on Leviticus 26: "You shall do them [the *mitzvot*]," *va-asitem otam*: "He who fulfills the commandments of the Torah . . . creates Him, as it were [*kivyachol*], in the world above. The Holy

One blessed be He says: It is as if he created Me. And they have explained this. Therefore [it is written], 'And you shall do them.'"[89]

Such symbolic—as compared to allegorical or spiritual—interpretation, of fundamental significance in the history of religions, is found in most of the major mystical traditions of the world. Christian mystical circles insist that the crucifixion and the resurrection, for all their possible allegorical interpretations, are historical—symbolic, irreplaceable—events. Jesus did die on the cross; his blood was shed to save humankind; he did rise physically on the third day. Stressing the absolute, mandatory, importance of Jesus' earthly life and death, Erigena teaches, "Without effort he created us through his divinity; with effort he created us through his humanity."[90] It is not sufficient, it is not acceptable, for Christians, even Christian mystics, to concentrate on what the crucifixion and resurrection mean "spiritually" if they neglect the actuality of the temporal crucifixion and resurrection. St. Anselm, meditating on these events in the life of Christ, explains, "As much as I can, though not as much as I ought, I am mindful of your passion, your buffeting, your scourging, your cross, your wounds, how you were slain for me, how you were prepared for burial and were burned."[91] "Would that I with happy Joseph might have taken down my Lord from the cross."[92] Indeed, the ongoing theological salience of the crucifixion and the resurrection depends, in the first instance, on their having been historical events.

This, of course, is not to deny that these acts do become what Ewert Cousins has aptly called "a mysticism of the historical event,"[93] that is, a mystical method of prayer and meditation based on Christ's life, death, and resurrection. Bonaventure's *Lignum vitae* and the anonymous *Meditations on the Life of Christ* (*Meditationes Vitae Christi*)[94] are just two of many examples of such mystical reflection and technique. But such meditation and related spiritual procedures are possible only because the particular, concrete events of Christ's life are irreplaceable symbols. So, for example, Bonaventure, whose *Itinerarium Mentis in Deum* (1259) is one of the major Neoplatonic works of the medieval Catholic mystical tradition, and who is no stranger to, or critic of, allegorical renderings of biblical material, feels compelled to teach:

> There is no other path but through the burning love of the Crucified, a love which so transformed Paul into Christ when "he was carried up to the third heaven" (2 Cor. 12:2) that he could say: "With Christ I am nailed to the cross. I live, now not I, but Christ lives in me" (Gal. 2:20). This love also so absorbed the soul of Francis that his spirit shone through his flesh when for two years before his death he carried in his body the sacred stigmata of the passion. The six wings of the Seraph, therefore, symbolize the six steps of illumination that begin from creatures and lead up to God, whom no one rightly enters except through the Crucified. For "he who enters not through the door, but climbs up another way is a thief and a robber." But "if anyone enter" through this door, "he will go in and out and will find pastures" (John 10:1, 9). Therefore, John says in the Apocalypse: "Blessed are they who wash their robes in the blood of the Lamb that they may have a right to the tree of life and may enter the city through the gates" (Apoc. 22:14). It is as if John were saying that no one can enter the heavenly Jerusalem by contemplation unless he enter through the blood of the Lamb as through a door.[95]

The shedding of the blood of Jesus in time, on the cross, in the worldly Jerusalem of circa 30 C.E., is not a metaphor,[96] an event that can be wholly allegorized. It can be the stuff of allegory, but only because it is, first and foremost, an irreplaceable historical-ontological reality. As the Dominican Johannes Tauler—the most influential medieval German Catholic mystic,[97] after Eckhart—taught, with a concentrated eye on the humanity of Christ and the historicity of the Passion: "No one can pass beyond the example set to us by Our Lord Jesus Christ."[98]

The entire tradition of *Amor Carnalis Christi* must also be given its due,[99] as part and parcel of this Christian spiritual totality, for, as Erigena insisted: "Divina non mendax . . . historia" (biblical history does not lie).[100] Likewise, the Marian piety that becomes so developed in the late medieval era represents this type of historical-ontic facticity in yet another form. Mary can be allegorized and spiritualized in all the wondrous senses connected with mothers and motherhood and mothering, but always the Catholic faithful must return to a view of Mary as the simple girl of first-century Palestine. As Tauler says at the outset of his sermon on the "Feast of Our Lady's Nativity": "Today we celebrate the lovely feast on which the Blessed Virgin, Our Lady, was born, free from sin, immaculate and holy from her mother's womb . . ."[101] Her Virgin Birth, the anunciation, her pregnancy, the birth of Jesus, her pain over his death, and her subsequent devotion provide the foundation for all later, grander claims for her as Queen of Heaven, mediatrix, the object of devotion in the liturgical Marian feasts, and for her putative appearances at various loci that became special shrines at which she was venerated.

The Catholic diagnosis of the Mass provides a paradigmatic insight into what is at stake in the difference between allegorical and symbolic exemplification. The sanctified wine and bread, representing the blood and body of Jesus, cannot be replaced by intellectual, spiritual, or moral appreciation of the death and resurrection of Jesus. It cannot be performed only "mentally"; its soteriological purpose cannot be accomplished by its allegorical or spiritual nonperformance. The holy *realia* of the ritual of the Eucharist constitute the literal meeting point of the present dialogue between Christ and the faithful. Jesus' words and actions, which provide the basis for this central ritual, "This is my body. . . . This is my blood" (Matthew 26:26–28), are translated into symbols—not allegories—through which the believer experiences transcendence and salvation. This act is not solely or wholly, or even primarily, an act of contemplation—though it can secondarily be seen and responded to in this way, as has been recommended by many distinguished interpreters in, for example, the Eastern Orthodox Community—but is, rather, a "magical" act in which material objects that cannot be replaced are mysteriously transformed into substances that participate directly and unequivocally in the divinity of Christ. Sacramental participation in this cardinal mystery rite is the entranceway to otherwordly life and bliss. To participate in the Mass is to gain Christ's grace, made possible by his death, which is now inexplicably but actually reenacted. Jesus is here present in the wine and bread.[102] The power of the Mass functions *ex opere operato*. So powerful, indeed, is it that it even benefits the dead; hence the tradition of the votive Mass—and the many cases of miracles connected to it.[103]

Similarly, the obligations imposed by the Qur'ān, and the sacrificial and ritual traditions of Hinduism, have been understood by the mystical teachers of these traditions as possessing the same sort of symbolic integrity that has been described vis-à-vis Kabbalah and medieval Christian mystical doctrine. The performance of *yajña* (the sacrifice), the offering of the drinkable soma over the holy fire (*agni*), which represents *prāṇa* (the vital energy force in the universe)—accompanied by the correct formulas (*yajus*) and hymns (*stotras*)—and through which the performer is purified and gains immortality, is not a metaphorical act, a behavior that is to be reduced to an allegorical meaning. Rather, it is an essential doing, the performing of which purifies and ennobles the self so that it can eventually become one with Brahman, the Ultimate One/Self. This metaphysical activity is repeated throughout the year—and one's life—by the Hindu in an elaborate round of rituals and sacrifices that are held to be soteriologically efficacious. Maṇḍana Mi'sra, Śaṅkara's seventh-century Advaitan contemporary (or disciple?),[104] argues, in his important *Brahmasiddhi*, that false appearances are removed by sacrifices (as taught by the Vedas) "in some unseen (*adṛṣṭa*) manner. Or else, as others say, sacrifice and the like accomplish their purpose by destroying impurities (*kalusa*) that get in the way of the highest good (*sreyas*); for the purpose of obligatory rites (*nityakarman*) is the washing away (*kṣaya*) of sins."[105] Neither faith, no matter how intense, nor psychological or subjective factors—paralleling the allegorical reading—can replace the actual fire, the drinkable soma, and the magical *yajus*, *samans* (songs), and *stotras*. *Yajña* (the Vedically prescribed sacrifice) has an intrinsic connection with the transcendental world, the nature of which cannot be duplicated or replaced by alternative acts of consciousness or, for example, moral behavior. It has restorative and salvific consequences for both the individual who performs the ritual—or has it performed for him—and the cosmic order as a whole. The gods and cosmic forces are themselves influenced by it. Though the state of *Brahmabhāva*—being in the state of Brahman or one with Brahman—is complemented by acts associated with the state of *Brahmacārya*, it is not simply equivalent to it and the latter cannot replace the former. Faith and good works cannot substitute for the globally consequential power (*prabhāva*) of the *yajña* and the mysterious theurgical efficacy of the verbal ritual-liturgical forms that accompany it. All of this ritual activity is entailed by the canonical literature of the tradition, particularly the Vedas, and therefore the Hindu spiritual adepts know they are bound by these sacrificial processes that no interpretive schema can explain away. They may use the sacred texts as pretexts for many things, but they are not free to turn the symbol into an idea, to reduce the sacrifice to an act of consciousness, essential as the transformation of consciousness is in this religious matrix.

In this context one also has to integrate the significance of the practice of reciting mantras. I have discussed this subject elsewhere,[106] and I therefore will not deal with it at length here, except that I should reaffirm the power of the mantra as such—that is, a power putatively embedded in the recitation of the Sanskrit sounds per se. The meaning of a mantra lies in its performance—a position with which even Śaṅkara agrees, in his commentary on the *Chāndogya Upaniṣad*, relative to the mantra *OM*. That he does so is significant evidence that must be factored into the overall equation in trying to reach a balanced understanding of how Hindu masters understand what the prescriptions of sacred texts entail.

Parenthetically, I also go farther to argue that though Śaṇkara and his disciples are regularly presented by scholars East and West as holding an essentially metatextual theological position that denigrates the obligatory performance of Hindu ritual, Śaṅkara himself would reject this characterization of his doctrinal claims—and this because his monism is the consequence of a searching conceptual analysis of the Vedas and the Upaniṣads, and not the end product of a direct and unmediated mystical experience. Śaṅkara's entire system, which, not for nothing, is technically described as *Advaita Vedānta*, results, as he would insist, from exegesis, not experience. Indeed, one is hard-pressed to find any evidence that Śaṇkara ever experienced the oneness he extols. Instead, this oneness is an ideal arrived at by arguing logically and otherwise about what certain Vedic and Upaniṣadic texts mean—it does not result from actual ecstatic moments in which Ātman is Brahman. (This circumstance is closely paralleled in the history of Kabbalah, wherein experiential reports, as compared to exegetical glosses and theoretical constructs, are very rare, as well as in the large corpus of Sufi writings that, on the whole, are considerably reticent about describing personal ecstatic experiences.[107] It is also distinctly paralleled in the history of Christian mysticism, though in this tradition experiential reports are more common. But even in this setting, one needs to go a step farther and understand that such reports represent, have the nature of, a stylized form of narrative in this tradition.)

In reflecting on these claims for *mitzvot* that are made by kabbalists, the claims regarding the life and death of Jesus and the Mass by medieval Catholic mystics, the role of *yajñas* and mantras in Hinduism—and, by extension, aspects of Sufi teaching about Qur'ānic doctrine and *ādāb* (rules of correct behavior)—one recognizes the truth of M. D. Chenu's observation on the nature of symbolic interpretation in the medieval era: "To bring symbolism into play was not to extend or supplement a previous act of the reason; it was to give primary expression to a reality which reason could not conceptualize."[108] The symbolic can be found everywhere in religious environments but it is present nowhere more than in the thought and teaching of the great mystical masters. For them it was an essential mode of being, a necessary form of decipherment, a discrete method of metaconceptualization and, to the degree possible, a required type of explanation. The "symbol," the symbolic modality—and the theurgical and magical possibilities they open up—comprise a fundamental channel of divine teaching through which humankind learns, glimpses, the irreducible Beyond.

Typology, or Metonymy

As a complement to the allegorical and symbolic readings, there is the separate method of interpretation known as typology, or metonymy. Here an individual or an event is not read simply as referring to, or standing for, something else (that is, *X* understood to mean *Y*), as in allegorical situations, but rather, the event or individual at issue is conceived of as a model, type, or sign of a specific sort of activity or characteristic that repeats itself, which thereby means that the future will be like the past and that the past prefigures the future. Quintilian, in his *Institutes of Oratory*, already observed that "metonymy . . . consists in the substitution of one name for another, and as Cicero tells us, is called *hypallagē* (exchange) by the rhetoricians."[109] Employing such an understanding, the Hebrew Prophets saw the Exodus, for example, as a sign of God's redemptive power, which would manifest itself again in the future redemption. "On that day, the Lord will extend his hand yet a second time [the Exodus having been the first] to recover the remnant of the people."[110] The saving God still saves.

The most essential implication of this hermeneutical method is summed up in a famous rabbinic maxim: "What occurred to the Fathers will occur to the sons."[111] A teaching glossed by Nachmanides—arguably the greatest medieval Jewish mystical Bible commentator—is as follows:

> I will tell you a principle by which you will understand all the coming portions of Scripture concerning Abraham, Isaac, and Jacob. It is indeed a great matter which our Rabbis mentioned briefly, saying: "Whatever has happened to the patriarchs is a sign to the children." It is for this reason that the verses narrate at great length the account of the journeys of the patriarchs, the digging of the wells, and other events. Now, someone may consider them unnecessary and of no useful purpose, but in truth they all serve as a lesson for the future: when an event happens to any one of the three patriarchs, that which is decreed to happen to his children can be understood. . . . It is for this reason that the Holy One, blessed be He, caused Abraham to take possession of the Land and symbolically did to him all that was destined to happen in the future to his children. Understand this principle. Now, with the help of G-d, I will begin to explain in detail the subject matter of the verses.[112]

Mekubbalim know that history, especially the history of the Jewish people, is not the result of accidents. It reflects and reveals an encompassing, providential plan that is organized according to a stylized pattern of divine initiatives and responses. As such, the past is the pointer to the future if the past, in keeping with its deep mystical structure, is properly comprehended. In its totality, history is the enactment and reenactment of transcendental purposes.

In similar fashion, the fundamental theological premise of Christianity, regarding its relation to Judaism, was its belief that the events described in the Hebrew Bible, the so-called Old Testament, "prefigure" those in the New Testament, and that the prophecies of the former are fulfilled in the latter. So Cain is the synagogue; Abel, the church. So Hagar and Sarah, Ishmael and Isaac, Leah and Rachel, Manasseh and Ephraim, Eli and Samuel, Saul and David are all, respectively, "typologically," the old and new covenants. So Jesus is a new Adam,[113] the sacrificial Isaac,[114] and a superior Moses.[115] His death and resurrection repeat the salvific act fo the Exodus.[116] His temptations repeat Israel's trials in the desert.[117] He is the "suffering servant" of Isaiah 53. In sum, the most important prophecies of the Hebrew Bible are directed to the future and for the sake of an event yet to happen—the life and death of Jesus. In Paul's phrase, Jesus "is the yes pronounced upon God's promises, every one of them" (2 Cor. 1:20). God's revelations in the past are for the sake of the Christian future. "The time is fulfilled" (Mark 1:15). Augustine clearly and paradigmatically described this interconnection: "In the Old Testament the new lies hid; in the New Testament the meaning of the Old becomes clear."[118] And Jerome made it a rule of his exegesis: "Let us follow the rule that all the prophets did much that was typical of our Lord . . . and whatever at the actual time happened concerning Jeremiah was a prophecy of the future concerning the Lord."[119] Developing this argument, Hilary, in his *Tractatus Mysteriorum*, wrote: "Christ begets the Church, . . . redeems it by true authentic prefigurations through the whole course of this world's history: in the sleep of Adam, in the flood of Noah, . . . the justification of Abraham. Everything which Christ would fulfill had then been prefigured since the beginning of the world" (1.1).[120] In any event, such typological readings are found in nearly all the major patristic authors; and through the work of Justin, Melito of Sardis, Tertullian, Clement, Origen, Ambrose, Hilary, Athanasius, Gregory of Nyssa, Chrysostom, Basil, Cyril of Alexandria, Cyprian, and

Augustine, it becomes a standard form of medieval Christian scriptural interpretation—mystical and nonmystical alike.

What is particularly significant about typological analyses, as against simply allegorical ones, is that they do not dissolve the concreteness of the (primarily) historical terms or events—for example, the Exodus or the Passion—being deciphered and compared. Indeed, it is essential to the metonymic model that the individual names of persons and events be retained to both individuate them and make possible a linear analysis. In such an interpretive schema, event A or person B is said to be like event X or person Y, and both A and X and B and Y are explicated as being part of a coherent, often historical, series that is tied together by an overarching value or principle, for example, Divine Love, Providence, God's redemptive power, or the power of evil. As a result, such exegesis differs from and negates (to varying degrees from case to case) the spiritualizing tendency found, for example, in the extreme allegorizing of Origen and his many heirs. Typology—if I may be allowed a certain simplification—compares (and contrasts) events and people, while allegory compares (and contrasts) disembodied metaphysical archetypes.

Kabbalists, and other Jewish exegetes, employed this mode of interpretation but less often and less centrally than did Christian scholars. The reason for this asymmetry lies in the differing historical-theological situations in which Jewish and Christian students of the Bible found themselves—that is, Jewish scholars did not have to find connections between two testaments and, therefore, had less need of such an interpretive procedure. Yet, insofar as they looked to the Bible for indications of Israel's future, of God's presence and activity in the ongoing life of the Jewish people, even in exile—and hopefully of Israel's final redemption and return to the Land of Israel—typology was a useful method of interpretation. So, for example, Esau is Rome for the Talmudic sages. And regarding Esau, Rabbi Simeon bar Yoḥai taught: "It is an axiom [that] Esau hates Jacob."[121] This is *the* explanation of anti-Jewish sentiment, and Jews need to have no illusions on this matter. The future is like the past. Again, the book of Daniel's typology of the fourth wicked kingdom was applied by the Talmudic sages to Rome,[122] by medieval Jews in Christian countries to Christendom, and by Jews in Muslim countries to Ishmael and the world of Islam.[123] Similarly, Nachmanides, in interpreting Jacob's encounter with Esau after many years (recounted in Gen. 32:4), links Jacob's actions on this occasion with the fall of the later Hasmonean state to Rome:

> Since the southern part of the Land of Israel adjoins Edom, and Jacob's father *dwelt in the land of the South*, he had to pass through Edom or near there. Therefore, he feared lest Esau hear of it, and he took the initiative by sending messengers to him in his country. But the Sages have already taken him to task for this, saying in Bereshith Rabbah: *"Like one that taketh a dog by the ears is he that he passeth by, and meddleth with a strife not his own*. The Holy One, blessed be He, said to Jacob, "Esau was going his way, and you send him messengers, and say to him, *Thus saith thy servant Jacob!*""
>
> In my opinion this too hints at the fact that we instigated our falling into the hand of Edom [Rome] for the Hasmonean kings during the period of the Second Temple, entered into a covenant with the Romans, and some of them even went to Rome to seek an alliance. This was the cause of their falling into the hands of the Romans. This is mentioned in the words of our Rabbis, and is well publicized in books.[124]

Furthermore, Jacob's plan to divide his camp (so that in case of an attack some of his family might survive) is indicative of Israel's history during the Exile:

> The intent of this is that Jacob knew that all his seed would not fall into Esau's hands. Therefore, in any case, one camp would be saved. This also implies that the children of Esau will not formulate a decree against us designed to obliterate our name entirely, but they will do evil to some of us in some of their countries. One of their kings will formulate a decree in his country against our wealth or our persons while simultaneously another king will show compassion in his place and save the refugees. And so the Rabbis said in Bereshith Rabbah: "*If Esau come to the one camp and smite it*—these are our brethren in the south. *Then the camp which is left shall escape*—these are our brethren in the Diaspora." Our Rabbis thus saw that this chapter alludes also to the future generations.[125]

Nor is Nachmanides' use of typology unique. Although, as noted, it was a minor trope among Jewish exegetes in comparison to allegory more generally understood, it was utilized effectively by, for example, Isaac ben Joseph Ha-Kohen in his fifteenth-century commentary on the Book of Ruth, and by a variety of late-medieval Jewish rationalist and kabbalistic biblical commentators. As Frank Talmage notes regarding Joseph Ha-Kohen's *Ruth*:

> There the book of Ruth is read as a prefiguration of the future history of Israel, and its characters are types (*mashal*) of those yet to come—Elimelech of the House of David, Naomi of the kingdom of Israel, Ruth of the faithful tribes of Judah and Benjamin, Orpah of the wayward ten tribes who followed Jeroboam, and so forth.[126]

The Zohar, too, despite its emphasis on theosophical forms of meaning, its concern with the secrets of the sefirothic realm and humankind's relationship to this esoteric domain, also employs typological readings. For example, it sees, in the very odd tale of Lot and his daughters, a prefiguration of the action of Ruth and Boaz that, through the special direction of heaven, eventuates in the Messiah.

> In regard to the names Moab and Ammon, R. Jose made the following comment. "The first-born daughter was bold-faced enough to call her son 'Moab,' thereby proclaiming that he was *meab*, i.e., the issue of her own father; whereas "the younger she also bore a son, and called his name Ben-Ammi": the mother out of delicacy gave him that name which being interpreted simply means "a son of my people," without betraying who his father was. Further, the words "and he knew not when she lay down, nor when she arose" occur twice in this passage, first in reference to the younger daughter, and then in reference to the elder. In the former case the word *b'qumah* (when she arose) occurring in it is *plene*, i.e., with the letter *vav*, which, moreover, is provided with a dot; this is to signify that heaven, as it were, was an accomplice to the act which ultimately was to bring about the birth of the Messiah. Contrariwise, the similar word in reference to the younger one is written defectively, without the letter *vav*, for the reason that none of her issue had any part in the Holy One, blessed He. R. Simeon said: "The underlying meaning of the words 'and he knew not' is that he was unaware that the Holy One intended to raise from her King David and Solomon and all the other kings and, finally, the Messiah." R. Simeon said further: "The expression 'when she arose' has its counterpart in the words used by Ruth, 'And she rose up before one could discern another' (Ruth 3:14). For it was on that day that Lot's daughter could be said to have risen to the height of her destiny in that [p. 3a] Boaz became attached to one of her lineage in order 'to raise up the name of the

> dead upon his inheritance,' by means of which there were raised from her all those kings and the elect of Israel. Again, 'And he knew not when she lay down' has its counterpart in the verse, 'And she lay at his feet until the morning.'" (Ibid.).[127]

In this gloss, the Zohar, through its exoteric hermeneutics, is able to tease out, through the spelling of words used in Genesis, the future course of the families that were descended from Lot's double act of incest, through Ruth and Boaz, and that culminated in the royal line from which would derive the future Redeemer. This is not an accidental or contingent chain of genealogical descent but one in which a deep mystery abides, one in which "heaven, as it were, was an accomplice."

I resist the temptation here to provide examples of similar forms of typological exegesis found in Islamic and other mystical traditions. I add, however, one last, more general, observation regarding typology as a form of mystical scriptural exegesis: such expositions are premised on the hermeneutical-*cum*-metaphysical assumption that historical reality is governed by transcendental forces and moves forward toward a more-than-historical teleology, even if it does so, in Eckhart's phrase, *innuit quasi latenter*, that is, obscurely and darkly. As a result, to engage in such textual study and analysis, to attempt to unpack these dense theosophical *midrashim*, is not only to seek to know the basic design of the created order but also, and still more, to seek out the One/It who/which is responsible for this design.

Paradox

A favored exegetical and descriptive technique of mystical authors is the use of paradox. In employing it, mystics do not believe themselves to be making propositions that are simply logically contradictory—that is, their utilization of such unusual locutions is not merely the result of intellectual ineptitude and linguistic sloppiness. Rather, paradoxes are understood as contradictions that result from holding to two true propositions that do not agree, while the disagreement between them cannot be resolved in any rational manner. To avoid a longer analysis of this conception of paradox, I remind readers that this is the classical definition resorted to, for example, by the church to defend its various Christological formulations of the Incarnation and the Trinity,[128] notions that, by definition, are claimed to ultimately defy logic and transcend the ordinary categories of grammar and language.

In trying to give voice to what are regularly claimed to be truths beyond language, mystics find that paradoxes, because of their unconventionality, are a valuable tool. To the degree that they break accepted linguistic and logical rules, they are seen as a fit vehicle for religious language insofar as such language relates to God and other Ultimate Objects or Subjects—*al Haqq, Ens Realisimum, Nicht, Mu, Esse, Eyn Sof, Nirvāṇa, Śūnyatā, Brahman*—that, by definition, cannot be captured in standard discourse or limited and explained according to the laws of logic.

Understanding this first principle that governs the employment of paradoxes reveals the further truth that mystics (and scholars) utilize the deviant language of paradox to indicate the metastatus of the referents of such language—that is, such language is not meant as a literal description of the metalinguistic, metalogical ultimate realities but as a way of "signing" them. As such, despite the use of language in such circumstances, paradox shares, a priori, the hermeneutical premises of the *via negativa*—

that no predicates properly apply to God or the Ultimate *X*—and of apophatic theology more generally: for any (proposition or attribute) *Y*, *X* (the ultimate reality) is not *X*. (For, according to their governing principles, to predicate anything of God or of the Ultimate *X* would be to limit and thereby diminish God or the Ultimate *X*.) In the language of Hinduism, one can only say, *nety, nety*, (not this, not this). Which is to recognize that paradoxes do not make substantive ontological pronouncements. Rather, they indicate, by a sort of indirection, that there is an ultimate reality whose being/Being is more than this or that, more than a single category, or many categories, can capture, and which can be known, if it can be known at all, only through forms other than ordinary linguistic forms and logical categories.[129] As Erigena argued, in defense of terms such as *superessentialis*: "[A term such as this is permissible] for it says that God is not one of the things that are but that he is more than the things that are, but what that 'is' is, it in no way defines."[130]

Mention of Erigena reminds us that this use of paradoxical formulations is deeply embedded in the Western intellectual tradition, especially that part of it that is connected to, and emanates from, Neoplatonism. In particular, the paradoxical pronouncements of, and support for, a radical *via negativa* by Pseudo-Dionysius the Aeropagite—so-called because this fifth–sixth-century author was confused with the figure mentioned in Acts 17:34—exerted an enormous influence on medieval Christian mystical tradition. For it was Pseudo-Dionysius who taught what would become the much recycled doctrine of an ultimate *extasis* beyond *panta ouk onta aki onta* (being and nonbeing), *pros tēn hyperousion tou theiou* (in accordance with the essence of God).[131] Gregory the Great; John Scotus Erigena, who translated Pseudo-Dionysius into Latin in 862; Hugh of St. Victor, who edited two commentaries on the celestial hierarchy between 1125 and 1137; Richard of St. Victor; Bernard of Clairvaux; Isaac of Stella; Bonaventure; Eckhart; Tauler; Ruysbroeck; Nicholas of Cusa; Cisneros; Francis of Osuna; and John of the Cross—all draw upon him, as did a host of Renaissance Platonists led by Pico dello Mirandola and Ficino. Repeatedly, Christian mystics, as well as kabbalists and Sufis, turned to this strategy of using paradoxical formulations to indicate *that* God was, but not *what* God was. (And as noted in the following discussion, a parallel approach was widely adopted in the major Eastern mystical traditions.)[132]

Frank Tobin, commenting on Eckhart's German sermon on the "poverty of spirit" ("Beati pauperes spiritu"),[133] provides a helpful first example of one type of paradoxical formulation. He notes that Eckhart urges us

> to beg God to rid us of God. God can be known to us in any positive way only through what he brings about. But as the cause of creatures God does not reveal himself as he really is. Creatures are too far from him, are in the region of dissimilarity. In knowing God as the cause of creatures, we grasp something that is little more than an arbitrary sing of the reality. By getting rid of this sign, by realizing through negative attribution that our notion of God contains hardly a hint of his true nature, we pass—paradoxically—to a better understanding of the God who is hidden from us.[134]

Only through the paradoxicality of negation can one provide meaning to God-language. The structure of things, the Godliness of God—that is, His essential nature, whatever and however it is, such as it is—creates this phenomenological circumstance that cannot be overcome. In consequence, Eckhart, in trying to think through the relationship of human speech to God's true nature, reflects on Augustine's famous position on this problem—in his *On Christian Doctrine* (1.6)—as follows:

> Augustine says "All writings are in vain. If one says that God is a word, he has been expressed (*gesprochen*); but if one says that God is unspoken (*ungesprochen*), he is ineffable (*unspechlich*)." And yet he is something, but who can speak this word? No one can do this, except him who is this Word. God is a Word that speaks itself. Wherever God is, he speaks this Word; wherever he is not, he does not speak. God is spoken and unspoken.[135]

In this highly peculiar, very difficult teaching, Eckhart is trying to convey something of the truth of God's presence, despite acknowledging our human incapacity, that is made possible by God's own mysterious nature that necessarily makes Itself known. In reflecting on the possible interpretation of this strange formulation, it is helpful to appreciate that Eckhart's language—his use of elaborate paradoxical constructions that involve positing positive and negative attributions to the divine—does not function as language functions in, for example, Zen *kōan*s, in which case language is pushed to such an extreme that it ceases to operate altogether. Instead, Eckhart utilizes language to indicate something of transcendental reality—of God's nature and speech—that must be "known" but cannot be known; that must be expressed but cannot be expressed in ordinary language; that *is* but whose "*isness*" is unlike that of any other reality.

From this starting point, Eckhart proceeds to demand that "whoever sees anything of God sees nothing of God";[136] that "if we really understood how creatures flow out [of God] yet remain within [God], it would not be true";[137] that "the more he [God] is in things, the more he is outside of things"[138] (a recycling of the old Neoplatonic paradox of *totus intus, totus foris*);[139] and that if God is being (*wesen*), then the proper description of God is "a being above being,"[140] or, perhaps still better, "a being without being" (*ein wesen weselôs*). Supporting and advancing his theological and metaphysical views through the use of his paradoxes, together with the additional stylistic devices of negation and the *via negativa*, antithesis—the contrasting of opposites—and the use of chiasmus, Eckhart strives to convey that mystical insight, "unknowing knowledge,"[141] which is, by its inherent nature (assertedly) supralogical and beyond the boundaries and limits of phenomenal reality.[142] In so doing he seeks to use language to make plain the incapacity of language to deal with the transcendent, and, at the same time, the necessity, however contradictory, to struggle to do just this.

What is particularly interesting is that Eckhart attempts this logically impossible possibility more often than not in the context of interpreting a biblical teaching. For example, in his *Commentary on Wisdom*, explicating his views on the crucial dialectic of God's immanence and transcendence, he writes: "Everything which is distinguished by indistinction is the more distinct the more indistinct it is, because it is distinguished by its own indistinction. Conversely, it is the more indistinct the more distinct it is, because it is distinguished by its own distinction from what is indistinct."[143] While on the central issue of the Word in the opening of John's Gospel—a theme to which Eckhart returns again and again, and which provides a basis for his cardinal doctrine that *deus est intelligere*—he expresses himself in this grand paradoxical formulation: "When the Father gave birth to all creatures, he gave birth to me, and I flowed out with all the creatures, and yet remain within in the Father. Just like the word I now utter: It arises within me; second, I abide upon its image; third, I utter it forth, and all of you discern it; yet it actually remains in me. Just so have I remained in the Father." (The full force of Eckhart's "illogical" argument, of his strange construal of the nature of the Word, is conveyed most powerfully through his own highly idiosyncratic German: "Do der vater gebor alle creaturen, do gebor er mich, und ich cloz uz mit allen creaturen und bleip doch inne in dem vater. Ze glicher wis, als daz wort, daz ich nu spriche, daz entspringet in mir, ze dem andern male so ruowe ich uf dem bilde, ze dem dritten male so spriche ich ez uz, und ir enpfahet ez alle; nochdenne blibet ez eigenliche in mir. Also bin ich in dem vater bliben.")[144] Insofar as the Bible is God's own speech, we must seek to understand its meaning—here the meaning of the Word—and in order to do so we are authorized to speak of that which the Bible speaks. Had God not spoken of these matters—of the birth of the Word and its emanation—we could not speak of them at all. However, God's speech being polysemous, and its subjects transcendental, it reveals something of the mystery of His relation to the Word but in a manner that always escapes full human comprehension. God's speech as in, for example, his revelation allows us an awareness of transcendental realia—without it we would be largely bereft of knowledge of God—but God reveals Himself in such a way, through paradoxes and negation, that we are constantly reminded not to mistake that which we do comprehend for the totality of that which is to be comprehended. The Bible and other scriptures, as these are read by mystical masters like Eckhart, are seen to make present the numinous, the transcendent, and the mysterious, without presenting strong, structured conceptualizations of these dimensions of being/Being.

For Eckhart, the Bible is a book of secrets, and the key to understanding it is an awareness that it reveals ultimate truths while concealing them and conceals them while revealing them. In commenting on it, as he repeated does, he wishes to convey the unconveyable by speaking of *X* and then denying *X*, leaving some trace of the meaning of *X* while not describing *X*. Through simultaneously affirming *X* and denying *X*, paradoxical language, in his understanding of it, paradoxically gives some direction toward which to look for *X* but does not picture *X* or literally attribute qualities or characterstics of *X*, though paradoxically the indescribability of the absolute becomes, in an inverted way, a description.

At the same time, Eckhart also wishes to use language as a medium of and for spiritual transformation, through which the reader/hearer will undergo a change of perspective, an alteration of consciousness, a modification in one's belief, a revolution in one's experience of the divine.

Eckhart's use of paradoxical formulations, and his motivations for using them, are, of course, phenomena he shares with many (indeed most) medieval Christian mystics, especially as they attempt to plumb the depths of scripture. For example, Isaac of Stella talks of the "unapproachable light . . . [that] itself produces our darkness";[145] and he proposes that if "we wish to speak about the Ineffable, about whom nothing can be properly said, it is necessary to be silent, or to use altered terms."[146] Commenting on the seraphim spoken of in Isaiah 6:2 he preaches:

> No wonder the seraphim, for all their holiness and towering nature and those wings that indicate the soaring of contemplation, are seen to cover their face and feet. It was to teach us that it was not their own ignorance that kept the beginning and the end from them; it was God's fathomless superwisdom. Just as by seeing nothing we behold invisible darkness, and by hearing nothing we hearken to inaudible silence, so, by neither seeing nor enduring the Light that is more than superabounding and cannot be borne, we do see the Invisible, not as blind men, but as those conquered by the Light.[147]

Likewise, Richard of St. Victor analyzes the cherubim over the ark as symbols of the coincidence of opposites—God is active-passive, light-darkness, revealed-hidden, like-unlike, a reality that ordinary reason cannot comprehend but that, in the higher awareness of mystical intelligentsia, becomes united and understood.[148] Again, in explicating the Gospel of John 1:5, Hadewijch writes: "The accident of multiplicity takes from us our singleness; as Saint John the Evangelist said: 'The light shines in the darkness and the dark darkness does not understand the clarity of the light shining in her.'"[149] Mechthild of Magdeburt, reflecting on the biblical conceptions of sin and finitude, praises alienation from God (*gotzvrömedunge*), claims that the more she accepts this alienation the closer God comes to her[150]—*Mere ie sich tieffer sinke, ie ich süsser trinke*[151] (the more I sink, the more I drink [of God]). And Tauler speaks of the *grundelos grunt* (the groundless ground); he also speaks of the Trinity as the imageless image;[152] of God who "becomes and unbecomes"; of him (the mystical soul) who "has died and is decreated (*entworden*), to him the Father is revealed."[153] To make sense, however oblique, of the mysteries revealed through God's revelation in the Bible, one must forgo, transcend, that which is regularly identified as sense, and the forms of language and logic that define this delimiting standard of intelligibility. Paradox—and negation resulting in paradox—are the signs of transcendence when transcendence is "perceived" by human beings from below.

John of the Cross, in chapter 8 of *The Ascent of Mount Carmel*, in explaining that "no creature or knowledge comprehensible to the intellect can serve as a proximate means for the divine union with God," tells us: "In order to draw nearer the divine ray, the intellect must advance by unknowing rather than by the desire to know, and by blinding itself and remaining in darkness rather than by opening the eyes."[154] In offering this gloss, John of the Cross emphasizes still another meaning of paradoxical utterances: the purpose of using language and paradox in the mystical context is not to present an objective description, and not even a nondescriptive description, or a trace, à la Eckhart, but rather to testify to an experience—which John labels a "wound," a "burn," a "spark," a "flame of love" in the soul—and to mark out the path, set out most clearly in scripture, to that experience. The usefulness of paradoxical formulations lies in their unique ability to lead the reader/hearer/seeker into contact with the mystery of the Ultimate. "This knowing which is unknown . . . is of such high excellence, this supreme knowing . . . and his knowledge so increase, that he is left unknowing."[155] The object of such discourse is not the transmission of an idea, the sharing of some form of gnosis, but rather the remaking of the reader/hearer/seeker as an appropriate partner for an intense, overwhelming love affair with God. There is no more efficacious way to accomplish this transformation than through an encounter with the divine enigmas of scripture. As John explains regarding biblical mysteries:

> The spirit and life is perceived by souls who have ears for it, those souls, as I say that are cleansed and enamored. . . . Those who do not relish this language [that] God speaks within them must not think on this account that others do not taste it; St. Peter tasted it in his soul when he said to Christ, "Lord, where shall we go? You have the words of eternal life" [John 6:69]. And the Samaritan women forgot the water and the water pot because of the sweetness of God's words [John 4:28]. Since this soul is so close to God, it is transformed into a flame of love, in which the Father, the Son, and the Holy Spirit are communicated to it.[156]

This transcendental communion, however, is very special, so special in fact that *no* human knowledge can lead to it. God is not accessible to human beings on our terms, through our wisdom, as a consequence of our way of knowing. Rather, God, the incomprehensible, reaches out to humankind in a supreme act of grace and lets His unknowability be "tasted" through His love rather than through our wholly inadequate comprehension. For this reason, given this metaphysical circumstance, to indicate such extraordinary Divine activity, to speak of it even though it is "incomprehensible," one can but use paradoxical constructions.

The diverse use of paradoxes as a preferred literary-religious form is also widely found in Sufism. Junayd, for example, in developing his theory of the preexistence of the soul and the final goal of mystical ascent, employs locutions such as the searching after the condition in which the soul is "as [it] was when [it] was before [it] was."[157] Again he describes the moment of ecstasy, of *fana*, extinction of the self, as a moment in which Allah "annihilated me in generating me as he had originally generated me in the state of my annihilation."[158] Likewise, in poetically explicating the Qurʾānic tale of Iblis's (Satan's) refusal to bow before Adam, al-Ḥallāj tells us, "I have attained certitude that distance and nearness are one."[159] Ibn ʿArabī's description of mystical witnessing (*shahada*) is put mysteriously as follows: "When I witness, O!—the-one-who-has-no-likeness / Guidance and error are the same to me."[160] Indeed, in a not too extended sense, much of Ibn ʿArabī's corpus can be classified as both exegetical in character and paradoxical in form. The four volumes of Ibn ʿArabī's commentary on specific verses and suras, compiled and published by Mahmud Ghurab, reveal both of these characteristics very clearly. Take, as an example, his theosophical-exegetical reflection on Qurʾān 19:86, "And he pushes criminals." Ibn ʿArabī explains the verse as follows:

> He pushes those who deserve that toward which they are being pushed, by means of the wind from the west [*rîh al-dabur*], with which he makes them die unto themselves. He seizes them by their forelocks and the wind—which is only their own passions—pushes them toward Gehenna, toward the separation [*al-buʿd*, "distance"] that they imagined. But when he has thus pushed them toward this place, they in fact arrive at proximity. The [illusory] distance ceases, as does, for them, that which is called "Gehenna" [*musammâ jahannam*, Gehenna retains its name—*ism*—but that which was "named" (*musammâ*) by this name, namely, an abyss, a place of exile, has changed its nature].[161]

Allah's love is such that He transforms all relationships with humankind according to a rule of divine mercy. In applying this rule, according to Ibn ʿArabī, Allah's actions and their consequences create an alternative reality to the one that is usually imagined as existing. The alienation (*al-buʿd*) from the Divine that sin, "their own passion," causes does not lead to a distant Gehenna, but paradoxically, because of

His compassion, brings men back to their Creator. What is particularly interesting about this reading is that Ibn ʿArabī, through his systemic, paradoxical exegesis of this single Qurʾānic verse, posits, and relies upon, the following inversions or transformations: distance = closeness; judgment = compassion; Divine causation = human sin; death = life external; separation = proximity; Gehenna = heaven; exile = return. Things are not what they appear to be; the correctly decoded meaning of reality is not the superficial meaning we regularly claim to apprehend. Paradoxes for Ibn ʿArabī, and nearly the whole of the Sufi tradition, are intended to help us recognize this truth and to point us away from the limited and the mundane to the unlimited *al haqq*.

In the rich mystical traditions of India, Japan, and China, similar types of textual investigation and interpretive techniques have a continual and repercussive presence. Consider, for example, the character of Zen *kōan*s (and *mondo*s) that present classic mystical paradoxes, if of a special sort, generated from within a very particular ontological mapping of reality and human consciousness. Based on the claim that language is wholly inadequate for describing and translating the truth of *nirvāṇa*, and the way to *nirvāṇa*, Zen took to using language primarily in a performative way. The *kōan* does not "mean" anything; its purpose is to break the bonds of normal consciousness and thereby permit the gaining of a different sort of consciousness, which might be capable of achieving *samādhi*, *prajñā*, and *nirvāṇa*.

Consistent with this position, "Shuzan Shonen once held up his *shippe* (a stick about one and a half feet long made of bamboo) to an assembly of disciples and declared: 'Call this a *shippe* and you assert; call it not a *shippe* and you negate. Now do not assert, nor negate, and what would you call it? Speak, speak!'"[162] And a second Zen master emphasized: "The true state is no state. The gate of *Dhamra* is no gate. Holy knowledge is no knowledge."[163] It is important to appreciate that in both of these instances the master was neither presenting information nor seeking it. Instead, on both occasions the Zen masters were actively seeking, through their strange, paradoxical, formulations, to induce a changed awareness among their disciples consistent with the fundamental tenets of Buddhist ontology—that is, the doctrine of *anātman* (no self), the essential theory of "dependent origination," and the foundational tenet that liberation is possible through the attainment of *nirvāṇa*. Their purpose was not to comment on the state of *anātman*, but to encourage it; not to speak of liberation, but to help in achieving it; not to speculate on *nirvāṇa*, but to assist others in becoming "nirvanaized."

The essential claim presented in the early canonical literature of Buddhism is that the Buddha did not reply directly to metaphysical inquiries and rejected the ontological claims of Hinduism (of Ātman and Brahman). This doctrine forms the basis for the Zen belief, which is central to the doctrine that underpins the Zen *kōan*, that *tathatā* (suchness) is "without words," that "suchness" is "transmitted outside the doctrine," and that "suchness" "does not set up letters," that is, it is inexpressible in words. It is the Buddha's insistence on the negation of self in the notion of no-self, combined with the claim that the nature of *satori*, *Wu*, or *nirvāṇa* cannot be put into words, that generates the following intriguing dialogue: "Tung-Shan asked Pen-Chi: 'What is your name, monk?' and received the reply, 'Pen-Chi.' 'Say something more,' said Tung-Shan. 'I won't.' 'Why not?' 'Because my name is not Pen-Chi.'"

In addition, there are the many Buddhist paradoxes that revolve around the category of desire: we must cultivate the desire to be free of desire as we desire to be liberated. And those that turn on the paradox of *nirvāṇa*—for example, the *Prajñāpāramitā* teaches:

> Thus, O Sariputa, all things, having the nature of emptiness, have no beginning and no ending. They are neither faultless nor not faultless; they are neither perfect nor imperfect. In emptiness there is no form, no sensation, no perception, no discrimination, no consciousness. There is no eye, no ear, no nose, no smell, no tastes, no touch, no mental process, no object, no knowledge, no ignorance. There are no Noble Fourfold Truths; no pain, no cause of pain, no cessation of pain, no Noble Path leading to the cessation of pain. There is no decay, and no death, and no destruction of the motion of decay and of death. There is no knowledge of Nirvāṇa, there is no obtaining of Nirvāṇa, there is no not obtaining of Nirvāṇa.[164]

And those that emerge from the report that the Buddha responded to the question of whether there is life after death, or whether death is annihilation, replied in the following way: "'The Perfect One exists after death,' this is not apposite; 'the Perfect One does not exist after death,' this also is not apposite; 'the Perfect One neither does nor does not exist after death,' this also is not apposite."

Then, again, there is Nāgārjuna's much admired, much copied employment of paradox. By pursuing the internal logic of the various interpretations of Buddhism encoded in the *Abhidharma*, especially those factors (*dharma*s), that relate to the analysis of existence and the notion of attributes, he showed each to be inconsistent, even nonsensical. It was against the background of this deconstructive effort that he was led to formulate his own views, especially those on *śūnyatā* (emptiness), in which he came to conclude: "The extreme limit (*koti*) of *nirvāṇa* is also the extreme limit of existence-in-flux (*saṃsāra*). There is not the slightest bit of difference between them."[165] To reach this challenging conclusion, he used contradictions and negative dialectics to disorient us, to confuse our awareness of how things are, and to free us from false notions of existence, so that we might be reoriented vis-à-vis reality, *satori*, *nirvāṇa*. In effect, paradox is used by Nāgārjuna to achieve a specific radical exegesis of Buddhism. (Parenthetically, I note that in the case of Nāgārjuna, as in the case of Śaṇkara, there is, despite early claims to the contrary in the Madhyamika school's account of its founder, no evidence that points directly to his having attained mystical enlightenment.)

The canonical literature of the Hindu tradition and its vast commentaries abound in paradoxes. The *Isā Upaniṣad* contends: "The One, the Self, though never stirring, is swifter than thought; . . . though standing still, it overtakes those who are running. . . . It stirs and it does not stir, it is far and likewise near. It is inside all this, and it is outside all this." The *Chāndogya Upaniṣad* insists that Brahman "moves, it moves not, it is far and near, it is in, it is out." The *Kena Upaniṣad* concludes its epistemological reflections on Brahman with this wisdom: "He who knows not, knows; he who knows, knows not"[166]; "Other indeed, is it than the known, and moreover above the unknown" (167). (See also *Muṇḍaka Upaniṣad* 3.1.7; *Kaṭha Upaniṣad* 1.25.20; and *Chāndogya Upaniṣad* 3.14.3.) These paradoxes take us beyond partial, limited, "incorrect" ideas of the ultimate (*Brahman paramartha*) and help guide us to that higher level of insight (*prajña*)—which is the deepest meaning of the Upaniṣads—where corrupt and inadequate notions of self and other and of Self and Other are replaced by a more adequate wisdom.

Given that the objects/subjects of concern—that is, Ātman and Brahman—are altogether *un*like objects/subjects in the realm of the everyday, the language used to approach them must likewise be *un*like the language of the everyday. It is this assumption that leads to the introduction of paradoxes as a way of signaling that the referents of the language, to the degree that the discourse is, in any sense, referential, are metaphysically anomalous, or alternatively, that the language in play is not intended to be referential at all. In the Vedas and Upaniṣads the allusions to these ultimates are marked by paradoxical constructions precisely because the writers are aware of, and wish to make others aware of, this exceptional metaphysical-linguistic status. There is thus a particular and coherent logic to the functioning of paradoxes in the canonical sources of the Hindu tradition.

It should also be recalled that it was in commenting on the *Bṛhadāraṇyaka Upaniṣad* that Śaṅkara argued that the only correct way to characterize Brahman was *neti, neti.* The use of negation, and the related technique of double exclusion—"neither this nor that"—are seen by him as the most suitable means for pointing toward, not describing, the Ultimate. As a pradigmatic example of this hermeneutical position, take his dialectical commentary on the Gita's famous paradox: "The highest Brahman . . . is not being (*sat*), nor is it nonbeing (*asat*).

> OBJECTION: How can the "unknowable" be described as "neither being nor nonbeing?"
>
> REPLY: As he is inaccessible to speech, the knowable Brahman is defined in all the Upaniṣads just by the denial of all distinctions.
>
> OBJECTION: Only that which is spoken of as being can be said to exist. If the knower cannot be spoken of as "being" (or "existence"), then it cannot exist as knower . . .
>
> REPLY: But neither is it nonbeing, since it is not an object of our consciousness of nonexistence.
>
> OBJECTION: But every state of consciousness is either consciousness of existence or nonexistence. The "knowable" therefore . . .
>
> REPLY: Not so, for it is beyond the reach of the senses, and thus is not an object of consciousness accompanied with the idea of either being or nonbeing. . . . As such it can only be known through the means of knowledge called testimony; it cannot be, like a jar, an object of consciousness accompanied by the idea either of existence or nonexistence.[167]

Through this procedure of questions and answers, involving the refinement, but not the dissolution, of the nature of the original paradox of the Gītā, Śaṇkara—never making any positive assertions about "higher Brahman," and never predicating any attribute to Brahman—advances our understanding by a process of elimination and indirection, consistent with the logic of paradoxical utterances.[168] In the employment of this logical technique, he reminds one of Eckhart, though readers must take care not to push this comparison too hard or too far. That is, for Śaṇkara, as for Eckhart, the logic of negation contains, paradoxically, a capacity to inform, while, at the same time, it does not allow the accumulation or formation of propositional knowledge or the direct attribution of predicates to the Divine (Brahman). Put another way, negation serves as an apophatic indicator—that is, its denials affirm the reality of that which is beyond speech.

One final observation of these differing traditions, and these differing techniques that are related to the employment of paradoxes: paradoxical formulations are, by design, intended to be logically indeterminate because they are employed in relationship to absolutes, the ultimate objects/subjects of mystical concern, which are, by definition, indeterminable. Paradoxes show this indeterminacy through their form, a form that finally has—on strict logical grounds—no content. But, at the same time, they do not become meaningless or wholly absurd, because they are utilized to express, to point toward, a truth that is revealed and confirmed normatively by revelation and scripture and they occur within a larger religious context in which all the negations and attributions, and the negations of attributions, and the attributions of negation receive meaning from the Weltanschauung that frames the entire, specific exegetical enterprise. So, for example, when Eckhart writes of a God who is not God, and the Word that is and is not God, and the Father who is and is not the Son, he is working from within a recognizably Christian Neoplatonic ontology that posits, a priori, a recognizably Christian trinitarian conception of God. Likewise, Nāgārjuna's dialectical negations that lead to an understanding of the doctrine of "dependent origination" (*pratītya-samutpāda*) and the related principle of *anicca* (impermanence) as equivalent to emptiness (*śūnyatā*), and again the radical paradoxical claim that "birth and death (*saṃsāra*) is identical in *nirvāṇa*," make some kind of sense because they presume and occur within a larger Buddhist context. In actuality, Nāgārjuna's comments on dependent origination, impermanence, and emptiness are best, and most fully, understood as commentaries on the Buddha's original teaching regarding *pratītya-samutpāda*. For this reason, no matter how complex, and sometimes apparently meaningless—because of its (il)logical turns—Nāgārjuna's thought possesses an overall coherence and intelligibility. He is, in effect, pushing Buddhist thought to its limits, but we can follow him because we understand the main structural claims of Buddhism that he shares and manipulates. Again, Saṅkara's *neti*, *neti* is a negation within the standing systematic theology of Hinduism. It is not just *neti*, *neti*, but "not this, not this" as *this* is conceptualized within the worldview of the Vedas and Upaniṣads. For this reason—that is, by virtue of this contextualization—the use of paradox by the world's mystics is more grounded than might appear to be the case.

Using Paradox to Hide Knowledge

There is one additional distinctive, mystical use of paradoxes to which I should call attention. This involves consciously utilizing, and understanding, paradoxes and paradoxical formulations as ways of purposely hiding certain types of knowledge, while simultaneously indicating this fact by hinting at, but only hinting at, the existence of such "secrets." Perhaps the best-known description of this position is set out in the "Introduction" to Maimonides' *Guide for the Perplexed*, which exerted a wide influence among the later Jewish rationalists and kabbalists, especially Abraham Abulafia and Shem Tov ibn Gaon, and among Christian scholastics such as Aquinas and mystics such as Eckhart. As part of his exploration of biblical language, Maimonides provides "seven causes that should account for the contradictory and contrary statements to be found in any book or compilation." Regarding the last of the seven, he writes:

> The seventh cause. In speaking about very obscure matters, it is necessary to conceal some parts and disclose others. Sometimes in the case of certain dicta this necessity requires that the discussion proceed on the basis of a certain premise, whereas in another

> place necessity requires that the discussion proceed on the basis of another premise contradicting the first one. In such cases the vulgar must in no way be aware of the contradiction; the author accordingly uses some device to conceal it by all means.[169]

Which is to say that, on at least certain occasions, the presence of contradictions-paradoxes does not prove a logical error or indicate the lack of conceptual power but is, rather, a sign intended to hint that the text that contains such constructions possesses deep spiritual resources not meant for everyone. Now, to the degree that we comprehend this function of contradictions-paradoxes, we generate yet another paradox. That is, while such formulations hide information, they also simultaneously, through the recognition of their distinctive form, reveal secrets, at least to the extent of calling the attention of the wise to the presence of esoteric doctrines in specific textual loci. This is most famously seen in a revised form in Nachmanides' biblical commentary wherein he does not publicly expose the putative core of the Torah and explicitly tells the general reader:

> Now behold I bring into a faithful covenant and give proper counsel to all who look into this book not to reason or entertain any thought concerning any of the mystic hints which I write regarding the hidden matters of the Torah, for I do hereby firmly make known to him [the reader] that my words will not be comprehended nor known at all by any reasoning or contemplation, excepting from the mouth of a wise Cabalist speaking into the ear of an understanding recipient. Reasoning about them is foolishness; and unrelated thought brings much damage and withholds the benefit. *Let him not trust in vanity, deceiving himself*, for these reasonings will bring him into nothing but evil as if they spoke falsely against G-d, which cannot be forgiven, as it is said, *The man that strayeth out of understanding shall rest in the congregation of the shades. Let them not break through unto the Eternal to gaze, for the Eternal our G-d is a devouring fire, even a G-d of jealousies*. And He will show those who are pleasing Him wonders from His Torah. Rather, let such see in our commentaries novel interpretations of the plain meanings of Scripture and Midrashim, and let them take moral instruction from the mouths of our holy Rabbis: "Into that which is beyond you, do not seek; into that which is more powerful than you, do not inquire; about that which is concealed from you, do not desire to know; about that which is hidden from you, do not ask. Contemplate that which is permitted to you, and engage not yourself in hidden things."[170]

Despite this warning, Nachmanides, when commenting on specific verses, many, though not all, of which are paradoxical or appear contradictory, gives his readers a clue as to which ones contain kabbalistic gnosis by remarking, "Ha-maven yaven" (Those who understand will understand). That is, while he does not reveal the actual nature of the encoded secrets, for they are not meant for the masses, readers should pay special attention to the verse under analysis, for its close study will reveal *chochmah nistarah*[171]—knowledge of the sefirothic realm and related theosophical wisdom. In this way the act of hiding also becomes, in part, an act of revealing.

Already in the *Celestial Harmony*, Pseudo-Dionysius had told his readers: "It is most fitting to the mysterious passages of scripture that the sacred and hidden truth about celestial intelligences be concealed through the inexpressible and the sacred and be inaccessible to the hoi polloi. Not everyone is sacred, and, as scripture says, knowledge is not for everyone."[172] Let these brief comments suffice—let readers take the hint that paradoxes are crucial indicators used to conceal, as well as to reveal, knowledge throughout the world's mystical literature.

Alphabets and Numbers

Many of the secrets of canonical texts are disclosed and retrieved through the application of intricate and unusual methods of numerical and letter permutation. Although it is not often discussed in the theoretical investigations of mystical phenomena that dominate the academic study of mysticism, the reality is that in at least certain major mystical traditions such exegetical techniques play an important role. The oldest tradition of this sort in the West is connected with Pythagoreanism and certain Neoplatonic teachers, including Plotinus. This practice was then adopted by Jews, Christians, and Muslims. Jewish thinkers began with three assumptions: (1) that God speaks Hebrew; (2) that the building blocks of the universe are the letters of the Hebrew alphabet, which God "spoke" in order to create the world; and (3) the letters, numbers, and sentences that God spoke in the process of creation are to be found in the Hebrew account of creation in Genesis. In consequence, the kabbalists held that the letters of the Hebrew alphabet, the numerical value of the letters, and the permutation of the letters (and, therefore, the words and sentences) contained and revealed elemental insights into the world above and the world below. Seen in this context, the *Sefer Yetzira*, for example, which was produced in the rabbinic era, should be considered, as its author intended it to be considered, a numerical-permutational commentary on Genesis 1—that is, an investigation of the mechanics by which God created the world. How, it asks, did God perform the wonder of creation through speech that is so simply and briefly described in Genesis? What did God say? What did He do? In answer to these primary queries, the *Sefer Yetzira* instructs its readers:

> 1. By means of thirty-two wonderful paths of wisdon, YH, YHVH of hosts, ELOHIM of Israel, Living ELOHIM, and Eternal King, EL SHADDAI, Merciful and Gracious, High and Uplifted, Who inhabits Eternity, exalted and holy is His Name, engraved. And He created His universe by three principles: by border and letter and number.
>
> Specifically as regard the letters of the Hebrew alphabet: 2. Twenty-two letters are the foundation: He engraved them, He hewed them out, He combined them, He weighed them, and He set them at opposites, and He formed through them everything that is destined to be formed.
>
> And these twenty-two letters then can be permutated and combined in a variety of ways: 4. And these twenty-two letters are the foundation: He set them in a wheel, like the kind of wall, with two hundred and thirty-one gates. And the wheel rotates forward and backward. And the sign of the thing is: there is no goodness above pleasure and there is no evil below pain
>
> 5. How did He combine them, weight them and set them at opposites? *Aleph* with all of them, and all of them with *Aleph*, *Bet* with all of them, and all of them with *Bet*. It rotates one turn, and thus they are in two hundred and thirty-one gates. And everything that is formed and everything that is spoken goes out from one term.[173]

Given the nature of this commentary, this mysterious doctrine of letters and numbers, and their myriad permutations, spawned a vast tradition of supercommentaries that continues into our own time.[174]

By the high medieval period, the notion that the creation account involved secrets necessarily linked to the Hebrew alphabet is widely attested. It is, therefore, well within the bounds of the tradition that the Zohar, in providing its theosophical rendition of Genesis 1, teaches:

"At the beginning," said Rav Hammuna Sava, "we find the letters in reverse order. The letter *bet* comes first, and then *bet* comes first again, namely, *bereshit* and then *bara*. After this we have *alef* coming first, and then *alef* coming first again, namely, *elohim* and then *et*. What happened was that when the Holy One, blessed be He, wanted to make the world, all the letters were sealed, and two thousand years before He created the world the Holy One, blessed be He, examined them and took delight in them. And when He wanted to create the world all the letters presented themselves to Him, from the end to the beginning."[175]

All the letters of the Hebrew alphabet are then described by the Zohar as to their esoteric significance, until the following:

The letter *bet* entered. She said to Him: "Master of the world, may it be Your will to create the world through me, because it is through me that they bless You in the upper and lower worlds." The Holy One, blessed be He, said to her: "Yes, to be sure, I shall create the world through you, and you shall be at the forefront of the creation of the world." The letter *alef* arose, but did not enter. The Holy One, blessed be He, said to her: "*Alef, alef*, why do you not come into My presence like the other letters?" She said to Him: "Master of the world, since I have seen all the other letters leaving Your presence without success, what point is there? Moreover, You have given this great gift to the letter *bet*, and it would not be right for a king to take away a present that he has given to his servant and give it to someone else." The Holy One, blessed be He, said to her: "*Alef, alef*, although I shall create the world through the letter *bet*, you will be the first of all the letters. I have no unification except through you. All calculations and every deed in the world will begin with you. No unification will be effected except through the letter *alef*." The Holy One, blessed be He, made large letters above and small letters below. Hence, we have *bet, bet: bereshit barā: alef, alef: elohim et*—the letters above, and the letters below, and they were all as one from the upper world and from the lower world.[176]

Then, further developing this theme, our kabbalistic commentator explains that the sequence of forty-two letters that begins with the *bet* of the first word in the bible, *Bereshit*, and continues to the letter *bet* in the word *Bohu*, comprises God's secret, mystical name:

Come and see. The world was engraved and established with forty-two letters, all of them a crown of the holy name. When they had become joined, they ascended by its letters to the realm above and then descended to the realm below. They were adorned with crowns in the four corners of the world, and (the world) was then able to survive. After this the letters went out and created the world above and below, the world of unification and the world of separation, and they are called "the mountains of Bether" (Song of Songs 2: 17), the mountains of separation, which are refreshed when the south side begins to draw near to them. Then the waters flow and, because of this force that flows above, everything rejoices. When thought arose in the joyful will of the mystery of mysteries a radiance came and flowed out of it, and they drew near to one another, and they have already explained it. These forty-two letters are a supernal mystery, and by them the upper world and the lower world were created, and they are the foundation and mystery of all the worlds. And concerning the fact that this is the mystery of the worlds, it is written, "The mystery of the Lord is for those that fear Him" (Psalm 25: 14). "And to make them known his covenant" (ibid.)—this is the mystery of the engraved letters (that stand out) revealed through their engraving.[177]

To know this name is a crucial matter that possesses, above all, theurgical significance, for it "is the foundation and mystery of all the worlds." Through the decipherment of these alphabetical configurations, especially those connected with the names of God, as these are revealed in the Torah, the Kabbalist knows himself to be laying bare the secret ontological skeleton on which the worlds above and below are constructed.

The a priori theory of the Hebrew language that is operative in this context also lends itself to other forms of letter manipulation that are used in pursuit of the discovery of the inner meaning of the Torah. The sequence of letters, their frequency, their repetition, and their reversibility are all taken to convey esoteric information. For example, the three letters *nun*, *gimmel*, and *ayin* can spell words for either distress or joy, depending on the order in which they occur. Being aware of this, the mystics argue that if we keep the Sabbath properly—that is, arrange the letters (which represent, and bring into being, reality) properly, we have joy (spelled *ayin*, *nun*, *gimmel*); if not, we experience distress (spelled *nun*, *gimmel*, *ayin*). Again the place that a letter occupies in the alphabet carries theosophical import—for example, *alef*, the first letter, is taken to be connected with divinity while the last letter, *taf*, has negative connotations. As a consequence, these letters and those words that contain these letters have to be carefully searched to decipher the positive and negative secrets they reveal. Similarly, in a much utilized argument, the letters that make up the divine names, especially the Tetragrammaton, are said to carry special meaningfulness, as do the divine names as names.

Parallel techniques, now predicated on the transcendental status of Arabic, are employed in multiple ways in Islamic, especially Sufi, exegesis of the Qur'ān. Ibn ʿArabī, for example, offers this explanation of the meaning of the letters of Muhammad's name:

> The first *mim* is the head, and that is the world of the supreme Sovereignty (*'alam al-malakut al-a' la*) and of the Greatest Intellect (*al-'aqlal-akbar*). The breast and the arms are under the letter *h*, and this is the Glorious Throne; its numerical value is 8, which is the number of the angels who carry the Throne. The second *m* represents the stomach, and that is the World of the Kingdom (*'alam al-mulk*). The hips, the legs, and the feet are from the *d*, and that is the stable composition by means of the Eternal Writ.[178]

Ibn ʿArabī intends this decoding to be taken very seriously, even literally, and sees in such alphabetical deconstructions the essential means for getting closer to the mystical core of Islam. Moreover, his employment of such hermeneutical methods is not incidental to this larger theosophical message. Indeed, it is as a result of the repeated application of such a method—and related methods—that he is able to establish the building blocks that support his capacious cosmological and anthropological vision.

A second example: Farīddiddīn 'Aṭṭār explains the name Aḥmad, another of Muhammad's names, in relationship to the *hadīth qudsī*, *Anā Aḥmad bilā mīm* (I am Aḥmad without the m) esoterically as follows: "Aḥmad is the messenger of Ahad [the One, Allah] . . . [and when] the radiance of the light of manifestation becomes evident, the *m* of Aḥmad becomes invisible."[179] There is then only Allah. Annemarie Schimmel, tracing the fame and importance of this extra-Qur'ānic tradition, notes:

> Scarcely any other *hadīth qudsī* has been used so frequently in the Persianate parts of the Muslim world, even though it is not attested in the early collections of traditions and appears only in the twelfth century. It seems to prove that Aḥmad-Muhammad is separated from God only by a single letter, the *m*. In the Arabic numeric system this letter has the value of 40, the number of patience, maturing, suffering, preparation. (Israel was for

> forty years in the desert; Jesus spent forty days in the desert; Muhammad was forty when his calling came; the forty days of Lent; the forty days of complete retirement as practiced by the Sufis, called *arbaʿin* or *chilla*; these and other similar customs and traditions are expressions of this special role of the number 40.) In Islamic mystical speculations 40 furthermore signifies the forty steps that man must pass on his way back to his origin—a topic elaborated by Attar in his *Muṣībatnāma*, and later by numerous mystics in the Ibn ʿArabī tradition. The *m* of Aḥmad points to all these mysteries; it is "the fountainhead of his teachings for which reason thirsts," as Jami says. A later poet in the Panjab has called the *m* "the shawl of humanity," which the One God put on when he created Muhammad in his exemplary role. Amir Khusrau, in a different vein of thought, found that the circular form of this *m* revealed it as "the Seal of Prophethood," and it is often called the "letter of contingency." Maulana Rumi, who sings that "Aḥmad is a veil" through which he wants to reach Ahad, dwells on the mystery of this *hadīth qudsī* in his prose musings, *Fīhi mā fīhi*: "Every addition to perfection is a diminution. . . . Aḥad is perfect, and Aḥmad is not yet in the state of perfection; when the *m* is removed it becomes complete perfection.[180]

This is the living stuff of mystical tradition—the way in which it is taught, commented on, expanded, learned, and transmitted from generation to generation. This is what Sufis, as compared to professors, are interested in. These are the sorts of gnostic insights that Sufis seek out, desire to master, and attempt to keep alive and pass on. Here we encounter one form of authentic commentary on *the* book, the Qurʾān, through which Sufism emerges and grows within the souls of Muslims and the heart of the Islamic community.

In addition, the same set of structural hermeneutical assumptions also supports exegetical techniques that depend on the idea of numbers. In nearly all the major mystical traditions that begin with Pythagoreanism in the West, and in the Hindu, Buddhist, Taoist, and Confucian commentary traditions in the East, numerological modes of interpretation of scripture are present. Hugh of St. Victor identified nine different factors that bear on the proper interpretation of numbers:

> The first way is by order of position: 1, for example, is connected with Unity and is the first number, the principle of all things. Alternately, one can look at their composition: 2, for example, can be divided and points to something transitory. Another meaning can be discovered through extension: since 7 follows 6, it means rest after work. Numbers can also have a meaning according to their disposition: thus, 10 has one dimension and points to the right faith, while 100 expands in width and thus points to the amplitude of charity, and 1,000 rises in height and can therefore be taken as an expression of the height of hope. One may also look at the numbers in connection with their use in the decimal system, in which case 10 means perfection. Another way to find a special meaning in a number is through multiplication: 12 is universal because it is the product of the corporeal 4 and the spiritual 3. Likewise, the number of its parts can be taken into consideration: 6, as is well known, is a perfect number because it is the sum of its integral components. It is also possible to look at the units that make up a number: 3 points to the Trinity, consisting of 3 units. And finally one may use exaggeration to understand why 7, under certain circumstances, grows into 77.[181]

Given this breadth of possibilities, the numerical and the numerological become as important in interpreting scripture as the alphabetical, the syntactical, and the semantical.

In Jewish tradition such methods, and related ones, are called *gematria*, or *notrakon*. These forms of analysis turn on the numerical value ascribed to the letters of the Hebrew alphabet; for example, *aleph* = 1, *bet* = 2, *gimmel* = 3. Given this alphetical sign-number link, words equal sums, and comparing the mathematical sum of a word (or letter) with other words (or letters) carries mystical import. So, for example, in searching out the meaning of the biblical phrase "Remember (*zachor*) the sabbath day, and hallow it," the mystics point out that the numerical value fo the word *zachor*, made up of the letters *zayin*, *chaf*, and *resh*, is 227, as is the numerical value of *berachah*, the Hebrew word for "blessing," made up of the letters *bet*, *resh*, *chaf*, and *hey*. This teaches that, given the mathematical equality, one who observes the Sabbath receives blessings. Again, in a more complicated play on numbers, the Hebrew letters that comprise the word for Satan, *ha-satan*, equal 364, which indicates that for 364 days of the year he causes problems for Israel and humankind, but that on the 365th day, Yom Kippur, the Day of Atonement, he is powerless against Israel's repentance and God's love.

Comparable and related numerical techniques are widely used in Pythagoreanism, Mithraism, and Zoroastrianism. For example, in Zoroastrianism, the number 7 represents the six *Amesha Spentas* (guiding spirits), and the high deity (*Ahura Mazda*), God of justice and goodness. In Sufi exegeses of the Qur'ān, in Christian mystical exegeses of the Hebrew Bible and of the Greek New Testament, and in Hindu interpretations of the Vedas and the Upaniṣads, the numbers 3 and 7 are of special value. Taoist and Confucian traditions assign a role to the pentagram, with its putative connections to the five planets, the five directions, the five seasons, the number of sacred mountains, and the degrees of nobility. And Buddhist texts and traditions interpret the number 7 as a magical-mystical number, so the Buddha searches for salvation for seven years and circles the Bodhi tree seven times before meditating beneath it.[182] Nearly everywhere, then, numbers, particularly as employed in scriptural narratives, carry substantive mystical content.

Conclusion

If one seeks to understand how mystical fellowships work and how individual mystics pursue their ambitious metaphysical goals,[183] then one not only has to concentrate attention on the rarified, and rare, moments of ecstasy, adhesion, supernal marriage, mindlessness, *satori*, *nirvāṇa*, and unity, but one also has to pay close attention to the sorts of exegetical techniques, and the ways of studying scripture, that are described in this essay. For the actual interpretation of sacred texts in these ways comprises a substantial part of what mystics actually do and plays a significant role in achieving those ultimate states of experience (and metaexperience) that mystics seek. It is therefore not surprising to find that the mystical exegesis of canonical texts constitutes a large, if not the largest, segment of what is usually identified as the collective body of the world's mystical literature.

The spatial constraints imposed upon an essay such as this forbid further exploration of the many additional important aspects related to the mystical exegesis of scripture. Among the relevant omissions, I think immediately of, for example, the not-yet-analyzed subjects of wordplay and the many ways in which changes of meaning take place; the cardinal role of analogy and analogical meaning in mystical texts; and the profound connections that are yet to be explored between meditation, prayer, and scripture. But such investigations must wait for other occasions. Instead, I conclude by emphasizing that exegesis, as understood by the world's mystical communities, by the world's mystical personalities, is a way of learning theurgical practices that can influence God or the Ultimate; a primary form, a main channel, of mystical ascent; a basic source of spiritual energy; a performative mystical act with salient experiential—transformational—consequences; a way of defining one's mystical path; and a way to meet and interact with God or the Ultimate(s). To engage scripture, as the mystical adept engages it,[184] is not only to participate in an intense dialogue with texts but also, and far more important, to reach out to, and sometimes even to feel and to touch—if only, as John of the Cross describes it, through a "gentle breeze, that art so delicate and gentle—"[185] those powers that lie at their origin.

NOTES

1. See my earlier studies: "Language, Epistemology, and Mysticism," in Seven T. Katz, ed., *Mysticism and Philosophical Analysis* (New York, 1978), pp. 22–74; "The 'Conservative' Character of Mystical Experience," in idem, ed., *Mysticism and Religious Traditions* (New York, 1983), pp. 3–60; and "Mystical Speech and Mystical Meaning," in idem, ed., *Mysticism and Language* (New York, 1992), pp. 3–41.
2. Cited in Carl W. Ernst, *The Shambala Guide to Sufism* (Boston, 1997), p. 49.
3. Ibid. For more on the tradition of Sufi exegesis of the Qur'ān, see Louis Massignon, *Essai sur les origines du lexique technique de la mystique musulmane* (Paris, 1968); Paul Nywa, *Exégèse coranique et language mysticque* (Beirut, 1970); Gerhard Bowering, *The Mystical Vision of Existence in Classical Islam; The Qur'ānic Hermeneutics of the Sufi Sahl at-Tustarī* (Berlin, 1980); Annemarie Schimmel, *Mystical Dimensions of Islam* (Chapel Hill, 1975); and the opening three chapters, especially the third, on "Traditional Esoteric Commentaries on the Quran," by Abdurrahman Habil in Seyyed Hussein Nasr (ed.), *Islamic Spirituality*, vol. 1: *Foundations* (New York, 1997).
4. For more on the study of grammar in the Hindu context, and on the interpretation of the work of grammarian as spiritual activity, see *The Vākyapadīya of Bhartṛhari with the Vṛtti*, trans. K. A. Suoramania Iyer (Poona, 1965 and 1971). Studies of this tradition include P. K. Chakravarti, *the Linguistic Speculations of the Hindus* (Calcutta, 1933); K. A. Subramania Iyer, *Bhartṛhari: A Study of the Vākyapadiya in the Light of Ancient Commentaries* (Poona, 1969); Harold K. Coward, *Bhartṛhari* (Boston, 1976); idem, *Sphota Theory of Language* (Columbia, Mo., 1980); and idem, "The Reflective Word" Spirituality in the Grammarian Tradition of India," in Krishna Sivardman, ed., *Hindu Spirituality: Vedas through Vedanta*, vol. 1 (New York, 1989), pp. 209-228.
5. Scholars have long debated which of the many (too many) works attributed to Śaṇkara are really his. Among those now generally agreed to be a authentic are the *Brahmasūtrabhāṣya*; the commentaries on the *Bṛhadāraṇyaka, Taittīrya, Chāndogya, Aitareya, Iśā, Kaṭha, Kena* (two), *Muṇḍaka*, and *Praśna Upaniṣads*; the commentary on the *Bhagavadgītā*; the commentaries on the *Māṇḍūkya Upaniṣad*, with the *Gauḍapādiyakārikābhāsya* and the *Upadesāsahasrī*. All other works, including the many devotional hymns attributed to Śaṅkara, are probably writings of later authors.
6. For more on these works by Śaṅkara and his disciples, see Karl Potter, ed., *Advaita Vedanta up to Śamkara and His Pupils* (Princeton, 1981).

7. For more on the debate over Rāmānuja's authentic corpus, see John Carman's discussion of the issue on his *The Theology of Rāmānuja: An Essay in Religious Understanding* (New Haven, 1974), pp. 49–64.
8. Both these authors and their work are discussed in Carman, *Theology of Rāmānuja*, pp. 225–230.
9. See, for further analysis, André Bareau, *Les premiers conciles bouddhiques* (Paris, 1955); and Jean Przyluski, *Le concile de Rajagrha* (Paris, 1926–1928).
10. For more on this literary and exegetical tradition, see K. R. Norman, *Pāli Literature* (Wiesbaden, 1983); Edward Conze, *Buddhist Thought in India*, part 2 (London, 1962); S. N. Dube, *Cross Currents in Early Buddhism* (New Delhi, 1980); Etienne Lamotte, *Histoire du bouddhisme indien* (Louvain, 1976); and G. C. Pande, *History of the Development of Buddhism* (Lucknow, 1962).
11. "The Sutras," in *Buddhist Spirituality*, vol. 1, edited by Takeuchi Yoshinori (New York, 1993), pp. 138–139.
12. I use these various locutions to be as inclusive as possible—that is, different traditions would describe the characterization of the ultimacy and authority of their canonical scriptures in different ways, given the larger ontology, the encompassing Weltanschauung, of which they are a part, but all would agree on the "fact" that their scriptures were the ultimate vis-à-vis their theological contexts.
13. *Didascalon*, book 5, chap. 10 (*Patrologia Latina*, Paris, 1844–1864), vol. 76, p. 698c. There is a more recent edition of this work, edited by Henty Buttimer, *Hugonis de Sancto Victore. Didascalion: De Studie Legendi* (Washington, D.C., 1939).
14. *Genesis Rabbah* 1.1.
15. *Zohar Chadash*, ad. loc.
16. *Jaiminya Upanīshad Brāhmana* 1.1–1.7, cited in Barbara A. Holdredge, *Veda and Torah: Transcending the Textuality of Scripture* (Albany, 1996), pp. 56–57.
17. Śaṇkara, *Brahmasūtra Bhāṣya* 1.3.28, cited in Holdredge, *Veda and Torah*, p. 126.
18. *Divine Names*, chap. 1, 588C.
19. Philo (of Alexandra), *De Migratione Abrahamie*, pp. 34–35. This, and all the other works of Philo cited in this essay, can be found in the Loeb Classical Library edition of Philo's corpus. I will refrain from providing individual citations for each text referred to or quoted.
20. Cited in Henri de Lubac, *Medieval Exegesis*, vol. 1: *The Four Senses of Scripture*, trans. Mark Sebanc (Grand Rapids, 1998), p. 61.
21. Meister Eckhart, *Liber Parabolarum Genesis*, in Josef Koch, ed., *Meister Eckhart, Die Deutschen und Latenischen Werke* (Stuttgart and Berlin, 1936), vol. 1, pp. 453–454.
22. Louis Massignon, *The Passion of al-Hallaj: Mystic and Martyr of Islam*, trans. Herbert Mason (Princeton, 1982), vol. 3, p. 39.
23. In Iamblichus's *Life of Pythagoras*, Pythagoras is said to have spent time in the Land of Israel, though it is referred to as Syria, in the sense of Greater Syria, "consorting with the descendents of Mochos the prophet and philosopher." Mochos has been identified with Moses most recently in John Dillon, *The Middle Platonists* (London, 1977) p. 143. A new English translation of Iamblichus's *Life* was published by Liverpool University Press (Liverpool, 1989). The reference to Mochos is found on p. 6. Porphyry, in his *Life of Pythagoras*, has Pythagoras learning Hebrew dream interpretation. See Porphyry, *Vie de Pythagore: Lettre à Marcella* (Paris: E. des Places, ed. and trans., Les belles lettres, 1982).
24. Albinus, *Didaskalikos*. In his discussion, Albinus repeats a theme that originated in Plato's *Republic*, esp. 7:52.

25. Holdredge, *Veda and Torah*, p. 357.
26. Ibn ʿArabī, as translated by William Chittick in his *Ibn Arabi's Metaphysics of Imagination: The Sufi Path of Knowledge* (Albany, 1989), p. 239.
27. On this standard rabbinic description of the Torah, see, for example, *Sifre on Deuteronomy*, no. 306.
28. *Taittiriyia Samhita* 7., 3.1.4.
29. *The Diamond Sutra and the Sutra of Hui-Neng*, trans. A. F. Price and Wong Mou-Lam (Boston, 1990), pp. 83 and 144.
30. I have dealt elsewhere with some interesting and unusual interpretive methods employed by mystics when they are deciphering canonical texts. For my earlier views, see S. T. Katz, "Mystical Speech and Mystical Meaning" and "The 'Conservative' Character of Mystical Experience."
31. Meister Eckhart, *Commentary on Exodus*, no. 211, in Josef Quint and Ernst Benz, eds., *Meister Eckhart, Die deutschen und lateinischen Werke* [Kohlhammer, 1936], vol. 2, p. 178, cited in Edmund Colledge and Bernard McGinn, eds., *Meister Eckhart, The Essential Sermons, Commentaries, Treatises, and Defense* (New York, 1981), p. 28.
32. *Al Futûhât al-Makkayya* (Cairo, 1919), vol. 4, p. 25.
33. Qurʾān 5:66: "Had they performed the Torah and the Gospel and what was sent down to them from their Lord, they would have eaten both what was above them and what was beneath their feet."
34. Bede, cited in H. de Lubac, *Medieval Exegesis*, p. 16.
35. There are well-known cases where individual mystics or mystical communities diverge from, or altogether reject, the moral norms of their larger, original community—for example, among the Sabbatians and Frankists, certain medieval Christian heretical groups, and tantric circles. However, in almost every case, this antinomian and "immoral" behavior is due to other beliefs held by the group—for example, messianic notions of a new age in which the "old law" and "old morality" are now overcome, rather than their mystical principles or experience as such. For more on the integral connection between ethics and mysticism in various traditions, see my two essays, "Ethics and Mysticism in Eastern Mystical Traditions" and "Ethics and Mysticism in Western Mystical Tradition," in, respectively, *Religious Studies*, vol. 28, no. 2 (June 1992), pp. 55–69 and vol. 28, no. 4 (September 1992), pp. 407–423.
36. I am indebted to Frank Tobin, *Meister Eckhart: Thought and Language* (Philadelphia, 1986), pp. 24–26, for this discussion of Eckhart's biblical exegesis.
37. *Al Futûhât al-Makkayya*, vol. 3, p. 158.
38. I note that Ewert Cousins quotes a slightly different version in his essay in this volume.
39. This is not to argue that moral readings are not to be found in the midrashic interpretations of the rabbinic era or in the medieval Jewish commentators, but to note that *derash*, as a full category, includes this type of exegesis and much more besides.
40. I am indebted to Frank Talmage's valuable essay "Apples of Gold; The Inner Meaning of Sacred Texts in Medieval Judaism," in Arthur Green, ed., *Jewish Spirituality: From the Bible to the Middle Ages* (New York, 1986), p. 319ff., for this nuance.
41. Augustine, *Confessions*, 12:18.27.
42. Gregory the Great, in 1 *Reg*, 1.78, cited in Bernard McGinn, *The Growth of Mysticism* (New York, 1994), p. 41.
43. For a full account of its Christian employ, see Henri de Lubac, *Medieval Exegesis*. See also Bernard McGinn, *History of Christian Mysticism* (Grand Rapids, 1998); and Marie-Dominique Chenu, *La Théologie au douzième siecle* (Paris, 1957).
44. *Breviloquium*, prol., Q5, 201.

45. Ibn ʿArabī, cited in Chittick, *Sufi Path*, p. 362.
46. *Midrash ha-Neelam, on Genesis* 1:3, in *Zohar Chadash* (Warsaw, 1885), p. 2.
47. Potter, ed., *Advaita Vedanta up to Samkara and His Pupils*, pp. 59–60.
48. An author whose biographical details and dates, and whose authorship of various works, are much in debate.
49. *Brahmasūtrabhāsya* 1.3.
50. Hermann Diels, *Die Fragmente der Vorsokratiker* (reprinted Berlin, 1985), Fragment 61.
51. See, for example, H. Diels (Berlin, 1903), *Fragmente*, 30D.
52. Plato, *Cratylus* 407A, *Republic* 378D, and elsewhere. For later criticism, see for example, Cicero, *de Natura deorum* and Sextus Empiricus, *adversus Mathematicos,* vol. 9.
53. Preceding him in this path were, for example, Pseudo-Aristeas and Aristobolous. For more on this Jewish Hellenistic tradition, see Moses Hadas, *Aristeas to Philocrates* (New York, 1951); Martin Hengel, *Judaism and Hellenism*, 2 vols. (Philadelphia, 1974); Jacob Lauterbauch, "The Ancient Jewish Allegorists," *Jewish Quarterly Review* (NS), vol. 1 (1910–1911), pp. 291–333; and Joseph Bonsirven, *Exégèse Rabbinique et Exégèse Paulinienne* (Paris, 1939). One should also note that allegorical interpretation finds an important place in the Dead Sea Scrolls. See, for example, the *Habbakkuk Commentary* and the *Damascus Document* (also known as the *Zadokite Fragment*).
54. See, for example, Philo's *Quod Deus sit immutabilis*; De Confusione Linguarum, 1.405; *De Opificio Mundi* 1.38; *Legum Allegoriarum* 1.128; *De Josepho* 2.59.
55. Philo understands the need to affirm the literal-historical level of the text, particularly where biblical personalities—for example, Abraham, Jacob, Joseph, Moses, and Samuel—are concerned. Thus, for example, in discussing the Patriarch Abraham, one of his favorite biblical characters, he takes pains to explain that both the literal and the allegorical readings of his travels are appropriate: "The migrations set forth by the literal text of the Scriptures are made by a man of wisdom, but according to the laws of allegory by a virtue-loving soul in its search for the true God." "I have employed both interpretations, the literal as applicable to man and the allegorical as applicable to the soul, and have shown both the man and the intellectual interpretation to be worth investigating" (*De Abrahama*, 68 and 88). In his exegesis of the lives of Joseph and Moses, he likewise gives due weight to the literal meaning of the biblical narrative (see *De Josepha* and *De Vita Moses*).
56. See, for example, Origen, *Homilies on Genesis and Exodus*, trans. Ronald E. Heine (Washington, D.C., 1982).
57. I have discussed the significance of the *Song of Songs*, in Jewish and Christian mystical traditions, in my essay "The Conservative Character of Mystical Experience," pp. 6–17.
58. *M. Yadaiim* 3.5; see also *T. B. Sanhedrin* 101A; and *Tosefta Sanhedrin* 3.10.
59. On Origen's commentary on the *Song of Songs* and its influence, see E. Ann Matter, *The Voice of My Beloved* (Philadelphia, 1990), pp. 20–48. On its relationship to earlier Jewish interpretations, see Ephraim E. Urbach, "The Homiletical Interpretation of the Sages and the Expositions of Origen on Canticles, and the Jewish-Christian Disputation," *Scripta Hierosolymitana*, vol. 22 (1971), pp. 247–275, and Nicholas De Lange, *Origen and the Jews* (Cambridge, Eng., 1976).
60. *Commentary*, "Prologue," in W. Bachrens (ed.), *Origines Werke*, vol. 8, in *Die Griechishen Christlichen Schriftsteller der Ersten drei Jahrhundert*, vol. 33 (Leipzig, 1901 ff.); there is also an English translation by R. P. Lawson, *Origen. The Song of Songs. Commentaries and Homilies* (New York, 1957), p. 61.

61. Cited in Matter, *Voice of My Beloved*, p. 59.
62. Ibid., p. 60.
63. Ibid., p. 131.
64. Bernard, sermon 31, cited in Matter, *Voice of My Beloved*, p. 129.
65. Ibid., pp. 128–129.
66. *Patrologia Latina*, ed. J. P. Migne, cited in Matter, *Voice of My Beloved*, p. 135.
67. In medieval Jewish tradition, too, this occurs both among mainline exegetes like Rashi and mystical adepts like Moses de Leon, author/redactor of the Zohar.
68. See, for example, the different interpretations of Robert Gordis, *The Song of Songs* (New York, 1974); Marvin Pope, *The Song of Songs: A New Tradition with Introduction and Commentary*; Michael V. Fox, *The Song of Songs and the Ancient Egyptian Love Songs* (Madison, 1985); and Roland E. Murphy, "Canticle of Canticles," in R. E. Brown et al., eds., *Jerome Biblical Commentary* (Englewood Cliffs, 1968), pp. 506–510.
69. This is the translation of the traditional Hebrew phrase, *kivyachol* which is customarily attached to such blatant anthropomorphic language to indicate that it should not be taken simply at face value.
70. *A. T. Tafsir al Rabir*, ad loc.
71. A basic claim of Eckhart's ontology, set out especially in his *Opus Tripartitum* (Tripartite works).
72. Meister Eckhart, *Book of the Parables of Genesis*, chap. 1.9, in Colledge and McGinn, *Meister Eckhart*, p. 96.
73. *In John*. 215. In Quint and Benz, *Meister Eckhart*, vol. 2, p. 354: "*Quod extra deum . . . nihil est nec est.*"
74. *Sermon 48*. In Colledge and McGinn, *Meister Eckhart*, p. 198.
75. As Eckhart's trial for heresy and excommunication indicates; for more on these events, see Colledge and McGinn, *Meister Eckhart*, introduction, pp. 10–15, and the sources on this matter in the accompanying notes.
76. Maimonides was not a mystic, despite later efforts by kabbalists to make him one. Nonetheless, his influence was so great that it was felt by Jewish mystics in a direct and powerful way. At the same time, he did believe in "secrets" being embedded in the Torah, especially in the "the account of the beginning" (*maʿaseh bereshith*) found in Genesis, and the vision of Ezekiel, "the account of the chariot" (*maʿaseh merkavah*), two biblical sources that had been central to Jewish mystical speculation from the rabbinic era onward. Even in the original Arabic version fo the *Guide for the Perplexed*, he refers to this esoteric material by the traditional Hebrew terms *sod* and *sithrey Torah*. In addition, he uses the Arabic terms *sirr* and *khafiyya* to indicate the notions of "secret" and "mystery." He also, complementarily, believed in a secret tradition of biblical interpretation that had been passed on by Moses to the intellectual elite of the Jewish people. See, for example, *Guide*, 1, 62, which refers to the tradition of "the men of knowledge" (in Shlomo Pines's English trans. [Chicago, 1963], p. 150). There is a tradition among the kabbalists that, late in his life, Maimonides realized the error of his rationalist ways and "converted" to a commitment to Kabbalah. This tradition is already found in R. Joseph ibn Shoshan's fourteenth-century *Commentary on Avot*, ed. M. Kasher and Yl Blacherowitz (Jerusalem, 1968), and in R. Shem Tob ben Abraham ibn Gaon's early-fourteenth-century commentary on Maimonides' *Mishneh Torah*, entitled *Migdal Oz*. By the late fifteenth and the early sixteenth centuries, this tale was widespread; see, for example, R. Elijah Gennazano's *Iggeret Hamudot*, published in London in 1912, Abrabanel's *Nahalat Avot* (New York, 1953), p. 209, and R. Meir ibn Gabbai's *Avodat ha-Kodesh* (Warsaw, 1883), p. 66. This tradition has

been critically studied by Gershom Scholem in his Hebrew essay "Mi-Hoker li-mekubbal," In *Tarbiz*, vol. 6 (1935), pp. 90–98; and in Michael A. Schmidman, "On Maimonides 'Conversion' to Kabbalah," in Isadore Twersky, ed., *Studies in Medieval Jewish History and Literature*, vol. 2 (Cambridge, Mass., 1984), pp. 375–386. Maimonides also used the term *kabbala* in its earlier etymological sense of "received tradition"—that is, the authoritative interpretation of the Torah that has been handed down from Moses through the Prophets to the rabbinic sages. In this he was seconded by the Sufi tradition that held that Muhammad had passed on the correct mystical interpretation of the Qur'ān to ʿAli. The Sufis called this tradition *naql*, a term also used by Maimonides in the original Arabic version of the *Guide*, I.5 and I.62.

77. Angus Fletcher, *Allegory: The Theory of a Symbolic Mode* (Ithaca, 1964), p. 2.
78. See, for more on this issue, M. D. Chenu, *Nature, Man and Society in the Twelfth Century* (Chicago, 1968), esp. p. 131.
79. I have discussed this hermeneutical strategy at some length in my *Holocaust in Historical Context* (New York, 1994), pp. 237–240; the discussion there contains an extensive bibliography.
80. Bruno of Segni, *In Genesis*, in Migne, *Patrologia Latina* 164:205C, cited in Henri de Lubac, *Medieval Exegesis*, p. 424, n. 26.
81. Migne, *Patrologia Latina* 167:1473D, cited in H. de Lubac, *Medieval Exegesis*, p. 424 n. 27.
82. Migne, *Patrologia Latina* 177:957A, cited in H. de Lubac, *Medieval Exegesis*, p. 425 n. 31.
83. Remi of Auxere, *Enarrationes in Psalmos 41*, in Migne, *Patrologia Latina* 131:393B, cited from H. de Lubac, *Medieval Exegesis*, p. 427, n. 66.
84. *Midrash ha-Neʿelam, Zohar Chadash*, 83A; my translation.
85. *Tikkunei Zohar, Tikkunim* 94A; my translation.
86. Zohar 2, 85B, cited in Isaiah Tishby, *The Wisdom of the Zohar*, trans. David Goldstein (Oxford, 1989), vol. 3, p. 158; see his entire analysis of this issue, pp. 1155–1167. And consult also Daniel Matt, "The Mystic and the Mitzvot," in Arthur Green, ed., *Jewish Spirituality* (New York, 1986), vol. 1, pp. 367–404.
87. Zohar 3, 38B, cited in Tishby, *Wisdom of the Zohar*, p. 1160.
88. Zohar 2, 153B.
89. Zohar 3, 113A, cited in Tishby, *The Wisdom of the Zohar*, p. 1160.
90. Cited in Bernard McGinn, *The Growth of Mysticism* (New York, 1994), p. 109.
91. *Prayers and Mediations of Saint Anselm* (New York, 1973), p. 95.
92. Ibid., p. 96.
93. Cited in Ewert Cousins, "The Humanity and Passion of Christ," in Bernard McGinn, et al., eds., *Christian Spirituality: High Middle Ages and Reformation* (New York, 1987), vol. 2, p. 378.
94. Though this work has been linked to Bonaventure as its author, this attribution is almost certainly incorrect.
95. Bonaventure, *The Journey of the Soul Into God*, "Prologue." For an English version of this work, see the translation by Ewert Cousins (New York, 1978), p. 383.
96. The details of the historical incarnation are seen clearly, for example, in Suso's *Buchlein der ewigen Weisheit* (Little book of eternal wisdom) of c. 1330 (translated into Latin as *Horologium Sapientae*). In setting out the "hundred meditations and petitions . . . which could be devoutly pronounced each day," he begins with this list of ten torments and indignities the historic Jesus suffered leading up to the crucifixion: "1. Ah, Eternal Wisdom, my heart reminds you how, after the Last Supper, you went to the mountain and were covered by a bloody sweat because of the anguish of your

loving heart. 2. And how you were captured by your enemies, roughly bound, and wretchedly led away. 3. Lord, how you were shamefully treated during the night, cruelly scourged, spat upon, and suffered your fair eyes to be blindfolded. 4. Early in the morning, you were condemned by Caiphas and delivered to death. 5. Your mother looked at you with boundless grief. 6. You were ignominiously brought before Pilate, falsely accused, and condemned to death. 7. You, Eternal Wisdom, clothed in white garments, were mocked as a fool before Herod. 8. Your comely body was cruelly disfigured and bruised by the savage lashes of the scourge. 9. Your tender head was pierced by sharp thorns, so that your loving face was covered in blood. 10. Thus condemned, you were miserably and shamefully led out to your death, bearing your own cross." And he then elaborates upon twenty items connected with the crucifixion. "1. Beloved Lord, on the high branch of the cross your clear eyes were dimmed, distorted. 2. Your divine ears were filled with mockery and insult. 3. Your refined sense of smell was offended with an evil stench. 4. Your sweet mouth was offended by a bitter potion. 5. Your delicate sense of touch was offended by hard blows. 6. Gentle Lord, your divine head was bowed down by pain and anguish. 7. Your lovely throat was rudely struck. 8. Your pure face was covered with spittle and blood. 9. Your clear complexion was pallid. 10. Your entire fair body was benumbed. 11. Beloved Lord, your right hand was pierced by the nail. 12. Your left hand was transfixed. 13. Your right arm was stretched out. 14. Your left arm was painfully dislocated. 15. Your right foot was dug through. 16. Your left foot was savagely torn. 17. You hung there helpless. 18. Your divine legs were extremely fatigued. 19. All your sensitive members were immovably riveted to the narrow halter of the cross. 20. Your body was bathed in hot blood." The mystical meditations that then follow these remembrances of the actuality of Jesus' suffering and death are predicated on the historical suffering of Jesus in his humanity. The flesh, Jesus' flesh, is not incidental to, or irrelevant for, authentic and profound Christian faith. Indeed such faith is impossible without it.

97. Tauler—contrary to the contemporary elevation of Eckhart, who was Tauler's teacher and main inspiration—was the mystic most read and the emulated in Germany over the centuries. Eckhart's extreme doctrines of detachment (*Abgeschiedenheit*) and of self-abandonment (*Gelassenheit*) that led to his papal condemnation by Pope John Paul XXII, in 1329, caused others to shy away from his doctrines, though, of course, he continued to be read—even if he was not always cited by name—and to exert a significant influence on the development of late medieval and early modern Christian mysticism.
98. Johannes Tauler, *Dies Predigten Taulers* (Zurich, 1968).
99. See, for example, Alfred of Rievaux's *De Iesu puero duodenni* (Jesus at the age of twelve) in Anselm Hoste and Charles Talbot, eds., *Aelredi Rievallensis Opera Omnia*, vol. 1, *Opera Ascetica* (Turnhout, 1971).
100. *Periphyseon* 953D, trans. J. P. Sheldom Williams (Washington, D.C., 1987).
101. Sermon 55, *Johannes Tauler, Sermons*, trans. Maria Shrady (New York, 1985), p. 158.
102. The dark side of this doctrine is evidenced most clearly in the medieval tradition of accusations that Jews, in particular, stole the wafers from the church in order to repeat the crucifixion. The first recorded instance in which the charge was leveled occurred in Belitz, Germany, in 1234, when a number of Jews were tried and burned at the stake. For more details on this accusation, consult Marie Despina, "Les accusations de profanation d'hosties portees contre les juifs," *Recontre*, vol. 5, nos. 22, 23 (1971), pp. 150–173, 180–196; and J. Stengers, *Les juifs dans le Pays-Bas au Moyen-Age* (Brussels, 1950). For further analysis, see Gavin Langmuir's two essays, "The

Knight's Tale of Young Hugh of Lincoln," in *Speculum* 47 (1972), pp. 459–482, and "L'absence d'accusation de meurtre rituel a l'ouest du Rhone," in *Juifs et judaisme de Languedoc, XIII siècle et au début XIV siècle*, *Cahiers de Fanjeaux*, vol. 12, (Toulouse, 1977), pp. 235–249.

103. The learned analyses and speculations of the later medieval works on the *quadriformis species sacramentorum* (the fourfold form/sense of the sacraments) also provide data that are relevant to a full discussion of the medieval notion of a symbol.
104. For details of the speculations about Maṇḍana Miśra's biographical details, see Potter, ed., *Advaita Vedanta up to Śaṃkara and His Pupils*, pp. 346–347.
105. This summary is quoted from Potter, *Advaita Vedanta*, p. 370.
106. See my comments on the role and meaning of mantras in my essay "Mystical Speech and Mystical Meaning," pp. 10–12.
107. The disproportionate prominence in the description and analysis of Sufism that is given to those masters who represent exceptions to this rule, especially that represented by the very greatest Sufi theosophist, Ibn ʿArabī, provides a distorted image of the character of the Sufi literary tradition in its totality.
108. M. D. Chenu, *Nature, Man and Society in the Twelfth Century*, p. 103.
109. Quintilian, *Institutes of Oratory*, trans. H. E. Butler (London, 1953), vol. 8, sec. 23.
110. Isaiah 11:11–15.
111. *Tanchuma, Lech Lecha*, 9.
112. Nachmanides' comment on this teaching is offered in his *Commentary on the Torah*, Genesis, 12:6. I cite the English translation by Charles B. Chavel, *Ramban Commentary on the Torah*, Genesis 12.6, (New York, 1971), pp. 168–169.
113. See, for example, Mark 1:1–13; 1 Cor. 15–21 and 44–49.
114. See, for example, Epis. to Hebrews 11:17–19.
115. Consider, for example, Matthew's account of the sermon on the mount, Matt. 5, cf. Exod. 20. See also, Matt. 8:23–27, 9–13, and 11:4–6.
116. See, for example, 1 Cor. 1:2, which marked the comparison to crossing the Red Sea. Also, see Acts 7.
117. See, for example, Matt. 4:1; and Heb. 3 and 4.
118. Cited in Geoffrey W. H. Lampe and K. J. Woollcombe, *Essays on Typology* (London, 1957), p. 13.
119. Jerome, *Commentary on Jeremiah*, 11.21–3.
120. Cited from Jean Danielou, *From Shadows to Reality: Studies in the Typology of the Fathers* (London, 1960), p. 11.
121. *Sifre*, Number 69, This will be found on p. 65 in the Horovitz edition of this midrash, which has been reprinted many times.
122. See, for example, *Mechilta de R. Ishmael, Baḥodesh* 9. This will be found in vol. 2, p. 268, of Jacob Z. Lauterbach's edition of this work (Philadelphia, 1933–1935).
123. See, for example, Abraham Ibn Ezra's commentary on Daniel 2:39.
124. Ramban, *Commentary on the Torah*, trans. Chavel, p. 394.
125. Ibid., p. 398.
126. F. Talmage, "Apples of Gold," p. 314.
127. *Zohar*, *Vayera*, 110B–111A. *Zohar*, trans. Harry Sperling and Maurice Simon (London, 1973), vol. 1, pp. 350–351.
128. Tauler puts this well in sermon 29: "When we come to speak of the Most Blessed Trinity, we are at a loss for words, and yet words must be used to say something of this sublime and ineffable Trinity. To express it adequately is as impossible as touching the sky with one's head. For everything we can say or think can no more ap-

proach the reality than the smallest point of a needle can contain Heaven and earth; indeed, a hundred, a thousand times, and immeasurably less than that.

It is utterly impossible for our intellect to understand how the lofty, essential Unity can be single in essence and yet threefold in Persons; how the Persons are distinct from each other; how the Father begets the Son; how the Son proceeds from the Father and yet remains within Him (by comprehending Himself the Father utters His Eternal Word); how from this comprehension that proceeds from Him, there streams forth an ineffable love, which is the Holy Spirit; and how these wondrous Processions stream back again in essential unity, in ineffable self-delight and self-enjoyment; how the Son is equal to the Father in power, wisdom, and love; how the Son and the Holy Spirit are also one. And yet there is an inexpressibly vast distinction between the Persons, although they proceed in an ineffable way in unity of nature. On this subject a staggering amount of things could be said, and yet nothing would have been said to convey how the supreme, superabundant Unity unfolds into Trinity."

129. There are many logical problems with this position that I will not discuss here. For an introduction to some of these difficulties, consult my essays, "The Language and Logic of 'Mystery' in Christology," in John Clayton and Stephen Sykes, eds., *Christ, Faith and History* (Cambridge, 1972), pp. 239–262; and "Utterance and Ineffability in Jewish Neoplatonism," in Lenn Goodman, ed., *Jewish Neoplatonism* (Albany, 1992), pp. 279–298.
130. Erigena, *Periphyseon* 1 (462D), cited in B. McGinn, *The Growth of Mysticism*, p. 98.
131. *Mystical Theology* chap. 1, 998B–1000A. A full translation can be found in *Pseudo-Dionysius: The Complete Works*, trans. Colm Luibheid (New York, 1987), p. 135.
132. One must not make the logical error of concluding, from these comparative data, that this use of paradoxical formulations in many different mystical traditions entails that the mystical experiences sought and had in the different traditions are the same. For more on this consequential error, see my remarks in "Language, Epistemology, and Mysticism," pp. 54–57. It must also be recognized that *parallel* does not always mean "equivalent" and that differences within specific Eastern traditions—for example, that are represented by Zen—are not to be too easily overlooked or diminished.
133. *Deutsche Werke* 2, 486–506, sermon 52.
134. F. Tobin, *Meister Eckhart*, p. 163.
135. *PR* 53, *Deutsche Werke* 2, 529, 3–7, cited in F. Tobin, *Meister Eckhart*, p. 164.
136. *PR* 62, *Deutsche Werke* 3, 66,4, cited in F. Tobin, *Meister Eckhart*, p. 165.
137. *PR* 30, *Deutsche Werke* 2, 94, 4–5, cited in F. Tobin, *Meister Eckhart*, p. 166.
138. *PR* 30, *Deutsche Werke* 2, 94, 6–7, cited in F. Tobin, *Meister Eckhart*, p. 166.
139. As suggested by Burkhard Mojsisch, *Meister Eckhart, Analogie, Univozität und Einheit* (Hamburg, 1963), p. 69.
140. *Patrologia Latina* 83, *Deutsche Werke* 3, 438, 1, cited in F. Tobin, *Meister Eckhart*, p. 166.
141. Meister Eckhart, *Deutsche Predigten und Tractate*, ed. and trans. Josef Quint (Munich, 1955), p. 430.
142. I use this term in its Kantian sense, referring to space, time, and causality.
143. *Commentarius ad Wisdom* in Migne, *Patrologia Latina*, vol. 82, p. 490.
144. Eckhart, *Ave, gratia plena*, *Deutsche Werke*, vol. 1, 376–377.
145. Isaac of Stella, sermon 22:5, cited in McGinn, *The Growth of Mysticism*, p. 292.
146. Isaac of Stella, sermon 22.10, cited in (McGinn) ibid., p. 292.
147. Isaac of Stella, sermon 22.12, cited in (McGinn) ibid., pp. 292–293.

148. For more on this, see McGinn, *The Growth of Mysticism*, p. 410.
149. Cited in Saskia Murk-Jansen, "Hadewijch and Eckhart: Amor Intellegere est," in Bernard McGinn, ed., *Meister Eckhart and the Beguine Mystics* (New York, 1994), p. 22.
150. *Mechthild of Magdeburg*, ed. Hans Neumann (Munich, 1990), vol. 3, pp. 65–68.
151. Ibid., vol. 4, p. 107.
152. "Sermon II on the Feat of the Blessed Trinity," in *Johannes Tauler Sermons*, p. 103.
153. See Tauler's poems (or pseudo-Tauler's?) in Laurentio Surius, ed., *Institutiones Taulerianae* (Cologne, 1548).
154. *John of the Cross, Selected Writings*, ed. Kieran Kavanaugh (New York, 1987), p. 100.
155. *Entrème*, in *Collected Works of St. John of the Cross*, ed. Kieran Kavanaugh and Otilio Rodriguez (Washington, D.C., 1973), p. 709.
156. *The Living Flame of Love*, vol. 1, p. 6, in *John of the Cross: Selected Writings*, ed. Kavanaugh, p. 296.
157. Abdel Kader, *The Life, Personality and Writings of Al-Junayd* (London, 1962), p. 57 (in Arabic). In an earlier work, Abu Bakr Kalabadi attributes this saying to Du'l-Nun, *Kitab al-ta'arrof*, ed. A. J. Arberry (Cairo, 1933), p. 105.
158. *Kitab al-Mithaq*, cited in Michael Sells, "Bewildered Tongue: The Semantics of Mystical Union in Islam," in Moshe Idel and Bernard McGinn, eds., *Mystical Union and Monotheistic Faith* (New York, 1989), p. 109.
159. *Kitab al-Tawasin*, ed. Louis Massignon (Paris, 1913), p. 45, no. 12.
160. *Rasa'il, Kitab a-Isra*, cited in Michael Sells, "Bewildered Tongue: The Semantics of Mystical Union in Islam," p. 107.
161. Michael Chodkiewicz, *An Ocean without a Shore* (Albany, 1993), p. 43.
162. Cited in Daisetz Teitaro Suzuki, *Introduction to Zen Buddhism* (New York, 1964), p. 66.
163. Cited in Junjiro Takakusu, *The Essentials of Buddhist Philosophy* (Honolulu, 1949), p. 163.
164. John Ferguson, ed., *Encyclopedia of Mysticism* (New York, 1977), p. 139.
165. *Mulamadhyami Kakarikas*, cited in Frederick Streng, *Emptiness: A Study in Religious Meaning* (Nashville, 1967), pp. 216–217.
166. *Kena Upaniṣad* 1, 2, 3.
167. Eric Lott, *Vedantic Approaches to God* (London, 1980), p. 72.
168. I note that in Jainism, too, the ineffable, *avaktavya*, is indicated by contradictory affirmations—that is, saying "yes" and "no" about *X* simultaneously. For more on the subtleties of the Jain position, see Bimal Matilal, *The Central Philosophy of Jainism (Anekantavala)*, (Ahmadabad, 1981).
169. *Guide for the Perplexed*, "Introduction," trans. S. Pines, p. 18.
170. Nachmanides' *Commentary on The Torah*, trans. C. Chavel, p. 16.
171. Nachmanides' *Commentary on The Torah*, trans. C. Chavel, p. 15, and see his explanation, p. 15 n. 58.
172. Pseudo-Dionysius, *Celestial Harmony*, in *Pseudo-Dionysius: The Complete Works*, trans. C. Leubheid, p. 149.
173. *Sefer Yetzira*, quoted from the English translation by David Blumenthal, *Understanding Jewish Mysticism* (New York, 1978), vol. 1, p. 15, Mishnah 1, and Mishnah 2, 4, and 5, pp. 21–31, 34–41.
174. See, for example, Aryeh Kaplan's translation and commentary, *Sefer Yetzirah* (York Beach, Maine, 1990); and Leonard R. Glotzer, *The Fundamentals of Jewish Mysticism: The Book of Creation and Its Commentaries* (Northvale, N.J., 1992). The ear-

lier commentary tradition on this work includes the efforts of such luminaries as Saadya Gaon (tenth century), R. Abraham ben David of Posquieres (thirteenth century)—though there are grounds for doubting the attribution of the work that usually is assigned to him, Nachmanides (thirteenth century), and R. Elijah of Vilna (the Vilna Gaon) (eighteenth century).

175. This is the English translation provided by D. Goldstein in the English edition of I. Tishby, *The Wisdom of the Zohar*, vol. 2, p. 562.
176. Ibid., pp. 566–567.
177. Ibid., p. 561.
178. Cited in Annemarie Schimmel, *And Muhammad Is His Messenger: The Veneration of the Prophet in Islamic Piety* (Chapel Hill, 1985), p. 115.
179. Cited in ibid., p. 116.
180. Ibid., p. 117.
181. *The Mystery of Numbers* (New York, 1993), pp. 21–22.
182. For further details on various numerological notions and usages, see A. Schimmel, *The Mystery of Numbers*, which includes a helpful bibliography for further study.
183. One might wish to substitute other terms for *metaphysical*, varying from tradition to tradition.
184. Though I use the singular terms *scripture*, *adept*, and *it* for reasons of style, it should be understood that I mean to refer to the wide variety of the world's scriptures, to the many sorts of mystical adepts, and that "it" is a reference to the plurality of sacred texts in the differing world's religions and mystical communities.
185. *The Living Flame of Love* (Garden City, N.Y., 1962), p. 47, n. 16.

2

Mystical Identity and Scriptural Justification

SHLOMO BIDERMAN

The role of scripture in religious traditions is often surrounded with a certain aura of ambiguity. Sometimes the ambiguity may even lead to a seeming paradox. In monotheistic creeds, such a paradox results from the need to adhere to two seemingly contradictory claims about the authority of scripture. According to one claim, the existence and nature of God are necessary requirements for the very validity of scripture. According to the other claim, the belief in God's existence stems from the testimony of scripture. To put this paradox in a somewhat more technical way, the existence of God is justified by scripture and the authority of scripture is justified by God.

At first glance it may seem that when we move away from the public space of scripture into the more private, secluded space of the mystic, we free ourselves from the yoke of certain theological assumptions that prevail within "institutional" religions, and therefore free ourselves as well from the sometimes disturbing paradox. The horizon of the mystic seems too accommodating to be clouded by mere paradoxes. There are, after all, countless ways in which mystics feel, experience, act, and react. Correspondingly, there are countless ways in which mystics may react to the existence and meaning of various scriptures. Indeed, one can easily detect a whole spectrum of mystical responses to scripture. Some mystics may declare themselves to be ardent followers of scripture, whether literally or spiritually. Other mystics may feel assured that their mystical experiences allow them to belittle the importance of the sacred texts of their tradition, viewing them as subsidiary in molding their religious outlook—some may see scriptures as merely relative, while others may (passively or actively) ignore them, and still others may even oppose them.

But beyond these diverse reactions there is a strange recognition that, while the theological paradox of scripture(s) fades into the cloud of mysticism, it is somewhat ironically replaced by another paradox. That is, the paradox reappears in another, pragmatic guise, this time as a disturbing inconsistency that can be manifested in the mystic's actions and reactions. On the one hand, mystics often see their mystical experiences as manifesting a superior degree of knowledge or a higher level of being than those expressed in the scripture(s) of their religious traditions. On the other hand, mystics often do *turn* to the scripture(s) of their tradition and, in many cases, are crucially dependent on them in the attempt to justify their mystical experiences by means of the scripture's infallible authority.

What are we to make of a mystic who is trying to reach or convey a unique mystical experience and, at the same time, to base this unique experience on the shared texts of religious tradition? In this essay I take a few steps toward an explanation of this dialectical relations between mystical experience and scriptural exegesis. My position is primarily philosophical, not phenomenological; therefore, I concentrate mainly on the two conceptual frames that are entangled in the dialectical relations that often seem to characterize the relationship between convictions based on mystical experience and those grounded in scriptural authority.

I begin by sketching the major arguments that have been given in favor of a dialectical presentation of mysticism and tradition. In emphasizing the dialectical relations between scripture and mysticism, I suggest a possible explanation of the nature and meaning of this conceptual entanglement. In the last section of the chapter, I turn to Śaṅkara, the great Hindu exegete and mystic, and show how the explanation of the dialectical mode that I have offered is clearly present in his writings.

Views of the Dialectical Relations between Mysticism and Scripture

As is widely known among those who study mysticism, many scholars hold that no valid dichotomy can be sustained between the mystical experience, as it is reported by the individual mystic, and the religious texts that constitute the tradition within which, or against which, the mystic is functioning. In the preface to his monumental study of Christian mysticism, Bernard McGinn states the antidichotomic argument explicitly. He argues that "mystical theology is not a more epiphenomenon, a shell or covering that can be peeled off to reveal the 'real' thing within." And he goes on to conclude that "rather than being something added on [to] mystical experience, mystical theory in most cases precedes and guides the mystic's whole way of life."[1]

Why is the dichotomy between mysticism and scripture inadequate? As Steven T. Katz has forcefully argued, it is often the case that the specific distinctions—by means of which religious phenomena are explained (or explained away)—are based on an all-too-sweeping general distinction between experience and interpretation. Katz argues that such a distinction cannot be maintained: "In order to understand mysticism it is not just a question of studying the reports of the mystic after the experiential event but of acknowledging that the experience itself as well as the form in which it is reported is shaped by concepts which the mystic brings to, and which shape, his experience."[2] He therefore concludes: "Mystical experience is 'over-determined by its socio-religious milieu: as a result of his process of intellectual acculturation in its broadest sense, the mystic brings to his experience a world of concepts, images, symbols, and values which shape as well as color the experience he eventually and actually has."[3]

Katz therefore views the distinction between experience and interpretation (as represented and defended by Walter T. Stace, among others) as oversimple.[4] If we apply Katz's contextual analysis to the apparent dichotomy of "scripture" and "mysticism," it is clear, I think, that there is no basis for maintaining an unequivocal demarcation line between mystical experience and scriptural exegesis. First, one cannot even hope to base such a demarcation line on some inherent mental differences between mystical experience and exegetical experience. It would surely be most unsound to base the demarcation line on some psychological mumbo jumbo about two distinct mental "types" of religious experience. Second, even a cursory glance at the reports of various religious experiences teaches us that the categories of "mysticism" and "scripture" are densely joined. In many instances, the so-called exegetical experience is reported in clearly mystical terms; in many other instances, the mystical experience is reported with the help of a direct reference to hermeneutical terminology.

The conclusion—which has initiated many recent discussions—is that it would be difficult, if not impossible, to draw a clear-cut distinction between the mystical and the exegetical practice. We need not necessarily adhere to the currently fashionable tendency to see interpretation as omnipotent to realize that the exegesis of sacred texts leads commentators to take a conscious or, more often, an unconscious part in a subtle process of rewriting the texts they interpret. The same holds in reverse for the reports of mystical experiences, many of which refer explicitly or implicitly to the relevant sacred texts of the reporter's own religious tradition. We may even generalize and conclude that, contrary to first appearances, there is in fact a close structural parallelism between the profile of "commentator" and that of "mystic." Both share the same substratum: they stand on the same floor, the same set of presuppositions. Both act and react while facing what they see as a perfect source of being, truth, light, or whatever other name is used. For both, the starting point of activity is the realization of the existence of some "presence," whether textual, visionary, auditory, or other.[5] The speech acts of the mystic who, as it were, tries to acquire or create an identity with this presence by grasping it, and the speech acts of the commentator, who tries to reach this presence by deciphering the code of scriptural language, may differ in scope and content (to borrow Austin's terminology, they are different locutionary acts), but they share the same status (or, again, with Austin, they have the same illocutionary force, both being performative utterances by means of which the longed-for presence is declared to be found).

Indeed, the dialectical characterization of mystical accounts has become a kind of "umbrella-notion" that covers a wide range of phenomena. It is often used by scholars of religion, in general, and those of mysticism, in particular. For example, it covers the relationship between experience and interpretation. We are advised not to see experience and interpretation as two consecutive terms, with experience being taken as logically prior to interpretation, but to give up any attempt to force a one-way logical order on these notions and to concede that the two relate to each other dialectically. While interpretation no doubt refers to prior experiences and tries to put them into meaningful verbal units, such interpretation also sometimes tries to establish the very possibility of the experience to which it refers.[6]

The general view of the dialectical relations between experience and interpretation is often enlarged to apply to more specific features of religion. Take, for example, the claim that although there is a distinction between the text and the liturgical activity of prayer, the text and the liturgical activity are closely and dialectically linked to each other. The same holds for the relations between revelation and scripture, on the one hand, and between vision and mystical experience, on the other hand. Dialectics, so it may seem, should supplant any dichotomic order (or, even more obviously, any hierarchical order) that we may have hoped to find in religion. The dialectical blending of mysticism and scripture has even led some scholars to doubt the very legitimacy of mysticism as a distinct defining notion.[7]

What are the reasons for preferring dialectical accounts of the relations been mysticism and scripture to any simpler explanation? The origins of this methodologically dialectical point of view are not doubt Kantian. The blending of the Kantian use of the term *dialectics* with Hegelian and post-Hegelian uses has led scholars to see dialectics as some sort of signpost. In adhering to a dialectical terminology, the scholar declares the inherent complexity of the phenomena being dealt with. More specifically, in using the terminology we are letting it be known that our subject matter cannot be coherently put into the procrustean bed of a linear explanation. We tread the closed border and single perspective of the one kind of explanation for the open border and multiple perspectives of the other kind. In claiming the situation to be "dialectical," the scholar abandons the expectation that it has any clear one-way conceptual direction, since any one-directional explanation is eventually self-defeating.

So far, so good. But what follows? It seems to me that we should not stretch the limits of our use of "dialectics" too far. To put it crudely, it would be a mistake to confuse the signpost for the road it marks. The claim that the relationship between two concepts is dialectical should not be regarded as a substitute for an attempt to analyze the nature and use of such a relationship. Roughly put, acknowledging a situation to be dialectical is by no means a sufficient condition for understanding it. On the contrary, in many cases such an acknowledgment is no more than a necessary condition for diagnosing the status of the subject being dealt with as a problematic one. There are not a few unfortunate instances in which a scholar claims a situation to be dialectical and therefore expects the reader, struck by this insight, to utter, "Ah? It's dialectical? So now I understand!" I would like to argue that this is only a pseudo-insight. For dialectics, as I have already said, is the signpost but not the road. Hence, to discover that there are dialectical relations between mystical vision and scriptural exegesis is no more than to provide a *pre*condition for a better understanding and to sharpen the focus of our attempt to explain the mutual relations of the two concepts. So, after proclaiming that the mystical vision and the scriptural exegesis are dialectically blended, we should not sigh with the relief of a scholar whose craving for explanation has been sated, but rather go on and search for the meaning of the dialectical relationship.

I would like to outline here a possible way to explain the entanglement of mysticism with scripture. Our departure point is the dialectical description of mysticism as it contains "elements of radical challenge to established religious authority and tradition" and, at the same time, "embodies characteristics that are anything but radical."[8] I ask, What can we understand by this dialectical approach? In answer, I suggest that we consider the mystic to be operating within two simultaneous frames—one of which separates the mystic sharply from scriptural tradition, and the other in which the mystic plays the same role as the exegetical guardian of the tradition.

Before I go on to a short description of the two frames, a methodological comment seems in order. In claiming that the mystic dwells in two frames, I am not making an empirical observation about mystics, whether in general or in some particular cultural context. It seems to me that the immense variety of mystical experience, found in so many cultures and during such extensive periods of time, defies any clear-cut categorization of mystical visions into classes or types. In trying to explain the dialectical relationship between mysticism and scripture, I therefore do not wish to make any empirical generalization. Rather, I hope to make conceptual clarification of the *possibility of one particular sort of relationship* between the individual mystic and his collective scriptural environment. As I will argue, this dialectical relationship shows that some mystics refer to their visions and offer a justification of these visions as a kind of *knowledge*. Evidently, we might find a mystic who, for instance, is deeply and exclusively absorbed in a private world of emotions and cares not at all about translating this inward experience into the terms of the more objective world of "externally" justifiable knowledge claims. For such a mystic, the dialectic in question is hardly applicable. In probing the dialectical relationship between mysticism and scripture, my purpose is to examine the uses made of these two notions in the various instances in which mystics have shown not only an exclusive interest in their own state but also the desire to present their state in epistemological terms. In short, I want to offer a conceptual clarification of a certain kind of *usage*, in which the terms *mysticism* and *scripture* are dialectically connected to one another.

The Mystic's *Frame of Identity*

I call the first frame in which the mystic operates the *frame of identity*. Seen within this first frame, the mystic is separated by a deep gulf from the religious environment—in particular, from its varied institutions. The gulf in question is basically one between the identity of the individual mystic and the collective profile of the tradition. I call this frame one of identity not because I think that mysticism should be reduced to a theory of personality or should exclusively involve a biographical or psychological account of the mystic. In my sense, *identity* refers to the borders through which an individual can distinguish herself from a society or a culture that is outside the borders. To be sure, there are various ways in which this distinction can be made. It generally involves a process of socialization, in the absence of which the very structure of one's personal identity would not be established. However, as far as mystical identity is concerned, it is clear that it is highly, profoundly, individualistic. Having a mystical experience is having something that is exclusively one's own. In a somewhat ironic way, the identity of the mystic is structurally very similar to the identity of the philosopher of reason, such as Descartes, who believes that he can draw all the consequences of thought from himself as an individual.[9]

The individualist nature of the frame of identity is well documented in mystics' descriptions of their (purportedly indescribable) experiences. The pages of mystical literature are full of accounts in which the mystic reports on a mystical experience in terms that show a psychological awareness of a change that transforms the mystic's identity as an individual. There is no need to dwell on these states in detail. It is enough to recall the numerous instances in which the mystic reports that his or her ego was either "filled" or "emptied." The mystical positions taken in the early Upaniṣads may serve as a striking example of the "filled" sort, while Mahāyāna mysticism fits the "emptied" one. "Filling" depends on the experience of superlative addition, as if all the possible qualities of experience had converged into an indescribable fullness. "Emptying," in contrast, depends on the experience of superlative subtraction, as if all the possible qualities of experience, all its characteristic distinctions, had vanished, leaving an indescribable residue, which is taken to be all that there really is—except that all the forms of the verb *to be* are inadequate to it. But the phenomenon of some redirection of identity is clearly present even in the mystical cases that cannot be so conveniently cataloged as either "full" or "empty." It would therefore be a mistake to approach mysticism conceptually or culturally without noticing the unique character of, I should say, many mystics' accounts of their mystical experiences.

As far as this uniqueness is concerned, consider, for example, the following account, taken from a popular collection of Bengali saints' biographies. The speaker is a "great sage," who described himself in these words:

> I was born in all castes, I drank the milk of all mothers. I experienced the joys and sorrows of innumerable wives, children, friends and relatives. I did undergo great sorrows of separation, deaths, floods, destruction and devastation . . . the joys and gains of friends, the sorrows of friends becoming enemies, and enemies causing great losers, the troubles of thieves and drunkards I experienced. I fell in many hells. . . .[10]

Clearly, this description manifests ecstatic states that are, first and foremost, an expression of being unique, of a way of constituting an identity with no parallel in the outside, nonmystic world. Indeed, the channel of ecstasy as one of the dominant features through which the identity of the mystic is proclaimed should not be underestimated. Ecstatic states, as Joan M. Lewis puts it, are "transcendental experiences . . . typically conceived of as states of 'possession,' [which] have given the mystic a unique claim to direct experiential knowledge of the divine and, where this is acknowledged by others, the authority to act as a privileged channel of communication between man and the supernatural."[11] Thus, ecstasy is, above all, an expression of singularity—a unique kind of behavior or state of mind.

The unique quality of mystical identity is expressed in various ways. Sometimes it is expressed not by means of ecstasy but, rather, by means of devotion. In a typical Śaivite bhakti hymn, composed by the south Indian poet Devara Dāsimayya, the mystical identity is not ecstatic but devotional:

> God of my clan,
> I'll not place my feet
> but where your feet
> have stood before
> I've no feet
> of my own.
>
> How can immoralists
> of this world know

the miracle, the oneness
of your feet
and mine.[12]

Another striking example of the uniqueness or individuality of mystical experience can be found in the sayings attributed to one of the strangest figures in the Jewish Hasidic movement: I am referring to Rabbe Menachem Mendel, from Kotzk, who is known as the Kotzker Rebbe. Living in Eastern Europe in the middle of the nineteenth century, he behaved, in some ways, in keeping with the Hasidic tradition of his time and place, as a father, a guru, and a social leader of his community. However, in other ways the Kotzker Rebbe was a strange and lonely figure, possibly even a borderline psychotic. The Hasidic tradition recalls many stories about his near-unusual behavior. It is told of him that he spent more than twenty years locked inside his room, going out of it quite rarely and sometimes in a fit of violence:

> For about twenty years he was shut inside his room. On Sabbaths and Holidays he did not come to the meal held in common. Sometimes he opened the door of his holy room and appeared before the group . . . looking like a terrible angel of God, and he spoke a few words in an extraordinarily loud voice . . .
>
> Once he opened the door to the study hall and shouted: "Ha, are these the people I have imagined? These, and not the handful dressed in white?!"[13]

Within his own frame of identity, the Kotzker Rebbe expresses his views in a wholly negating way, or in a way that at least separates his religious experience from any usual core, common to himself and his coreligionists, around which religious beliefs and practices may revolve. His example shows the extent to which the mystic is likely to be a lone figure, for whom society as a whole, and not infrequently the community of the faithful, in particular, are obstructions, blocking the way toward the full expression of the mystical truth, whatever it may be.

From this standpoint, any turning away from the inner mystic core of experience toward the surface of communal experience is an act of retreat, not to say betrayal. Socialization in this respect is an act of alienation from the mystic's reality (or "emptiness"). The attitude can easily be found in the many homilies on the Torah that are attributed to the Kotzker Rebbe. A typical example is his attitude to the figure of Moses as one human who had a direct encounter with God on Mount Sinai and who was then obliged to return to the earthly society of his community. The Bible says that Moses turned from God and went back to the people of Israel. Depending on the similarity of the two verbal roots in Hebrew, the Kotzker Rebbe interpreted the verb *turn* as "pretended." Such a mystic, like most mystics, I think, takes his social experience, that of the religious society in which he lives, as no more than a veiling or a masking that is superimposed on the true nature of things, to which he feels he has penetrated. In the same vein, the Kotzker Rebbe says that "when Moses put a veil on his face, it was not the case that he actually put on a mask, but only that he hid himself in his inwardness."[14]

The following tale is perhaps the one most indicative of the uniqueness through which the mystic is portrayed within a frame of identity:

> One night, at midnight, after the holiday of Rosh ha-Shana was over and the devotees, who were tired, fell asleep on the benches of the Study House, he all of a sudden opened

the door and cried out, "Do you know what I want? I want this: even if heaven falls on the earth and the earth cracks, the [true] man should not depart from his own way. This is what I want." And all of them replied, "Yes, yes."[15]

In another version of the same tale, the Kotzker Rebbe speaks even more harshly: "I want this: even if heaven falls, earth cracks, man's heart breaks into pieces, and man's shoulders fracture, the [true] man should not change his own course."[16]

In the present context, however, it is most important to emphasize the gulf that the mystic feels between his individual self-portrait and the collective understanding in the mystic's own religious tradition of the sacred scriptures. In this respect, the tension between the scriptures and the individual is far from being resolved, or even from being eased. Consider, for example, the almost brusque words of the Hindu mystical poet Kabir:

> Vedas, Purāṇas, why read them?
> It's like loading an ass with sandalwood!
> Unless you catch on and learn how Ram name goes
> how will you reach the end of the road?[17]

Another example of the belittling of scriptures comes from the words of an eighteenth-century Punjabi:

> Reading and reading knowledge, the muftis give judgment,
> But without love they have remained ignorant, Sir!
> By reading knowledge the secret of God is not known,
> Only one word of love is efficient, Sir![18]

Many other examples of such derogation of scriptures and traditions can be found in Tantric Hinduism. In their defense, they are likely to claim that their superior kind of insight can in fact be found in the Vedas, but only in a deliberately hidden form.[19] We find similar attitudes in Meister Eckhart and, of course, in Ch'an (Zen) Buddhism.

By referring to the frame of identity, I do not mean to contend that mystical experience is not contextual. Indeed, the mystic may rely heavily on tradition, scripture, history, and communal norms. But as long as we examine the procedure by which mystical experience constitutes the identity of the experiencing agent, notions like "history," "tradition," and "scripture" remain parasitic, or, at best, instrumental, since mystical identity is by nature internal. Of course, a mystic may use culturally revered icons and sacred words to describe her or his experience; a mystic may even use such icons and words in the course of the arousal of the experience itself. Nonetheless, mystical vision as such requires a personal author. As far as the frame of identity is concerned, the way in which the mystic treats the tradition is typically as a sort of wall—the external barrier between himself or herself as an individual and the external world. Whether or not the mystic comes to terms with this wall or tries to break through it, it is only the perimeter of the mystic's circle, whereas the mystic's individual identity lies at the center of the circle.

To put it directly, if socialization is to be considered a common channel for achieving personal identity, mystical experience constitutes an alternative (sometimes even a negating alternative) to socialization. Hence, within Hinduism, for example, mystical experience is often described as *mokṣa*—as freedom from dharma, that blanket notion that covers both cosmic harmony and social norms. And even in those instances in which *mokṣa* is identified with a way of action (karma-yoga) and presented as a perfect manifestation of dharma, achieving *mokṣa* necessarily involves a personal act of internalization.[20] As Ben Ami Scharfstein vividly describes the mystic in this respect, "Whereas he used to look out through his windows and go out through his door, he now pulls his windowshades down and locks his door. His lights he keeps on and his eyes open, but they are inverted into himself."[21]

Within the frame of identity, then, mystical identification is reached from the inside and takes the form of an individuality in constant opposition to religious communal practices. There are instances in which such opposition eventually changes its status and, in one way or another, becomes the established view, but of course, a change of status is not a change of identity. Therefore, the instances in which mystical experience draws from a tradition tell us something important about the epistemic framework of the tradition; but it is scarcely relevant to the mystic's frame of identity.

As far as the frame of identity of the mystical experience is concerned, what we encounter is a distinctive drive for individuality, a drive deeply rooted in the very conceptual scheme through which a meaningful account of mystical experience is given. What is the purpose and significance of this individuality? Does it express a yearning for authenticity? Or a craving for power? Or a fierce battle for (or against) sanity? Or does it, perhaps, express something different? All these intriguing contextual questions can be given a plausible answer only when related to a specific time, place, experience, and other relevant circumstances. But such a contextual consideration does not affect the identification of the mystical vision as an intensive, sometimes an all too intensive, attempt at individuality.

The Mystic's *Frame of Justification*

There is, however, a second, simultaneous framework within which the mystic usually dwells. I call this the *frame of justification*. Whereas the frame of identity is the one within which the individuality of mystical experience is proclaimed, the frame of justification is the one within which the mystic justifies and, as well, communicates the justification of the knowledge claims that are by nature embedded in individual mystical experiences. This justification leads the mystic to exhibit what Steven Katz describes as a "conservative character."[22] Within the frame of justification, there are very striking similarities between the attitudes of the mystic and those toward scripture expressed in religious tradition.

In most religious traditions, scriptures play more than one role. They are acknowledged to be sacred, both as texts and as objects. As texts, scriptures are usually conceived to hold endless meanings. This multiplicity of meanings is likely to be presented as a necessary condition for regarding a text as a scripture. In this respect, the essence of scripture lies in its (intended) ambiguity. Because of its intended ambiguity, scripture stands in constant need of commentary. Thus St. Augustine declares, in a much-quoted passage:

> There is only one God, who caused Moses to write the holy Scriptures in a way both suited to the minds of the great numbers of men who would all see truths in them, though not the same truths in each case, For my part I declare resolutely and with all my heart that

> if I were called upon to write a book which was to be vested with the highest authority, I should prefer to write it in such a way that a reader could find re-echoed in my words whatever truths he was able to apprehend. I would rather write in this way than impose a single true meaning so explicitly that it would exclude all others.[23]

The road of the commentator therefore seems to be wide open. Commentary indeed has its various genres, methods, styles, and ephemeral fashions. Mystical commentary is one of the commentarial genres, and the mystic shares with other religious practitioners the role of the exegete: the face of the traditionalist and the face of the mystic are often fused beyond separation in the commentator of sacred texts. As Elliot R. Wolfson nicely puts it, "The visionary is, first and foremost, an exegete, whose visions are primarily, not secondarily, informed by visionary accounts in canonical texts."[24]

But scriptures are not only texts. It has been argued recently that sacred texts should be understood within a much wider human context.[25] According this view, we should characterize scripture as a sacred object, not as a collection of sacred texts. The textual character of a scripture is only a manifestation of its extralinguistic sacredness. In fact, the sacredness of scripture is due to a web of historical, social, and cultural considerations that reflect the whole religious situation, and not only the more particular question of intelligibility or meaning. Thus scripture is often conceived as having a sacred physical being. Religious objects have generally possessed physical holiness and been treated with intensive respect and even fear. The words and the letters that make them up are regarded as themselves sacred. Here, too, we find the mystic to be an active participant in such "scriptural practices." It is to be expected that a mystic for whom the mode of contact (with God, some divine presence, the world, or something else) is so very central will find it natural to transfer this contact need to the physical body of scripture as well. The rather amusing biblical story about the prophet who, while in a mystical trance, we asked to eat God's divine words and did so (and found them tasty) is indicative of the mystic's possible reverence for the physical body of scripture.

As I have argued elsewhere,[26] these two faces of scriptures—the textual and the functional—are in fact two aspects of the epistemic role that scripture plays in religious traditions. One of the frequent errors of scholars has been to ignore one side or the other of this Janus-faced phenomenon, or, even worse, to consciously favor one of the two as the more representative for an understanding of the role that scripture plays in religious life. The scholarly search for the particular and singular too easily leads us to belittle the relevance of Peter Berger's conclusion concerning the essential role that knowledge plays in forming the inner structure of society. One central common feature of all societies is that each of them provides its members with an objectively available body of knowledge. "To participate in the society is to share its 'knowledge,' that is, to co-inhabit its nomos."[27] Both as texts and as functioning objects, scriptures *refer to the world* and aim at making it *known*.

Religions, then, are deeply conditioned by the notion of knowledge, and knowledge and scripture are most often strongly linked in different religious traditions. Notice that the term *knowledge* is often embedded in the names of particular scriptures. For example: In Judaism, the word *mishnah*, used as the name of the oral Torah, comes from the root *to repeat* in the sense of "to repeat in order to learn." In Christianity, the word *evangel*, meaning "the Christian gospel," comes from the Greek *evangelion*, meaning "good news." The word *gnōsis*, the esoteric knowledge that believers in Gnosticism seek, means, simply, "knowledge." Likewise, the Sanskrit *Veda* means "knowledge." We can safely conclude that scripture could not be what it is in the absence of its claim to superlative knowledge. More specifically, scripture is, as a rule, taken by tradition and practice as the means by which knowledge is claimed to be known and the certainty of its truth guaranteed. The epistemic framework that scripture provides is meant to portray a worldview that includes both facts and their significance.

When knowledge is related to scripture, what is usually sought is some kind of epistemic justification of the worldview portrayed by religious traditions in their sacred works. Scripture is usually seen as itself constituting the justification for the knowledge claims that it includes. This self-justification is one of the most visible traits of the whole phenomenon of scripture. The epistemological status is granted to scripture as being both the instrument by which knowledge is gained and the procedure by which knowledge is justified. What does such scriptural justification involve? The answer to this question requires the authority of scripture as the foundation on which scriptural justification rests. The justification of scriptural knowledge claims is offered by means of an appeal to the authority of scripture.[28] Justification by scriptural authority is an indirect procedure in which scripture is taken to include the evidence for the truth of its own knowledge claims. The result is that the declaration of the authority of scripture amounts to a declaration of the validity of the evidence it provides. From a philosophical point of view—at least from that of the modern Western theories of knowledge—authority has been regarded as a very dubious, not to say despised, means of justification. But the justification of scriptural knowledge cannot restrict itself to the standard empirical ways by which perceptual and inferential knowledge are justified. Scriptural authority expresses the willingness of religious communities to see their scriptures as sources of knowledge both of the world and of what is assumed to lie beyond it. This willingness is not restricted to abstract intellectual assent but is embedded in many modes of human action and reaction. Authority (in the sense of such a far-reaching willingness) has deep roots in scripture and is inseparable from the way in which it presents itself.

There are numerous instances, taken from different mystical traditions, in which mystics refer to the scriptures of their respective traditions to justify their mystical views. This turning to scripture has many modes, some of them conscious and perhaps sophisticated, and some unconscious or perhaps unreflective. On the more sophisticated level, we find the mystical commentaries on scriptures. The Zohar, which presents itself as a true interpretation of the sacred texts, is a striking example of a sophisticated approach. Similar accounts can be found in many mystical traditions, from both East and West. On a less sophisticated level, scripture sometimes serves, perhaps unreflectively, as an object of devotion or a source of emotional exaltation, the devotion or the exaltation itself confirming the inherent value of the mystical experience. To give one example of a devotional and emotional attitude, Rumi, the mystical Persian poet of the thirteenth century, sees the imagery of the Qurʾān as a revelation of its mystical secrets.[29] An example of what I take to be less sophistication is that of the Hindu sects that concentrate their mystical efforts on sacred sounds—that is, on the sound of mantras.

It is precisely within this frame of justification that the mystic often expresses the conservative constituent of mystical experience. The reliance of the mystic on the scriptural authority of his or her tradition was rightly pointed out by Katz as a central feature of the mystical hermeneutics of scriptures:

> Mystics *do* stretch texts in all directions through their employment of allegorical and symbolic readings; yet this very use of allegory and symbolism, as well as other varied hermeneutical devices, functions to *maintain* the authority of the canonical sources under interpretation rather than to destroy or transcend them, as is usually assumed. That is to say, the presupposition on which the mystical use of allegory and symbolic modes of exegesis depends is that the canonical books of one's tradition do in fact possess the *truth* and *authority* claimed for them. . . . The community is seen to have been all the time in possession of the "truth" revealed a second time to the contemporary initiate. In this way, the mystical hermeneutic reinforces, even exaggerates, the significance of canonical texts to a degree unheard of in the non-mystical hermeneutical tradition.[30]

Seen in the light of this frame of justification, the traditionalist and the mystic share the same enterprise. They both endeavor to establish, maintain, and defend a picture of the world to which the status of knowledge, truth, or being (and the like) is attributed. In this respect, then, the mystic is no different from the mainstream exegete. Both offer a justification of religious knowledge and both turn to scripture as the authority on which such justification is based. And even when the mystic exhibits less interest in elucidating the content of scriptural texts and more interest in cherishing and adoring scripture by quoting it, or chanting or singing it, or even venerating some physical manifestations of scripture—even then the mystic is in practice no different from the mainstream religious practitioner. It is true that the content of mystical exegesis of scripture may indeed be uncommon, highly symbolic, or eccentric, and the behavior of the mystic in relation to scriptural manifestations may be extraordinary. But though it may stem from a highly individual cast of mind, the mystic's verbal and nonverbal activity is structurally very mundane. The mystic is in fact also the vehicle of tradition, taking part in the complex procedure of justifying the knowledge claims on which the relevant tradition bases its image of persons, of their worlds, and of whatever may lie beyond them. Again, the mystic may draw from this omnipresent epistemic picture an exceedingly unusual conclusion, but nonetheless remains an integral part of the traditional religious community, at least in adopting its epistemic picture. Mystics therefore employ exegetical strategies in reading scripture, as well as liturgical and ritualistic devices in using scripture, in an effort to preserve and strengthen the authority of scripture, which, as I have contended, is necessary for acceptance of the authority of religious knowledge claims.

Śaṇkara's Mysticism: An Example of the Dialectical Relationship

As I have been arguing, we should regard the dialectical relationship between mysticism and scripture as conceptually based on the operation of two simultaneous frames within which the mystic dwells. I now give one striking example of the dialectical relationship between mysticism and scripture, in terms of the two frames, the frame of identity and the frame of justification. For my example, I cite the Indian philosopher and mystic Śaṅkara, since I think that his writings clearly manifest the struggle the mystic may undergo between his own mystical identity and the traditional need for giving scripture an epistemic justification. Given the limits of this chapter, I can make only a cursory examination of Śaṅkara's rich, complicated thought.

The absolute existence of Brahman is, beyond any doubt, the main target of Śaṅkara's mysticism. Brahman is described, according to Śaṇkara's understanding of the Upaniṣads, as uniform, unchanged, and unmoved. From this mystical standpoint, all knowledge about the phenomenal world or the individual soul is regarded as illusory and unreal. The realization of the identity between Brahman and Ātman (as the highest, nonindividual self) constitutes the final release (*mokṣa*) from the suffering and misery of "beginningless" cycles of births and rebirths. According to Śaṅkara, *mokṣa* is the total annihilation of the world and brings *saṃsāra* and karma to a final end. It can be obtained by the removal of ignorance (*avidyā*), which is then replaced by right intuitive knowledge of the identity between Brahman and Ātman.

Śaṅkara emphasizes that the attainment of *mokṣa* does not involve the adoption of any explicit theological or philosophical ontology. The realization of the identity of Brahman and Ātman is a wholly intrinsic affair, in which the person having the mystic vision of the identity can be marked (if not characterized) by the mental conversion to which his or her mind is subject.[31] Throughout his writings, Śaṅkara portrays mystical conversion in very strong terms, by means of which he explicitly contrasts it with the life in the outside world, including the religious Hindu world, where the notion of dharma is key.

Mystical experience is a strong expression of negation; it is the negation of life—as understood by the philosopher, as interpreted by the exegete, and as lived by the practitioner. In contradistinction to some reported mystical experiences, the mystical ideal of Śaṅkara must possess not only a noetic quality but also the certainty that this noetic quality is permanent and, most important, not subject to change or replacement by anything else. There is felt to be some mystical inner guarantee that makes the mystical state immune from the wear and tear of outer reality, including the religious tradition that the mystical state negates. More specifically, the very uniformity and the irreversible certainty of the mystical experience function as the perfect guardians against the interference of the nonmystical world. Hence, as soon as the mystical state has been attained, "this whole world of names and forms, which had been hiding Brahman from us, melts away like the imagery of a dream."[32] This inner, intuitive knowledge of the Brahman–Ātman identity is the sufficient condition for recognizing the mystical experience as internally "valid" and therefore avoids the frustrating situation in which "you may say a hundred times, 'I experience Brahman! Dissolve this world!' and yet we shall be unable to do either the one or the other." Thus Śaṅkara concludes this commentary on the *Brahma Sūtra* by claiming that "it is a settled matter that those who, through perfect knowledge, have dispelled all mental darkness and are devoted to the eternally perfect Nirvāṇa do not return.[33]

What we see here is an account of the mystical state given from the point of view of the frame of identity. Within this frame, the mystical state is totally different from, and opposed to, the empirical realm, and therefore its nature can never but put into meaningful words, including scriptural words. (According to Śaṅkara, any apparently positive description of it that is to be found in the scriptures has a purely secondary, didactic purpose.) Seen in the light of Śaṅkara's mystical identity, Brahman–Ātman lies beyond the limits of the ordinary valid means of knowledge (*pramāṇas*) around which the epistemological view of Śaṅkara revolves.

But when we move from the frame of the identity of the mystic to the frame in which the epistemic justification for the validity of the mystical experience is examined, we encounter the second aspect of Śaṅkara's Janus-faced mysticism. Here Śaṅkara is far from the great annihilator of ordinary experience and normative society. To the contrary, he appears as a conservative traditionalist who spares no effort to anchor the very possibility of the mystical state well within the body of scripture of his own religious tradition. Indeed, scriptural texts, mainly the Upaniṣads, are seen by Śaṅkara as the sole authority for justifying the mystical viewpoint. Just as one face in a photograph can be faded into that of another, the face of the mystic is faded into the face of the religious exegete. And the reclusive identity of the mystic fades into the orthodox chain of traditional scriptural commentaries made throughout the ages. When Śaṅkara deals with the epistemic justification of his mystical claims, he is therefore a conservative heir of the Hindu scriptural tradition. In this respect he is the ardent follower of the Mīmāṃṣā school—the ritualistic Hindu school that, somewhat anachronistically and somewhat heroically, tried to preserve the ancient Vedic tradition and devotes very many exegetical pages to the task of scriptural interpretation. This school's main objective is to establish dharma as an ultimate value, on the claim that dharma requires a total obedience to all the injunctions that can be discovered in the Veda.[34] Śaṅkara, of course, does not imitate the Mīmāṃṣā's obsessive concern with the normative notion of dharma. he trades it for the soteriological notion of *mokṣa*, on the assumption, which he takes to be certain, that the attainment of the mystical experience of Brahman–Ātman identity is possible. He turns to scripture to help him affirm the truth of the mystical experience. But although he strongly differs from the Mīmāṃṣā exegetes in his interest, like them, he is bound to attempt a metascriptural justification—that is, a validation of scripture by the affirming of its authority.

Let me briefly follow Śaṅkara the mystic in his persistent attempt to validate the knowledge claims of scripture. According to Śaṅkara, the authority of scripture is found in its status as a *pramāṇa*—that is, as a means of right knowledge. Like the other means that Śaṅkara accepts (sense-perception and inductive inference), the scriptures, regarded as a means of knowledge, are meant to prove something that is not already known; should they be grasped as restating something that is already known they will lose their validity. In other words, Śaṅkara understands scripture as a means of knowledge in the strict sense of this term. Although it refers to a completely different sort of *content* than the ordinary means of knowledge, it nevertheless shares with them the same status of validation. Hence the definition of scripture as a means of knowledge brings it under the same framework within which the "ordinary" means of knowledge operate.

Śaṅkara thus deals mainly with questions such as "In which cases can the information supplied by scripture (*śruti*) be regarded as valid?" and "What is the relation between knowledge attained through scripture and knowledge obtained through the ordinary means of obtaining knowledge (perception and inference)?" The answers he provides for these questions are crucial not only for a comprehensive understanding of his thought but also, and more relevant to our present purpose, for clarifying the importance that Śaṅkara as mystic attaches to a right understanding of the role and status of the scriptures as the epistemic validators of mystical knowledge.

To exhibit the importance that Śaṅkara attributes to the epistemic role of scripture—that of justifying mystical knowledge—I briefly state four of the major conditions that Śaṅkara posits for the possibility of obtaining mystical knowledge through scripture. These conditions all deal, in one way or another, with the status of scripture as *pramāṇa* (means of knowledge). I call them the conditions of autonomy, uniqueness, restriction, and compatibility.

First, Śaṅkara is eager to establish scripture—as a means of knowledge—as *autonomous*, for example, totally independent of the other valid means. Following the orthodox Mīmāṃṣā view, Śaṅkara argues that the authority of scripture is inherent—it lies within itself and does not stand in any need of being justified either by perception or by inductive inference: "The authoritativeness of the Veda with regard to the matters stated by it is independent and direct, just as the light of the sun is a direct means of our knowledge of form and colour."[35] Being autonomous, scripture is further seen by Śaṅkara as *unique*, since it is the only source of knowing Brahman. Hence Śaṅkara emphasizes that "Brahman, though it is of nature of an accomplished thing, cannot be an object of perception and the other means of knowledge; for the fact of everything having its Self in Brahman cannot be grasped with the aid of the scriptural passage 'That are thou.'"[36]

Against the prima facie view (*pūrvapakṣa*), which claims (in what can be described as a version of "rational theology") that Brahman can be known through the ordinary *pramāṇa*s Śaṅkara argues:

> It has indeed been maintained by the pūrvapakshin [theoretical interlocutor] that the other means of proof . . . also apply to Brahman, on account of it being an accomplished entity (not something to be accomplished as religious duties are); but such an assertion is entirely gratuitous. For Brahman, as being devoid of form and so on, cannot become an object of perception; and as there are in its case no characteristic marks (on which conclusions, etc., might be based), inference also and the other means of proof do not apply to it; but, like religious duty, it is to be known solely on the ground of holy tradition.[37]

The autonomy and uniqueness of scripture as a means of knowledge do not mean that its scope is limitless. To the contrary, Śaṅkara emphasizes that the scope of scripture is indeed *restricted*, its jurisdiction being valid only within the epistemological framework of the phenomenal world. Śaṅkara emphasizes this point while defending his Advaita viewpoint against possible objections. In this context he writes: "We [do not] mind your objecting that if perception ceases to be valid, scripture itself ceases to be so; for this conclusion is just what we assume. . . . We ourselves assume that when knowledge [here, referring to the highest intuitive knowledge of Brahman] *springs up* scripture ceases to be valid.[38]

Last, scripture as a means of knowledge must be *compatible* with the other means of knowledge. More specifically, it cannot produce statements that contradict statements derived from perception and inference. The result is that, speaking hypothetically, in any case in which scripture contradicts perception and inference, its statements must be regarded as invalid. Śaṅkara writes:

> The scripture seeks not to alter things, but to supply information about things unknown, as they are. . . . Things in the world are known to possess certain fixed characteristics such as grossness or fineness. By citing them as examples the scriptures seek to tell us

> about some other thing which does not contradict them. They would not cite an example from life if they wanted to convey and idea of something contradictory to it. Even if they did, it would be to no purpose, for the example would be different from the thing to be explained. You cannot prove that fire is cold, or that the sun does not give heat, even by citing a hundred examples, for the fact would already be known to be otherwise through another means of knowledge. And one means of knowledge does not contradict another, for it only tells us about those things that cannot be known by any other rmeans.[39]

It is clear that Śaṅkara's thought can be used as a conspicuous illustration of the two frames within which the notion of mysticism is anchored. Śaṅkara is one of the best-known Indian philosophers and is perhaps the most noteworthy among Indian thinkers for the vast number of misrepresentations that have been made of his writings. I think that some of these stem from the failure to realize that his thought must be interpreted with the aid of the two frames and should not be reduced to either one of them alone. Can Śaṅkara be classified as a philosophical realist, or, instead, as the realist's opponent, the idealist? Since he seems to be holding both positions, the most promising understanding of his thought would be, I suppose, to take him at his different words and realize that, as a philosopher of the mystical, he appears with a different distinctive face in each of the two frames. As far as his mystical identity is concerned, Śaṅkara no doubt represents the mystic in highly individualistic terms, as a recluse who commits an irreversible act of retirement and seclusion by which the whole structure of tradition—its language, social institutions, moral norms, religious laws, beliefs, and practices—is challenged. Dharma, scripture (Veda and Upaniṣads alike), karma, and ritual—all these are declared *māyā*, that is "illusory," and are canceled out when confronted with the mystical yearning for "apersonal" individuality, that of Ātman–Brahman. But insofar as Śaṅkara is preoccupied with providing an epistemological justification, the knowledge conveyed to him by his mystical experience, he makes extensive use of all the linguistic distinctions that he rejects within the first frame of identity. The hermeneutical task he takes on himself leaves him locked in the collective epistemic endeavor of the religious tradition to which he belongs. By maintaining and cultivating the authority of scripture, Śaṅkara is seen to be deeply rooted in classical Hinduism.

Conclusion

What can we learn from the dialectical relationship between scripture and mysticism? First, I would like to reemphasize that the distinction between the two frames, those of identity and justification, is not meant to be a sharp, exclusive one. The distinction is not empirical but conceptual. Phenomenologically speaking, mysticism defies any clear-cut attempt at classification of its different types. Accordingly, by explaining the dialectical relations of the mystic and his culture in terms of the two frames, I submit that a possible explanation of the epistemic element is hidden inside the mystical phenomenon. In pointing out the dialectical relations between creating a mystical identity and justifying a mystical knowledge claim, I have used the theoretical distinction between the two frames for a specific purpose—namely, to clarify the strange manner in which mystical experiences are referred to by mystics themselves, as experiences that contain knowledge in the strictest, superlative sense of the term *knowledge*. Further, in using the two-frames model, my purpose has been to suggest a clarification of a certain kind of usage, the usage in which the terms *mysticism* and *scripture* are dialectically connected with one another. I must add that the distinction between the two frames is meant to be a provisional one and, as such, to lead us to reconsider the use of the concepts of tradition and culture within the two different frames (that of identity and that of justification).

When we examined the dialectical relationship between mysticism and scripture, we were able to see that the mystic can be viewed as dwelling in two frames, or, if you wish, as playing two different simultaneous games, each in a different court. In each court, scripture, as a distinctive mark of the mystic's religious tradition, is grasped in a different way: in one, that of identity, it is pushed aside, belittled, and even, so to speak, annihilated; in the other, the game or framework of justification, it is taken with full seriousness and endorsed with hardly any qualification. We may now ask, however, What is really meant by the reference to "tradition" in this context? The prevailing answer to this question often leads us to view tradition as some sort of blanket term—that is, as a notion that covers anything and everything that is retained as religiously relevant. To use Wittgensteinian terms, "culture" is often regarded as the bedrock of our thoughts and actions, as a notion that is presupposed whenever we attempt to give a coherent account of a human practice.

To return to the distinction between the two frames, it seems that tradition, far from being the bedrock of our thoughts and actions, is grasped, oddly enough, in a quite different way in each of the two different frames. Such a conclusion contextualizes the very idea of tradition, contradicting the notion that it is presupposed bedrock of our thoughts and actions and leaving its meaning dependent on the frame within which it has been used. Thus, by using the two-frames model, we may perhaps become more critical of the uncritical way in which we take the terms *culture, tradition*, and *scripture* as basic and relatively fixed.

I wonder if we have not been subject to some mistake of orientation, the result of our attempt to grasp religion as an unambiguous whole. We have too often looked at religion, in all its variety, as a majestic tree or, rather, a majestic grove of majestic trees, all of which stem, like great fig trees, from a common root. This view of religion leads us to assume that by discovering the oldest root, the mother-root, we may discover the essential nature, the simple truth, in terms of which we can explain the whole needless complex of religious phenomena. By realizing that the notion of "scripture" (taken as a central manifestation of "tradition") functions differently within the two frames here hypothesized, we can avoid drawing a simple linear picture based on the notion of a single root. Then perhaps we will be able to view tradition and scripture as *complex notions* that do not necessarily involve the need to imagine a majestic grove of trees with a single root or, to change the image, the need to erect a great, Babel-like tower on the bedrock of a single set of presuppositions. The complexity of these notions may be more a matter of depth and perspective than the treelike branching of a conceptual tree of relations. What is suggested is that the frame of identity and the frame of justification are *differences in perspective*. To understand the conception of tradition, what we need to do is to merge or remerge identity and justification, not like two different pictures hung side by side but, rather, like two transparent images—slides, perhaps—that are superimposed, one on the other, and, when projected, are seen as one. The dialectical relationship between mysticism and scripture shows us that tradition and culture are less a matter of ultimate, bedrock terms than one of different modes of perspective by which to view the same phenomena.

NOTES

1. Bernard McGinn, *The Foundations of Mysticism* (New York, 1991), p. xiv.
2. Steven T. Katz, "Language, Epistemology, and Mysticism," in Katz, ed., *Mysticism and Philosophical Analysis* (London, 1978), p. 26.
3. Ibid., p. 46.
4. Walter T. Stace, *Mysticism and Philosophy* (London, 1961). Katz, "Language, Epistemology, and Mysticism." Katz further explains that Stace arrived at this incorrect distinction due to his "failure to appreciate the complexity of the nature of 'experience.'" He comments that Stace ignored the fact that experience and interpretation are mutually dependent and thus have a "two-directional symmetry: beliefs shape experience, just as experience shapes belief" (p. 30).
5. William P. Alston characterizes as mystical "any experience that is taken by the subject to be a direct awareness of (what is taken to be) Ultimate Reality or (what is taken to be) an object of religious worship." See Alston, "Literal and Nonliteral in Reports of Mystical Experience," in Steven T. Katz, ed., *Mysticism and Language* (New York, 1992), p. 80.
6. The dialectical relations between the radical and the conservative, between experience and interpretation, and between vision and exegesis are based on an exaggerated polarization. This dialectic is not to be taken as a mental relationship, as a characterization of the mind of the mystic (at least as the mystic experiences it). As far as the vague "direct" description of the mystic's mental state is concerned, far from being dialectical, it is assumed by the mystic to be some (more or less) straightforward contact with a divine presence. Such contact is considered to be not merely abstract but superlatively real.
7. See, for example, Hans H. Penner, who regards "mysticism" as "a false category which has distorted an important aspect of religion." Penner, "The Mystical Illusion," in Steven T. Katz, ed., *Mysticism and Religious Traditions* (New York, 1983), pp. 89–116.)
8. Steven T. Katz, "The 'Conservative' Character of Mystical Experience," in Katz, *Mysticism and Religious Traditions*, p. 3.
9. See the intriguing account given by Ernest Gellner of Descartes and Hume as highly individualistic philosophers, in Gellner, *Reason and Culture: New Perspectives on the Past* (Oxford, 1992), chap. 1.
10. Quoted in McDaniel, *The Madness of the Saints: Ecstatic Religion in Bengal* (Chicago, 1989), p. 255.
11. Joan M. Lewis, *Ecstatic Religion: A Study of Shamanism and Spirit Possession*, 2nd ed. (London, 1989), p. 15.
12. A. K. Ramanujan, trans., *Speaking of Śiva* (Harmondsworth, 1973), p. 106.
13. *Emet ve-Emuna* [Truth and faith] 3rd ed., assembled by I. J. Arten (Jerusalem, 1972), pp. 38, 100 (in Hebrew).
14. Ibid., pp. 19–20.
15. Ibid., p. 127.
16. *Emet me-Eretz Titzmakh* [Truth will rise from earth], ed. M. Schoenfend (Benei Berak, 1994), p. 226 (in Hebrew).

17. John Stratton Hawley and Mark Juergensmeyer, trans., *Songs of the Saint of India* (New York, 1988), p. 51.
18. Annemarie Schimmel, *Mystical Dimensions of Islam* (Chapel Hill, 1975), p. 385.
19. Douglas Renfrew Brooks, *The Secret of the Three Cities* (Chicago, 1990), p. 55.
20. "Internalization" is one of the main tactics used in Indian philosophy (both Hindu and Buddhist), but I cannot go into this matter here.
21. Ben Ami Scharfstein, *Mystical Experience* (Oxford, 1973), p. 147.
22. Steven T. Katz, "The 'Conservative' Character of Mystical Experience," in Katz, *Mysticism and Religions Traditions*, p. 3.
23. Saint Augustine, *Confessions*, trans. R. S. Pine-Coffin (Harmondsworth, 1961), p. 308.
24. Elliot R. Wolfson, *Through a Speculum That Shines: Vision and Imagination in Medieval Jewish Mysticism* (Princeton, 1994), p. 123.
25. See Wilfred Cantwell Smith, *What Is Scripture? A Comparative Approach* (Minneapolis, 1993), p. 223. See also William A. Graham, *Beyond the Written Word: Oral Aspects of Scripture in the History of Religion* (Cambridge, 1987), pp. 47–49; and Jonathan Z. Smith's attack on historians of religion, who, by ignoring its communal dimension, have portrayed religion as an essentially inhuman activity, one in which, according to Smith, what has been left is "the impossible generic abstraction of Homo religious." See Smith, "Sacred Persistence: Towards a Redescription of a Canon," in *Imagining Religion: From Babylon to Jonestown* (Chicago, 1982), p. 42.
26. Shlomo Biderman, *Scripture and Knowledge: An Essay on Religious Epistemology* (Leiden, 1995).
27. Peter L. Berger, *The Social Reality of Religion* (Harmondsworth, 1973), p. 30.
28. As Ben Ami Scharfstein argues, belief in authority of certain otherworldly omens, dreams, or sacred texts is present in every tribal culture. See Scharfstein, *Ineffability: The Failure of Words in Philosophy and Religion* (Albany, 1993), pp. 145–149.
29. Annemarie Schimmel, *The Triumphal Sun* (Albany, 1993), p. 173.
30. Katz, "The 'Conservative' Character of Mystical Experience," p. 30.
31. See, for example, Śaṅkara's commentary on *Bṛhadāṇyaka Upaniṣad* 4.4.7.
32. Śaṅkara's *Brahma-Sūtra-Bhaṣya* 3.2.21 in George Thibaut, trans., *The Vedānta Sūtras of Bādarāyaṇa, with the Commentary by Śaṅkara* (New York, 1962) part 2, p. 163.
33. Śaṅkara's *Brahma-Sūtra-Bhaṣya* 4.4.22 (in ibid., part 2, p. 419).
34. *Mīmāṃsā Sūtra* I.1.1–2.
35. Śaṅkara's *Brahma-Sūtra-Bhaṣya* 2.1.2 (in Thibaut, part 1, p. 295).
36. Śaṅkara's *Brahma-Sūtra-Bhaṣya* 1.1.4 (in ibid., part 1, p. 22).
37. Śaṅkara's *Brahma-Sūtra-Bhaṣya* 2.1.6 (in ibid., part 1, pp. 306–307). See also, 2.1.27.
38. Śaṅkara's *Brahma-Sūtra-Bhaṣya* 4.1.3 (in ibid., part 1, p. 340).
39. Śaṅkara's commentary on *Bṛhadāṇyaka Upaniṣad.* 2.1.20, in S. Madhavananda, trans. *The Bṛhadāṇyaka Upaniṣad with the Commentary of Śaṅkaracārya* (Calcutta, 1965, pp. 301–302.

3

The Zohar as Exegesis

MOSHE IDEL

The Zoharic Corpus

The Zohar is the canonic work of Jewish mysticism. Written during the last quarter of the thirteenth century, it has traditionally been attributed to a second-century Jewish master, Rabbi Simeon bar Yoḥai, himself a personality inclined to mysticism. However, as some Kabbalists at the end of the thirteenth century had already suspected, and as proven conclusively by modern scholarship, the Zohar is a medieval work, written in Castile.[1] It consists of numerous smaller treatises that can be divided into three main layers:

1. The earliest, written during the seventies of the thirteenth century, was designated as *Midrash ha-Ne'elam*. This is an esoteric midrash, written mainly in an allegorical vein and reminiscent of Jewish philosophical exegesis; it includes several portions of Genesis, as well as a commentary on the books of Ruth and the Song of Songs.
2. The main bulk of the Zohar consists primarily of an extensive commentary on most of the parts of the Pentateuch—the commentary is based on a theosophical-symbol exegetical approach. It also includes several smaller, though nevertheless important, theosophical tracts.
3. The latest layer is composed of two larger treatises—the *Tiqqunei Zohar* (Amendments of the Zohar), which consists of seventy associative interpretations of the first word of the Bible; and the *Ra'ya' Mehemna'*, a commentary on the mystical intentions that inform biblical commandments. These two treatises were authored by a later Kabbalist, that is, someone other than the author of the first two strata.[2]

Modern scholarship has identified Rabbi Moshe ben Shem Tov de Leon as the author of the majority of the Zohar, though some other contemporary Kabbalists might also have contributed to the present structure of the text of the Zohar, or—as suggested by Yehuda Liebes—even to the writing of the book.[3]

As even this very brief description of the contents of the Zohar shows, the work represents one of the most elaborate and influential attempts in any tradition, to interpret the Bible, and certainly the most important effort among Jewish mystics. Like many other kabbalistic commentaries on the Bible, the Zohar surmises that what happens during the exegetical enterprise is the retrieval of the ancient truths that comprise the esoteric core of the Jewish tradition, as these are embodied in a paramount way in the Bible. That is, these "secrets" are not innovations contrived by a medieval group of Kabbalists. In fact, what seems to be unique about the status of the Zohar is that it is seen as having transformed a literature that is interpretive in a deep sense—in fact, a conglomerate of esoteric interpretations on various parts of the Bible—into a canonic literature. However, despite the very substantial resort of the various parts of the verses, its special status was not derived from its being printed together with the biblical text, or from the fact that, due to the more usual form that biblical commentaries take, the Zohar was studied as part of the weekly regimen of studying the Bible. Rather, biblical verses have been absorbed into the mystical text and recycled as part of a mythical parable and theosophical interpretations that only very rarely assume the form of a linear commentary. It is significant, for the understanding of the interpretive nature of Jewish traditional culture, that a commentary indeed became a canonic writing.

In this essay, I attempt to discern the most important exegetical devices that were characteristics of the bulk of the Zohar and that informed the highly imaginative hermeneutics of this book.

The Zohar: The First Comprehensive Arcanization of the Bible

In the earlier Jewish esoteric literature, the so-called heikhalot literature of the third to the seventh centuries, as well as in the rabbinic views of esoterics, the operative assumption is that there are esoteric topics that are limited to some few passages in the Bible: the first chapter of Genesis, designated as "Maʿaseh Bereshit"; the first chapter of Ezekiel, known as "Maʿaseh Merkavah"; the discussions of interdicted sexual relations, ʾArayiot; and the secrets related to the divine names. In the Kabbalah of the thirteenth century this rather limited view of the domain of the esoteric evolved toward the assumption that each and every part of the Bible contains secret knowledge that concerns either divine or demonic worlds and the human relationship to them. This process may be described as one of comprehensive "arcanization." Found in a more modest manner in the earlier Kabbalah, arcanization is more evident in the Zohar, which proposes the more extended view that the divine name is identical to the Torah.[4] This identity means, to a certain extent, that the entire biblical literary corpus is the name of God and also contains God's form and power and should, therefore, be studied in all its detail. So, for example, the Zohar assumes that in each and every word of the Torah there are many profound truths and that these truths are like pearls that shine in all directions.[5] This view, and many others, imply a polysemic attitude to the biblical text.[6] According to one of the most far-reaching expressions, attributed to Rabbi Simeon bar Yoḥai, the alleged author of the Zohar:

> If people only knew the words of the Torah then they would comprehend that there is no word or letter in the Torah that does not contain supernal, precious secrets. Come and see: it is written, "Moses spoke and God answered him in a voice" [Exodus 9:19].[7] It has been taught: What is [the meaning of] "with a voice"? With the voice of Moses! This is correct [indeed], the voice of Moses precisely, the voice to which he was attached, and through which he was superior to all other prophets.[8]

This view, which has some parallels in the Hebrew writings of Rabbi Moses de Leon, has important repercussions for the attitude to the details of the biblical text: each and every one of its components must be carefully analyzed in the ongoing effort to fathom its secret recesses—for example, the forms of letters as used in the traditional writing of the text; the mystical etymology of proper names; and the peculiar expressions found in the text as commented on in the passage. Let us consider this last issue in more detail. The biblical formulation in Exodus is quite difficult: Did God speak with the voice of Moses? This was the answer accepted by the Talmudic sages and by many medieval interpreters. The Zohar, however, goes beyond this general statement. The voice, designated in the Bible by the word *be-Qol*, does not specify whether it is divine or human, and the Zohar offers an intermediary solution: "voice" stands for a divine manifestation to which Moses has been attached and which used Moses' throat to express itself. This voice being higher than other voices—or other divine manifestations—ensured the superiority of Moses as a prophet. This is a supernal secret because it reveals something not only about the relationship between God and man but also about the inner structure of the divine, and all this comes to light by means of a very close inspection of the formulations in the biblical verse. Divine and, alternatively, demonic, secrets lie hidden behind or above every detail of the biblical corpus.

It should also be understood that the study of the Torah is envisioned as a theurgical activity—that is, as a way of maintaining the world and of affecting the divinity. For this reason, and in order to attain their maximal efficiency, the commandments of the Bible (which are conceived of as paralleling the limbs of the body) have to be performed with the correct kabbalistic intention (*kavvanah*).[9]

PaRDeS: The Fourfold Zoharic Integrative Exegesis of the Bible

Centered on the details of the biblical text far more than Christian mystics, and perhaps even more than the Sufis, the medieval Kabbalists in general, and the Zohar, in particular, offered a plethora of mystical interpretations whose relationship to the already existing corpus of traditional nonmystical interpretations of Scripture had to be worked out and clarified. The major expression of the Kabbalists' attempt to establish an explicit scheme that would explicate the hierarchical relationship between the different types of Jewish exegesis is known by the acronym PaRDeS.[10] Originally meaning an orchard, this term is mentioned as part of an ancient rabbinic legend about four sages who entered a state of mystical contemplation of a supernal, and dangerous, realm named PaRDeS. As an acronym it designates a fourfold system of exegesis, used mostly in Kabbalistic writings. PaRDeS stands for *P*(*eshat*), or "plain sense"; *R*(*emez*), or a "hint," sometimes designating allegorical explanations; *D*(*erash*), or "homiletic expositions"; and finally *S*(*od*), or "secret—namely, symbolic—interpretations."

Two main theories attempt to explain the emergence of the PaRDeS type of exegesis among Kabbalists at the end of the thirteenth century: W. Bacher maintained that the Kabbalists adopted and adapted the Christian fourfold theory of interpretation; and P. Sandler claimed that this exegetical system emerged as the result of an inner development that began among Jewish exegetes of the twelfth century.[11] In his earlier work, Gershom Scholem adopted the theory of Bacher, though later he did not explicitly reject the view of Sandler.[12] Now, it needs to be said that Sandler did not make a very strong argument for his own view. However, it is difficult to simply accept the Bacher-Scholem position because of the simple fact, already pointed out by Sandler and reiterated by Frank Talmage and A. van der Heide, that the kabbalistic fourfold method does not correspond in certain crucial details with the Christian fourfold method.[13] Though it is always possible that an individual Kabbalist would accept an alien type of exegesis, either Christian or Muslim,[14] it seems less than plausible to assume that several Kabbalists, at exactly the same time and apparently independently of one another, adopted a very similar exegetical method. And if this is correct, then we need to look for a common factor that would explain the concomitant resort of several Jewish authors to this exegetical method.

The fact that the Kabbalists, rather than the Jewish philosophers, were those who espoused such a fourfold method is highly significant. The term *PaRDeS* stands, in some kabbalistic texts that date from the late thirteenth century, for the four methods of exegesis. However, in the period when this exegetical system emerged, PaRDeS designated methods that were already applied, separately, in different types of Jewish literature. The plain sense was the main subject of the exegetical literature produced by the northern France school of exegetes during the eleventh and twelfth centuries. Homiletical literature, the midrash, was already voluminously produced between the third century and the early Middle Ages. Since the eleventh century, Jewish philosophers like Solomon ibn Gabirol, Abraham ibn Ezra, and Maimonides had often resorted to allegorical interpretation; its floruit can be established in the thirteenth century. Finally, kabbalistic (mainly symbolic-theosophical) interpretations of the Bible and of other canonic Jewish writings were already known in the middle of the thirteenth century. In other words, the PaRDeS fourfold exegetical method, as sometimes cultivated by the Zohar, incorporated a variety of types of Jewish literature that already existed when the first formulations of this exegetical method were articulated. The latest type of exegetical literature was Kabbalah, and it is no accident that the exponents of this mystical lore were those who first exposed the method of PaRDeS. By contrast, we have sufficient evidence to suggest that some of the Kabbalists who proposed the PaRDeS, or other systematic exegetical methods, underwent a certain spiritual development before they became Kabbalists and that they became acquainted with the three other forms of interpretation before resorting to the various forms of kabbalistic exegesis. An inspection of the Zoharic literature immediately reveals a strong innovative form of exegesis, even when it is compared to the earlier kabbalistic literature. However, the Zohar was often anxious to point out that, novel as its interpretations of the Bible were, they are found in some manner within the interpreted text, thus subscribing to a much more conservative rhetoric.[15] In many cases the Zohar is inclusive, allowing an important role for all the existing achievements of Jewish cultural creativity as preparatory approaches, while presenting the respective mode of interpretations that corresponds to the Kabbalistic system in whose framework it was articulated as the highest achievement. However, de facto, we may describe the specifically Kabbalistic exegesis itself, according to the versions found in the various discussions of the Zohar, as integrating elements from the other three sorts of exegesis. It should be emphasized that the Zohar does not resort, systematically, to the four exegetical methods as separate types of interpretation but uses various elements together as part of its commentaries on the Bible.[16] No doubt, the author, or authors, of the Zohar had been aware of the contributions of the various earlier layers of Jewish exegetical literature to the formation of the Zoharic text. The second conclusion, which is derived from the first one, involves the relatively conservative nature of even some of the innovative Kabbalistic literature, most especially the Zohar. That is, these Kabbalists strove to integrate the earlier strata into still more comprehensive exegetical systems, safeguarding their importance and survival,[17] even when some of them, like Rabbi Abraham Abulafia, considered these "lower" types of exegesis relevant only to the vulgar masses.[18] Kabbalists very often attempted to articulate their hermeneutics in concert rather than in conflict with the traditional one. This responsible attitude to the spiritual heritage of Judaism also ensured the special role of Kabbalah in those Jewish circles that were not identical with more narrowly defined Kabbalistic groups.

Moreover, the symbolic recasting of external reality, as performed in the Zohar, allowed the emergence of what one scholar has aptly called "a transindividual unity of experience."[19] No wonder that the Zohar, the most important source of objective symbolism, also became a canonical work: it shaped an additional level of experience of the biblical text, shared by many individuals qua part of a religious community. This was the key element in the revitalization of Jewish spirituality achieved by the dissemination of the Zohar in its various interpretations, especially since the middle of the sixteenth century. Not only did the symbolic vision formulate an audacious theosophy that contributed to the canonization of the Zohar but also, and even more important, it contributed to an even more profound interpretation of both the Bible and Jewish tradition.

The Hidden Layer of Torah as a Maiden

The most famous of the Zoharic discussions of the fourfold exegetical method is found in a remarkable parable, one of the most fascinating stories in the whole Zoharic corpus, where the Torah, on its esoteric level, is symbolized as a young maiden and the Kabbalist is viewed as her lover.[20] The different possible relationships between the two are indicative of the four ways of interpretation that culminate with the symbolic-theosophical one, which is represented in the parable by the wedding of the two. The erotic union, however, does not invalidate the alternative and preliminary forms of communication between the two, and the Zohar emphatically indicates that plain sense is not dispensed with by the arrival of the esoteric one. The involvement of the mystic with the text is to be understood, on the basis of the parable, as a deeply experiential reading, a penetration of the body into the text, which has obvious sexual connotations. It is quite emblematic that the Zohar, unlike other Kabbalistic texts that were produced earlier, and unlike other contemporary works, uses the view of the female human body to make its point. Unlike the geometrical metaphors of Abraham Abulafia and the younger Joseph Gikatilla, or the resort to the male body in the later work of Gikatilla, the Zohar is creating a view of the beloved that is reminiscent of medieval court love.[21] An interesting reverberation of the maiden parable is found in a vision of the eighteenth-century mystic Emmanuel Swedenborg:

> There appeared to me a beautiful girl with a fair countenance, advancing quickly towards the right, upwards and hurrying a little. She was in the first bloom of youth—not a child nor a young woman. She was dressed attractively in a black shining dress. So she hastened cheerfully from light to light. I was told that the interior things of the Word are such when they first ascend. The black dress stood for the Word in the letter. Afterwards, a young girl flew towards the right cheek, but this was only seen by the interior sight. I was told that those are the things of the internal sense that do not come into the comprehension.[22]

The girl, when veiled, is compared to the literary level of the Torah; in both cases, the initiative is taken by the girl, who approaches the man. It is perhaps significant that the second girl's dress is not mentioned; she may correspond to the woman who discloses her secrets in the Zoharic parable. Therefore, I would suggest that Swedenborg has once again interiorized Kabbalistic material into his visions. Significantly enough, the most striking difference between Swedenborg's version of this experience and that of the Zohar is that for the Christian mythic the parable involves an understanding of the reality related to the Holy Scripture, while the Kabbalist's focus is on experiencing the meaning of the parable and thereby becoming the "husband" of the Torah.

This integrative, or inclusive, approach of the authors of the Zohar notwithstanding, in the later layer of the Zoharic literature, the so-called *Ra'ya' Mehemna'* (Faithful shepherd), an important example posits the Kabbalah as at the apex of the Jewish curriculum in a way that is ostensibly disjunctive vis-à-vis the earlier exegetical tradition. When dealing with the four types of interpretations, the anonymous Kabbalist of this text assumes that the only correct understanding of the Torah is the kabbalistic one, while other forms of interpretation are not only inferior but even, at times, deleterious.[23] It is in this context that an explicit relationship between the four methods of interpretation and the story of the four sages that entered the PaRDeS is established, to the effect that only one of the four sages, Rabbi 'Aqiva, has a correct approach to the Bible, namely, the kabbalistic one.

Massive Remythologization of the Biblical Text in the Zohar

Biblical literature constitutes a fabric made up of complex crosscurrents: efforts to demythologize the earlier religious traditions and to propose another myth, that of the divine will. The process of demythologization of the ancient Near East, however, was never complete; even when attempts were made to obliterate the mythical contents of some traditions, vestiges of the mythical imagery remained. Those vestiges served as starting points for the mythopoeic imagination of the Zohar, which created, and sometimes perhaps even re-created, out of the biblical verses and phrases, new myths. I discuss the following passage of the Zohar, part of the *Midrash ha-Ne'elam*, which exemplifies this trend in the Zoharic use of the Bible.

> When a man departs [more precisely, dies], the angels cause the soul to ascend up to a distance of three hundred years as it is said in our sages [*B.T. Pesaḥim*, fol. 94b] "from the earth to the firmament there are five hundred years," and they cause the soul to ascend to the highest heaven and they say: "If the soul has [done] a virtuous deed she will ascend." But before she ascends, they set her in a place where there are thirty two thousands of paths, some of them straight [forward], the other awkward, and all of them are called "traps of Death" and "ways of the Sheol." And on each and every path there is a consuming fire, and they say to each other: "If you see any soul entering any of those ways tell me." And there is there another way and over this way a power [is in charge], which is similar to a dog, and when the soul enters any of those paths the dog sees it and immediately barks and when the noxious [powers] and the pernicious angels [*Mal'akhei habbalah*] hear its voice [then] they know that there is a soul [arriving there] and they immediately arrive and seize the soul and sling her as it is written [Samuel I, 25:29] "And the souls of thy enemies, them shall He sling out, as out of the hollow of a sling" until they throw her to Gehenna. And David, the king of Israel, blessed be his memory, implored the Holy One, Blessed be He, that He should rescue him from the dog, as it is said [Psalm 22:21]: "Deliver my life from the sword; my only one from the dog." Is it possible that David, the king of Israel, would be afraid of a dog? But of that power [was he afraid] which is called dog. And they said that the souls of [the children of] Israel do not enter to that place and to these paths, and this dog does not damage them, as it is said [Exodus 11:7]: "But against any of the children of Israel not a dog whet his tongue."[24]

The special understanding of the dog, mentioned in two biblical verses quoted in the text, will show how the Zoharic imagination worked. On the one side, David, the quintessential hero of the Bible and the author of the Psalms, is afraid, according to the verse from the psalm, of the dog. This fear is interpreted as pointing to the extraordinary nature of the dog: it is not an ordinary animal, which would not impress the heroic king at all, but a personification of an evil power. Thus, a dramatic encounter between the soul of David and the mythical dog is created. This encounter, according to the logic of the situation, takes place in the underworld, or perhaps in a certain kind of purgatory. However, if understood in such a manner, the dog of the Zohar is reminiscent of Cerberus, the mythological dog of Greek mythology who is the guardian of Hades. Thus, the Zohar imports a Greek mythological phenomenon in order to better understand a verse of the Bible; and in so doing, it not only clarifies a verse but also creates a new myth. How is the image of the Zoharic Hades, or the Jewish *Gehenna*, produced? Again, with biblical *verses* and expressions. So, for example, the phrase "ways of Sheol" found in Proverbs 14:12 and the phrase "traps of death" found in Psalms 18:6 are personified in a way that creates a myth. Together with the verse from Samuel, a concatenation is produced that creates a web of dramatic events related to the odyssey of the soul in the underworld. While these references have a half-metaphorical and, sometimes, even half-mythical status in their original biblical contexts, here they become proper names describing pernicious powers that populate a labyrinthine underworld. To a certain extent the Zoharic reading of these mythical pre-biblical vestiges reinvests them with renewed mythical values.

Sexual Polarization as a Hermeneutical Device

One of the most outstanding characteristics of the Zoharic exegesis of the Bible is the exploitation of the biblical stylistic phenomena of parallelism between the different parts of a verse, in order to introduce a bipolar reading that is in many cases seen as representing the polarity between male and female. This approach is related to the comprehensive arcanization of the biblical text as it implies that mere repetition of synonymous terms would diminish the semantic cargo of the text. By reading a dual vision into the parallels in the verse, which are synonyms in the biblical style, the Zohar creates a drama, often implying a sexual or erotic mythical event that occurs in the sefirotic realm. However, central as this exegetical device is for the hermeneutics of the Zohar, it is not something original to it; it had already been found in several instances, in the early thirteenth century theosophical Kabbalah—for example, in Rabbi Ezra of Gerona's *Commentary on the Song of Songs*. In the following passages, I show how the Zohar exploits the interpretive possibilities that were opened much earlier by the *Targum Onqelos*, one of the early canonical, Aramaic translations of the Bible:

> "Great is the Lord and highly to be praised, in the city of our God, in the mountain of his holiness" [Psalm 48:2]. When is the Lord called "great"? When *Knesset Yisrael* is to be found with Him, as it is written, "In the city of our God is He great." "In the city of our God" means "with the city of our God" . . . and we learn that a king without a queen is not a [real] king, and is neither great nor praised. Thus, so long as the male is without a female, all his excellency is removed from him and he is not in the category of Adam, and moreover he is not worthy of being blessed. . . . "Beautiful for situation, the joy of the whole earth: mount Zion, the side of the North, the city of the great King." The meaning of "beautiful for situation, the joy of the whole earth" stands for the excellency of their [sexual] intercourse. "Beautiful for situation [stands] for Him [who is] Holy, blessed be He, who is the righteous, [who is] the joy of the whole earth" and then it is the delight of All and *Knesset Yisrael* is blessed [Hedwetah de-Kullah, ver. 3].[25]

Let me start my analysis here with the Zoharic interpretation of verse 3 of Psalm 48, which is more easily deciphered. The term *Yefe nof*, which means, literally, "a beautiful view," is understood as a symbol for divinity, more precisely, the ninth *sefirah*, that of *Yesod*—that is, the male divine power par excellence, identified with the membrum virile. This limb, which is to be used only in holiness—an imperative often recurring in the Zohar—is representative in the Zoharic symbolism of the righteous, that is, both the righteous in the world above, meaning the ninth *sefirah*, and the righteous in the world below. This sexual reading has been fostered by the occurrence of the term *masos* in the verse—translated here as "joy and delight"—that occurs in several texts in the context of the desire of the bridegroom for the bride. Indeed, the reading of *Yefe nof* as a bridegroom has been inspired by the Aramaic translation of this verse, where it is written: "Beautiful, like a bridegroom, who is the delight of the inhabitants of the whole earth." The biblical term *masos* has been translated as *hedwetah*, which is followed by the term *kol*, a fact that inspired the emergence of the Zoharic phrase *hedwetah de-kullah*. I suspect that the term *earth* (*ha-'aretz*) has been understood by the Zohar as a symbol for the last, or the tenth, *sefirah*—namely, *Malkhut*, which is synonymous with *Knesset Yisrael*, all of them serving as symbols for the feminine divine manifestation.

Let us turn now to the Zoharic interpretation of verse 2 of Psalm 48. Also in this case, the sexual polarity is involved. This time the pattern of interpretation, similar to that of many other passages in kabbalistic literature, involves a differentiation between the meaning of two divine names: the Tetragrammaton, signifying the Lord—standing for the *sefirah* of *Tiferet*, or the male divine attribute—and *ʾElohenu*, referring to *Malkhut*, or the female attribute. However, the novelty here is not to be found in this widely employed distinction in the Kabbalah. Rather, the focus of the exegetical effort is on the word *great*, which articulates the relationship between these attributes. Greatness is not a quality inherent in the male but a quality that is acquired through his relation to the female; only by the act of intercourse, as hinted in our discussion, is the quality of "great" and of "praised," made applicable to the male, whereby he becomes "man." The sexualization of the relationship between the divine attributes is a well-known kabbalistic exegetical device that presupposes a discovered reality even in those places in the Bible where synonyms were misinterpreted, as pointing to different entities.[26]

Moreover, beyond the investment of divine names with sexual qualities, a move common in kabbalistic literature, this passage of the Zohar adds something quite specific: how the greatness and excellency of the male is attained, both in the human and the divine realms. The gist of this exegetical endeavor is that it explains the appearance of a quality through the establishment of a certain relationship. However, the ultimate message of the Zohar is not the mere understanding of the condition required for perfection; that is, while its symbolism may invite contemplation, the awareness of certain theosophical and anthropological ideas does not change the nature of man. To attain both his perfection and the perfection of the divine realm, man must also act appropriately; otherwise, the very purpose of the exegetical process is not fulfilled. The experiential aspect of apprehending the Zoharic exegesis, therefore, is only the first step toward the ultimate goal; for the Kabbalist, understanding is an inescapable invitation to act. Without the appropriate action, the male does not reach the status of "man," nor can he perform the theurgic activity intended to influence the supernal syzigies. The definition of *man* is adduced in a very peculiar context, that is, from the occurrence of the term *ʾAdam* in the verse, "If any man of yours brings an offering to the Lord . . ." [Leviticus 1:2]. Therefore, symbolism in Zoharic exegesis is to be viewed as part of an effort to deepen both the significance of the biblical text and the understanding of human ritualistic activity, which has now come to be understood as theurgical and thus oriented to the higher world. Therefore, symbolization is much more than the disclosure of a static meaning carried by certain words.

We may distinguish three distinct steps that constitute the inner structure of the biblical text: (1) "gnostic" perfection, which stands for the understanding of the theosophical and theurgical significance of the text; (2) an operative achievement, namely, the acquisition of the status of "man"—that is, the realization of an ongoing way of life that is achieved together with his wife, just as two *sefirot* are to be brought together by kabbalistic activity; (3) finally, as a perfect man, the Kabbalist induces divine harmony through the performance of the commandments.

As we have seen in the parable of the palace of the maiden, according to the Zohar even the fathoming of the depths of the biblical text has an experiential aspect—that of becoming a complete man. And this is accomplished through the lived reality created and cultivated through one's relationship with one's wife.

To return to the previously cited passage: the plain sense of verse 2 is apparently simple and obvious—that the Lord is great and, as a separate assertion, that His mountain is located in His holy city. The former is a theological assessment, unconditional and absolute; the latter indicates that the sacred mountain is geographically located in the sacred city. The relationship between God's greatness and the sacredness of the mountain is not even alluded to; these two theological statements can easily be understood separately, and so I assume that there is no intention of describing any peculiar dynamic interaction between God and His city. Even though the biblical conception of the holy city as the city of God is quite explicit, no changing relationship pattern is implied by this assertion—it is chosen forever. The relationship pattern is a "vertical" one; divine holiness, stemming from the supernal world, is imposed on a material entity that is thereby metamorphosed into a sacred center. The Zohar radically changes this pattern: the vertical relationship is transposed on the divine plan, where it can now be viewed as horizontal—that of two sexually differentiated entities that are both understood as divine attributes. To determine the relationship between the two parts of the verse, the Hebrew prefix *be*, meaning "in," is interpreted as meaning "with"; these dynamics emerge from the sexualization and the interrelation of the two divine names found in the biblical comparison with other types of Jewish exegeses. Theosophical Kabbalah alone could put into relief divine attributes whose affinity with one another gradually turns at times into semimyths and at other times even into full-fledged myths. However, the transformation of the vertical relationship into an intradivine polarity does not obliterate the previous vertical understanding of the relationship of God to the city.

As we have already noted, the corporeal reality was not ignored by the Zoharic Kabbalist and was interpreted in such a way as not to detract from its substantiality. Symbolism, as cultivated in the Zoharic Kabbalah, does not supersede the importance of material reality or of the interpreted text; it only adds a new layer of significance. The real city is holy since it represents a higher entity of female nature in the lower world. We may, therefore, speak here of a "horizontal descending symbolism,"[27] which, on the level of corporeal reality, turns into a vertical symbolism, as a Kabbalist would put it. Or, as a modern reader would formulate it, the vertical relationship of God to His city is transformed into an ascending symbolism on the horizontal divine level, without attenuating its primary significance.

The Canonization of the Zohar

How the audacious literature of the Zohar became a classic of Jewish mysticism, and ultimately of Judaism is general, is a crucial question presently under investigation.[28] Here we cannot deal with the historical stages of a gradual process that culminated in the Zohar's canonization in the middle of the sixteenth century. However, the main facts relevant to an understanding of this historical process should be adduced in this context. In the generation of the emergence of the Zohar at the end of the thirteenth century, parts of the text were translated into Hebrew,[29] and other parts began to be commented on,[30] while the Zoharic language began to be imitated by other Kabbalists,[31] and Rabbi Menahem Recanti quoted extensively from the bulk of the Zohar in his own mystical writings.[32] A certain revival in the interest in the book may be discerned in the generation of the expulsion of the Jews from Spain in 1492, both before and after the expulsion.[33] Though printed in Italy in 1558 in two different printing houses, one in Mantua and one in Cremona, the book did not attract special attention from the Italian Kabbalists for the rest of the century. However, in the second half of the sixteenth century many of the Kabbalists in Safed, in northern Israel, wrote commentaries on the book—indeed, they wrote more commentaries than had been written elsewhere over the previous century and a half.[34] Written in close proximity to the Galilean village of Meron—the place where the kabbalistic tradition believed that the book had originally been written, by Rabbi Simeon bar Yoḥai—these new commentaries owe much to their belief that their authors might make direct contact with the soul of the ancient "Kabbalist," whose tomb was visited for just this mystical purpose.[35]

The two most eminent figures of Safed who were crucial in this development were the great kabbalistic luminaries of the century: Rabbi Moses Cordovero, the author *ʾOr Yaqar*, the longest commentary on the *Zohar*, which comprises dozens of volumes still in the process of being published,[36] and Rabbi Yitzhaq Luria Ashkenazi, who displayed an unrestricted reverence toward the book. The latter immersed himself for weeks in concentrated attempts to fathom the theosophical and experiential meaning of its content. One passage preserved by his main disciple, Rabbi Ḥayyim Vital, appropriately illustrates Luria's influential—and reverential—attitude toward the Zohar:

> The worlds change each and every hour, and there is no hour which is similar to another. And whoever contemplates the movement of the planets and stars, and the changes of their position and constellation and how their stand changes in a moment, and whoever is born in this moment will undergo different things from those which happen to one who was born in the preceding moment; hence, one can look and contemplate what is [going on] in the supernal infinite, and numberless worlds . . . and so you will understand the changes of the constellation and the position of the worlds, which are the garments of *ʾEyn Sof*; these changes are taking place at each and every moment, and in accordance with these changes are the aspects of the sayings of the book of the Zohar, changing [too], and all are words of the Living God.[37]

The Zohar is here held to be an inexhaustible and continually changing text that reflects the nature of its eternal and ever-changing composition. The organic vision of the Zoharic text as a body that changes, just as its author does, is reminiscent of the rabbanic vision of the Torah, whose dialectical nature has been described in similar terms. Elsewhere, Luria asserts that "each and every moment the [meaning of the] passages of the Holy Zohar are changing."[38] Hence for a Kabbalist the Zoharic text has achieved a status very similar to that of the Bible itself. Rabbi Israel Baʿal Shem Tov (1700–1760), the founder of Hasidism, envisioned this book as changing its meaning every day. He was reported by his grandson to have asserted, in a way quite consonant with the previous view of Isaac Luria that "the book of the Zohar has, each and every day, a different meaning."[39] Rabbi Eliezer Tzevi Safrin, a mid-nineteenth-century Hasidic commentator on the Zohar, quoted his father, Rabbi Yitzhaq Aiziq Yehudah Yeheil Safrin of Komarno—himself a renowned commentator on the book—to the effect that, "in each and every day, the Zohar is studied in the celestial academy, according to a novel interpretation."[40]

In addition to the literary activity of interpreting the Zohar, which generated a very rich literature that has yet to be explored as it deserves to be—that is, as a special literary genre—parts of the book have been, and continue to be, recited ritualistically, especially in the Jewish communities of Morocco and in the Middle East, even by persons who were not acquainted with its substantial theosophical content.[41] Here the recitation acts like a mantra that possesses rich possibilities of and for mystical experience.

NOTES

1. For an elaborate description of the corpus of writings belonging to the Zohar, see Gershom Scholem, *Major Trends in Jewish Mysticism* (New York, 1967), pp. 156–243; Isaiah Tishby, *The Wisdom of the Zohar*, English trans. by David Goldstein (Oxford, 1989), 3 vols.; Charles Mopsik, "Le corpus Zoharique ses titres et ses amplifications," in Michel Tardieu, ed., *La formation des canons scripturaires* (Paris, 1993), pp. 75–105; and the innovative treatments of the writing of the Zohar by Yehuda Liebes, mentioned here, in notes 3, 34, and 44. For a description of the Kabbalah in the period when the Zohar was written, see Moshe Idel, "Kabbalah and Elites in Thirteenth-Century Spain," *Mediterranean Historical Review*, vol. 9 (1994), pp. 5–19.
2. On this layer, see Pinchas Giller, *The Tiqqunim: Symbolization and Theurgy* (Albany, 1993).
3. See the important analysis of this issue in Yehuda Liebes, *Studies in the Zohar* (Albany, 1993), pp. 85–138.
4. Zohar, vol. 3, fol. 35b. For more on this issue, see Moshe Idel, "The Concept of the Torah in Heikahalot Literature and Its Reverberations in Kabbalah," *Jerusalem Studies in Jewish Thought*, vol. 1 (1981), pp. 58–60 (in Hebrew).
5. Zohar, vol. 3, fol. 202a.
6. See Umberto Eco, *Semiotics and the Philosophy of Language* (Bloomington, 1984), pp. 153–154.
7. On this verse in Jewish mysticism, see Moshe Idel, *The Mystical Experience in Abraham Abulafia* (Albany, 1987), pp. 84–85.
8. Zohar, vol. 3, fol. 265a. For more on this passage see Elliot R. Wolfson, "Beautiful Maiden without Eyes: Peshat and Sod in Zoharic Hermeneutics," in Michael Fishbone, ed., *The Midrashic Imagination* (Albany, 1993), p. 175.
9. Zohar, vol. 1, fol. 134b; vol. 2, fol. 162b. See also Gershom Scholem, *On the Kabbalah and Its Symbolism* (New York, 1969), pp. 46–47; Idel., "The Concept of the Torah," pp. 58–59.
10. The following paragraphs draw on an earlier discussion in Moshe Idel, "PaRDeS: Some Reflections on Kabbalistic Hermeneutics," in J. J. Collins and Michael Fishbone, eds, *Death, Ecstasy, and Other Worldly Journeys* (Albany, 1995), pp. 249–264.
11. See, respectively, Bacher, "L'Exégèse biblique dans le Zohar," *Revue des Etudes Juives*, vol. 22 (1891), pp. 33–46, especially pp. 37–40. See also Bacher, "Das Merkwort PRDS in der Jüdischen Bibelexegese," *Zeitschrift für die alttestamentliche Wissenschaft*, vol. 13 (1893), pp. 294–305; Sandler, "On the Question of PaRDeS and Fourfold Method," *Sefer Eliahu Auerbach*, (Jerusalem, 1955), pp. 222–235 (in Hebrew). See also A. van der Heide, "PaRDeS: Methodological Reflections on the Theory of Four Senses," *Journal of Jewish Studies*, vol. 34 (1983), pp. 147–159, and the further analytic comments on the PaRDeS in Steven T. Katz's essay, in chap. 1 in this volume.

12. On the Kabbalah, p. 61: "I am inclined to agree with Bacher." However, several years earlier, Scholem's opinion was much more explicit in favor of the Christian influence: "I have no doubt that this method [PaRDeS] was taken from the Christian medieval exegesis," in Gershom Scholem, *Explications and Implications: Writings on Jewish Heritage and Renaissance* (Tel Aviv, 1975), p. 249 (in Hebrew).
13. Talmage, "Apples of Gold: The Inner Meaning of Sacred Texts in Medieval Judaism," in Arthur Green, ed., *Jewish Spirituality* (New York, 1986), vol. 1, pp. 319–320; van der Heide, "PaRDeS," pp. 154–155. For more on the Christian understanding, see the essay by Ewert Cousins, chap. 5 in this volume.
14. See Talmage, "Apples of Gold," p. 349 n. 48; Moshe Idel, *Language, Torah and Hermeneutics in Abraham Abulafia* (Albany, 1989), pp. 93 and 191 n. 52.
15. On this issue, see Daniel Ch. Matt, "New-Ancient Words: The Aura of Secrecy in the Zohar," in Peter Schaefer and Joseph Dan, eds., *Gershom Scholem's Major Trends in Jewish Mysticism, 50 Years After* (Tübingen, 1993), pp. 181–207. For more on Zoharic hermeneutics, as part of the more general discussion of Kabbalistic hermeneutics, see also Elliot Wolfson, "By Way of Truth: Aspects of Nahmanides' Kabbalistic Hermeneutic," *AJS Review*, vol. 14, no. 2 (1989), pp. 103–178; Wolfson, "Circumcision, Visionary Experience and Textual Interpretation: From Midrashic Trope to Mystical Symbol," *History of Religions*, vol. 27 (1987), pp. 189–215; Wolfson, "Left Contained in the Right: A Study in Zoharic Hermeneutics," *AJS Review*, vol. 11, no. 1 (1986), pp. 27–52; Wolfson, "The Hermeneutics of Visionary Experience: Revelation and Interpretation in the Zohar," *Religion*, vol. 18 (1988), pp. 311–345; Ithamar Gruenwald, "From Talmudic to Zoharic Homiletics," in Joseph Dan, ed., *The Age of the Zohar* (Jerusalem, 1989), pp. 255–298 (in Hebrew); Daniel Ch. Matt, "Matnita Dilan: A Technique of Innovation in the Zohar," in Dan, *The Age of the Zohar*, pp. 123–145 (in Hebrew); and Steven D. Benin, "The Mutability of an Immutable God: Exegesis and Individual Capacity in the Zohar and Several Christian Sources," in Dan, *The Age of the Zohar*, pp. 67–86.
16. See Bacher, "L'Exegeses bliblique."
17. See, e.g., one of the most important discussions of Zoharic hermeneutics, the maiden parable, to be discussed immediately below.
18. Idel, *Language, Torah and Hermeneutics*, pp. 83–87.
19. John E. Smith, *Experience and God* (Oxford, 1968), p. 159.
20. Zohar, vol. 2, fols. 99ab, that has been analyzed in detail by several scholars. See Bacher, 'L'Exégèse biblique, pp. 36–38; Scholem, On the Kabbalah, pp. 55–56; Talmage, "Apples of Gold," pp. 316–317; Tishby, *The Wisdom of the Zohar*, vol. 3, pp. 1084–1085; Moshe Idel, *Kabbalah: New Perspectives* (New Haven, 1988), pp. 227–229; Wolfson, "Beautiful Maiden"; and Daniel Ch. Matt, trans. and intro., *Zohar—The Book of the Enlightenment* (New York, 1983), pp. 121–126.
21. See Talmage, "Apples of Gold," p. 316 and n. 21.
22. *Arcana Caelestia*, par. 1872, translated in *Internal Sense of the Word*, (London, 1974), p. 41. See also Moshe Idel, "Infinities of the Torah in Kabbalah," in Geoffrey H. Hartman and Sanford Budick, eds., *Midrash and Literature* (New Haven, 1986), pp. 150–151.
23. See Zohar, vol. 1, fols. 25b–26a. For more on this passage, see Moshe Idel, "Metatron, Remarks on Jewish Mythology," In Haviva Pedaya, ed., *Eshel Beer Sheva*, vol. 4 (Beer Sheva, 1996), pp. 29–44 (in Hebrew).
24. First printed in Moshe Idel, "An Unknown Text from Midrash ha'Neʿelam" in Dan, *The Age of the Zohar*, pp. 73–87 (in Hebrew).
25. Zohar, vol. 3, fol. 5a.

26. Idel, *Kabbalah: New Perspectives*, pp. 128–136. On the erotic and sexual symbolism in the Zohar, see also Liebes, *Studies in the Zohar*, pp. 19–25, 37–43, 63–65, 67–74; Liebes, "Zohar and Eros," *Alpayim*, vol. 9 (1994), pp. 67–119 (in Hebrew). Compare the elaborate exposition of the view presented by Elliot Wolfson, *Circle in the Square, Studies in the Use of Gender in the Kabbalistic Symbolism* (Albany, 1995), pp. 95–110—adumbrated already in earlier studies of this scholar—which assumes a tendency to obliterate the difference between the male and female divine powers, as part of the absorption of the female within the male. This thesis, which may sometimes be helpful in understanding some few texts of Zoharic Kabbalah, does not hold, however, for many other Zoharic treatments of the sexual polarity.
27. On "ascending" versus "descending" symbolism, see Erich Kahler, "The Nature of the Symbol," in Rollo May, ed., *Symbolism in Religion and Literature* (New York, 1960), pp. 50–75. For a more general exposition of the two forms of sexual symbolism in the Kabbalah, see Moshe Idel, "Sexual Metaphors and Praxis in the Kabbalah," in David Kraemer, ed., *The Jewish Family*, (New York, 1989), pp. 179–224.
28. See Boaz Huss, "*Sefer ha-Zohar* as a Canonical, Sacred, and Holy Text: Changing Perspectives in the Book of Splendor between the Thirteenth and Eighteenth Centuries," *Journal of Jewish Thought and Philosophy*, vol. 7 (1998), pp. 257–307.
29. Moshe Idel, "Major Currents in Italian Kabbalah between 1560–1660," *Italia Judaica*, vol. 2 (Rome, 1986), p. 251.
30. See Daniel Ch. Matt, *The Book of Mirrors: Sefer Mar'ot ha-Zove'ot by R. David ben Yehudah he Hasid* (Missoula, 1982), pp. 13–17; M. Idel, "Targumo shel R. David ben Yehudah he-Hasid le-*Sefer ha-Zohar*," *ʿAlei Sefer*, vol. 8 (1980), pp. 60–73; vol. 9 (1981), pp. 84–98 (in Hebrew).
31. The above-mentioned R. David wrote a commentary on *Iddra ʿRabba ʿ*: see Matt, *The Book of Mirrors*, p. 4.
32. R. Joseph Angelet's *Sefer Livnat ha-Sappir* (Jerusalem, 1904), for example.
33. See Zevia Rubin, *The Zohar Citations in R. Menahem Recanati's Torah Commentary* (Jerusalem, 1992) (in Hebrew).
34. On this issue, see Huss, "Sefer ha-Zohar."
35. On this issue, see Yehuda Liebes, "New Directions in the Study of Kabbalah," *Peʿamim* vol. 50 (1992), p. 165 (in Hebrew).
36. At this point, twenty-three folio volumes have been published, with still more volumes forthcoming.
37. R. Hayyim Vital, *ʿEtz Ḥayyim* 1, 1, 5, fol. 15a; quoted with few slight changes, in R. Eliezer Tzevi Safrin of Komarno's preface to his father's comprehensive commentary on the Zohar entitled *Zohar Ḥai* (Lemberg, rpt. Israel, 1971), vol. 1, fol. 1b.
38. *Zohar Ḥai*, vol. 1, fol. 3a.
39. Quoted in Rabbi Moshe Hayyim Ephrayyim of Sudylkov's *Degel Maḥaneh Ephraim* (Jerusalem, 1963), p. 98.
40. *Zohar Ḥai*, vol. 1, unnumbered, first folio. It is possible that the title of the collection of Zoharic material printed under the name of *Zohar Ḥadash*—the new Zohar—may have influenced the emergence of the new interpretations of the Zohar, as formulated by R. Ytizhaq Yehudah Safrin.
41. Abraham Stahl, "Ritual Reading of the Zohar," *Peʿamim*, vol. 5 (1980), pp. 77–86 (in Hebrew); Harvey Goldberg, "The Zohar in Southern Morocco: A Study in the Ethnography of Texts," *History of Religion*, vol. 29 (1990), pp. 249–251.

4

The Book of Zohar and Exegetical Spirituality

MICHAEL FISHBANE

The book of Zohar is the masterpiece of Jewish mysticism. Ostensibly a commentary on the Torah, it pulses with the desire for God on virtually every page. One may even say that the commentary is carried by this desire and that its protean creativity is primarily motivated by a longing to experience the divine realities uncovered by mystical interpretation.[1] Toward this end the full range of tradition is activated, which runs from late antiquity to the thirteenth century, when the book of Zohar appeared in Castile.[2] Recovering theosophical truths in the teachings of the Torah, the mystics ascend exegetically to God.[3] This process invites attention.

According to the teaching of the Zohar, the spiritual powers of all-being descend from the highest realms in diverse patterns of appearance. The Torah is one such manifestation. Considering it not merely law and lore and religious expression, the mystics proclaim its inner essence to be the vitality and wisdom of God Himself. Scripture may therefore be many things to its readers—folly and fable to the scoffer; secret and source to the wise at heart.[4] Those with plain sense are content with the straightforward context, while the religious seeker looks more deeply for hints of heavenly illuminations. "How splendid are the ways and paths of the Torah," says Rabbi Pinḥas ben Yair in a Zoharic homily—"for in each and every word there are so many thoughts and good things for humankind, so many pearls shining light on every side." And then, comparing the Torah to a tree with roots, bark, pith, branches, leaves, flowers, and fruit, the sage exults: "So the words of the Torah have plain-sense, exegetical derivations [legal and homiletical], speculative allusions, numerical tallies, hidden mysteries, impenetrable mysteries, one above the other, [and laws dealing with] unfit and fit, unclean and clean, forbidden and permitted."[5]

In this catalogue of exegetical bounty, the language of Scripture contains transcendental meanings that far exceed the concerns of normative rabbinic piety. A quick glance at *Song of Songs Rabba* is instructive. Near the beginning of this midrash we read about how the divine words of the Decalogue came to the people at Sinai and that each and every word appraised the listeners of the vast system of law that would stem from these roots. "Do you accept this word upon yourself?" says each word. "There are such and so many rules in it, such and so many penalties in it, such and so many decrees in it, and such are the religious duties in it, and such are the lenient and stringent features of it, and such and so are the rewards in it."[6] For Rabbi Pinḥas, even this vast potentiality may be superseded. The Torah conceals infinite truth, as befits a word of God.

Three Types of Zoharic Exegesis

In great textual cultures like Judaism, the process of thought is always exegetical—be it simply the reformulation of older tradition or the detailed derivation of a new scriptural sense.[7] This is profoundly true of the Zohar as well. No summary is therefore adequate for its content or pertinent to its character. Rather, the mystical theology of this work unfolds word by word, in the thickness of semantic solutions. Inspired by a bold exegetical impulse, the teachings of the Zohar combine imagination with explanation in unexpected ways. This is as true for the primary circle of teachers (the mystical fellowship in the text) as it is for the widening circle of disciples who retrieve the original teachings and transform them through study.

Exegetical spirituality is thus grounded in the hermeneutical process. As a result, the interpretative imagination is linked to the concrete language and images of scripture and is sustained by their syntax and intertextual relations. To this extent, the exegetical spirituality of the Zohar is a species of the midrashic imagination. What distinguishes Zoharic exegesis is its search for esoteric layers within scripture—esoteric layers of the Godhead, of Torah, and of the self. This concern affects its peculiar dynamism. For while midrashic exegesis activates the letters and words of scripture along a horizontal plane, Zoharic exegesis adds a vertical axis—through its belief that the grammar of scripture conceals traces of a hidden, supernal truth.[8] The verbal dynamics of biblical sentences are thus expressions of esoteric processes deep within the Godhead. This being so, mystical exegesis rings true when this divine reality is revealed to one's consciousness.

Throughout the book of Zohar the disciples meet and meditate on the words of scripture, hoping to achieve spiritual and theosophical instruction through exegetical means. Overall, three types of instruction are exemplary. The first type takes the Torah itself as its subject and seeks to reveal the benefits of Torah study for humans, as well as the theurgical effects of such exegetical piety on God. The second type focuses on more personal matters and provides spiritual counsel for the worshiper, as well as an elucidation of dangers on this path of piety. Such piety is particularly concerned with the perfection of the human self, achieved through a rejection of negative instincts that diminish its worth. This endeavor leads to an enhancement of ones' divine soul and to a neutralization of the demonic forces that assault it from within and without. The third type of Zoharic exegesis has a different goal—an understanding of the nature and dynamism of the Godhead. Theosophical truth thus flashes forth from the words of scripture, as exegetical inspiration penetrates its arcane essence. The ritualization of these divine truths in personal prayer is a significant but derivative aspect of their exegetical recovery.

A Cycle of Teachings by Rabbi Pinḥas

To appreciate the vastness of Zoharic exegesis and its spiritual dimensions, each of these types is taken up here in turn. A striking example of the first type, in which the Torah and its study are the subject of hermeneutical reflection, is a cycle of teachings by Rabbi Pinḥas ben Yair.[9] His comparison of the mystery of the Torah to a tree is found in that cycle. His choice of that image—an archetypal one that recurs throughout the Zohar—was not accidental. In fact, the analogy was directly conditioned by the biblical verse that was taken up for discussion by the disciples, Deuteronomy 20:19—which contains a rule prohibiting the destruction of trees during a prolonged military siege. In his spiritual exegesis, Rabbi Pinḥas converts each textual element to new theological ends. Gradually its symbolic meaning unfolds. The discourse proceeds as follows:

> When you besiege a city many days in order to capture it, you must not destroy its trees [*ʿetzah*; lit., "its tree'], by wielding an ax against them. For you eat of them, (therefore) you may not cut them down. Are trees of the field human against which you would lay siege?" [Deuteronomy 20:19]. . . . This verse has a literal meaning and a homiletical meaning. And it also has supernal wisdom to instruct whoever needs it.[10] Happy is the portion of those continually preoccupied with Torah. What does the Torah say of one so preoccupied? "For his delight is in the Torah of the Lord, and in His Torah he meditates day and night. He will be like a tree [Psalm 1:2–3].[11]

As the homily develops in classical midrashic form, a connection between these two biblical verses is established. At the outset they are simply linked by their common rhetorical identification of a person with a tree. But such a comparison is static, and not yet transformed by dynamic exegesis. The process begins when the teacher turns to the simile in Psalm 1. Starting with comparison, in which a Torah scholar is likened to a productive and well-rooted tree, Rabbi Pinḥas adds a deeper dimension. In his figuration the student of scripture will become a tree of wisdom, deeply rooted in the wide-branching areas of Torah. It follows that such a sage will also benefit his city in times of danger. The point brings the homily back to the biblical law, which is now read in an entirely new way. No longer just an order addressed to soldiers during a siege (the plain sense), the command is now allegorically revised and interpreted as conditions imposed by God on His angel of destruction (the homiletical sense.[12] He tells this angel that only the sinners of a city may be destroyed, not "its trees" (*ʿetzah*), which symbolize the scholars of Torah, "the tree of life" of the community.[13]

At one level, then, the teacher interprets the biblical rule in terms of the prophylactic power of study for the individual; but he quickly adds a social dimension through the trope of the tree. Adding a verbal play to his symbolic reading of *ʿetzah* (its trees), the homilist says that the scholars will be saved because they provide the people with spiritual "counsel" (*ʿetzah*) for their collective salvation. In this respect, Ben Yair's interpretation parallels a reading of Deuteronomy 20:19 that is found in the Babylonian Talmud. In that context Rabbi Zeira teaches that the Torah compares a person to a tree from which on may eat, implying that "if a scholar is a worthy man, one may eat [learn] from him"—but if not, one may not learn from him and he should be cut down.[14]

In our homily, Rabbi Pinḥas goes further. Not content to linger on the worldly benefits of Torah study, he immediately shifts to a mystical plane. From this perspective the boon of exegesis transcends earthly needs and feeds "the mighty Rock, from whom emerge all the holy and powerful spirits."[15] This figure in the Zohar alludes to the lower feminine gradation in the divine hierarchy called *Shekhinah*, the matrix of all the powers that vitalize divinity in its ontological manifestations.[16] Accordingly, the Torah scholar is at once a tree of the Torah in this world and a source of sustenance to the Shekhinah on high.

This mystical interpretation itself is deepened later in the passage. We are told that since the destruction of the Temple, God on high has been nourished solely by the words of Torah that the scholar renews "in his mouth." The particular divine cognomen used here is "the Holy One, blessed be He," a denomination for the masculine gradation of divinity (called *Tiferet*), which is the heavenly consort of the Shekhinah. This gradation is also called the Tree of Life, a symbolic archetype for the all-inclusive Torah in the divine realm. Accordingly, through the tree of the Torah that he embodies while he is engaged in study, the Torah scholar serves as a spiritual conduit to the heavenly powers. In this capacity he provides a bipolar role "above and below"—nourishing the supernal sources of his creativity from below and transmitting their powers downward to the people. As a symbolic "tree of the field," the scholar is nothing less than a mystical consort of the Shekhinah (symbolically known as the heavenly "field") and serves as the earthly counterpart of *Tiferet* in the heights of heaven.

Through this higher service, as it were, the "advice" of scholars is also transformed. At the level of midrashic truth, the spiritual counsel of sages was valued for its capacity to induce the repentance of sinners and thus save them from divine punishment. The mystical effect of their actions is greater. As heavenly mediators imbued with saving powers, Torah scholars may also bring the repentant sinners to that most narrow of heavenly realms where complete forgiveness is granted—a realm symbolically designated as the place of "siege" (*matzor*) in the biblical text.[17] It is in this transformed sense that we may read the first part of Deuteronomy 20:19 in terms of the saving role of God's agent on earth (the sage), going beyond a reading of it as a condition imposed on His heavenly angel of destruction. The biblical verse thus serves as a complex symbolic prism for Rabbi Pinḥas, refracting different mystical meanings simultaneously. Correspondingly, the Torah encodes several aspects of a myth of salvation: scholars are to be saved from divine doom so that they may restore sinners to absolute atonement in heaven.

It should be added that the symbolic sphere of *matzor* also refers to the "mighty rock" above—this in turn being a symbol for the most exalted mother of the highest gradations (*Binah*, or understanding). Like her lower feminine counterpart, the Shekhinah, this divine "rock" is also nourished by the scholar, though now through the very sinners who are restored by him to her womb. Heeding the words of "counsel" of the sages, which are the words of the Torah used for social benefit, the wayward return to their most supernal source.[18]

Rabbi Pinḥas ben Yair began his exegesis of Deuteronomy 20:19 with the exhortation that "this verse has a literal meaning and a homiletical meaning. And it also has supernal wisdom to instruct whoever needs it." His interpretations trace this multiple trajectory, moving successively from a reading of the words as a military rule to the personal and communal benefits of Torah study, and ultimately to a perception of the human role in the sustenance of the Godhead. In the process, the rhetorical thrust of the central metaphor (linking me to trees) is transformed. At the initial level of practical action, the earthly warrior needs to be told not to destroy the trees of the field during a siege—for "are trees . . . human [literally, a man] against which you would lay siege?" Surely not; the rhetorical question reinforces the prohibition of the rule. But at the midrashic or homiletical level, this correlation changes, and with it the rhetorical purpose of the comparison. Read as an independent phrase after the opening admonition, the Hebrew words *ki ha-ʾadam ʿetz ha-sadeh la-boʾ ʿaleykha be-matzor* lend themselves to an entirely positive assertion: "Man is a tree fo the field who goes on your behalf in the siege." In this reading the Torah scholar is the archetypal man, a human mediator who serves his community in times of travail.

The mystical meaning builds on the literal dimension of this reading, even as it simultaneously interprets the images symbolically. Through such a characteristic interfusion of hermeneutical registers (the literal and symbolic), a mythic dimension emerges from scripture. In this case the scholar assimilates the properties of the Torah he studies and becomes a tree—a cosmic tree, in fact, that links the earthly and divine realms into one divine whole. When so viewed, scriptural study is an act that virtually transforms the practitioner into a symbolic configuration of divine powers.

Exegesis and Religious-Ethical Values

The spiritual transformation of the exegete *through exegesis* is the profound truth repeatedly dramatized in the Zohar. This is so principally because scripture is a configuration of divinity; accordingly, the interpreter is affected by the transcendental features he penetrates in the course of study. In other respects, the Zohar reveals religious ideals and values that the adept must attend to. Once again, these deeper truths are not mere surface instructions, but deep wisdom recovered through exegesis.

An instructive example is the Zohar's concern with the purification of the inner self, which usually takes expression through homilies or exegeses that warn the seeker of the dangers of impurity and natural desire. In fact, just these two dangers are the subject of an exhortation delivered by Rabbi Simeon bar Yoḥai in a teaching launched by the textual conjunction of two apparently unrelated topics. The first of these is a negative commandment, "You shall not make molten gods for yourself [*lakh*]", while the second is a positive injunction, "You shall keep the feast of unleavened bread [*matzot*]" [Exodus 34:17 and 18).[19] "What has the one [rule] to do with the other?" the master asks, and then answers his own rhetorical question by alluding to an old exegetical solution that said, "One who eats leaven [*ḥametz*] on Passover is like an idol-worshiper."

This pithy admonition arises from an old homiletical technique for interpreting sequential verses. It recalls the nearly similar Talmudic teaching of Rabbi Eleazar ben

Azariah, who reportedly said (based on the same sequence), "Whoever despises the festival times is like an idol-worshiper."[20] Rabbi Simeon develops this point here and adds to it a new mythic dimension.[21] He says that when the Israelites left Egypt, they left the "other domain," called *ḥametz* (leavened bread), belonging to the demonic Other Side.[22] In so doing, they went from the realm of idolatry to that of pure worship, a realm unencumbered by alien forces. But this action is not a onetime achievement, since the domain of *ḥametz* can also become manifest through *se' or*—this being another term for "leaven" (in Exodus 12:15) and an old rabbinic metaphor for the evil inclination.[23] Indeed, the Other Side uses this *se'or* as an agent to penetrate the human will, insinuating itself as an alien force that "little by little" overwhelms its host and perverts him, moving him away from piety. According to the teacher, this false presence is nothing less than a "molten god" or idol made within the "self" (Exodus 34:18)—a recurrent eruption of the "other domain" in the human heart. Hence one must "keep the feast of unleavened bread" (Exodus 34:19), to guard perpetually against this danger.

At this point Rabbi Judah offers a different approach to the conjunction of Exodus 34:18 and 34:19 and takes his homiletical starting point at a different verse: "Desist from man, who has [but] breath in his nostrils, for by what is he to be [highly] accounted?" (Isaiah 2:22).[24] At first glance, this blast against human pretense has little to do with our theme. But the sage deftly exploits the prophetic passage in order to mediate between the two verses in Exodus. In so doing, he provides another instruction about self-made idols. The teaching begins with the first clause, "Desist from man," and proceeds incrementally through the several clauses of the verse until his point is established. The exegetical process takes him from social rules to a theosophy of the soul and, finally, to the spiritual effects of one's inner psychological state.

Starting with the obvious, Rabbi Judah wonders just what the injunction to "desist from man" could mean, since it is hard to suppose that its purpose is to counsel people to cease from associating with human company altogether. He therefore initially proffers an explanation that reads the verse as advice to worshipers not to greet their fellows before praying to God. This instruction alludes to a teaching of Rav that is found in the Talmud: "Whoever greets his fellow before he prays is as if he made him [the neighbor] into a place of idolatry [*bamah*]; as is said, 'Desist from man, who has breath in his nostrils, for by what [*ba-meh*] is he to be accounted?' [Isaiah 2:22]. [Hence] do not read *ba-meh* but *bamah* [that is, desist from one who regards another as an idol, greeting him before God]."[25] But this bold interpretation is passed over without comment, since it does not explain the middle clause, which deals with the breath in one's nostrils.[26] As the homilist explicates this section, the exegesis deepens and Rav's explanation returns with unexpected force.

Rabbi Judah's discourse of the middle phrase, "who has breath in his nostrils [*neshamah be-'apo*]," is a tour de force. He begins by giving the verse a spiritual turn, so that the interdiction serves as a warning to keep away from people who have strayed toward evil and defiled their divine soul (neshamah). Having raised this issue, the teacher then begins a more esoteric interpretation. It is based on the belief that each human being is created in the image of the divine hierarchy, such that he receives "in his nostrils" a holy spirit comprised of three divine elements—*nefesh* (soul), *ruaḥ* (spirit), and *neshamah* (super-soul).[27] Ideally, this triadic soul structure is unified on the basis of the model of the supernal structure of divine gradations[28] and constitutes the person as a "whole" and a "faithful servant" of God. One may associate with such a person, says Rabbi Judah, "and become his companion in order to learn his ways." But one must desist from associating with someone who clearly defiles this unity, and who thereby brings his *neshamah* into ruin.

At first glance this interpretation of the phrase is puzzling. One can hardly suppose that the sage wished to instruct his fellows to desist from associating with those who have a "soul" in their nostrils—for this manifestly contradicts his intention. Still, how does he find a negative treatment of the *neshamah* in this passage? The answer lies in a powerful pun. In speaking of a person who destroys his soul, the sage says that he succumbs to the force of "his anger" (*rugzeih*). By this (Aramaic) turn of phrase, it is clear that the (Hebrew) word *'apo* in Isaiah 2:22 has been reinterpreted. In the preacher's mind, the term no longer refers to the "nostrils" of all mortals but to the "anger" of the emotionally unbalanced. This metaphorical extension of the noun for "nose" or "nostrils" is common enough in biblical usage, but its exegetical employment here transforms Isaiah's instruction altogether. No longer giving a word to the wise to desist from relying on mere humans (a widespread biblical theme), Rabbi Judah offers new spiritual counsel. He advises the true worshiper to desist from associating with those who corrupt their divine souls through anger, by allowing this force to enter them like "an idol." Such persons are no longer servants of their divine Master but idolators, and one must steer clear of them.

With this last assertion, the homily arrives at its main point. Significantly, Rabbi Judah does not adduce the old rabbinic dictum that "one who is angry is lie an idol-worshiper."[29] He rather makes his argument from scripture, taking the exegetical comment of Rav (cited earlier in the homily) and giving it a new twist. As will be recalled, this sage interpreted the interrogative *ba-meh* ("by what?") in Isaiah 2:22 as *bamah*, a site of idolatry. His interpretation was concerned with the case of a person who greets humans before prayer. Now, in light of the focus on one's divine soul and the corrupting power of anger, Rabbi Judah makes a new observation: the pious must desist from all association with those who uproot their divine souls so that alien spirits might grow in their place. Such a person is himself "accounted a *bamah*," an idolatrous object of defilement against which a servant of God must stand guard. In Rabbi Judah's understanding, this was precisely the reason that scripture juxtaposed the warning not to make molten idols "for oneself" with the injunction to "keep the feast of unleavened bread." Exegetically recovered, the sequence of commands in Exodus 34:18 and 34:19 serves as an exhortation to the worshiper to "preserve the power of holiness and not exchange it for the Other Side."

With this explanation, Rabbi Judah adds a new peril to Rabbi Simeon's initial warning: more dangerous than the insidious quality of the evil inclination—which grows like leaven in one's nature—anger destroys the divine harmony of one's soul and replaces it with an alien spirit. Both Rabbi Judah and Rabbi Simeon present these dangers in mythic terms, as demonic powers that may invade the worshiper whose mind or emotions stray. Spiritual constancy and watchfulness are thus absolutely necessary, lest a man be transformed into an idol. Our homily serves these hortatory ends through an exposition of the dangers to the self and a warning to take care. Notably, both the danger and the antidote are revealed through textual exegesis—a way of truth on the way to truth.

Scriptural Exegesis and Supernal Realities

The Structure of Emanation

The foregoing examples of Zoharic interpretation were developed through the exegetical transformation of biblical passages—the dynamics of the Bible's surface sequence were used to ascend in spiritual wisdom. Indeed, the verbal dynamics of the Torah and its changing images were repeatedly converted into possibilities for spiritual instruction. At the highest end of the spectrum, these insights focus on the mystery of the Godhead—its primordial and sempiternal truths. A profound example of this is an esoteric exegesis of a verse in the book of Genesis. The teaching unfolds in stages:

> "And God said: Let the waters be gathered," etc. [Genesis 1:9]—by way of a line [*qav*], in order that it should be by a straight path; for all emerged, while still hidden, from the mystery of the primal point, until it reached and gathered in the supernal Palace. From there it emerged in a straight line to the remaining gradations, until it reached that "one place" which gathered all together into the totality of male and female. And what is that? The "Life of the Worlds." "The waters"—that emerged from above, from the upper [first] letter *he* [of the Tetragram, Y-H-V-H]. "Under the heavens" [is symbolized by] the small *vav*, which explains [the spelling of] the letter *vav* [of the Tetragram. The word *vav* is spelled with the letter *vav* twice.]: one [*vav*] is heavens, the other [smaller one] is [the region] "under the heavens." [After this occurs,] then: "let the dry land appear"—this is the lower [final] letter *he* [of the Tetragram]. This [one] is revealed, all the other [letters are] concealed; and from this final [element] one may perceive [the wisdom] that is concealed. "To one place"—since *here* is the bond of unity of the upper world.[30]

The mystical exegesis of this passage is a meditation on Genesis 1:9—overtly about one act of divine creation, it is now revealed as an esoteric process that traces the emergence of divinity from the most supernal and hidden of mysteries to all the successive gradations of divine Being. This is figuratively described in the Zohar as the extension of the primal point into a straight line, the gradual and dynamic transformation of undifferentiated unity into "the totality of male and female." Esoteric concealment marks this entire process until we see the manifestation of the lowest gradation, through which alone the upper realities may be perceived. The beginning of the divine emanation is encoded in the scriptural words "And God said: Let the waters be gathered"—words that express the divine will that Being flow toward its cumulative reservoir in "the one place." The end of the sequence is found in the phrase "and let the dry land appear"—which expresses God's desire that the concluding gradation become manifest, to reflect all the higher processes on its plane.

In developing his interpretation, the mystic draws on esoteric and exoteric traditions. For example, he can rely on his hearers' knowing that the primal point is supernal wisdom (*Ḥokhmah*) and that the appellation God (ʾElohim) is the gradation of understanding (*Binah*), the heavenly palace. Further, the "heavens" stand for the gradation called "splendor" (*Tiferet*), the male "line" (*qav*) that connects the upper feminine gradation of *Binah* with the lower feminine one, called here the "dry land"—this being the Shekhinah. This line spans six gradations; hence *Tiferet* is symbolized by the letter *vav*, which is the sixth letter of the alphabet. Spelled indeed with two *vav*s, the letter *vav* thus symbolizes both *Tiferet* (the first and extensive *vav*) and the gradation called "foundation" (*Yesod*), this being the principle of masculine vitality that is symbolized by the second and (so-called) smaller *vav*. It is structurally found below *Tiferet* (the "heavens"), and hence referred to in Genesis 1:9 as the area "under the heavens."

We thus see that our biblical verse is a sequence of symbolic clusters encoding the mysterious flow of divinity out of primal hiddenness and into revealment. A similar truth, depicting the emergence of divine Being from the primal point of *Ḥokhmah*, and thence *Binah*, is revealed by the Zohar pages earlier, in connection with the opening words of scripture: "In the beginning, God created." In that case the teaching is simply asserted, without clarification or justification. Similarly, the Zohar also spoke there of how the primal spark "measured out a measure" (*medid meshiḥa'*)[31]—but without elaboration. By contrast, in our case, this mythic assertion is exegetically justified by the verb *yiqavu* ("to be gathered"), which is understood as implying the extension of a "line" or "measure" (*qav*) from the upper spheres of wisdom to the gradation called foundation, marked in scripture as "one place." This interpretation of the verb is derived from an ancient rabbinic comment on the divine delimitation of the primal waters at the creation of this world.[32] It is now applied to a process within divinity. Hence the teaching provides a mystical reinterpretation of a midrashic observation and widens the mythic opening provided by that tradition.

But the esoterism of Genesis 1:9 is even more complexly configured. As the Zohar's interpretation unfolds, it is clear that the line is only one theosophical coordinate of the phrase; the other is the holy divine Name (the Tetragram) Y-H-V-H, which is coordinated with the symbolic language of the verse. Thus the straight line descends from "the waters" of the well of understanding—this being the first *H(e)* of the Name—to the "place" known as "the life of the worlds," the divine gradation called "foundation" (*Yesod*), symbolized by the small *V(av)*.[33] After this happens, the "dry land" can appear: the revealed manifestation of divine kingship (*Malkhut*), symbolized by the second *H(e)* of the Name. Accordingly, the biblical phrase encodes the supernal structure of divinity as symbolized by the letters H-V-H of the divine Name. Although the initial Y (*Yod*) is not explicitly mentioned in this exposition, it is always implied in kabbalistic parlance by the primal point of origination, the source of the line.[34]

Fusions between Myth and Ritual

This way of studying scripture results, at once, in a revelation of esoteric knowledge and a contemplation of the eternal process of divine creativity.[35] And since all of scripture is one truth, other passages may deepen the discussion. This is precisely what happens in the present case, where one can virtually observe the teacher associate from one phrase to another. Thinking about the gathering of the waters into "one place" brings to mind the words of the prophet Zechariah: "YHVH is one, and His Name one" (Zechariah 14:9).[36] Why the doubling of the creed here? What does the second assertion add to the first, and how does this relate to Genesis 1:9? The teaching explains:

> "YHVH is one and His Name one." There are two unities here—one is the upper world [of the supernal structure], which is unified in its gradations; and one is the lower world [of the divine structure], which is unified in its gradations. The bond of unity of the upper world extends until [the gradation called] "Life of the Worlds," where the upper world is

> established and unified in its unity:[37] and it is therefore called "one place," [for] all the gradations and extensions gather there and become one, with no division whatever. And this is the only gradation where there is such a unification, where all the gradations are concealed in a hidden manner with one desire.[38]

This interpretation of Zechariah's words allows the exegete to go further in this exposition of Genesis 1:9, and to identify the "one place" of that verse with the first of two supernal unities. The first, as we learn, is the ingathering of all the higher gradations in a bond of concealment—or, as the text immediately adds, in a gradation that "unifies the world of revealment in the world of concealment." It is here (in the gradation of *Yesod*) that the upper powers are balanced in a hidden way, yet with a desire to disseminate into the final divine gradation (*Malkhut* or *Shekhinah*) where they become manifest to humans. Accordingly, this bond is also called the Life of the Worlds, since it receives the gradations in the higher world and channels them to the world below. It is in this lower sphere that the second unity occurs, in the image of the first. This constitutes the mystery of the appearance of the "dry land."

The dry land is thus the symbolic locus of mystical vision, and the place where the upper unity, gathered in the gradation of *Yesod*, may be perceived. To mark this truth, the exegete cites several texts in which the verb *ra'ah* (to see), used in Genesis 1:9 to denote the appearance of the dry land, is also used for the visualization of the divine Glory in the final gradation and for the appearance of the rainbow (*qeshet*) in the cloud—this being the manifestation of the upper unity in the lower one.[39] The teaching adds that the three colors of the rainbow (white, red, and green) show the radiance of the semblance of the divine Glory,[40] united in their manifestation below as they are in their concealment on high.[41] What is more, this configuration of colors is said to be "an illumination concealed in the rotation of the closed eye."[42] It is thus not restricted to the mystical vision of the few.[43] Rather, a rolling of the eyes may result in a manifestation of colors for the practitioner—an illumination whose esoteric truth is the dynamic unity of God. The mystery of the appearance of the dry land in scripture thus includes the potential visualization of the divine Glory by the inner eye of contemplation. Exegesis and spiritual practice serve the same ends and confirm their reciprocal truth.

Further Dimensions of Myth and Ritual

The teacher speaks further. The idea of the triune colors in the upper and lower unities leads him to another expression of this truth found in the credal formula "Hear, O Israel, YHVH is our God, YHVH is one" (Deuteronomy 6:4). Struck by the triune assertion of divinity made here (reading: "YHVH–Eloheinu [our God–YHVH is one"), he says:

> YHVH Eloheinu YHVH (The Lord our God the Lord). [These words refer to] the hidden colors that are not visible and bound to [the gradation of] "one place," [forming] one unity above.[44] The [three] colors of the rainbow below unite . . . just like the hidden colors [on high]. And these constitute another unity [and are the] secret of [the words] "and His Name is one" [Zechariah 14:9]. [Further:] "Blessed be the name of His glorious kingdom forever" is the lower unity; [whereas] "Hear, O Israel, YHVH our God, YHVH is one" is the upper unity: one parallel to the other, here six words [*Barukh shem kavod malkhuto le-ʿolam va-ʿed*—"Blessed be" etc.] and there six words [*Shemaʿ yisrael YHVH*

> *ʾEloheinu YHWH ʾeḥad*—"Hear, O Israel," etc.]. [Just so is the secret of] "Let [the waters] be gathered" [*yiqavu*]—[this is] the measurement [*medidu*] of the line [*qav*] and a measure [*mishḥetaʾ*]. Here six words, and there six words. The measure [*mishḥetaʾ*] is the [mystery of] the hardened spark, as it is written, "Who has measured [*madad*] the waters in the hollow of His hand?" [Isaiah 40:12]. And this is [the mystery of what scripture means by] "Let the waters be gathered." This is the measurement [*shiʿuraʾ*] of the Creator of Worlds, *Yod He' Va'v He'* [*Y-H-V-H*].[45]

This passage provides a further glimpse into the exegetical theology of the Zohar. The hermeneutical pivot is the word *ʾeḥad* (one), first found in Genesis 1:9. Through a correlation of it with Zechariah 14:9 and with the phrase "YHVH is *ʾeḥad* [one]" in Deuteronomy 6:4, the verse in Genesis is said to refer to the upper of two supernal unities. Contrasted with these passages is the lower unity—designated in Genesis 1:9 by the word "dry land" and by the phrase "and His name is *ʾeḥad* [one]" in Zechariah 14:9.

A third reference to this lower divine unity is said to be found in the formula "Blessed be His glorious kingdom forever," which is normally recited sotto voce after the declaration of the upper divine unity by means of Deuteronomy 6:4.[46] The identification of this formula with the lower unity is presumably based on the phrase God's "kingdom," since that term symbolizes for the Jewish mystic the final divine gradation, called kingship (*Malkhut*). In light of the previous discussion, it is even possible that the reference to God's "glorious kingdom" (*kavod malkhuto*; literally, "the glory of His kingship") was understood to designate the mystical appearance of the divine Glory *kavod* within the gradation of kingship, as part of the complex unity below.

This striking correlation between liturgy and theosophy is even more precisely indicated through the correlation made between the six (Hebrew) words in each of the two formulas, "Hear, O Israel" and "Blessed be His glorious kingdom," and the six upper and lower divine gradations, respectively. At first glance this link appears to be merely numerological; but on a second viewing it appears to be a mystical reinterpretation of an ancient rabbinic practice. According to a report preserved in the Babylonian Talmud, in the context of determining the proper intention for reciting the *Shemaʿ* prayer ("Hear, O Israel," etc.), the following exchange took place:

> Rabbi Jeremiah was once sitting before Rabbi Zeira, and the latter saw that he was prolonging the word *ʾeḥad* ["one," in the formula "Hear, O Israel . . . the Lord is *ʾeḥad*"] excessively. He said to him: "Once you have made Him king [*ʾamlikhteih*] above and below and the four quarters of the heaven, no more is required."[47]

This admonition is puzzling as well as intriguing. It is puzzling because there was already an established tradition that explained why the *Shemaʿ* heads the paragraphs that follow: because by its recitation the worshiper would "receive upon himself the yoke of the kingdom (*Malkhut*) of Heaven."[48] What is the relationship between this liturgical acceptance of divine kingship and its ritual establishment? Presumably, Rabbi Zeira's words hint at some mental or gestural enactment of the encompassing reality of God.[49] This may be deduced from an intriguing Talmudic reference to the practice of waving the heave offerings, as well as the palm fronds (on the feast of Tabernacles), in six directions—above and below, and in the four compass directions.[50] This suggests the possibility of a parallel practice in connection with the daily recitation of divine kingship, which is performed by bodily gestures or mental intentions.

Further confirmation of just such a ritual enactment of divine kingship comes from its formal legitimation in the important twelfth-century halakhic codification Sefer Ha-ʾEshkol, by Rabbi Abraham ben Isaac of Narbonne (the Rabi Abad). He cites the ritualization of the *Shemaʿ* formula transmitted by Rabbi Judah ben Barzillai al-Barceloni, and explains that "one must enthrone [God]" during the recitation of the final two letters of the word *ʾeḥad*, through head movements (nodding up and down while enunciating the second letter, *ḥet* , and in the four compass directions while prolonging the final letter, *dalet*).[51] These movements were presumably accompanied by meditative intentions as well—and the whole matter, I would suggest, serves as the background for our Zoharic passage (cited above). In this case, building on a theosophical metaphysics, the worshiper is told that the recitation of the six words of the *Shemaʿ* formula will establish the unity of the upper divine realm, even as the recitation of the six words of the "Blessed be His glorious kingdom" formula will do the same in the lower realm. The Zohar further links these contemplative intentions to Genesis 1:9 and specifically indicates that this double unification is found in the Hebrew term *yiqavu* (Let [the waters] be gathered).

What is confusing is that there are not two series of six words here. Indeed, the meaning of the assertion "Here six words, and there six words" is opaque even for this esoteric passage. The solution may lie in the explanation that the word *yiqavu* is "the measurement of the line (*qav*) and a measure." Accordingly, one may suppose that the author was struck by the fact that the word *yiqavu* is spelled *y-q-v-v*—that is, with two *vav*s (the first, to mark the consonant; the second, to mark the vowel). And since for him every jot and tittle in scripture has significance, it is possible that the word (*yi-qav-vu*) was interpreted as containing a mystical hint of the upper and lower realms. In that case, the element *qav* would indicate the "line" that descends through six upper gradations from *Binah* (wisdom) to *Yesod* (foundation [the "one place"]); and the final letter *vav* (which is, numerically, six), alludes to the measure that includes the entire expanse of the "hardened spark"[52]—a metaphor for the impulse of will that arises in the hidden recesses of divinity and that gives rise to all the gradations of divine Being, from the highest crown (*Keter*) in nothing (*ʿAyin*) to the lowest one (*ʿAtarah*) in the kingdom (Malkhut).

The totality of divinity marked by the verb *yiqavu*—"the measurement of the line and the measures"—thus includes the manifestation of the six upper gradations in the lower realm of the supernal hierarchy. It is called here a *shiʿuraʾ* (measurement), a fairly undisguised allusion to the Shiʾur Qomah, "infinite stature" of God.[53] Accordingly, when the Zohar instructs the worshiper to contemplate the divine gradations in prayer, the entirety of the Godhead is intended—above and below, in all the forms imagined by kabbaslistic interpretation. In this respect, scriptural exegesis and spiritual practice are complementary; what the one discovers, the other enacts.[54]

Final Reflections

The exegetical spirituality made manifest in the Zohar is thus a complex fusion of myth and ritual. First, and most important, the seekers' quest for divine truth is bound up with the myths of God imagined through the work of exegesis—an achievement that puts him in mind of the hidden mysteries, and in connection with them. In turn, these esoteric myths are enacted in liturgical recitation and mystical contemplation—for the sake of God and man. The circularity of this spirituality is as paradoxical as it is profound: a search for certainty through the theological myths of the exegetical imagination.

"Blessed are those who study the Torah in order to know the wisdom of their Master, and who know and understand the supernal mysteries." But how can a person learn to "know his body . . . and how [it] is arranged; or "understand the secrets of his super-soul [*neshamah*], [and] the soul [*nefesh*] that is in him"; or even "the world in which he lives, and upon what it is based; and after this, the supernal mysteries of the world above, in order that he might recognize his master"?[55] The lesson of the Zohar is that everything depends on the integrity of tradition and the authenticity of exegesis. Of the two, the first is primary and establishes a connection between the spiritual fellowship of Rabbi Simeon's circle and all earlier seekers from whom they derive trust and direction on their path. They thereby form a chain of tradition, which is the very meaning of the word *Kabbalah*. But the desire to penetrate the mysteries of scripture goes beyond tradition by its innovative nature. Accordingly, everything depends on the capacity and character of the interpreter, on his spiritual composure and imaginative powers. This adds a paradoxical dimension to our subject, for it reveals that the whole project of exegetical spirituality repeatedly risks failure—both the failure of exegetical nerve and the perversion of exegetical desire.

In the book of Zohar, therefore, the test of truthfulness lies with the fellowship of the faithful. Only they can determine, through intuition and their evolving tradition, whether any act of exegesis is an authentic creation or the bluster of human vanity.[56] Accordingly, one of the signs of successful exegesis in the Zohar is the cry of joy among the disciples when they sense that they have heard a "portion" of divine truth from their fellows. Another sign occurs when an interpretation is sealed by a kiss from the friends, whose mutual love inspires them on their exegetical way to God.[57] The Zohar is the great product of this love—and the gift of tradition to all who would follow on this path.

NOTES

1. In a penetrating exploration, Yehuda Liebes, "Zohar ve-ʾEros," *ʾAlpayyim* 9 (1994), pp. 67–119, considers the multifaceted aspects of Zoharic creativity and its sources of inspiration. This study is an important first step toward an ars poetica of the Zohar. Here I stress the primacy of the spiritual desires that generate this creativity through exegetical forms.
2. For considerations of this medieval dating, see the classic discussion of Gershom Scholem, *Major Trends in Jewish Mysticism* (New York, 1946), lecture 5, in which a case is made for individual authorship by Rabbi Moses de Leon; see also the compelling analysis by Yehuda Liebes, "Keitzad Nitḥaber Sefer Ha-Zohar?," *Jerusalem Studies in Jewish Thought*, vol. 8 (1989), pp. 1–71, in which a case for a circle of authors is advanced. An English rendition, "How the Zohar Was Written," appears in Liebes, *Studies in the Zohar* (Albany, N.Y., 1993), pp. 85–138, 194–227.
3. For two explorations of exegetical renewal in the Zohar, see Daniel Matt, "Matnitin Di-lan: Tekhniqah shel Ḥidush Be-Sefer Ha-Zohar," *Jerusalem Studies in Jewish*

Thought, vol. 8 (1989), pp. 123–145; and "'New-Ancient Words': The Aura of Secrecy in the Zohar," in Peter Schäfer and Joseph Dan, eds., *Gershom Scholem's Major Trends in Jewish Mysticism: 50 Years After* (Tübingen, 1993), pp. 181–207.

4. Cf. Zohar, vol. 3, fol. 152a; also, vol. 3, fol. 149a/b.
5. Zohar, vol. 3, fol. 202a.
6. *Song of Songs Rabba* I.2.ii.
7. I have shown this in many writings. Regarding the Hebrew Bible, see Fishbane, *Biblical Interpretation in Ancient Israel* (Oxford, 1985); and for various forms of later Jewish spirituality, see Fishbane, *The Kiss of God: Spiritual and Mystical Death in Judaism* (Seattle, 1994).
8. For this idea in the context of kabbalistic symbolism, see Moshe Idel, *Kabbalah: New Perspectives* (New Haven, 1988), pp. 222–229.
9. See Zohar, vol. 3, fols. 200b–202b.
10. The verb "to instruct," *le-ʾizdaharah*, provides a multilevel pun, for it evokes both the Hebrew nouns for legal warning (*ʾazharah*) and for spiritual illumination (*zohar*). The Torah scholar is associated with both qualities in this homily.
11. Zohar, vol. 3, fol. 202a.
12. The change of addressee required no change to scripture; the reconception of the siege as an act of destruction did. It assumes that the verb *tatzur* was midrashically construed as meaning "(when) you act as an enemy"—from the same stem (*tz-w-r*). This virtual change is implied by the thematic shift from human warfare to divine doom.
13. For the semantic survey of tree symbolism in the Zohar, see Yehuda Liebes, *Sections of the Zohar Lexicon* (Jerusalem, 1976), pp. 107–131, and for this instance, see p. 118, no. 69 (in Hebrew).
14. Babylonian Talmud (= BT), Tractate *Taʿanit* fol. 7a.
15. Zohar, vol. 3, fol. 202a.
16. For a wide-ranging characterization, see Gershom Scholem, *On the Mystical Shape of the Godhead* (New York, 1991), chap. 4.
17. This is due to a play on *tzar* or *metzar* (narrow place).
18. Zohar, vol. 3, fol. 202b.
19. See Zohar, vol. 2, fol. 182a.
20. BT, *Pesaḥim* 118a; and see BT *Makkot* 23a; Jerusalem Talmud (= JT), Tractate *Ḥagigah*, chap. 3, 1. According to Rabbeinu Bahye, the juxtaposition refers to the divine attributes of judgment and mercy; see Hayim Chavel, ed., *Rabbeinu Baḥye: Beʾur ʿal ha-Torah* (Jerusalem, 1982), vol. 2, p. 356.
21. Significantly, the Zohar does not develop a theosophical explanation or interpret the passages in terms of the heavenly gradations of judgment and mercy. This line was taken by the contemporary commentator Rabbeinu Baḥye ben Asher on Exodus 34:17; see Chavel, *Rabbeinu Baḥye*, vol. 2, p. 356.
22. On this power, see Scholem, *On the Mystical Shape*, chap. 2.
23. Rabbi Simeon calls the evil inclination *ḥamir ba-ʿisah*, thus giving an Aramaic rendition of the common idiom *seʾor sheba-ʿisah* in rabbinic literature; cf. BT, *Berakhot* 17a. His rendition draws on the Targum of Exodus 12:15; and cf. BT, *Pesaḥim* 5a.
24. The teaching continues through Zohar, vol. 2, fol. 182 a/b.
25. BT, *Berakhot* 14a. On this theme of blessing God before greeting men, see Zohar, vol. 1, fol. 228a.
26. The prooftext used is from Proverbs 27:14: "He who greets his fellow loudly early in the morning shall have it accounted for him (*teḥashev lo*) as a curse." This proof fits well thematically and verbally with Isaiah 2:22 (cf. *neḥshav lo*—"will he be accounted?"). See also, Zohar, vol. 2, fol. 226b. Rabbi Moses de Leon cites mystical

explanations received for both passages; see *R. Moses de Leon's Sefer Sheqel ha-Qodesh*, critically edited and introduced by Charles Mopsik (Los Angeles, 1996), fol. 36b, p. 42 (in Hebrew).

27. *Nefesh* and *neshamah* occur with nostrils in Genesis 2:7; *ruaḥ* and *neshamah* occur with nostrils in Genesis 7:22.
28. The triad parallels, in ascending order, *Malkhut* (dominion; the lower mother, Shekhinah); *Tiferet* (splendor; the husband of the bride, the Holy One, blessed be He); and *Binah* (supernal wisdom; the upper mother).
29. See BT, *'Eruvin* 65a.
30. Zohar, vol. 1, fol. 18a.
31. This tradition is also found later in the present passage, where the verb *yiqqavu* is glossed by the hyperphrase *medidu de-qay u-meshiḥta'* (the measurement of the measuring-line and the measurement).
32. See *Midrash Bereshit Rabba* 5.2 and 28.2, Juda Theodor and Chanokh Albeck, eds. (Jerusalem, 1965), vol. 1, pp. 32 and 260. In both cases the noun *middah* (measure) is used.
33. The letter *vav* usually symbolizes the middle column of the line, known as *Tiferet* (splendor), and when it suits exegetical purposes, the lower gradation of *Yesod* is called a small *vav*. Since *Tiferet* is regularly symbolized by "heaven," "under the heavens" would symbolize the next lower gradation, *Yesod*. The fact that the letter *vav* is spelled with two *v(av)*s marks this esoteric point orthographically.
34. In some printed editions the four letters of the Tetragram are variously marked in the first four words of the verse (Genesis 1:9). Cf. the annotation of the Derekh Emet in the margin of Zohar, vol. 1, fol. 18a.
35. See the fine formulation in *Zohar Ḥadash* 105c, where it is said that "those who are engaged in Torah [study], and contemplate the words of Torah with intention and deliberation . . . do not contemplate the word alone, but rather the [supernal] place upon which the word depends; for there is no [scriptural] word that is not dependent upon another supernal mystery." For the passage and a discussion, see Elliot Wolfson, *Through a Speculum that Shines: Vision and Imagination in Medieval Jewish Mysticism* (Princeton, 1994), 390–391.
36. The phrase is given there as an eschatological promise; the Zohar cites it as a theological reality.
37. I prefer the reading *'itbesis* (established) to *'itbesim* (perfumed, or purged of the dross of judgment).
38. Zohar, vol. 1, fol. 18a.
39. See Zohar, vol. 1, fol. 18a/b. All the classical sources are cited: Exodus 24:10, Numbers 14:10 and 17:7, Isaiah 6:1, and Ezekiel 1:28. In a brilliant addition, the teaching supplements this series with a citation from Genesis 35:16: "And Rachel was in childbirth, and had difficulty (*va-tiqash*) in her labor." With this verse the letters of *qeshet* (rainbow) are inverted as the teacher makes the esoteric point about the manifestation of the lower gradation of *Malkhut* (in which the bow of the upper world is revealed) through the arousal of the left side (the side of judgment, limitation, and, hence, restriction or difficulty).
40. It would appear that these colors symbolize the supernal triad of grace (*Ḥesed*), power/judgment (*Gevurah/Din*), and splendor (*Tiferet*). If so, this configuration is understood to be reflected in the manifestation of the divine Glory in *Yesod* (the upper unity) and *Malkhut* (the lower unity). For the color symbolism of the bow, see also Zohar, vol. 3, fol. 215a and the comment of Rabbi Baḥye ben Asher (Chavel, *Rabbeinu Baḥye*, vol. 1, p. 122), on Genesis 9:13. Our passage is considered within a wider framework

in Gershom Scholem, "Colors and Their Symbolism in Jewish Tradition and Mysticism," *Diogenes* 109 (1980), 69–71.

41. The imagery of the bow in the cloud has commonly been understood as a symbol of sexual conjunction (the union of the final masculine gradation of the upper world, *Yesod*, with the receiving feminine gradation in the lower world, *Malkhut*), insofar as the *qeshet* (bow) is an old rabbinic euphemism (based on Genesis 49:24) for the *membrum virile*; see BT, *Soṭah* 36b. For this passage, see Scholem, "Colors," 70–71; and more broadly (based on Zohar, vol. 2, fol. 99a), Idel, *Kabbalah*, 227. A reading of the symbolism in terms of the unveiling of the "androgenous phallus" in the lower gradation, as "the basic phenomenological presupposition of theosophic Kabbalah and zoharic Kabbalah in particular" is presented in Wolfson, *Through a Speculum*, pp. 336–345. I would nuance the matter differently—despite the erotic valence—since the bow is called here the ""appearance of the semblance of the divine Glory"; that is, despite the metonymic aspect of the bow as symbolic of male sexual potency, this arc of colors is perceived as the *whole* divine Glory in a form like a man. It is this anthropomorphic configuration as a whole that enters the kingdom (*Malkhut*) of the beloved, symbolized by the cloud.
42. This rotation of the closed eye is called here *gilgulaʾ de-ḥeizu de-ʿeiynaʾ*; for an analysis, see Liebes, *Sections of the Zoharic Lexicon*, pp. 291–293. Among other formulations of the praxis, note the instruction *ʾasḥar galgalakh* in Zohar, vol. 2, fol. 23b.
43. For other modes of color visualization in prayer, see Moshe Ideal, "Kabbalistic Prayer and Colors," in David Blumenthal, ed., *Approaches to Judaism in Medieval Times* (Atlanta, 1988), vol. 3, pp. 17–27.
44. There is reason to suppose that the triune assertion of YHVH-Eloheinu-YHVH has been influenced by Christianity; see the analysis of Yehuda Liebes, "Christian Influences on the Zohar," *Jerusalem Studies in Jewish Thought* 2 (1983), 40–45 (in Hebrew); English translation in Liebes, *Studies in the Zohar*, pp. 140–145. Liebes cites a passage from Moses de Leon's *Sheqel ha-Qodesh* that, like our Zohar passage, deals with the mystery of unity of the three Names in Deuteronomy 6:4 and adduces Zechariah 14:9; see Mopsik, *R. Moses de Leon's Sefer Sheqel ha-Qodesh*, p. 103. An extended discussion there (pp. 82–92) is very similar to our Zoharic formulation, and the language of the unity of the three Names is similar to Zohar, vol. 3, fol. 43b. On this text, see Adolph Jellinek, "Christlicher Einfluss auf die Kaballah," *Der Orient* 12 (1851), 580–583.
45. Zohar, vol. 1, fol. 18b.
46. The verse is recited aloud only on Yom Kippur. It is derived from Psalms 72:19 and 145:11 and was the response formula in the temple to the recitation of the ineffable Name by the high priest on Yom Kippur. See *M. Yoma* 3.8. The phrase was transferred to the recitation of the *Shemaʿ* at an early date. Its silent recitation in conjunction with the *Shemaʿ* is presented with an aggadic anecdote in *b. Pesaḥim* 56a. The passage at Zohar, vol. 2, fols. 133b–134b is an extended parallel to our discussion; the author says there that the silent recitation of the phrase is for this world alone, not the eschatological world to come. See also the brief formulation, but one linked to Genesis 1:9, in the third *Piquda'* in Zohar, vol. 1, fol. 12a. On this genre, see Ephraim Gottlieb, "Ma' amarei ha-'Piqudin' sheba-Zohar," *Kiryat Sefer* 48 (1972–73), 499–508.
47. This version of the episode follows BT, *Berakhot* 13b; but I read Rabbi Zeira here as per the JT, *Berakhot* chap. 2, halakha 1, since Rabbi Jeremiah was Rabbi Zeira's pupil, as also in this piece. The manuscripts of the Babylonian Talmud vary; see Rabbinovicz, *Diqduqei Soferim*, *Berakhot* 2.1.
48. *M. Berakhot* 2.2 (the verb there is *yiqabbel*, "receive"; "accept").

49. On Rabbi Zeira and certain ritual practices, see Avraham Goldberg, "Rabbi Zeira u-Minhag Bavel be-ʿEretz Yisra'el," *Tarbiz* 36 (1966–67), 319–341.
50. See BT, *Menaḥot* 62a and BT, *Sukkah* 37b–38a, respectively, and the illuminating discussion in Meiron Bailik Lerner, "Ba-shamayim uva-ʾAretz uva-ʾArbaʿ Ruḥot ha-ʿOlam," in Ezra Zion Melamad, ed., *Sefer Zikaron le-Binyamin de-Vries* (Jerusalem, 1969), 101–109.
51. See, in the edition of Shalom Albeck (Jerusalem, 1984), vol. 1, p. 14. For al-Bargeloni's discussion, see S. J. Halberstam, ed., *Peirush le-Sefer Yetzirah* (Berlin, 1885), 204. The letter *dalet* is, Numerically, "four" and thus is deemed fitting to indicate divine totality. A comprehensive review of the sources of this head gesture appears in Yitzhak Zimmer, "Tenuḥot ve-Tenuʿot ha-Guf be-Shaʿat Qeriʾat Shemaʿ," *Asufot* 8 (1994), 359–362.
52. This spark is the *botzinaʾ de-qardinutaʾ*, which is mentioned in this creative capacity in the opening myth of creation, Zohar, vol. 1, fol. 15a and vol. 2, fol. 133b. The spark is sometimes referred to as *botzinaʾde-qadrinutaʾ*, (spark of darkness). On these terms, see Liebes, *Sections of the Zohar Lexicon*, 145–151, 161–164, respectively (in Hebrew).
53. On this comprehensive figure, see Scholem, *On the Mystical Shape*, chap. 1.
54. The passage concludes with one further correlation between scripture and liturgy: a correlation between a tripartite reading of Genesis 1:9 and the *trishagion* formula (from Isaiah 6:3) recited during the *Kedushah* recitation.
55. See *Zohar Ḥdash, Midrash Shir Ha-Shirim*, 70d.
56. Cf. the famous exposition on this subject in Zohar, vol. 1, fols. 4b–5a. This passage is emphasized by Yehuda Liebes in his aforementioned exploration of the imaginative impulses of the Zoharic creativity. See "Zohar ve-'Eros," 71, and the wider discussion on pp. 70–80. See Liebes's comprehensive treatment of this passage in "The Messiah of the Zohar" (in Hebrew), in *The Messianic Idea in Jewish Thought: A Study Conference in Honor of the Eightieth Birthday of Gershom Scholem* (Jerusalem, 1982), 182–187.
57. This observation is indebted to the discussion of Yehuda Liebes in "Zohar ve'Eros," 104–112. He rightly stresses the highly eroticized dimension of the fellowship's relation to Rabbi Simeon as a manifestation of the *Shekhinah* through the kiss (cf. Zohar, vol. 3, fols. 59a and 201b); indeed, the love of the friends is deemed fundamental to the eros of creativity. Powerful sublimations are clearly involved. The issue of the "latent homoeroticism" of the fellowship has been taken up by Wolfson (*Through a Speculum*, 368–372).

5

The Fourfold Sense of Scripture in Christian Mysticism

EWERT COUSINS

Through the twenty centuries of Christian history, theologians and spiritual writers have drawn diverse resources from their scriptures. For example, they have gathered formulas for their creeds and doctrinal statements; they have forged concepts for their theologies and verbal weapons for their debates with those they considered heretics and schismatics. They have mined the scriptures for use in their liturgies and in their communal and private prayers. Readings from scripture have played an essential role in the liturgy of the Mass, in the monastic chanting of the divine office, and in the administration of the rites of the sacraments.

From the early centuries the scriptures have been central in Christian spirituality. Saints and spiritual teachers drew mystical texts from scripture; developed methods of meditation on scripture; and, through the symbolic interpretation of texts, penetrated beyond the literal level to explore the deeper mystical meaning of their scriptures. In doing this, they believed that their explorations were not mere flights of fancy but the discovery of meanings that God had implanted in the texts and that could be brought to light by the devout soul who allowed the text, with God's grace, to penetrate and illumine his or her soul.

Different periods of history have produced different approaches to scripture. In the era of the early councils, scriptural texts were marshaled to define and defend doctrines. This polemic use of scripture emerged again with vigor at the time of the Reformation. With the rise of science and the Enlightenment, much effort was expended to relate and reconcile the scientific and scriptural worldviews. Out of this ferment emerged the historical-critical method of interpreting scripture, which flourished in the twentieth century. The pervasiveness of this method in academic circles has overshadowed the classical symbolic and mystical reading of scripture. However, with the widespread awakening of spirituality since the 1960s, along with the parallel discovery of the spiritual practices of the world's religions and the growing interest in the academic study of mysticism, fresh attention has been given to scripture and mysticism.

In this study, I explore several aspects of the relationship between mysticism and scripture in Christianity, focusing chiefly on the patristic and medieval periods. It is necessary to begin with an exposition of the patristic worldview derived from scripture, since the early fathers of the church saw scripture as providing an all-encompassing environment. In such a context, it is not surprising to find that they identified theology with scripture. Such an understanding of scripture differs sharply from the perceptions of later periods. In this context, I give examples of how the patristic and medieval writers explored the mystical dimensions of this all-encompassing worldview. I focus on the emergence of the fourfold sense of scripture, beginning with the literal level and moving into the three mystical levels. To bring this to its completion, I examine the five spiritual senses of the soul, which are activated as one progresses in the spiritual journey and which are often awakened by reading scripture.

Scripture as a Worldview

Although in later doctrinal controversies, individual texts, phrases, and even words were the focus of theological debate, scripture played a much more organic role in the earlier periods. Taken as a whole, the canonical books of scripture provided a holistic vision of the spiritual universe in which Christians lived and participated in the mysteries revealed by God. This vision encompassed the Trinity; creation; the fall; the incarnation of Christ; his death, resurrection, and ascension; the sending of the Holy Spirit; and the life of the church. It was this vision, which was both cosmic and personal, that was articulated in scripture and ritually enacted in the cycle of the liturgical year. And within these larger horizons of scripture, Christian mysticism was evoked and then flourished.

The major scripture scholar in early Christianity was Origen, who flourished in the first half of the third century C.E. His contribution to the study of scripture was monumental in its scope and depth and in its pervasive presence in the other areas in which he excelled—in speculative theology and in spiritual and mystical teachings. For example, he wrote the first Christian mystical commentary on the Song of Songs and contributed in a foundational way to the allegorical interpretation of scripture, which opened a broad spectrum of mystical meanings. Basing himself on scripture, Origen also formulated the doctrine of the spiritual senses of the soul, which has played a significant role in the history of Christian mysticism. According to this doctrine, in addition to their five external senses, human beings also have five internal senses—for example, the spiritual sense of sight and touch. In a person's spiritual journey, one or another of these spiritual senses may be awakened, providing an immediate mystical experience of God.

Building on the work of Origen, later patristic writers made their own distinctive contributions toward creating a common comprehensive vision of the spiritual universe of scripture that was typical of the patristic era and that flowed into the High Middle Ages. It is not surprising, then, to see that Bonaventure, in the thirteenth century, identified scripture and theology and wrote a short treatise on scripture as a prologue to his abbreviated summa of scholastic theology.

In his study for a doctorate in theology at the University of Paris, Bonaventure was required to write commentaries on several books of scripture, to produce a massive commentary on the four books of *The Sentences of Peter Lombard*, and to successfully defend sets of disputed questions. Overwhelmed by the quantity of this material, his students asked him to write a brief summary, which he entitled *Breviloquium* (literally, a brief statement). As he explains in its prologue, "Beginners in the study of theology, in fact, often dread the scripture itself, feeling it to be as confusing, orderless, and uncharted as some impenetrable forest."[1] What follows his prologue to the *Breviloquium* is a summary of theology that runs the length of a modern book of some three hundred pages; it has the extraordinary density and clarity that only the emerging scholastic method at the University of Paris could produce—a method which, ironically, eventually separated theology as a discipline from the integral view of scripture of the patristic era.

In the prologue to the *Breviloquium*, Bonaventure identifies scripture with theology and produces what is considered a classical description of the integral patristic view of scripture. He begins his prologue with a text from Paul (Ephesians 3: 14–19) that closes with the following statement: "Being rooted and grounded in love, you may be able to comprehend with all the saints what is the breadth and length and height and depth, and to know Christ's love, which surpasses knowledge, in order that you may be filled unto all the fulness of God." He continues, "In these words, the origin, development and end of holy scripture, *which is called theology* [emphasis mine], are exposed by the great teacher of nations and preacher of truth."[2]

Bonaventure then develops the four aspects of scripture: its breadth, length, height, and depth. He is clearly using the image of the four dimensions as an archetypal symbol for totality, thus affirming the all-inclusive nature of the patristic vision of scripture. The breadth of scripture consists of the Old and New Testaments and the four kinds of writing found in both Testaments: "legal, historical, sapiential, and prophetical." "Holy Scripture," Bonaventure observes, "is like an immense river: the farther it flows, the greater it grows by the addition of many waters."[3] He states that "in holy scripture we find also length, for scripture describes all times, and periods from the beginning of the world until the day of judgment."[4] He divides the history of the world into seven stages and compares the stages of history to "a beautifully composed poem" in which we can discover the beauty and rectitude of "God's wisdom ruling the universe. But as no one can appreciate the beauty of a poem unless his vision embraces it as a whole, . . . the Holy Spirit has given us the book of Scriptures whose length corresponds to the whole duration of God's governing action in the universe."[5]

Bonaventure then explores the height of scripture, which reveals the nature of the angelic hierarchies and leads us to Christ as the Word and the Eternal Art of the Father, through whom all things are made. Elsewhere, he speaks of two books: the book written within the Trinity, namely, the Son, Word, and Art of the Father; and a second book, written without, namely, creation, which externalizes the eternal ideas generated within the Son as an expression of the Father's fecundity. In another text, Bonaventure speaks of scripture as a third book, which can lead us to see creation as an outer expression of the Son, who draws us up to union with the Father.[6]

Bonaventure next turns to the depth of scripture. Here mysticism and scripture connect most intimately. Following the patristic and medieval tradition, he distinguishes between the literal and the three spiritual, symbolic, or mystical senses of Scripture. Since I explore these mystical senses in some detail in following discussions, I do not examine them further here. Bonaventure concludes his prologue on the breadth, length, height, and depth of scripture with a powerful archetypal Christocentric image. "Scripture, then," he claims, "deals with the whole universe, the high and the low, the first and the last, and all things in between. It is, in a sense, an intelligible cross in which the whole organism of the universe is described and made to be seen in the light of the mind."[7]

Moses and the Cloud

Within this rich and complex view of scripture, theologians and spiritual writers in the patristic and medieval periods drew from scripture narratives, images, and dynamics in charting the spiritual journey and in describing mystical states of consciousness. For example, the narrative in Exodus that describes Moses' ascent of Mount Sinai was used as a classical symbol of the ascent of the soul to mystical consciousness. In the fourth century, Gregory of Nyssa wrote a treatise entitled *The Life of Moses,* in which he presents the biblical account of the life of Moses as a model of virtue and a paradigm for the mystical ascent. He describes Moses at the summit of Mount Sinai: "Since he was alone, by having been stripped as it were of the people's fear, he boldly approached the very darkness itself and entered the invisible things where he was no longer seen by those watching."[8] Having gone through a process of purgation and separation, Moses, at the summit of the mountain, enters into the "inner sanctuary of the divine mystical doctrine," and

> there, while not being seen, he was in company with the Invisible. He teaches, I think, by the things he did that the one who is going to associate intimately with God must go beyond all that is visible and (lifting up his own mind, as to a mountaintop, to the invisible and incomprehensible) believe that the divine is *there* where the understanding does not reach.[9]

The biblical narrative of Moses' ascent of Mount Sinai became the major source for the Christian ascent to apophatic mystical consciousness through the *via negativa.* The Pseudo-Dionysius made it the central image in his *Mystical Theology*, one of the most influential texts in the history of Christian mysticism. It is important to note here that the term *mystical* in the ancient Greek mystery religions, and in the Christian patristic and medieval periods, merely meant "hidden" or "secret." It did not denote or connote "rapture" or "ecstasy," as it began to do in the late-medieval and into the modern periods.

Like Gregory of Nyssa, the Pseudo-Dionysius presents the narrative of Moses' ascent of Mount Sinai as a path to apophatic mystical experience, where those who make this ascent "leave behind them every divine light, every voice, every word from heaven, and who plunge into the darkness where, as scripture proclaims, there dwells the One who is beyond all things." The author says that "it is not for nothing that the blessed Moses is commanded to submit first to purification" and then he leaves behind those who have not been purified. After this he hears the blasts of trumpets and he sees many lights streaming abundantly. He then stands apart from the crowd, and with chosen priests, "he pushes ahead to the summit of the divine ascents. And yet he does not meet God himself, but contemplates, not him who is invisible, but rather where he dwells." Then Moses breaks free from all that is perceived with the eye of the body and the mind, from what sees and is seen:

> And he plunges into the truly mysterious darkness of unknowing. Here, renouncing all that the mind may conceive, wrapped entirely in the intangible and the invisible, he belongs completely to him who is beyond everything. Here, being neither oneself nor someone else, one is supremely united by a completely unknowing inactivity of all knowledge, and knows beyond the mind by knowing nothing.[10]

The Pseudo-Dionysius has had an enormous influence on the mystical and theological writings of both the Greek East and the Latin West. For example, he has influenced Maximus the Confessor and Gregorius Palamas in the East, along with John Scotus Erigena, the Victorines, Bonaventure, and Thomas Aquinas in the West. His *Mystical Theology*, with the image of Moses at its center, has become the locus classicus for apophatic mysticism in Christianity. His direct influence on the West reached a high-water mark with the writing of the fourteenth-century anonymous handbook of practical spiritual guidance entitled *The Cloud of Unknowing*. The English author of this handbook had translated *The Mystical Theology* of the Pseudo-Dionysius from Latin to Middle English. It is not surprising, then, that he would develop a form of apophatic spirituality based explicitly on the image of the darkness of the cloud that envelops Moses ("the darkness of unknowing") in his mystical ascent, as described in *The Mystical Theology* by the Pseudo-Dionysius. In his key passage, the author of *The Cloud* claims that no one can reach God by thinking. He continues: "Therefore, it is my wish to leave everything that I can think of and choose for my love the thing that I cannot think [of]. Because he can certainly be, but not thought. He can be taken and held by love but not by thought."[11]

He admits that at times it is good to think of God's kindness and worthiness. However, in the exercise he is teaching in his book, he says firmly that this must be cast down and covered over with a cloud of forgetting. He continues: "You are to step above it stalwartly but lovingly, and with a devout, pleasing impulsive love strive to pierce that darkness above you. You are to smite upon that thick could of unknowing with a sharp dark of longing love."[12] In this passage the author of *The Cloud* is proposing a type of apophatic mysticism that is not identical with that of *The Mystical Theology* of the Pseudo-Dionysius. The latter merely suppresses the mind, whereas the former, while suppressing the mind, awakens love to penetrate the darkness of the cloud of unknowing. This is not original with him; for both Thomas Gallus and Bonaventure, who base their apophatic mysticism on *The Mystical Theology* of the Pseudo-Dionysius, awaken ecstatic love within the darkness of unknowing.

The Four Senses of Scripture

With these mystical texts as a background, I now explore the fourfold sense of scripture. This approach opens the door to the symbolic interpretation that reveals the many levels of scripture and their correlation with mysticism. Found in scripture itself, in both the Old and New Testaments, this symbolic interpretation was developed during the patristic period in the East and in the West, and it reached its fullest articulation in the High Middle Ages. Taking their point of departure from the literal meaning, patristic and medieval theologians proceeded to interpret the text on three other levels: the moral (or tropological), the allegorical, and the anagogic. These three latter senses were called spiritual, symbolic, mystical, or allegorical in a generic sense of *allegory*. In this usage, as just indicated, the term *mystical* meant "hidden or secret," and not "ecstatic," as it came to mean later. In the early centuries the senses of scripture were not yet divided into the fourfold pattern that was to become standard in the later periods. For example, Origen used a threefold division: "For just as a human being," he writes, "is said to be made up of body, soul, and spirit, so also is sacred scripture, which has been granted by God's gracious dispensation for man's salvation."[13] Hence, according to Origen, there are three senses of scripture: the somatic, the psychic, and the pneumatic—that is, the literal, the moral, and the spiritual. Gregory the Great is regarded as the principal initiator of the medieval division into four senses. In a homily on Ezekiel, he compared the words of scripture to a square stone, which can stand on each of four sides because there are no rough spots on any side. This image is not unlike that evoked by Bonaventure (noted above), of the breadth, length, height, and depth of scripture. While retaining the literal and moral sense of Origen, later medieval theologians divided his spiritual sense into the allegorical and the anagogic. This division is summed up in the celebrated distich by the Dominican, Augustine of Dacia (d. 1282):

> Littera gesta docet, quid credis allegoria,
> Quid agis moralis, quo tendis anagogia.[14]
>
> (The literal sense teaches historical events,
> Allegory what you believe, the moral sense
> What you should do, and the anagogic sense
> That toward which you are striving.)

It would be wise here to give in full the classical source in Dante of the meaning of the four senses of scripture. Writing to Can Grande della Scala, Dante claims that his *Commedia* should be read according to the allegory of the theologians—that is, according to the fourfold sense of scripture:

> For the clarity of what will be said, it is to be understood that the meaning of this work is not simple, but rather it is polysemous, that is, having many meanings. For the first meaning is that which one derives from the letter, another is that which one derives from the things signified by the letter. The first is called "literal" and the second "allegorical," or "mystical." So that this method of exposition may be clearer, one may consider it in these lines: 'When Israel went out of Egypt, the house of Jacob from people of strange language, Judah was his sanctuary and Israel his dominion' [Psalm 114:1–2]. If we look only at the letter, this signifies that the children of Isreal went out of Egypt in the time of Moses; if we look at the allegory, it signifies our redemption through Christ; if we look at the moral sense, it signifies the turning of the soul from the sorrow and misery of sin to a state of grace; if we look at the anagogical sense, it signifies the passage of the blessed soul from the slavery of this corruption to the freedom of eternal glory.[15]

The position of Dante was shared by the theologians of the scholastic period of the Middle Ages. For example, Thomas Aquinas describes the four senses of scripture as follows: "Therefore that first signification whereby words signify things belongs to the first sense, the historical or literal. That signification whereby things signified by words have themselves also a signification is called the spiritual sense, which is based on the literal, and presupposes it." He continues by citing the other senses. "Now this spiritual sense has a threefold division. . . . So far as the things of the Old Law signify the things of the New Law, there is the allegorical sense; so far as the things done in Christ, or so far as the things which signify Christ, are signs of what we ought to do, there is the moral sense. But so far as they signify what relates to eternal glory, there is the anagogical sense."[16]

In the same vein, Bonaventure writes in his prologue to the *Breviloquium*: "Many scriptural passages have, besides the direct sense, three other significations: the allegorical, the moral, and the anagogical." He goes on to describe the specific meaning of each of these senses." Allegory consists in this: that one thing signifies another thing which is in the realm of faith; moral teaching, or tropology, [consists] in this: that from something done, we learn another thing that we must do; anagogy, or lifting up, [consists] in this: that we are given to know what to desire, that is, the eternal happiness of the elect."[17]

Medieval exegetes interpreted a number of central symbols on four levels. For example, in addition to the Exodus as treated in Dante, Jerusalem was interpreted literally as the city of David; morally, as the soul adorned with virtue; allegorically, as the church on earth redeemed by Christ; anagogically, as the heavenly Jerusalem or the souls of the saved enjoying the beatific vision. In a similar fashion the words in Genesis, "Let there be light," describing God's creation of light, were interpreted as referring literally to corporeal light; morally, to the illumination of the soul by virtue; allegorically, to the illumination of the church by Christ; anagogicially, to the illumination of the blessed in heaven by the beatific vision. Not all such symbols were interpreted on four levels. At times a literal sense would yield chiefly a moral meaning, as, for example, in Richard of St. Victor's interpretation of the Mercy Seat in the tabernacle as a symbol of the contemplative self.[18] This same symbol was interpreted allegorically in Bonaventure as a symbol of Christ in his *Soul's Journey into God*.[19]

Lectio Divina

The fourfold interpretation of scripture was nourished by *lectio divina*, a method of prayerful reading that has been practiced in the Christian monastic tradition for centuries. *Lectio divina*, which in Latin means "divine reading," was part of the daily schedule of the monastery. Each day the monks would spend an hour or two, or more, privately reading scripture or some spiritual book in a prayerful manner. The key to the method was its pace—the monks read very slowly, sometimes aloud, sometimes in silence or by forming the words silently with their lips. Their goal was not to finish a passage, but to enter prayerfully into its depths by dwelling on a sentence, a phrase, or even a word—mulling over it, ruminating on it, allowing it to sink into their being and resonate on many levels of meaning. The monks were instructed that if something struck them, they were to pursue it, moving from the text into meditation, affective prayer, and contemplation—in the Latin terms: *meditatio*, *oratio*, *contemplatio*.

As this method has been practiced since the early centuries, it has not been directed to one prayerful attitude alone—for example, meditation. Rather, it has provided a gateway to many such attitudes evoked spontaneously in the course of the reading. For example, the reader might move from the text to meditate on a specific point, which would lead to a spontaneous affective prayer of praise, gratitude, or petition. This in turn might lead to a contemplative attitude: a wondrous gaze, a loving response, or a silent dwelling in the divine presence. After this, the reader might return to the text, letting a word or a phrase draw him directly into the silent presence.

A distinction was made between meditation and contemplation by Richard of St. Victor, in *The Mystical Ark*. One of the most highly esteemed psychologists of the spiritual life, Richard claims that meditation examines an object and contemplation marvels at it. He defines the terms as follows: "Contemplation is a penetrating and free gaze of a soul extended everywhere in perceiving things; but meditation is a zealous attention of the mind, earnestly pursuing an investigation concerning something. Or thus: Meditation is the careful gaze of the soul employed ardently in a search for truth." Meditation is goal oriented and proceeds with energy and focus toward what it seeks, for as Richard says, "Meditation presses forward with great activity of soul, often through arduous and rough places, to the end of the way it is going. Contemplation, in free flight, circles around with marvelous quickness wherever impulse moves it."[20]

In *lectio divina* one is drawn ever more deeply into contemplation through the symbolic interpretation of scripture. From the literal and historical level one can be led into the moral and allegorical level and ultimately into the anagogical or mystical realm, where God is experienced in ecstatic immediacy. This can be seen in a number of examples. Returning to Dante's text on the Exodus, we can cite a graphic description that, through symbolism, draws one from the literal to the moral level. In *The Life of Moses* (cited above), Gregory of Nyssa, referring to the army of the Egyptians, states: "For who does not know that the Egyptian army—those horses, chariots and their drivers, archers, slingers, heavily armed soldiers, and the rest of the crowd in the enemies' line of battle—are the various passions of the soul by which man is enslaved?" He goes on to specify his symbolic meaning: "For the undisciplined intellectual drives and the sensual impulses to pleasure, sorrow, and covetousness are indistinguishable from the aforementioned army. Reviling is a stone straight from the sling and the spirited impulse is the quivering spear point. The passion for pleasures is to be seen in the horses who themselves with irresistible drive pull the chariot."[21]

Gregory's entire treatise is a symbolic interpretation of scripture. He first summarizes the life of Moses as recorded in scripture; then he seeks out "the spiritual understanding which corresponds to the history in order to obtain suggestions of virtue."[22] He presents Moses as an example for us, drawing rich symbolic meaning about the life of virtue, such as we saw above. Although his symbolic interpretation is chiefly on the moral level, he deals as well with the other two levels: the allegorical and anagogic.

Echoing Gregory's treatment of Moses, Richard of St. Victor, in his treatise *The Twelve Patriarchs*, gives a moral interpretation of the account of the sons of Jacob. For example, he treats Joseph as a symbol of discretion and Benjamin as a symbol of contemplation. In his companion treatise, entitled *The Mystical Ark*, he continues the moral interpretation through the symbol of the ark of the covenant. At the outset, he indicates that he is following the moral interpretation, not the allegorical: "The mystical meaning of the ark in the allegorical sense, that is, as it represents Christ, has been articulated by learned persons and investigated by more penetrating minds before. Despite this, we do not presume to be guilty of carelessness by now saying something about it in the moral sense."[23] By "moral" here he intends not the virtues he had examined in *The Twelve Patriarchs*, but the stages of contemplation, which he sees symbolized in the building of the ark.

One of the most cultivated examples of the symbolic approach is found in the interpretation of the Song of Songs. As already mentioned, in the third century Origen laid the foundation for this tradition in his *Commentary on the Song of Songs*, in which he interpreted the bridegroom symbolically as Christ, the Word. He interpreted the bride in two ways: as symbolizing the individual soul and as symbolizing the church. In the prologue he states. "This book seems to me an epithalamium, that is, a wedding song, written by Solomon in the form of a play, which he recited in the character of a bride who was being married and burned with a heavenly love for her bridegroom, who is the Word of God." He then indicates the two symbolic meanings of the bride. "For whether she is the soul made after his image or the church, she has fallen deeply in love with him."[24]

Through the centuries many spiritual writers followed Origen's symbolic interpretation in their own commentaries on the Song of Songs. In the twelfth century, Bernard of Clairvaux made this the theme of his *Sermons on the Song of Songs*, which is considered one of the masterpieces of the commentary genre. In the hands of a great spiritual master like Bernard, the symbolic interpretation becomes a framework for an exploration of the entire spiritual life. He traces the movement of the soul through the phases of growth to the final stage of union with Christ, which he designates as the "kiss of the mouth."[25]

This mystical symbolism is found richly developed in John of the Cross and in Teresa of Ávila. In *The Interior Castle*, Teresa blends the scriptural symbolism with her own. She bids us to "consider our soul to be like a castle made entirely out of a diamond or of very clear crystal, in which there are many rooms, just as in heaven there are many dwelling places." She then leads us through the castle of the soul until we come to the seventh area, which is the dwelling place of Christ, the spouse of the soul. It is here that the mystical marriage is consummated. "When our Lord is pleased," she says, "to have pity on this soul that he has already taken spiritually as his spouse, because of what it suffers and has suffered through its desires, he brings it, before the spiritual marriage is consummated, into his dwelling place, which is the seventh."[26] Note here that the distinction between the moral, the allegorical, and the anagogic is not so sharply drawn, for the soul and Christ as bridegroom are part of an integral narrative that depicts the growth of the soul toward ecstatic union with the Beloved.

Meditations on the Life of Christ

In the High Middle Ages, meditation on the life of Christ was developed as a distinct form of prayer that involved considerable precision of method. In the Franciscan milieu of the thirteenth century, a devotion to the humanity of Christ flourished.

This produced a desire to meditate on the concrete historical details of the life of Christ in order that one might draw out a moral lesson. Although this form of prayer differs from contemplation and the use of the symbolic imagination in the interpretation of scripture, it deserves mention here because it is based in scripture and can be the object of *lectio divina*, which leads one to move into the more mystical levels of consciousness. Because of its power to bring one into the events of Christ's life, I have called it elsewhere "the mysticism of the historical event."[27]

A classic example of this type of meditation is found in Bonaventure's *The Tree of Life*. With a symbol drawn from scripture, Bonaventure presents the life of Christ as the Tree of Life, on whose branches twelve fruits blossom, including such virtues as humility, piety, patience, and constancy, which are presented to us for imitation.

In his meditation on the birth of Christ, Bonaventure summarizes the Gospel accounts of the nativity, choosing details that draw into focus the virtues of poverty and humility: "Although he was great and rich, he became small and poor for us. He chose to be born away from a home in a stable, to be wrapped in swaddling clothes, to be nourished by virginal milk, and to lie in a manger between an ox and an ass."[28] Through vivid details, Bonaventure paints a graphic scene and even draws us as participants into the drama of the event. In the following passage, note how he evokes a response of love for the infant, then elicits contemplative admiration at the host of angels and calls forth a prayer of praise: *Glory to God in the highest* (Luke 2:14). Thus he passes over from meditation to prayer—blending in the classic method of *lectio divina* the three prayerful attitudes summed up in the Latin terms *meditatio*, *contemplatio*, *oratio*:

> Now, then, my soul,
> embrace that divine manger;
> press your lips upon and kiss the boy's feet.
> Then in your mind
> keep the shepherds' watch,
> marvel at the assembling host of angels,
> join in the heavenly melody,
> singing with your voice and heart:
> *Glory to God in the highest*
> *and on earth peace*
> *to men of good will.*[29]

This method was given another expression in the work entitled *Meditations on the Life of Christ*, which grew out of the early Franciscan tradition and which was erroneously attributed to Bonaventure. These meditations were incorporated into the work of Ludolf of Saxony, which was read by Ignatius of Loyola, who in turn built this form of meditation into his *Spiritual Exercises*. In the hands of Ignatius, meditation was worked into a formal method. He applied the three faculties of memory, understanding, and will, especially to scenes from the life of Christ, from which moral lessons would be derived. As in the case of Bonaventure, this method also led to contemplative wonder and to spontaneous affective prayer. In fact, Ignatius used the term *contemplation* for his meditations on the life of Christ, which were less sharply focused on a specific goal.

The Four Levels of the Psyche

We now turn from medieval exegesis to contemporary research into states of consciousness. I point out a correlation between the four levels of the psyche I discovered in the course of this research, and the four senses of scripture. From this correlation, I make a fundamental claim: the symbolic method of interpreting scripture is not arbitrary but is based on the very structure of the psyche. In actual fact, it is a method designed to allow a text to reveal its meaning on each of the four levels of the psyche. From this basic claim, a number of further claims are derived: In light of the correlation, a comprehensive hermeneutic can be determined with greater precision than was available to patristic and medieval theologians, for the rules of this hermeneutic can be ascertained from the structure and dynamics of each of the levels of the psyche. Once brought to light, this hermeneutic context can clarify the various types of symbolism used in the interpretation of scripture. I show that the levels of the psyche correspond to the three levels of the interpretation of scripture, whose very structure and dynamics follow a symbolic pattern that opens to mystical consciousness. This reveals that symbolic and mystical thinking is not alien or peripheral to the psyche, but a constitutive element of its most profound dimensions. Thus in light of contemporary psychological research, the symbolic interpretation of scripture can be seen rooted in the structure and dynamics of the psyche itself.

I base my discussion here chiefly on the research of Robert Masters and Jean Houston, which is reported in their book *The Varieties of Psychedelic Experience*.[30] Although the cases studied in their book involved psychedelic drugs, the same patterns of consciousness were revealed by their later research, which was performed without the use of drugs. Similar patterns have emerged in the work of Stanislav Grof.[31]

The research of Masters and Houston has revealed that the psyche has four levels, which are described as follows: (1) the sensorium, or the level of heightened sense experience; (2) the ontogenetic, or recollective analytic level, where the subject recalls his or her personal history, and which corresponds to Freudian psychoanalysis; (3) the phylogenetic, or symbolic level, which corresponds to the collective unconscious of Jung, and where the subject relives the great myths and rituals of humankind; and (4) the level of integral consciousness, or the mysterium—the level of deep mystical consciousness, which is similar to that described by the mystics of the world.[32] These levels are all markedly different, with their own horizons, structure, logic, and dynamics. Although there is a certain interpenetration of each in the other, they remain sufficiently distinct; yet one leads to the other.

After taking a dosage of a psychedelic drug, a subject usually first experienced heightened sensation. For example, having been handed an orange by a guide, the subject contemplated it for several minutes and said: "Magnificent. . . . I never really saw color before. . . . It's brighter than a thousand suns. . . . (Feels the whole surface of the orange with palms and fingertips.) But this is a pulsing thing, . . . a living, pulsing thing. . . . And all these years I've just taken it for granted."[33]

After some time on the sensory level, the subject usually moved to the ontogenic, or recollective analytic level. For example, the subject experienced his deep emotions at the time of the death of his grandmother, when he was not quite four years old.

"Suddenly," he said, "I felt as if some obstacle were coming up to me—something large, dark, and vague, but very powerful—as if it were knocking on the walls of consciousness. . . . It's Granny's death! I must examine Granny's death!" The subject then felt a surge of guilt that he had experienced years before over his grandmother's death, but which he had repressed. In the course of the session he was able to free himself from the burden of this unconscious guilt.[34]

Because of the importance of the third level, I cite at length the case of a subject who relived the rites of Dionysus:

> The guide initiated the ritual process by suggesting to the subject the he was attending the rites of Dionysus and was carrying a thyrsus in his hand. When he asked for some details the subject [S] was told only that the thyrsus was a staff wreathed with ivy and vine leaves, terminating at the top in a pine cone, and was carried by the priests and attendants of Dionysus, a god of the ancient Greeks. To this S nodded, sat back in his chair with eyes closed, and then remained silent for several minutes. Then he began to stamp the floor, as if obeying some strange internal rhythm. He next proceeded to describe a phantasmagoria consisting of snakes and ivy, streaming hair, dappled fawn skins, and dances going faster and faster to the shrill high notes of the flute and accelerating drums. The frenzy mounted and culminated in the tearing apart of living animals.
>
> The scene changed and S found himself in a large amphitheater witnessing some figures performing a rite or play. This changed into a scene of white-robed figures moving in the night towards an open cavern. In spite of her intention not to give further clues, the guide found herself asking the subject at this point: "Are you at Eleusis?" S seemed to nod "yes," whereupon the guide suggested that he go into the great hall and witness the mystery. He responded: "I can't. It is forbidden. . . . I must confess. . . . I must confess . . ." (The candidate at Eleusis was rejected if he came with sinful hands to seek enlightenment. He must confess, make reparation, and be absolved. Then he received his instruction and then finally had his experience of enlightenment and was allowed to witness the mystery. How it happened that this subject was aware of the stages of the mystery seemed itself to be a mystery.) S then began to go through the motions of kneading and washing his hands and appeared to be in deep conversation with someone. Later, he told the guide that he had seemed to be standing before a priestly figure and had made a confession. The guide now urged the subject to go into the hall and witness the drama. This he did, and described seeing a "story" performed about a mother who looks the world over for her lost daughter and finally finds her in the world of the underground (the Demeter-Kore story which, in all likelihood, was performed at Eleusis).
>
> This sequence dissolved and the subject spoke of seeing a kaleidoscopic pattern of many rites of the death and resurrection of a god who appeared to be bound up in some way with the processes of nature. S described several of the rites he was viewing, and from his descriptions the guide was able to recognize remarkable similarities to rites of Osiris, Attis, and Adonis. S was uncertain as to whether these rites occurred in a rapid succession or all at the same time. The rites disappeared and were replaced by the celebration of the Roman Catholic Mass. Seeking to restore the original setting, the guide again suggested the image of the thyrsus. S imaged the thyrsus, but almost immediately it "turned into" a man on a tree (the Christ archetype). The guide then said: "You are the thyrsus," to which S responded: "I am the thyrsus. . . . I am the thyrsus. . . . I have labored in the vineyard of the world, have suffered, have died, and have been reborn for your sake and shall be exalted forevermore."[35]

Another remarkable experience is recorded by Grof in an LSD session, involving a clergyman, that also reveals the fundamental dynamic level of the psyche, which is the dynamic of transformation:

> I began to experience the passion of our Lord Jesus Christ. I was Christ, but I was also everyone as Christ and all men died as we made our way in the dirgelike procession toward Golgotha. At this time in my experience there was no longer any confusion; the visions were perfectly clear. The pain was intense, and the sorrow was just, just agonizing. It was at this point that a blood tear from the face of God began to flow. I did not see the face of God, but his tear began to flow, and it began to flow out over the world as God himself participated in the death of all men and in the suffering of all men. The sorrow of this moment is still so intense that it is difficult for me to speak of it. We moved toward Golgotha, and there in agony greater than any I have ever experienced, I was crucified with Christ and all men on the cross. I was Christ, and I was crucified, and I died.

This was followed by a resurrection experience: "When all men died on the cross, there began the most heavenly music I have ever heard in my entire life; it was incredibly beautiful. It was the voice of angels singing, and we began slowly to rise."[36]

Although a relatively large number of subjects reached the third level, only a small proportion attained the fourth—the level of integral consciousness, or the mysterium. Those who did reported experiences similar to those of the acknowledged mystics of the world's religions. For example, one subject reported:

> I, who seemed to have no identity at all, yet experienced myself as *filled with God*, and then as (whatever this may mean) *passing through God* and into a Oneness wherein it seemed God, Being, and a mysterious unnameable One constituted together what I can only designate the ALL. What "I" experienced as this ALL so far transcends my powers of description that to speak, as I must, of an ineffably rapturous Sweetness is an approximation not less feeble than if I were to describe a candle and so hope to capture with my words all of the blazing glory of the sun.[37]

Correlation with Senses of Scripture

We now explore the correlation between the four levels of the psyche and the four sense of scripture. The sensorium corresponds to the literal sense, since the latter deals with the meaning of a text in its concrete, particular facticity, similar to our sense data. The second level, the ontogenetic or recollective analytic, corresponds to the moral sense, since this level of the psyche involves a consciousness of the individual subject in his or her personal history, affectivity, and personal commitments. The third level, the phylogenetic or symbolic, corresponds to the allegorical sense, for this level of the psyche links early historical ritual material with Christ. The fourth level—the mysterium, or the realm of integral consciousness—corresponds to the anagogical sense, for the latter deals with the ultimate union of the soul with God.

It would be especially interesting to explore the allegorical sense in light of the data drawn from the phylogenetic level of the psyche. The case from Masters and Houston that I just presented gives a striking example of the material from this level. It is highly symbolic, consisting of clusters of archetypal symbols and primitive rituals. Most strikingly, these rituals emerge in a temporal sequence that culminates, in the case cited, in the image of Christ and the Mass. The very fabric and dynamic of this level reveal the logic of the process of allegorizing scripture. Christian theologians drew events and symbols from the Old Testament and saw them as culminating in Christ. From one point of view, this could be seen as an arbitrary procedure; but from the standpoint of the dynamics of the third level of the psyche, the logic is completely coherent. It is not by chance, then, that the early Christian community incorporated the Old Testament into their prayer, liturgy, and belief precisely by allegorizing—that is, by seeing this data as symbolically culminating in Christ. In fact, in light of the phylogenetic level of the psyche, it is possible to extend the procedure back beyond the Old Testament and into the entire context of primal religious ritual and symbol. As in the case cited, the many transformation rituals from the Greek world can be seen as culminating in the person of Christ and in the continuing transformation ritual of the Mass.

The Spiritual Senses of the Soul

After examining the fourfold sense of scripture, we should not close without including at least a brief treatment of the spiritual senses of the soul. In this phrase the term *sense* refers to a faculty of mystical perception or experience. According to this teaching, just as we have five physical senses, so we have five spiritual senses, which can be awakened in the spiritual journey, thereby enabling human beings to experience God in a variety of mystical ways.

Although the spiritual senses of the soul have played a significant role in the history of Christian mysticism, they have not been sufficiently tapped in recent times to throw light on the nature and varieties of mystical experience. Moreover, they can be easily confused with the spiritual or mystical senses of scripture that we have been studying. The ambiguous term here is *sense*. In the fourfold sense of scripture, as we saw, *sense* refers to *meaning*, usually the symbolic or mystical meaning of a text. It is important also to deal with the spiritual senses of the soul in the context of the overarching topic of this book: mysticism and scripture. The doctrine of the spiritual senses of the soul in Christianity originated in scripture. If we were to fail to acknowledge it, we would be ignoring one of the major factors in the practice of *lectio divina*, which also functioned significantly in the contemplative interpretation of scripture through the symbolic, spiritual, and mystical senses.

The teaching on the spiritual senses is very ancient, having been developed by Origen in the third century. In his history of Western Christian mysticism, Bernard McGinn calls Origen's doctrine of the spiritual senses of the soul "one of his most important contributions to the history of Christian mysticism."[38] This is indeed high praise in view of Origen's monumental influence on the entire subsequent tradition of the mystical reading of the Song of Songs. The doctrine of the spiritual senses has had a continuous history in Christianity—for example, flowing in the patristic period through Basil the Great, Gregory of Nyssa, and Evagrius Ponticus in the East and Augustine and Gregory the Great in the West; and in the twelfth century through Bernard of Clairvaux, William of St. Thierry, and Alcher of Clairvaux. After Origen, Bonaventure is considered its major exponent. In the twentieth century, Karl Rahner revived interest in the spiritual senses through a seminal article he wrote in 1932 on Origen's doctrine of the spiritual senses, followed by another in 1934 on Bonaventure's doctrine of the spiritual senses.[39] The spiritual senses also play a major role in the thought of Hans Urs von Balthasar.[40] In 1996, Stephen Fields published an article in *Theological Studies* that was entitled "Balthasar and Rahner on the Spiritual Senses," focusing on the way that von Balthasar and Rahner have given different interpretations of Bonaventure's ideas on the spiritual senses. Fields points out how these two different approaches to the spiritual senses found in Bonaventure reflect the differences in von Balthasar's and Rahner's systems.[41] Rich though this focus is, I believe that the clarification of the doctrine of the spiritual senses, as launched by Origen—and then further elaborated upon by Bonaventure—can also enormously enhance the study of mystical experience as expressed in mystical texts. Although there has been an awakening of the doctrine of the spiritual senses of the soul, it has not had a major impact on the recent academic study of mysticism. Much attention has been paid to language and contemporary epistemology, but not enough has been paid to this s ancient position as espoused by the mystics themselves.

Origen and Augustine

As far as scholars can determine, the creation of the doctrine of the spiritual senses originated with Origen. Although there is some anticipation of the doctrine in the ideas of Philo, of Clement of Alexandria, and of Tertullian, Origen's development of the doctrine of the spiritual senses flows out of his interest in psychology and principally out of his monumental work in scripture and in a special way from his own mystical interpretation of the Song of Songs. He formulates his position follows: "After thorough investigation one can say that there exists, according to the word of Scripture, a general sense or faculty for the divine. Only the blessed know how to find it, as we read in the Wisdom of Solomon, 'You discover the divine faculty of perception' (Prov. 2:5)." He describes how the spiritual sense unfolds:

> This sense, however, unfolds in various individual faculties: sight for the contemplation of immaterial forms, as is evidently granted in the Cherubim and Seraphim, hearing for the discrimination of voices, which do not echo in the empty air, taste in order to savour the living bread which came down from heaven to bring life to the world (John 6:33), and even a sense of smell, with which Paul perceived those realities which caused him to describe himself as a sweet odour of Christ (2 Cor. 2:15), and finally touch, which possessed John when he states that he has touched with his own hands the Word of life (1 John 1:1).[42]

Origen claims that the prophets had discovered these two modes of sense perception—one mortal and the other immortal, spiritual, and divine.

We turn now to Augustine and the account of his mystical experience, which he describes in book 7 of the *Confessions*. This experience was decisive in his life—it was the turning point in his labyrinthine spiritual search and the catalyst for his conversion. Augustine had joined a group of Christian Neoplatonists who had gathered around Ambrose, the bishop of Milan. In this milieu, Augustine tells us, he read the books of the Platonists, where he found the Trinity but not the Incarnation. Although his primary focus was on the books of the Platonists, he read these with an eye on

Christian scripture. For he tells us how the Platonic writings called to his mind the prologue of the Gospel of John. He explicitly mentions "the light that shines in darkness"; he says that the Word of God is "the true light which enlightens every man that comes into this world." It is not surprising that in recalling these verses of scripture, he has awakened his spiritual sense of sight in a mystical experience of God as light. He continues:

> Being thus admonished to return to myself, under your leadership I entered into my inmost being. This I could do, for you became my helper. I entered there, and by my soul's eye, such as it was, I saw above that same eye of my soul, above my mind, an unchangeable light. It was not this common light, plain to all flesh, nor a greater light, as it were, of the same kind, as though that light would shine many, many times more bright, and by its great power fill the whole universe. Not such was that light, but different, far different from all other lights. Nor was it above my mind, as oil above water, or sky above earth. It was above my mind, because it made me, and I was beneath it, because I was made by it. He who knows truth, knows that light, and he who knows it knows eternity. Love knows it, O eternal truth, and true love, and beloved eternity! You are my God, and I sigh for you day and night![43]

Note Augustine's own comments on the "unchangeable light." "It was not this common light, plain to all flesh," and therefore not a sense image symbolizing God. "Nor a greater light, as it were, of the same kind"; therefore, it was not ordinary light used analogously. It was, rather, on a different ontological plane, in fact, on the highest ontological plane—namely, the plane of divinity—because, as he says, "it made me." Finally, he names the light: "You are my God." He uses the strongest possible statement, saying equivalently: This light is God. It is not a symbol for God, an analogy for God—it *is* God.

This example, I believe, clearly reveals the nature of a spiritual sense. With his inner eye, Augustine saw an unchangeable light, but what he experienced was not primarily the light, but the reality of God.

Bonaventure on the Spiritual Senses

With this in mind, we now turn to Bonaventure's major text on spiritual senses, which is found in chapter 4 of the *Itinerarium mentis in Deum*. Its context is very important since Bonaventure situates his teaching on the spiritual senses at a stage of the spiritual journey. After describing, in chapter 3, the reflection of God in our memory, understanding, and will, he turns in chapter 4 to the transformation of the soul by grace: "The image of our soul, therefore, should be clothed with the three theological virtues, by which the soul is purified, illumined, and perfected. And so the image is reformed and made like the heavenly Jerusalem and a part of the Church militant which, according to the Apostle, is the offspring of the heavenly Jerusalem." He then describes the spiritual senses:

> When by faith the soul believes in Christ as the uncreated Word and Splendor of the Father, it recovers its spiritual hearing and sight: its hearing to receive the words of Christ and its sight to view the splendors of that Light. When it longs in hope to receive the inspired

> Word, it recovers through desire and affection the spiritual sense of smell. When it embraces in love the Word incarnate, receiving delight from him and passing over into him through ecstatic love, it receives its senses of taste and touch.[44]

The soul can then encompass the Spouse:

> Having recovered these senses, when it sees its Spouse and hears, smells, tastes, and embraces him, the soul can sing like the bride of the Canticle of Canticles, which was composed for the exercise of contemplation in this fourth state. *No one* grasps this *except him who receives* (Apoc. 2:17), since it is more a matter of affective experience than rational consideration. For in this stage, when the inner senses are restored to see the highest beauty, to hear the highest harmony, to smell the highest fragrance, to taste the highest sweetness, to apprehend the highest delight, the soul is prepared for spiritual ecstasy through devotion, admiration, and exultation."[45]

One of the richest applications of Bonaventure's doctrine of the spiritual senses is found in his treatment of Francis's nature mysticism as he describes it in his *Legenda major* (or major biography of St. Francis). This passage is sprinkled with phrases from scripture and reflects the many passages in scripture dealing with nature. Speaking of Francis, he says:

> Aroused by all things
> to the love of God, he
> *rejoiced* in all *the works*
> *of the Lord's hands.*
> and from these joy-producing manifestations
> he rose to their life-giving
> principle and cause.
> In beautiful things
> he saw Beauty itself
> and through his *vestiges* imprinted on creation
> *he followed his Beloved* everywhere,
> making from all things a ladder
> by which he could climb up
> and embrace him *who is utterly desirable.*
> With a feeling of unprecedented devotion
> he savored
> in each and every creature—
> as in so many rivulets—
> that Goodness
> which is their fountain-source.
> And he perceived a heavenly harmony
> in the consonance
> of powers and activities
> God has given them,
> and like the prophet David
> sweetly exhorted them to praise the Lord.[46]

In this remarkable passage, Bonaventure refers to the five senses in such a way that they abundantly suggest the spiritual senses of the soul. The passage occurs in his chapter on Francis's fervent love and on the way that creatures stimulated Francis's love of

God. Bonaventure speaks of creatures also awakening Francis's spiritual sense of sight so that in beautiful things he saw beauty itself—the kinesthetic sense through which he followed his beloved's footprints everywhere, climbing up the ladder of creation to embrace his beloved through the spiritual sense of touch. Next comes the spiritual sense of taste and smell through which he savored each and every creature, as flowing from the "fountain-source" of divine goodness. Finally, Bonaventure awakens the spiritual sense of hearing through the heavenly order of the universe, suggesting the tradition of perceiving the "harmony of the spheres." At the climax of this passage, having awakened the five spiritual senses, Bonaventure obliquely refers to Francis's *Canticle of Brother Sun*, saying, "And like the prophet David sweetly exhorted them to praise the Lord."[47]

In the final stage of his *Soul's Journey,* Bonaventure evokes love and the spiritual sense of touch, quoting *The Mystical Theology* of the Pseudo-Dionysius, in order to bring about the transformation into ecstasy. However, unlike the Pseudo-Dionysius, he guides the reader into the darkness where mystical love is enkindled:

> But if you wish to know how these things come about,
> ask grace not instruction,
> the groaning of prayer not diligent reading,
> the Spouse not the teacher,
> God not man,
> darkness not clarity,
> not light but the fire
> that totally inflames and carries us into God
> by ecstatic unctions and burning affections.
> This fire is God,
> and *his furnace is in Jerusalem*;
> in the heat of his burning passion,
> which only he truly perceives who says:
> My soul chooses hanging and my bones death.[48]

Bonaventure reaches a climax and closes with images of darkness and death.

At this point I would like to make an observation about the spiritual senses that, to my knowledge, is not found articulated in the tradition but that, I think, is coherent and plausible. The level we have reached is above and beyond the kataphatic and even the apophatic. I believe that, here on the level of the highest spiritual senses, the negation of a spiritual sense such as sight or hearing, produces another spiritual sense—namely, darkness or silence—which I claim is positive, not negative. For on the level of our physical senses, in the case of sighted or hearing beings, to close one's eyes or one's ears produces not mere emptiness but the positive other side of sight and hearing. Thus the spiritual senses of the soul, even in darkness and silence, bring the soul into the immediate experience of God.

NOTES

1. Bonaventure, *Breviloquium*, prologue 6, 5, trans. José de Vinck, in *The Breviloquium* (Paterson, N.J., 1963).
2. Ibid., 1.
3. Ibid., 1, 1; 1, 4.
4. Ibid., 2, 1.

5. Ibid., 2, 4.
6. Ibid., 3, 1–3; *Disputed Questions on the Mystery of the Trinity*, q. 1, a. 2, corpus.
7. Ibid., 6, 4.
8. Gregory of Nyssa, *The Life of Moses*, trans. Abraham Malherbe and Everett Ferguson, in *Gregory of Nyssa: The Life of Moses* (New York, 1978), vol. 1, 46.
9. Ibid.
10. Pseudo-Dionysius, *The Mystical Theology*, trans. Colm Lubheid and Paul Rorem, in *Pseudo-Dionysius: The Complete Works* (New York, 1987), vol. 1, p. 3.
11. *The Cloud of Unknowing*, trans. James Walsh (New York, 1981), p. 6.
12. Ibid., p. 00.
13. Origen, *On First Principles*, trans. Rowan Greer, in *Origen: An Exhortation to Martyrdom, Prayer, and Selected Works* (New York, 1979), 4, 2, 4.
14. Augustine of Dacia, cited in the *New Catholic Encyclopedia*, s.v. "Exegesis, Medieval."
15. Dante, "Epistle to Can Grande della Scala," trans. Nancy Howe, in Mark Musa, ed., *Essays on Dante* (Bloomington, 1964), p. 37.
16. Thomas of Aquinas, *Summa Theologiae*, ed. Anton C. Pegis (New York, 1948, 1, q. 1, a. 10, corpus.
17. Bonaventure, *Breviloquium*, prologue, 4, 1.
18. Richard of St. Victor, *The Mystical Ark*, 1, 1; 4, 17–21.
19. Bonaventure, *The Soul's Journey into God*, 6, 4–7.
20. Richard of St. Victor, *The Mystical Ark*, trans. Grover Zinn, in *Richard of St. Victor: The Twelve Patriarchs, The Mystical Ark, Book Three of the Trinity* (New York, 1979), 1, 5.
21. Gregory of Nyssa, *The Life of Moses*, vol. 2, 122.
22. Ibid., vol. 1, 15.
23. Richard of St. Victor, *The Mystical Ark*, 1, 1.
24. Origen, *Commentary on the Song of Songs*, prologue, trans. Rowan Greer, in *Origen: An Exhortation to Martyrdom, Prayer, and Selected Works* (New York, 1979).
25. See Bernard of Clairvaux, *Sermons on the Song of Songs*, esp. sermon 7.
26. Teresa of Ávila, *The Interior Castle*, trans. Kieran Kavanaugh and Otilio Rodriguez, in *Teresa of Ávila: The Interior Castle* (New York, 1979), vol. 1, p. 1; vol. 7, pp. 1, 3.
27. See Cousins, "Francis of Assisi: Christian Mysticism at the Crossroads," in Steven T. Katz, ed., *Mysticism and Religious Traditions* (New York, 1983), pp. 166–169.
28. Bonaventure, *The Tree of Life*, in *Bonaventure: The Soul's Journey into God, The Tree of Life, The Life of St. Francis,* trans. Ewert Cousins (New York, 1978), p. 4.
29. Ibid.
30. R. E. L. Masters and Jean Houston, *The Varieties of Psychedelic Experience* (New York, 1966).
31. Stanislav Grof, *Realms of the Human Unconscious* (New York, 1975).
32. Masters and Houston, *The Varieties*, p. 308.
33. Ibid., p. 181.
34. Ibid., p. 207.
35. Ibid., pp. 218–19.
36. Grof, *Realms*, p. 147.
37. Masters and Houston, *The Varieties*, p. 308.
38. Bernard McGinn, *The Foundations of Mysticism: Origin to the Fifth Century* (New York, 1991), p. 121.
39. Karl Rahner, "The 'Spiritual Senses' According to Origen," *Theological Investigations*, vol. 16, pp. 81–103; see also "The Doctrine of the 'Spiritual Senses' in the Middle Ages," pp. 104–134.

40. Hans Urs von Balthasar, "Bonaventure," *Studies in Theological Style: Clerical Styles, The Glory of the Lord*, vol. 2, pp. 260–362.
41. Stephen Fields, "Balthasar and Rahner on the Spiritual Senses," *Theological Studies* 57 (1996), 224–241.
42. Origen, *On First Principles*, 1, 1c., no. 9, trans, in Karl Rahner, *Theological Investigations* (Baltimore, 1949), vol. 16, p. 83.
43. Augustine, *Confessions*, 8, 10, trans. John Ryan (New York, 1960).
44. Bonaventure, *The Soul's Journey into God*, trans. Ewert Cousins, in *Bonaventure: The Soul's Journey into God, The Tree of Life, The Life of St. Francis* (New York, 1978), chap. 4, no. 3.
45. Ibid.
46. Bonaventure, *Legenda maior* (The life of St. Francis), chap. 9, no. 1.
47. Ibid.
48. Bonaventure, *The Soul's Journey*, chap. 7, no. 6.

6

Classical Sufi Approaches to Scripture

PETER AWN

Historians of religion often equate scripture in Islam solely with the Qur'ān. But if scripture is understood to include those texts for which a claim of divine inspiration is made by the Muslim community, other bodies of Islamic religious literature must be included. Scripture in Islam encompasses the Qur'ān, which is understood by Muslims to be God's actual word transmitted though Muhammad; the divinely inspired Hadīth (tradition literature); and, arguably, the Sharīʿah (divinely revealed religious law) which is derived primarily from the Qur'ān and the Hadīth. This essay explores key strategies employed by Islamic mystics from the eighth through the fourteenth centuries to interpret these various genres of Muslim scripture.

Qur'ān

To appreciate the role of the Qur'ān in early Sufism, it is first necessary to describe the complex literary structure of this unique text. Arabia was an oral society before Muhammad, during his lifetime, and after his death. Memory, more frequently than writing, was the primary storage mechanism for fables, heroic tales, and complex poetry; transmission was done through recitation, which gave rise to a professional class of reciter/apprentices.

The revelations of God to Muhammad, through the mediacy of the Angel Gabriel, began at Mecca in the year 610 C.E. and lasted until his death at Medina in 632 C.E. According to Muslim sources, the revelations were preserved in the minds and hearts of the faithful, along with perhaps some few revelations written on bones, palms, barks, and parchment during Muhammad's lifetime. While non-Muslim scholars continue to explore the extent to which Muhammad may have been involved with the collection and codification of the Qur'ānic revelations, Muslim scholars generally affirm the following traditional account.

Because of the dispersion of the rapidly expanding Muslim community and the deaths of close companions of the Prophet in battle, there was concern that the process of oral transmission of the revelations would be disrupted or, worse, that some revelations would be lost. The early caliphs who succeeded to Muhammad's role as guardian of the community began a complex process of collection, thus initiating the move from orality to text. Muslim tradition records that, during the reign of the third caliph ʿUthmān (644–656 C.E.), the process of collection and codification was completed.

Muslims insist that there was no editing of the Qur'ān text by humans and that Muhammad was illiterate (*ummī*) (see Qur'ān 7:157), which thus made it impossible for him to have written the revelations. All efforts at collection focused on preserving God's actual words as they were transmitted to Muhammad. Consequently, the written Qur'ān vividly reflects its oral origins. The text is structurally fluid, with key phrases being repeated; moreover, the revelations are composed in a rhymed prose, which thus facilitates memorization. The chapters, (*suras*), which range from only a few to several hundred verses, are rarely narrative in structure. Longer *suras*, especially, appear to be compilations of contemporaneous revelations.

Because of the imprecise and ambiguous nature of the Arabic orthography of the period, the ʿUthmānic recension of the Qur'ān could not reproduce what was stored in the memory of the faithful. There were no diacritical marks that could have distinguished consonants of similar shape, and there were few indications of vowels. Reliance on memory, therefore, was essential for interpreting the written text. Over several centuries, diacritics and vowel marks were added, so that eventually the written document mirrored closely the Qur'ān of the oral tradition.

By the time orthography was able to accurately reproduce what was preserved in memory (by the ninth–tenth centuries), a number of different readings or vowelings of the Qur'ān had achieved prominence, seven of which, with a long and distinguished pedigree, were eventually canonized. At a relatively early date, the affirmation of multiple readings of even a few verses or sections of the Qur'ān established the possibility that God intended verses of the Qur'ān to have not only one meaning but also potentially a constellation of legitimate interpretations.

Alongside the recognition of the protean quality of Qur'ānic orality and of the principle of multiple readings, in the eighth and ninth centuries there emerged two main genres of Qur'ānic exegesis. The first, *tafsīr* (exoteric interpretation), is based on analyses of grammar, philology, historical context, relation to earlier scriptures of the Christians and Jews, dogmatics, and law. A classic of this genre is the *Tafsīr* of at-Tabarī (d. 932 C.E.).

The second exegetical method is *ta'wīl* (esoteric interpretation), which is associated primarily with the Shīʿah community and with Sufi exegetes. For the Shīʿah, the focus on hidden meanings of the Qur'ān was intended to legitimate the claims of ʿAlī (d. 661 C.E.) to the caliphate and to explore the theology of the Imām (infallible guide). For Sufis, *ta'wīl* unlocked the hidden (*bātin*) mystical meanings of the Qur'ān. A classic study of the emergence of Sufi *ta'wīl* is Paul Nwyia's *Exégèse coranique et langage mystique*, in which he demonstrates persuasively that early Sufi Qur'ān commentaries range from a more exoteric analysis of Qur'ānic terms, evident in the work of Muqātil ibn Sulaymān (d. 767 C.E.), to the fully developed esoteric Sufi commentary of the Shīʿah Imām and Sufi, Jaʿfar as-Sādiq (d. 765 C.E.):

> As an exegete, Muqātil focuses on the exoteric dimensions of the Qur'ān in which a symbol is situated alongside a Qur'ānic word, while Jaʿfar reads the Qur'ān through the mediacy of his own experience in which both symbol and word are synthesized. From that moment on, a new form of exegesis was established, which is no longer the reading of the Qur'ān but the reading of experience within [the context of] a new interpretation of the Qur'ān.[1]

Sufi *ta'wīl* is predicated on the conviction that the Qur'ān is a living document, a "thou" rather than an "it." Esoteric insight depends on the continued spiritual growth of the individual Sufi. The relationship between Sufi and sacred word is dynamic: as the Sufi achieves greater levels of spiritual insight, the word reveals more of its hidden meanings.

The Divine–human relationship in the Qur'ān is cemented by a covenant though which Lord (*rabb*) and servant (*ʿabd*) are bound.[2] God's sovereignty and His transcendence echo throughout the text. Scholars have argued that one of the catalysts for the emergence of Islamic mysticism in the eighth century was the desire on the part of some Muslims to balance the Qur'ānic emphasis on God's radical otherness with an exploration of His immanence, which led to the establishment of a relationship of intimacy between the soul and the Creator.

The Qur'ān does not focus in any major way on spiritual interiority or mystical transformation but stresses faith in the oneness of God and in Muhammad's role as messenger and seal of the prophets; the consequences of unbelief and hypocrisy; eschatology and apocalypticism; an elaborate system of ethics; the building of community; and ritual/legal obligations. As Annemarie Schimmel has pointed out, however, the Sufis mined the text for verses on which to base their claims for union with the divine. Most creative was the Sufi exegesis of Qur'ān 7:172, known as the verse of the primordial covenant, in which God calls forth, from the children of Adam, their seed—that is, all potential human souls—and asks, "Am I not Your Lord?" They cry out in unison, "Yes, we witness [to it]."[3] Sufi theorists argue that there is no more significant expression of mystical union than this primordial covenant. And the goal of Sufism as a spiritual method is to recapture that moment and place it in a time before time, when God and the souls of all potential humans were most fully united. The verse is so well known among Sufi poets that the Arabic phrase *Alastu* (Am I not?) is all that is needed to evoke the image. In Persian and other non-Arabic mystical poetry, references to the "Day of Alast" (*rūz-i alast*) are common.

Qur'ānic verses that can be interpreted as affirming an ontological relationship between God and the soul are equally cherished. One of the most well known of these is *sura* 50:16: "We (God) are nearer to him than (his) jugular vein." Literally, the pulsating life force is created by God at every moment, confirming His immanence within humankind. Equally as influential are *suras* 15:28–29 and 32:7–9, in which, at the moment of creation, God breathes into humans "of His Spirit" (*min rūhihi*), which thus establishes an ontological link between Creator and created that is essential if the soul is to come to know and experience the divine.

Farīd ad-Dīn ʿAttār (d.c. 1220 C.E.), in his sophisticated mystical fable *The Conference of the Birds*, compares the divine to the mythic bird, Simourgh. The birds' souls' ability to progress along the Sufi path is predicated on their essential ontological link with the Simourgh, without which they would have no recollection of the existence of the Simourgh and would not know that he can be sought. As ʿAttār describes it, the Simourgh in a distant past let one of his feathers fall to earth. The feather's fame spread and each individual believed he or she knew its true form:

> If the trace of his feather had not been made visible,
> This worldwide uproar would not have occurred.
> All of these signs were produced from its splendor,
> All human souls (spring) from the trace of His feather.[4]

Ontology is not the only major focus of early Sufi theorists in their Qurʾānic exegesis. Perhaps more widespread are commentaries in the form of word studies, exploring individual Qurʾānic terms for their exoteric and/or esoteric implications for mysticism. Here again, Nwyia is particularly helpful. He discusses at length the work of the Sufi exegete Tirmidhī Hakīm (d.c. 932 C.E.), contrasting his approach to word analysis with that of the earlier commentator Muqātil ibn Sulaymān (d. 767 C.E.):

> It is clear, in fact, that Muqātil was content to align different meanings of the same word without making the effort to establish a hierarchy among these meanings. This [approach] gives at times an arbitrary quality to his inventory (of terms). The methodology that he followed, [namely], only to comment on the Qurʾān using the Qurʾān, and only to interpret a word by its context, probably did not allow him to discover a principle of order by which to hierarchize its various meanings (lit., *wujūh*, "faces").
>
> Tirmidhī was able to discover this principle thanks to a century of history during which Muslim consciousness moved from the stage of naive objectivity to that of subjective experience. Compared to this [commentary] of Muqātil, his [Tirmidhī Hakīm's] work possesses major interest for us because it allows us to witness, as it covers the same ground where Muqātil worked, the transformation of a methodology, thanks to the insights that a new principle of exegesis afforded him: religious experience.[5]

One of the many Qurʾānic terms whose richness is revealed through Sufi exegesis is *dhikr* (remembrance). The root *dh-k-r* appears well over 250 times in the Qurʾān. But the phrases "remembrance of Allah" and "remember Allah" are the most evocative and ripe for Sufi interpretation.[6] The exoteric analysis of Qurʾānic "remembrance" focuses on believers' remembering God at all times; and on the acknowledgement by the faithful of God's grace and blessing, manifest through His creative power and sovereignty over the cosmos. Sufi *taʾwīl*, in contrast, emphasizes interior transformation through the ritual repetition of divine names. Nwyia's summary of Tirmidhī Hakīm's commentary on *dhikr* is illuminating: "*Dhikr*, writes Tirmidhī, is the heart racing towards God, inflamed with His love (*hubb*) and (with) desire (*shawq*) for Him."[7]

Sufi exegesis of Qurʾānic technical terminology is the basis for the evolution of another foundational genre of Sufi literature, namely, manuals of the spiritual life. The writers of Sufi manuals often included analyses of critical terms, both Qurʾānic and extra-Qurʾānic, in their overall exposition of the Sufi path. One of the most well known early manuals is the *Kitāb at-ta ʿarruf* of Abū Bakr Muhammad al-Kalābādhī (d. 990 C.E.), whose discussion of *dhikr* encompasses a number of themes that have become standard within the Sufi tradition. "True remembrance (*dhikr*)," explains al-Kalābādhī, "is that you forget everything except the One Remembered in the act of remembrance."

Dhikr is a multifaceted practice with numerous hierarchical divisions.[8] Al-Kalābādhī, relying on the famous Sufi Ibn ʿAtā' (d. 922 C.E.), outlines one model of the stages of *dhikr*:

> The first is *dhikr* of the heart, meaning that the One Remembered is no longer forgotten but is now remembered. The second is *dhikr* of the attributes of the One Remembered. The third is contemplation of the One Remembered, which [requires] that one annihilate *dhikr* because the attributes of the One Remembered annihilate you from your own attributes, and thus you annihilate *dhikr*.[9]

There are many other classifications of Sufi *dhikr* that are found in the manual literature, but most emphasize that *dhikr* begins as an audible, rhythmic remembrance of God—*dhikr* of the tongue (*lisān*)—and progresses to *dhikr* of the heart (*qalb*), a soundless repetition of divine names in unison with the natural rhythm of heartbeats, culminating in *dhikr* of one's innermost essence (*sirr*), wherein the seeker's whole being resonates with the repetition of divine names.

Ḥadīth

The richness of Sufi theory based on Qur'ānic sources is equaled only by the Sufi hermeneutics of the second most important body of scripture in Islam—the tradition literature, or Ḥadīth. As a literary genre, the traditions mirror the fundamental orality of the Qur'ān. Not only did the early community focus on the preservation in memory of God's Word, but also, Muslim sources insist they memorized the teachings of Muhammad and his earliest companions as well. During the ninth and tenth centuries, a number of scholars scoured the Islamic world to collect hundreds of thousands of these traditions, evaluating them for authenticity and preserving them in written form.

The process of authentication focused primarily on the chain of transmitters (*isnād*) for each Ḥadīth. Were the transmitters historically able to transmit to one another? Were they individuals of probity and sound learning? Ḥadīth scholars developed categories of varying reliability in order to classify Ḥadīth: *Sahīh*, sound; *Hasan*, good; *Daʿīf*, weak; *Saqīm*, infirm. Muslim Ḥadīth scholars did not scrutinize, in any significant way, the actual texts of the Ḥadīth as a means of verifying authenticity. If the *isnād* is affirmed as sound, the body of the text (*matn*) is presumed to be fundamentally accurate.

The reason for this reluctance to subject the *matn* to internal criticism was Muslim scholars' insistence that, as with the Qur'ān, the Ḥadīth are divinely inspired—it is not for humans to tamper with either of these genres of Islamic scripture, only to preserve and interpret them. As the famous theologian al-Ghazālī (d. 1111 C.E.) argues:

> God does not have two words, one expressed in the Qur'ān style which we are bidden to recite publicly, and called the Qur'ān, while the other word is not Qur'ān. God has but one word which differs in the mode of its expression. On occasions, God indicates His Word by the Qur'ān, on others, by words in another style, not publicly recited, and called Sunna (i.e., Ḥadīth). Both were mediated by the Prophet.[10]

The move from orality to text in the tradition literature evolved over several centuries, culminating in the ninth and tenth centuries, at which time a number of extensive collections of Ḥadīth were prepared by Muslim scholars. The two best-known ones are the multivolume collections of al-Bukhārī (d. 870 C.E.) and of Muslim (d. 875 C.E.), although a number of others achieved prominence in both Sunnī and Shīʿah circles.[11]

The question of the authenticity of Ḥadīth is perhaps most contentious between Muslim and non-Muslim scholars. The majority of traditional Muslims are committed to the belief that the Ḥadīth are historically accurate. The process of collection, evaluation, and codification of Ḥadīth, they insist, was fundamentally sound, preserving only those Ḥadīth that are, on the whole, reliable. Non-Muslim scholars argue a substantially different position—namely, that many, if not most, Ḥadīth came into existence later than the period of Muhammad's life and that their contents often reflect theological and legal debates of a significantly later period. Unfortunately, several prominent non-Muslim scholars described this process of Ḥadīth creation as "fabrication," asserting that most Ḥadīth are fraudulent constructions employed by lawyers, theologians, and politicians to foist their positions on the Islamic community. The term *fabrication* is offensive and understood by Muslim scholars as a blatant attempt to derogate Islamic scripture.

There is a certain irony in the fact that European and American scholars, many of whom are Christians and Jews, continue to use the term *fabrication* for Ḥadīth without describing their own scriptures in similar fashion. Modern New Testament scholarship, for example, has proven without a doubt that the Christian scriptures are texts produced considerably later than the period of Jesus' lifetime and are a fascinating combination of history and myth, in which critical theological questions are resolved by putting solutions into the mouth of the founder.

While the narrative structure of the New Testament is different from the *isnād-matn* structure of Ḥadīth, the function of both scriptures is similar, for they ground change and theological development in the original experience that spawned the movement. These texts are sophisticated and successful attempts to ensure that the later community, different though it may be from the community that existed during the lifetime of the founder, understands that it is fundamentally continuous with the original vision.

The use of *isnād*s for authenticating traditions carries over into biographical and historical texts, as well as into Qurʾān commentary. A myth of critical importance both for the Muslim community and for Sufi theorists is the story of the night journey and the ascension of Muhammad. It appears in the early biography of Muhammad, *Sīrat rasūl Allah*, by Ibn Isḥāq (d. 767 C.E.), in Ḥadīth form. After listing the major figures, both male and female, on whose testimony he relies for details of the story, Ibn Isḥāq explains how he will organize the material:

> The following account reached me from. . . ; [the lengthy list of transmitters follows]. It is pieced together in the story that follows, each one contributing something of what he was told about what happened when he [Muhammad] was taken on the night journey. . . . It was certainly an act of God by which He took him by night in what way He pleased to show him His signs, which He willed him to see so that he witnessed His mighty sovereignty and power by which He does what He wills to do.[12]

Ibn Isḥāq's version covers the basic outlines of the myth: Muhammad falls asleep near the sacred cube (*Kaʿbah*) in Mecca and is carried miraculously by Gabriel from Mecca to Jerusalem, from where he ascends through the seven heavens while being mounted on the fabled steed Burāq; and he encounters the prophets of the Jewish and Christian traditions, who acknowledge that Muhammad supersedes them. In some later versions Muhammad actually enters the divine presence and sees God.

Over time, the night journey and the ascension evolved into the subjects of an elaborate and multilayered myth, examples of which exist in all Islamic languages.[13] Interestingly, however, later versions include only a radically abridged *isnād* or none at all, perhaps because the story was so widely accepted and no longer needed authentication. Many of the complex elements of the myth of the night journey and the ascension lent themselves in a very creative way to Sufi interpretation. Muhammad's ascent through the seven heavens (which in the original myth is concerned with affirming Islam's continuity with, and supersession of, the Abrahamic faiths and with Muhammad's role as seal of the prophets) is interpreted by Sufis as an allegory of the spiritual path. The soul mounts through seven stages of mystical transformation, which culminate in the vision of the Beloved.

ʿAttār's mystical fable, *The Conference of the Birds*, mirrors this seven-tiered structure in its description of the seven valleys through which the birds must pass in order to reach the Simourgh.[14] In another of his epic poems, *the Ilāhī-nāma, or Book of God*, ʿAttār states, in greater detail, his mystical interpretation of Muhammad's night journey and ascension in the traditional introductory encomium that cites the Prophet:

> When the Holy Prophet set out upon Burāq, he rose with the speed of lightning to the seventh heaven.
> He rose, thus mounted, up to the throne of God, for he was lord of Burāq and of the pulpit.
>
> . . . .
>
> He unfurled his banner over the empyrean and took his stand on the "seat of truth." [See Qurʾān 54:544–555]
> There came a cry from the denizens of the heavens: "The Lord of the World has come to the trysting-place."

After a description of Muhammad's encounters with the Abrahamic prophets, and the ecstasy of the cosmos in response to his ascension, the poet brilliantly translates Muhammad's traditional encounter with God during his ascension into an allegory of mystical union.

> So did his soul perspire with longing for God that he rent his robe into a hundred pieces.
> Aye, since the sky was his robe he rent it all, for that night he could do nothing else.
> The proof of this is the Milky Way, which is made up of small pieces of the nine curtains.
> Those nine curtains were rent to pieces during his ascension, because he was the intimate of God forever.
>
> . . . .
>
> The Prophet said: "Lord, Thou knowest how I feel, Thou hast no need to question me.
> Thy favours are so continuous that I cannot count them; my tongue is tied.
> Nothing is left of my being; all is now sun, the shadow is gone."[15]

Annemarie Schimmel points out that in ʿAttār's mystical interpretation of the night journey and the ascension, Gabriel plays a unique role. Despite his angelic nature, Gabriel is not permitted to enter the divine presence, but must wait "at the lote tree of the farthest boundary" (Qurʾān 53:14). Only Muhammad is permitted to enter, demonstrating Muhammad's superiority over both the material and spiritual worlds:

> In the famous *ḥadīth* connected with this mystery the Prophet said *Lī ma'a Allah waqt . . .*, "I have a time with God to which even Gabriel, who is pure spirit, is not admitted."[16] This remark is interpreted as pertaining to the mystery of the heavenly journey, in which the Prophet was taken out of serial, created time and touched by the Eternal Now of God. The term *waqt*, "time," then, became a central concept in Sufi life: The Sufi is called to give himself over completely to this Divine moment, to be *ibnu'l-waqt*, "son of the moment," that is, to live in the moment of Divine inspiration.[17]

It is Muhammad who epitomizes the "son of the moment"; and al-Hujwīrī (d.c. 1071 C.E.), in his renowned Sufi manual, *Kashf al-mahjūb*, understands Muhammad's ascension as his mounting to the mystical station of proximity to the divine:[18]

> He [Muhammad] desired that his body should be destroyed and his personality be dissolved, but God's purpose was to establish His proof. He bade the Apostle remain in the state that he was in; whereupon he gained strength and displayed the existence of God from out of his own nonexistence and said, "I am not as one of you. Verily, I pass the night with my Lord, and he gives me food and drink"; and he also said, "I am with God in a state in which none of the cherubim nor any prophet is capable of being contained with me."[19]

The exaltation of Muhammad within Sufi circles was the catalyst for a fascinating process of revisionist history, which argues that Muhammad was himself a Sufi saint who underwent spiritual transformation before his appointment by God to the prophetic office. The link between sainthood and prophecy was explored by numerous classical Sufi authors like al-Hujwīrī, who defends the moderate view that saints are never superior to prophets; rather, the saint's role is to confirm the prophetic mission. The final stage of saintship is only the beginning of prophecy and, while all prophets are saints, not all saints rise to the prophetic office.[20]

Many of the most creative Ḥadīth employed by Sufi poets and theorists are not found in the early canonical collections but most probably emerge out of later Sufi circles. When Ḥadīth appear in a Sufi text, they frequently lack full *isnād*s; the text is simply introduced by indicating that the Apostle Muhammad said such and such. The creation of Ḥadīth by Sufis, in order to substantiate their theoretical claims for mysticism, is analogous to the creation of canonical Ḥadīth in an effort to argue particular theological and legal positions. One of the most interesting subgenres of Ḥadīth, which Sufis employed with great skill to promote their mystical theory, is known as Ḥadīth Qudsī—that is, Ḥadīth whose *isnād*s go back not to Muhammad but to God himself. While some Ḥadīth Qudsī appear in the canonical sources, many that are fundamental to Sufism are noncanonical.

The most famous of these Sufi Ḥadīth Qudsī is one whose philosophical core resonates throughout thirteenth-century mystical poetry and philosophy: God said, "I was a hidden treasure and I desired to be known, so I created creation in order that I might be known."[21] In some Sufi versions of this Ḥadīth Qudsī, the phrase "I desired to be known" is replaced by "I desired to be loved."[22] The renowned poet Jalāl ad-Dīn Rūmī (d. 1273 C.E.) integrates this Ḥadīth Qudsī into one of his well-known poems, vividly capturing the significance of his Ḥadīth Qudsī for Sufism:

> David[23] said, O King [of the universe], since you have no need of us,
> Tell us at last what wisdom there was in creating the two worlds.

> The [God who is] Truth answered him, "O temporal man, I was a hidden treasure,
> I desired that that treasure of beneficence and favour be revealed,
> I made manifest a mirror, its face the heart, its back the world,
> Its back is better than its face if you have no knowledge of the face.[24]

This particular Ḥadīth Qudsī reinterprets in dramatic fashion the traditional creation myth in the Qur'ān. As in the Hebrew and the Christian scriptural traditions, God in the Qur'ān is understood to create ex nihilo (out of nothing). In contrast, the Sufi understanding of creation enshrined in this Ḥadīth Qudsī is considerably more reminiscent of Hellenistic emanation theory than of *creatio ex nihilo*. This emanationist model is foundational to the mystical philosophy of Ibn ʿArabī (d. 1240 C.E.) and of his school, and to his key concept of *wahdat al-wujūd* (the unity of being). All created reality, which is a projection of God, will eventually return to the source from which it emerged, the undifferentiated One. Created reality, including the soul, possesses only an illusory independence. Eventually the soul will return to the One, like a drop of water returning to the ocean. As the Persian poets of the period repeat time and time again, *Hamé ūst* (All is He).

Rūmī's identification in his poem of the face of the mirror with the heart of the Sufi points once again to the fundamental ontological link between God and humans. Another well-known Sufi Ḥadīth reinforces this ontological vision: "He who knows his inner self, knows his Lord." Schimmel explains that mystical theorists have relied heavily on this particular Ḥadīth: "To know one's innermost heart means to discover the point at which the divine is found as the *dulcis hospes animae*, the meeting point of the human and the divine."[25]

For Sufi theorists like al-Hujwīrī, this particular Ḥadīth points first to the realization that humans are finite and perishable, while God is infinite and eternal; that God is the Almighty Lord and humans are humble servants. Second, this Ḥadīth evokes the experiences of gnosis (maʿrifah) and of annihilation (fanāʾ), in which the self is obliterated in the divine:

> In this sense the Apostle said: "He who knows himself has come to know his Lord," i.e., he who knows himself to be annihilated knows God to be eternally subsistent. Annihilation destroys reason and all human attributes, and when the substance of a thing is not accessible to reason it cannot possibly be known without amazement (*hayrah*)."[26]

In Rūmī's work, creation, while clearly a reflection of the divine, can become a trap if the Sufi does not progress through the signs of God in the material world to an encounter with Him in the heart/soul. In the Sufi quest for union with the divine, the role of the world and materiality is a hotly contested issue. Perhaps the greatest contrast to Rūmī's love of nature is found in the writings of one of the earliest and best-known Sufi ascetics, Hasan al-Basrī (d. 728 C.E.). In a letter to the Umayyad caliph ʿUmar ibn ʿAbd al-ʿAzīz, who ruled the empire from 717 to 720 C.E., Hasan quotes a tradition from God that is more reminiscent of gnosticism than of traditional Islam: "For this world has neither worth nor weight with God; so slight it is, it weighs not with God so much as a pebble or a single clod of earth; as I am told, God has created nothing more hateful to Him than the world, and from the day He created it He has not looked upon it, so much He hates it."[27] While Rūmī's understanding of the role of the world in mysticism is the more prevalent, there is no doubt that Sufis in general were highly suspicious of the world's enticements and feared its ultimately corrupting influence.

Sharīʿah

During Muhammad's lifetime, the reign of the first four caliphs, and the Umayyad dynasty (661 C.E.–750 C.E.), Muslim legal practice was based primarily on the general ethical principles and specific regulations articulated in the Qurʾānic revelations and on the pre-Islamic customary law of Arabia, Syria, and Iraq. As Joseph Schacht points out in his seminal work on Islamic law, the legal debates in the eighth and ninth centuries were over whether local customary law would be the principal basis for evolving legal theory, or whether Ḥadīth that went back to Muhammad would be the principal foundational element.[28] The former position argued for diversity by canonizing long-standing local legal practices; the latter argued the need for a universal legal theory that would apply in all cultural areas and would mirror the universality of the Qurʾān. The latter position prevailed, due particularly to the brilliant work of the legal theorist ash-Shāfiʿī (d. 820 C.E.).

Four classical schools of Islamic law (*Sharīʿah*) eventually emerged as the primary repositories of canonical legal theory, each school being named after a prominent theorist of the period: the Hanafī School (named after Abū Hanīfa, d. 767 C.E.), the Mālikī School (after Mālik ibn Anas, d. 796 C.E.), the Shāfiʿī School (after ash-Shāfiʿī, d. 820 C.E.), and the Hanbalī School (after Ahmad ibn Hanbal, d. 855 C.E.). Shīʿah religious law is often included by scholars as a fifth school. The differences among the four canonical Sunnī legal schools are considerably fewer than the areas in which they agree. One or the other school tends to predominate in a particular geographical region, although in complex urban environments all schools are represented.

Islamic legal theory (*fiqh*) is founded primarily on the Qurʾān and Ḥadīth, while *qiyās* (the use of analogy) and *ijmāʿ* (community consensus) are recognized by scholars as key parts of the process as well. Since Sharīʿah is derived from revealed and inspired scripture (the Qurʾān and Ḥadīth), it too is understood to be divinely inspired. Islamic law, argue traditional legists, is not a human construct that can be altered or changed at will. On the contrary, the ideals and prescriptions of Sharīʿah are universally applicable and ahistorical, in the sense that they are not bound or conditioned by any historical moment but have been true in the past, are true now, and will be true in the future.

Despite the centrality of this divinely revealed legal tradition in Islam, Sufis debated, sometimes fiercely, the appropriate role of Sharīʿah in mysticism. While the debate is interesting, more relevant are the different ways various classical Sufis actually dealt with religious law in their mystical theory. For example, one early group known as the Malāmatiyya (seekers after blame) engaged in private strict observance of the law, while in public they acted in ways shocking to the community. Schimmel recounts a story related by the poet Jāmī (d. 1492 C.E.) about a famous Sufi, who, on entering a town, was hailed by the inhabitants. But as the entourage progressed down the road, the Sufi urinated in a ritually objectionable fashion. The crowd dispersed and people never again believed in his spiritual accomplishments. The Malāmatiyya were so committed to *ikhlās* (total sincerity) that they deliberately chose to keep secret their spiritual progress and good deeds. Moreover, the condemnation of them by the community prevented their succumbing to excessive pride.[29]

The Malāmatiyya represents a clear minority among Sufis of the classical period. A considerably more complex and sophisticated reinterpretation of the role of Sharīʿah is epitomized by the writings of one of the great Sufis of the tenth century, Husayn ibn Mansūr al-Hallāj (d. 922 C.E.), whose "*Ana ʾl-Haqq*" (I am the divine truth!) rings throughout the history of Sufism as the paradigmatic ecstatic utterance.

For many in the Islamic community, both Sufi and non-Sufi, al-Hallāj's ecstatic cry "*Ana ʾl-Haqq*" was tantamount to self-divinization, equating himself with God, one of whose ninety-nine names is al-Haqq. Al-Hallāj defends himself by comparing his state to two figures from the Qurʾān: the devil (Iblīs) and Pharaoh. In a masterful exercise of Qurʾānic *taʾwīl*, al-Hallāj argues that both Iblīs and Pharaoh attained unique levels of spiritual intimacy with the divine.[30] Despite the fact that both are condemned in traditional sources as prideful sinners, al-Hallāj insists that their actions were morally correct and dictated by the Beloved:

> My friend and my teacher are Iblīs and Pharaoh. Iblīs was threatened with the fire, but he did not go back on his preaching. And Pharaoh was drowned in the Red Sea, but he did not acknowledge any mediator at all. . . . And if I were killed, or if my hands and feet were cut off, I would not go back on my preaching.[31]

Al-Hallāj's paradoxical spiritual elevation of Iblīs and Pharaoh, and his insistence that God's curse is in fact a sign of His unique favor, are key elements in his understanding of the role of Sharīʿah in mysticism. Al-Hallāj's writings imply that two levels of legal observance exist, one exoteric and the other esoteric. Exoteric law—that is, traditional Sharīʿah—applies primarily to the masses of the Muslim community. For the ecstatic Sufi, in contrast, behavior is dictated not solely by Sharīʿah but also by the beloved, who reveals His will to the lover in the experience of mystical union.

What is most interesting about al-Hallāj's approach to law is his affirmation that both the exoteric and esoteric models are true, but that they apply to different people according to their spiritual accomplishments. In one of his most famous poems, al-Hallāj expresses this position dramatically by insisting that his own execution is sanctioned by the exoteric law, while his ecstatic utterances, for which he is being condemned, are sanctioned by the hidden guidance of the beloved—both the community and al-Hallāj act in accordance with God's will. He writes:

> Kill me my trusted friends,
> for in my death is my life!
> Death for me is in living, and
> life for me is in dying.
> The obliteration of my essence
> is the noblest of blessings.
> My perdurance in my human attributes,
> the vilest of evils.[32]

Other Sufis of the classical period expressed even more radical reinterpretations of Sharīʿah. Abū Saʿīd ibn Abī ʾl-Khayr (d. 1049 C.E.), for example, began his life as a Sufi ascetic who meticulously observed the Sharīʿah. It is said that he never ate during the day, nor did he sleep at night except by standing up. In one story, his father discovers him hanging by his feet in a pit while he recites the Qur'ān.

Yet when Abū Sa'īd attained gnosis (*ma'rifah*) during his fortieth year—a state he enjoyed until his death—he abandoned his asceticism because he was now totally detached from worldly realities. Whether he dressed in rags or brocade, it was all the same because of his spiritual state.

In addition to his rejection of the ascetic life, Abū Sa'īd also challenged pivotal ritual practices enshrined in the Sharī'ah. The tradition reports that, on one occasion, Abū Sa'īd and his disciples were engaged in *samā'*, listening to music and performing ritual dance, when a pious Muslim interrupted to announce the time of prayer. Abū Sa'īd replied that they were already at prayer and ordered that the rapturous music and dance continue.

Another fable focuses on Abū Sa'īd's refusal to perform the required hajj, or pilgrimage to Mecca: "Why have I not performed the Pilgrimage? It is no great matter that thou shouldst tread under thy feet a thousand miles of ground in order to visit a stone house." More shocking is his proclamation that the celestial archetype of the *Ka'bah* comes several times a day to circumambulate him![33]

There is real danger in interpreting these Sufi fables literally. Whether or not Abū Sa'īd in fact said and did what his biographer claims he said and did is impossible to verify. There is no doubt, however, that this particular genre of Sufi fable in which Sharī'ah was challenged was relatively common. More often than not, however, the point of the challenge is not to suggest that Sufis reject Islamic law, but to illustrate vividly that, while traditional legal practice is appropriate for the majority of Muslims, Sufis must not lose sight of their higher calling—the attainment of mystical union.

This challenge of Sharī'ah can be found in the works of Sufis who are themselves archconservatives in terms of law and Qur'ānic exegesis. 'Abdullāh Ansārī (d. 1089 C.E.), whose book of prayerful colloquies, *Munājāt*, is a classic of the spiritual life, was a follower of the most conservative intellectual tradition in law and theology—that of Ibn Hanbal. Yet his embracing of textual literalism resulted in Ansārī's refusal to require logic from scripture. On the contrary, he gloried in the paradoxes inherent in his literalism:

> Whether the Beloved gives us agony or pleasure,
> Whatever comes from the Beloved is good.
> We do not think of good or evil—
> Our intent is His pleasure and contentment.[34]

Ansārī, like Abū Sa'īd, criticizes traditional ritual practice in order to jolt the Sufi initiate into taking seriously the goals of mysticism. The five pillars of Islam, he suggests, are a distraction for the Sufi. The pilgrimage appears an occasion for tourism; almsgiving is something that should be left to philanthropists; fasting is a fine way to conserve food; and ritual prayer should be left to old women.

> Fall in love:
> That is doing something![35]

While Abū Sa'īd's and Ansārī's use of Sharī'ah is especially creative, it is important to realize that most Sufis expressed a more moderate position, emphasizing that the mystic must remain faithful to the religious obligations embodied in Islamic law even as he continues on the quest for gnosis and union. Al-Ghazālī takes the argument one step further, arguing that obligatory rituals and, by extension, all religious laws are essential to spiritual growth and should be compared to complex medical remedies employed by physicians. While medicines cure the body's ills, ritual practices are cures for the soul. It is impossible to fully understand why medicines are effective, so the patient must blindly obey the physician who has learned his art from the prophets, who, because of their prophetic powers, came to understand the medicinal properties of natural substances:

> In a similar fashion it became necessarily evident to me that the reason for the effectiveness of the remedies of the acts of worship, with their prescriptions and determined quantities ordained by the prophets, cannot be perceived by means of the intellectual resources of men endowed with intellect. On the contrary, they must be the object of blind obedience to the prophets who perceived those qualities by the light of prophecy, not by intellectual resources.[36]

Rather than relegate the efficacy of religious law solely to the exoteric realm of the nonmystic, al-Ghazālī insists that legal observance keeps the Sufi immersed in the broader community that mediates spiritual power. To abandon the legal tradition is to abandon any link to the Islamic community (*Ummah*) and thus to be incapable of true spiritual growth. Sharīʿah, contrary to being a barrier or, worse, superfluous, is essential to progress along the Sufi path.

NOTES

1. Paul Nwyia, *Exégèse coranique et langage mystique* (Beirut, 1970), pp. 160–161.
2. See especially Qur'ān 2:83–96, 3:81, 5:7, 5:12–14, 5:70–71, 7:172–173, 20:115, and 33:7–8.
3. Annemarie Schimmel, *Mystical Dimensions of Islam* (Chapel Hill, 1975), pp. 23–26.
4. Farīduddīn ʿAttār, *Mantiqu 't-tayr*, ed. Muhammad Javād Mashkūr (Tehran, 1353 A.H./1968 C.E.), p. 47, ll. 6–7. For a very readable free translation in verse of this particular work, see *The Conference of the Birds*, trans. and intro. Afkham Darbandi and Dick Davis (New York, 1984).
5. Nwyia, *Exégèse coranique et langage mystique*, p. 120.
6. The phrase "remembrance of Allah" occurs in *sūra*s 5:91, 13:28, 24:37, 29:45, 39:22, 39:23, 57:16, 58:19, 62:9, and 63:9; the phrase "remember Allah" occurs in *sura*s 2:198, 2:200, 2:203, 2:239, 4:103, 33:41, and 62:10.
7. Nwyia, *Exégèse coranique et langage mystique*, p. 130.
8. Abu Bakr Muhammad al-Kalābādhī, *Kitāb at-ta ʿarruf li madhhab ahli 't-tasawwuf*, ed. ʿAbd al-Halīm Mahmoud and Taha ʿAbd al-Bāqī Sarūr (Cairo, 1380 A.H./1960 C.E.), p. 103. For an English translation of this Sufi manual, see A. J. Arberry, *The Doctrine of the Sufis* (Cambridge, 1966).
9. al-Kalābādhī, *Kitāb at-ta ʿarruf*, p. 106. For an interesting discussion of various kinds of *dhikr* and its role in Sufism, see Schimmel, *Mystical Dimensions of Islam*, pp. 167–178.
10. Abū Hāmid Muhammad al-Ghazālī, *Kitāb al- Mustasfā*, 2 vols. (Cairo, 1322 A.H.), vol. 1, p. 125. This passage is quoted by John Burton in *The Collection of the Qur'ān* (Cambridge, 1977), p. 57.

11. Among the Sunnīs, the following individuals are credited with the most authentic collections of Ḥadīth: al-Bukhārī (d. 870 C.E.), Muslim (d. 875 C.E.), Abū Dawūd (d. 888 C.E.), at-Tirmidhī (d. 892 C.E.), Ibn Māja (d. 886 C.E.), and An-Nasā'ī (d. 915 C.E.). In addition to the above, the Shīʿah community canonized a number of collections of traditions whose *isnāds* focus primarily on ʿAlī and his descendants, the later Shīʿah Imāms. Among these collections are those of al-Kulaynī (d. 939 C.E.), al-Qummī (d. 991 C.E.), at-Tūsī (d. 1067 C.E.), and ash-Sharīf al-Murtadā (d. 1044 C.E.). In the same way that Shīʿah *ta'wīl* was used to legitimate the claims of ʿAlī and his family, so too do Shīʿah Ḥadīth function as critical sources of political and religious legitimation.
12. Muhammad ibn Ishāq, *The Life of Muhammad: A Translation of Ibn Ishaq's Sirat Rasul Allah*, trans. Alfred Guillaume, (Oxford, 1955; rpt. Lahore, 1974), pp. 181–182.
13. One of the most popular Arabic versions is the *Miʿrāj al-kabīr* of Najm ad-Dīn al-Ghaytī (d. 1574 C.E.), trans. Arthur Jeffery, in *A Reader on Islam* (The Hague, 1962; rpt. New York, 1980). See also the translation of a Swahili version of the myth in *Textual Sources for the Study of Islam*, ed. and trans. Andrew Rippin and Jan Knappert (Chicago, 1990), pp. 68–72. A superb illuminated manuscript from Central Asia of the night journey and the ascension has been edited by Marie-Rose Séguy, *The Miraculous Journey of Mahomet: Miʿrāj-Nāmeh* (New York, 1977).
14. Farīd ad-Dīn ʿAttār, *The Conference of the Birds*, pp. 166–229.
15. Farīd ad-Dīn ʿAttār. *The Ilāhī-nāma or Book of God*, trans. John Andrew Boyle (Manchester, 1976), pp. 12–13, 15–16.
16. This Ḥadīth, Schimmel indicates, can be found in Badī ʿuzzamān Furūzānfar's *Ahādīth-i Mathnawī* (Tehran, 1955), n.100.
17. Annemarie Schimmel, *And Muhammad Is His Messenger* (Chapel Hill, 1985), pp. 168–169.
18. There continued to be a serious debate among classical Sufi writers about whether or not Muhammad actually saw God during his ascension. Al-Kalābādhī, in his *Kitāb at-taʿarruf*, summarizes the different positions and argues for the more moderate view, asserting that Muhammad did not see God with his eyes. Yet he acknowledges that some Sufis insist that Muhammad saw God and that he was unique among humans for having been granted this vision by God. See Arberry's translation of the *Kitāb at-taʿarruf*, in *The Doctrine of the Sufis*, pp. 29–30.
19. Alī ibn Uthmān al-Hujwīrī, *The Kashf al-mahjūb*, trans. Reynold A. Nicholson, Gibb Memorial Series, no. 17 (Oxford, 1911; rpt. Delhi, 1982), p. 283. See also pp. 380–381, where al-Hujwīrī describes Muhammad's actual encounter with God during his ascension: "The Apostle conversed secretly with God, and when he reached the goal his tongue became dumb before the revelation of God's majesty, and his heart was amazed at His infinite greatness, and he said, "I cannot tell Thy praise."
20. al-Hujwīrī, *The Kashf al-mahjūb*, trans. Nicholson, pp. 235–236.
21. The Arabic form of this Ḥadīth is "kuntu kanzan makhfiyyan, wa ahbabtu an uʿrafa fa khalaqtu 'l-khalqa likay uʿrafa."
22. Annemarie Schimmel, *I Am Wind, You Are Fire* (Boston, 1992), p. 74.
23. The reference is to King David of the Hebrew Bible, the author of the Psalms (*zabūr*). David was a particular favorite because of his involvement in poetry, music, and dance.
24. See Reynold A. Nicholson, *Selected Poems from the Dīvāni Shamsi Tabrīz* (Cambridge, 1898; rpt., 1977), pp. 14–15. Nicholson provides the Persian text of the poem and his translation, which differs slightly from mine.
25. In Arabic the Ḥadīth reads, "man ʿarafa nafsahu faqad ʿarafa rabbahu." See Schimmel, *Mystical Dimensions of Islam*, pp. 189–190.
26. See al-Hujwīrī, *The Kashf al-mahjūb*, trans. Nicholson, pp. 197 and 275.

27. For a translation of excerpts of this letter, see A. J. Arberry, *Sufism: An Account of the Mystics of Islam* (London, 1950), pp. 33–35.
28. Joseph Schacht, *An Introduction to Islamic Law* (Oxford, 1964), p. 48. See also Schacht's earlier work, *The Origins of Muhammadan Jurisprudence* (Oxford, 1950).
29. For a brief discussion of the Malāmatiyya and various Sufi writers' opinions on this movement, see Paul Nwyia, *Ibn ʿAtāʿAllah (709/1309) et la naissance de la confrérie shâdhilite* (Beirut, 1972), pp. 243–244, and Schimmel, *Mystical Dimensions of Islam*, pp. 86–87.
30. See Qur'ān 7:12, 38:76, and 79:24.
31. Husayn ibn Mansūr al-Hallāj, *Kitāb at-tawāsīn*, ed. Louis Massignon (Paris, 1913), p. 49, #19.
32. Husayn ibn Mansūr al-Hallāj, *Le diwan d'al-Hallāj*, ed. Louis Massignon (Paris, 1955), pp. 33–34.
33. Reynold A. Nicholson, *Studies in Islamic Mysticism* (Cambridge, 1921; rpt., 1978), pp. 60–62.
34. Abdullāh Ansārī, *Munājāt* (Intimate conversations), trans. Wheeler M. Thackston in *The Book of Wisdom and Intimate Conversations*, trans. Victor Danner and Wheeler M. Thackston (New York, 1978), p. 193.
35. Ibid., pp. 216–217.
36. Abū Hāmid al-Ghazālī, *Freedom and Fulfillment: An Annotated Translation of al-Ghazālī's al-Munqidh min al-Dalāl and Other Relevant Works of al-Ghazālī*, trans. Richard J. McCarthy, S. J. (Boston, 1980), pp. 101–102.

7

Ibn al-ʿArabī's Hermeneutics of Mercy

WILLIAM C. CHITTICK

No doubt the predominant interpretative methods of today, at least in academic circles, belong to the category of the "hermeneutics of suspicion." In contrast, Islamic civilization is characterized by a hermeneutics of trust, albeit a trust in God alone. One can observe a tension between the interpretative approach of the experts in Kalam (dogmatic theology) and the Sufis, however: the Kalam authorities were more likely to trust in God's wrath and vengeance, while the Sufis preferred to trust in his mercy and forgiveness. The stance of the Kalam experts, and of the jurists along with them, is not unrelated to their chosen role as guardians of religious and social order; they appealed to a God who will punish all those who stray from the straight and narrow, while the Sufis called on a God who is inclined to forgive all sins. One major reason for this difference in perspective lies in individual religious experience. Dogmatic theologians made no claim to know God other than by way of rational interpretation of the Qur'ān and the tradition. Many of the Sufis claimed to know firsthand that God's fundamental reality is mercy and compassion.

In his voluminous writings, the Andalusian sage Ibn al-ʿArabī (d. 1240) combined the intuitive, mystical perspective of Sufism with the rational analysis of the experts in Kalam, in jurisprudence, and in other Islamic sciences.[1] However, he held that rational analysis drives God far from the world and the soul, abstracting him from his creation. Rational minds find it easy to prove God's transcendence and "incomparability" (*tanzīh*), but—in contrast to direct mystical perception—they are utterly incapable of grasping his immanence and "similarity" (*tashbīh*). "Those who know God through their rational faculties look upon Him as far removed from themselves through a distance that demands the declaration of incomparability. They put themselves on one side and the Real on the other side, so He calls to them 'from a far place'" (Qur'ān 41:44; and see Ibn al-ʿArabī, III 410.18).[2] In contrast, God called to Ibn al-ʿArabī and other Sufis from "a near place," for they found, through their own experience, that God was "nearer than the jugular vein" (50:16).

Later Sufis often referred to Ibn al-ʿArabī as *al-shaykh al-akbar* (the greatest master). Part of the reason for this was that his massive corpus of writings contained consistently erudite and profound expositions of the meanings of the Qurʾān that had few precedents and, indeed, no serious later challengers. Recent studies have brought out the intimate connection between his spiritual life and his understanding of the Qurʾān. For him, the Qurʾān was the vivifying word of God, an infinite ocean that constantly replenished his soul, a living presence that would embody itself to him and appear in visions.[3] The dependence of his writings on the Qurʾān is obvious to careful readers, and he frequently reminds us of this fact. As he says in one passage, everything he writes "derives from the presence and the storehouses of the Qurʾān," because God gave him "the key to understanding it and taking aid from it" (III 334.32). His works are based not on rational analysis of the Qurʾān but on the direct "unveiling" (*kashf*) of its meanings, a visionary knowledge of its varied senses given by God.

Ibn al-ʿArabī began his career as the Greatest Master suddenly, as a pure grace, when he was little more than a boy. He tells us that the "one look" that he was given at the outset became the basis for everything he wrote in later life, even though he continued to experience unveilings of the unseen world, and, indeed, from the year 1193 onward, lived in what he calls "God's vast earth," seeing God's face in all things.[4] But Ibn al-ʿArabī is not simply a "mystic." He repeatedly assures his readers that reason (*ʿaql*) is unveiling's necessary complement. Without the balanced vision of "the two eyes"—reason and divine unveiling—the traveler to God runs the risk of going astray. Much of Ibn al-ʿArabī's great appeal over the centuries lies in his own rational exposition of his visionary knowledge. Even those who did not trust unveilings had to contend with his arguments in defense of what he saw, arguments that drew not only from the Qurʾān and the Ḥadīth, but also from the diverse Islamic sciences.

Since Ibn al-ʿArabī offered most of his writing as the fruit of divine unveiling and as explicit or implicit commentary on the Qurʾān, he claims to present us with inspired and indisputable interpretations of the revealed book. Nevertheless, this does not imply that he means to preclude other interpretations. Quite the contrary, from his standpoint, a true understanding of a Qurʾānic passage can never be exclusive. He goes so far as to claim that anyone who reads a Qurʾānic verse in the same manner twice has not understood it as it should be understood. After all, the Qurʾān is God's word, and God's word is the self-disclosure of his infinite Essence. God's infinity demands that he never disclose himself in the same form twice—this is Ibn al-ʿArabī's famous doctrine of the "renewal of creation at each instant." Hence, to the degree that we understand the Qurʾān, we have understood God's self-disclosure, which is to say that our understanding has been illumined by God. Given that no two human beings are identical images of God, no two understandings can possibly be illumined in exactly the same way. Moreover, no individual remains exactly the same for two successive moments. As Ibn al-ʿArabī notes: "When meaning repeats itself for someone who is reciting the Qurʾān, he has not recited it as it should be recited. This is proof of his ignorance. But when someone's knowledge is increased through his recitation, and when he acquires a new judgment with each reading, he is the reciter who, in his own existence, follows God" (IV 367.3).

Diverse interpretations of the Qur'ān answer to the diverse modes in which God discloses himself to the book's readers. One could, of course, claim that this characteristic is not specific to the Qur'ān since no two readers will understand *any* book in exactly the same way. Ibn al-ʿArabī would not dispute this, but he points to one grand difference between divine and human books. When the omniscient God reveals a book, he intends every meaning that will be understood from it, but no human authors can possibly anticipate, much less intend, all the meanings that their readers will find: "The Qur'ān is an ocean without shore, since He to whom it is ascribed intends all the meanings demanded by the speech—in contrast to the speech of created things" (II 581.11). This does not imply that every interpretation is equally valid, since Ibn al-ʿArabī adds a number of conditions to this blanket approval—most notably, that the interpretation must be sustainable by the language of the revelation. If the language does indeed support it, "No scholar can declare wrong an interpretation that is supported by the words. . . . However, it is not necessary to uphold the interpretation or to put it into practice, except in the case of the interpreter himself and those who follow his authority" (II 119.24).[5] Responsibility for interpretation rests with the interpreter.

If interpreters of the divine speech will be held responsible—by God, of course—for their interpretations, they should naturally take care to interpret the Qur'ān in a way that is appropriate to its author. Ibn al-ʿArabī often quotes the Ḥadīth Qudsī: "I am with My servant's opinion of Me, so let his opinion of Me be good." Those whose opinion of God is good (*khayr*) will be given good by God, just as those who have an evil opinion will find evil: "That God may chastise the hypocrites, men and women alike, those who associate others with Him, men and women alike, and those who opine evil opinions of God—against them shall be fortune's evil turn" (48:6). Perhaps the best opinion that one may have of God is represented by the famous Ḥadīth Qudsī, "My mercy takes precedence over My wrath." This *ḥadīth* is the leitmotif of Ibn al-ʿArabī's writings. When he saw God in all things, he saw mercy, and God's mercy is nothing but his goodness, bounty, kindness, love, and solicitude toward all creation.

In analyzing the *ḥadīth* of the servant's opinion, Ibn al-ʿArabī points out that opinion (*ẓann*) occupies an intermediary position between knowledge and ignorance. A given context will alert the reader to whether the side of knowledge or that of ignorance predominates. This specific *ḥadīth* tells us explicitly that we must make a choice between good and evil:

> God says, "I am with My servant's opinion of Me," but He does not stop there, because "His mercy takes precedence over His wrath." Hence He said, in order to instruct us, "So let his opinion of Me be good"—by way of commandment. Those who fail to have a good opinion of God have disobeyed God's commandment and displayed ignorance of what is demanded by the divine generosity. . . . When people have a bad opinion of the actual situation, what overcomes them is their own bad opinion, nothing else. (II 474.26)

Ibn al-ʿArabī is famous for his claim that he is the "seal of the Muhammadan saints." The claim implies that he would be the last person (before Jesus at the end of time) to inherit all the sciences, spiritual stations, virtues, and visionary experiences of Muhammad.[6] The Qur'ān says that God sent Muhammad only as a mercy (*raḥma*) to the creatures, and the fact that practically every chapter of the Qur'ān begins by citing God's two primary names of mercy—*al-raḥmān* and *al-raḥīm*, the "All-merciful" and the "Compassionate"—was lost on no one. If Ibn al-ʿArabī considered himself Muhammad's last plenary inheritor, he also saw his own role as that of spreading mercy. He writes, "God created me as a mercy, and He made me an heir to the mercy of him to whom He said, 'We sent thee only as a mercy to the worlds' [21:107]" (IV 163.9). What is especially interesting here is Ibn al-ʿArabī's next sentence, in which he clarifies his understanding of what this mercy implies: "God did not specify those with faith to the exclusion of others." In other words, God sent Muhammad as a mercy to everyone, not just to the Muslims or the faithful. This all-inclusiveness of the divine mercy has implications that many theologians—not only Muslim theologians—would find difficult to accept. As Ibn al-ʿArabī puts it, such people would like to exclude some of God's creatures from his mercy, but their evil opinion of God can only redound upon themselves: "He who curtails God's mercy curtails it only from himself. Were it not that the actual situation is otherwise, those who curtail and limit God's mercy would never reach it" (III 532.22).[7]

Ibn al-ʿArabī's constant stress on the precedence and predominance of God's mercy has many Qurʾānic roots, but no doubt his own experience of the unveiling of God's mercy is his deepest motivation. One of his visions is especially striking in this respect. He witnessed the divine throne, upon which, according to the Qurʾān, the "All-merciful" is sitting, and he saw that it was supported by four columns. He found himself standing in the ranks of the angels who held up the most excellent of these columns, which is "the storehouse of mercy," because God had created him "compassionate [*raḥīm*] in an unqualified sense" (III 431.32). Of the other three columns, one was pure wrath, severity, and hardship, while the other two were mercy mixed with wrath.

In short, Ibn al-ʿArabī's Qurʾānic interpretations—and all his writings are Qurʾānic interpretations—are permeated by the idea of the divine mercy. His metaphysics, theology, cosmology, and spiritual psychology are rooted in the good opinion that God's mercy predominates over his wrath. Where this stress on mercy comes out with special clarity is on the issue of hell. The Qurʾān declares that hell is a place of divine wrath and punishment. The general understanding among Muslims is that the chastisement of the Fire will last forever, though many theologians offer dissenting views.[8] Ibn al-ʿArabī's own good opinion is categorical, however. Although certain types of unbelievers will remain in the Fire forever, even they will cease to suffer after a certain period of time, however long this may take in earthly terms. He often comes back to this idea in his *Futūḥāt al-makkiyya.* I have mentioned some of his arguments in a survey of his teachings on the afterlife; here I touch on a few more, paying special attention to the manner in which he reads the Qurʾānic text.[9]

One of Ibn al-ʿArabī's most basic arguments to prove the impermanence of hell's punishment is simply that God is, in Qurʾānic terms, "the Most Merciful of the merciful" (12:64). After all, there are people who could never agree that anyone, even the most evil of men, should suffer forever. God is certainly more merciful than they are:

> I have found in myself—who am among those whom God has innately disposed toward mercy—that I have mercy toward all God's servants, even if God has decreed in His creating them that the attribute of chastisement will remain forever with them in the cosmos. This is because the ruling property of mercy has taken possession of my heart.

> The possessors of this attribute are I and my peers, and we are creatures, possessors of caprices and personal desires. God has said about Himself that He is the Most Merciful of the merciful, and we have no doubt that He is more merciful than we are toward His creatures. But we have known from ourselves this extravagant mercy. So how could chastisement be everlasting for them, when He has this attribute of all-inclusive mercy? God is more generous than that. (III 25.19)[10]

In this context, God's "generosity" or "nobility" (*karam*) is one of Ibn al-ʿArabī's frequent themes. God has commanded his servants to acquire "noble character traits" (*makārim al-akhlāq*). How could he ask his servants to acquire attributes that he himself lacks? The Qurʾān ascribes many of the noble character traits to God by calling him compassionate, forgiving, patient, just, pardoner, and so on. These traits demand that God keep the best interests of his creatures in view. Hence the "final issue" (*maʾāl*) of the creatures will be at God's mercy.

According to a *ḥadīth*, God has rights (*ḥaqq*) against his servants, and his servants have rights against him: "God's right against the servants . . . is that they should worship Him and not associate anything with Him, . . . and the servants' right against God" is that "if they do that, He will bring them into the Garden," that is, paradise. The Qurʾān says that people will not be blamed for claiming their own rights, but it also states that it would be better to forgive. According to Ibn al-ʿArabī, "God has set down in the Sharīʿa, concerning some of our rights that, if we abandon them, it would be best for us, and He placed this among the noble character traits." To prove this, Ibn al-ʿArabī cites the verse "And the recompense of an ugly act is an ugly act the like of it, but whoso pardons and makes wholesome, his wage falls upon God" (42:40). The next verse indicates that a person may claim what is due to him: "Whosoever helps himself after he has been wronged, against them there is no way" (42:41). If it is better for the servants to pardon so as to observe God's law, then God himself will certainly pardon the sin of not worshiping him: "He will pardon, show forbearance, and make wholesome. Hence the final issue will be at God's mercy in the two abodes. Mercy will embrace them wherever they may be" (III 478.20).

Mercy's Precedence in *Wujūd*

To say that God has noble character traits is to say that reality itself is rooted in these traits and demands that they become manifest. The key term here is *wujūd*, which is the standard theological and philosophical term for "existence" or "being." God is "the Necessary *Wujūd*," which is to say that he is and cannot not be. In contrast, everything else is a "possible thing" (*mumkin*), which is to say that nothing other than God has any inherent claim on existence. Thus the "cosmos" (*al-ʿālam*), which is defined as "everything other than God," owes its existence to God's bestowal, which is his mercy. Ibn al-ʿArabī's extensive teachings on cosmology are based on the idea that the universe itself, the whole domain of possible existence, is nothing other than "the Breath of the All-merciful" (*nafas al-raḥmān*). The Qurʾānic passage that he cites most often in support of the all-pervasiveness of mercy is 7:156: "My mercy embraces all things." From this passage Ibn al-ʿArabī concludes as follows:

> The cosmos is identical with mercy, nothing else. (II 437.24)
>
> God's mercy is not specified for one locus rather than another, or for one abode rather than another. On the contrary, it embraces all things. Hence the abode of mercy is the abode of existence. (IV 4.32)
>
> The name All-merciful protects us. Mercy has been given preponderance, so its ruling property exercises influence, for it is the root in giving existence. As for vengeance, it is an accidental property, and accidents have no fixity. After all, existence accompanies us, so our final issue will be at mercy and its property. (II 157.23)
>
> The final issue will be at mercy, for the actual situation inscribes a circle. The end of the circle curves back to its beginning and joins it. The end has the property of the beginning, and that is nothing but *wujūd*. "Mercy takes precedence over wrath," because the beginning was through mercy. Wrath is an accident, and accidents disappear. (IV 405.7)

Inasmuch as the cosmos is everything other than God, it is everything other than the merciful, the compassionate, the permanent, the living, the powerful, the knowing, and the generous. It is, in short, everything other than the Real (*al-ḥaqq*), who is God himself, *wujūd*. Hence the cosmos has nothing of its own to support its existence. At the same time, we all recognize that supporting the underdog is a noble character trait. How could God, who is merciful, compassionate, and generous in essence, do anything but help the weak? "And all creatures are weak at root, so mercy envelops them" (III 255.33).

The Qur'ān states, "There is no fault in the blind, and there is no fault in the lame, and there is no fault in the sick" (48:17). This is normally taken to mean that the Sharīʿa makes allowances for human weaknesses and handicaps. But the Sharīʿa is God's law, and, as such it expresses the nature of *wujūd* itself. It follows that a deeper meaning of this verse is that God makes allowances for those who are weak and disabled. But weakness and disability are the attributes of the whole universe, which is other than the real, the strong, and the powerful.

> He who is stricken by some blight has no fault, and all the cosmos is stricken by a blight, so it has no fault in the view of him whose insight has been opened by God. This is why we say that the final issue of the cosmos will be at mercy, even if they take up an abode in the Fire and are among its folk. "There is no fault in the blind, and there is no fault in the lame, and there is no fault in the sick." And there is nothing but these. . . . For the cosmos is all blind, lame, and sick. (IV 434.34)

Ibn al-ʿArabī finds allusions to mercy's final triumph throughout the Qur'ān. For example, the text tells us that the "felicitous" will remain in paradise forever, as "a gift unbroken" (11:108). In the same place it tells us that the "wretched" will remain forever in the Fire, but, as Ibn al-ʿArabī points out, God "does not say that the state within which they dwell will not be cut off, as He says concerning the felicitous." He continues: "What prevents Him from saying this is His words, 'And My mercy embraces all things' [7:156], and His words, 'My mercy takes precedence over My wrath' in this configuration. For *wujūd* is mercy for all existent things, even if some of them suffer chastisement through others" (II 281.26).

To say that mercy takes precedence over wrath is to say that God takes precedence over his creatures; that light takes precedence over darkness, reality over unreality, and good over evil. Or it is to say that, by embracing all things, mercy also embraces wrath, employing it in its own service: "God says, 'My mercy embraces all things' [7:156], and His wrath is a thing. Hence His mercy has embraced His wrath, confined it, and ruled over it. Hence wrath disposes itself only through mercy's ruling property. So mercy sends out wrath as it wills" (III 9.23).

Although the Qur'ān asserts that mercy embraces all things, it never suggests that wrath is all-pervasive. Thus, when it tells us in several verses that all things will be taken back to God, this can mean only that they will go back to God's all-embracing mercy:

> God's mercy includes all existent things and "embraces all things" [7:156], just as He "embraces all things in mercy and knowledge" [40:7]. Wrath was not mentioned in this divine and merciful all-embracingness. So the final issue of the cosmos must be at mercy, since the cosmos has no escape from returning to God, for He is the one who says, "To Him the whole affair is returned" [11:123]. When its return reaches Him, the affair goes back to the beginning, the origin, the originator. The beginning is a mercy that "embraces all things," and the originator "embraces all things in mercy and knowledge." Hence, in going back, the affair is immersed in mercy. (III 119.35)

Ibn al-ʿArabī pays extraordinarily close attention to the meaning of Qur'ānic words. He often tells us that the best way to understand the words is to grasp how they would have been understood by the Arabs to whom the Qur'ān was addressed. In his investigations of the etymological sense of particular terms, he invariably looks at the concrete images conveyed by the words rather than at the abstract meanings, the latter having been derived by the rational minds of the theologians and grammarians. The *ḥadīth* of the "precedence" (*sabq*) of mercy provides a good example. The basic meaning of this word is to outstrip and surpass, to come first in a race. In one verse the Qur'ān employs the word as follows: "Do they reckon, those who do ugly deeds, that they will precede Us?" (29:4). Commentators typically understand this as a warning to sinners that they will not be able to escape God's punishment. Ibn al-ʿArabī offers a much more interesting explanation by paying close attention to the verb *precede*, which was typically used in horse racing (which provides, by the way, the only sort of gambling that the Sharīʿa permits):

> When people disobey, they expose themselves to vengeance and affliction. They are running in a race to vengeance for what has occurred from them. But God races against them in this racetrack in respect of the fact that He is ever-forgiving, pardoning, overlooking, compassionate, and clement. Through acts of disobedience and ugly deeds, the servants race the Real to vengeance, and the Real precedes them. So He will have preceded them when they arrive at vengeance through ugly deeds. God passes them through the ever-forgiving and its sisters among the divine names. When the servants reach the end of the race, they find vengeance, but the ever-forgiving has preceded them and has come between them and their acts of disobedience. They had been judging that they would reach it before this. This is indicated by God's words: "Do they reckon, those who do ugly deeds, that they will precede Us?" [29:4], that is, that they will precede My forgiveness and the envelopment of My mercy through their ugly deeds? "Ill they judge!" [29:4]. On the contrary, precedence belongs to God through mercy toward them. This is the utmost limit of generosity. (III 252.7)[11]

The Qur'ān tells us that the wrongdoers, even if they possess the whole universe, will not be able to ransom themselves from the ugliness of their actions. "There will appear to them from God what they had never reckoned with . . . and they will be encompassed by what they mocked at" (39:47). Theologians of evil opinion read this as a guarantee of the "implementation of the threat" (*infādh al-waʿīd*), but, Ibn al-ʿArabī rejects this out of hand: God, after all, is "sheer good, in whom there is no evil" (II 478.9).[12] The wrongdoers, having been immersed in evil, reckon to receive the same from God. But, what appears to them is reality in itself: "'There will appear to them from God what they had never reckoned with,' and that is the witnessing of the affair as it is in itself. God will relieve them through what appears to them from Him, for nothing appears from the Good save good" (II 478.12).

As already suggested, one of the most obvious Qurʾānic assertions of God's good intentions is found in the *basmala*, the formula of consecration that begins practically every Qurʾānic *sūra*: "In the name of God, the all-merciful, the compassionate." The name God itself embraces all the divine attributes, which are often divided into two categories—the severe and the gentle, or the majestic and the beautiful. But the fact that this name is followed by the two primary names of mercy tells us that the merciful side of God predominates in revelation and creation. Ibn al-ʿArabī compares the *basmala* to the intention (*niyya*) that undergirds every human activity. According to the Sharīʿa, if one is deficient in one's practice "through heedlessness or inattention, this has no effect on the correctness of the activity, for the intention makes up for it." In the same way, God's intention, asserted in the *basmala*, makes up for "every threat and every attribute that demands wretchedness mentioned in the sura. . . . So the final issue will be at mercy, because of the *basmala*. It is a statement of good news" (III 147.31).

> None of the names of severity are manifest in the *basmala*. On the contrary, He is "God, the all-merciful, the compassionate." Even if the name God includes severity, it also includes mercy. So the names of severity, dominance, and harshness that the name God comprises are countered measure for measure by the names of mercy, forgiveness, pardon, and forbearance that it contains in itself. There remains for us the surplus . . . and that is His words, "the all-merciful, the compassionate." . . . Thus His mercy is all-inclusive, and hope is great for everyone. . . . After all, He has made mercy three—the nonmanifest mercy within the name God, the all-merciful, and the compassionate. (III 9.24)

The *Fiṭra*

People win paradise by obeying the commandments that God has sent through the prophets, just as they earn hell by disobeying these commandments. The prophets bring instructions on how to become proper "servants" (*ʿabd*) of God, or on how to "worship" (*ʿibāda*) him, as is his due. However, the Qurʾān also tells us that all things are servants by nature: "Nothing is there in the heavens and the earth that comes not to the All-merciful as a servant" (19:93), for all things are creatures of the all-merciful, created by him out of mercy. He says to them, "Be!," and they come into existence. "Our only speech to a thing, when We desire it, is to say to it 'Be!,' and it is" (16:40). Nothing can disobey this command, so the first act of every creature is to say, "I hear and I obey." In other words, the primary characteristic of everything, because of its created nature, is obedience to the divine command and service to the all-merciful. This characteristic must exercise its ruling property, sooner or later.

> The possible thing comes to be from the divine power in a manner that it does not know. It hurries to engendered existence, so it comes to be. Hence its own self makes manifest hearing and obeying toward Him who says to it, "Be!" so it acquires praise from God for its obe-

> dience. Thus the possible thing's first situation is its hearing God and its obeying Him in coming to be, so every act of disobedience that becomes manifest from the possible thing is an accident that occurs to it, while its root is hearing and obeying. This is like the wrath that occurs accidentally, while precedence belongs to mercy. . . . The possible thing's obedience has precedence, and the end and conclusion always have the property of the precedent. The precedent belongs to mercy, so there is no escape from the final issue at mercy for every possible thing for which wretchedness occurs, for the thing is obedient at root. (IV 296.10)

There are two basic sorts of worship and obedience: The first is the "essential" (*dhātī*) worship of all things to their Lord, which follows upon their created nature; and the second is the "accidental" (*ʿaraḍī*) worship, which God commands through the prophets. Accidental worship is a human characteristic that depends on a number of factors, not the least of which is free choice (*ikhtiyār*). Other creatures, lacking this gift, never cease worshiping God through their own essential worship. In the next world, whether people enter the Garden or the Fire, they will lose their power of free choice and return to worship through their essences, making manifest their essential property of service to the all-merciful: "It is through the essential worship that the folk of the Gardens and the folk of the Fire will worship. This is why the final issue for the wretched will be at mercy, for the essential worship is strong in authority, but the command [to worship God in this world] is accidental, and the wretchedness is accidental. Every accidental thing disappears" (III 402.11).

Although human beings are free when gauged against other creatures, they have no freedom when compared to God. They are his absolute servants, like everything else. They are, as Ibn al-ʿArabī often remarks, "compelled to have free choice."[13] They never leave their essential worship, even if they employ their free choice to reject accidental worship. Hence God will forgive them for their accidental disobedience. "Since the excuse of the world is accepted in actual fact—because they are compelled in their free choice—God placed the final issue of everything at mercy" (III 433.4).

The Qur'ān refers to the fundamental created nature of human beings as their *fiṭra*, a word that can be translated as "primordial nature" or "original disposition." Typically, Muslims have understood the term to mean that all people are born with a disposition toward *tawḥīd*, the acknowledgment of God's unity, and if they fail to acknowledge it, they are flying in the face of their own nature. The *fiṭra* is associated with the Covenant of Alast, when all human beings stood before God before their entrance into this world and acknowledged his lordship over them (Qur'ān 7:172). Ibn al-ʿArabī often identifies people's *fiṭra* with their essential worship of God, and hence he makes it their guarantee of ultimate felicity. Those in hell will reap the fruit of the covenant when they finally come to understand that they, like everything else, were created as servants of the all-merciful. At this point they will cease "making claims" (*iddiʿā*)—asserting lordship and mastery when, in fact, they are nothing but creatures and servants. They will recognize that everything real belongs to the Real and will thereby be delivered from ignorance, illusion, and pain.

> The sinners will never cease witnessing their servanthood. Even if they claim lordliness, they will know from what they find in themselves that they are liars. Hence making claims will disappear with the disappearance of its appropriate time, and the relationship of servanthood that they had had, both in the state of making claims and before making claims, will remain with them. Then they will pluck the fruit of their words [at the Covenant of

> Alast], "Yes [we bear witness]" [7:172]. . . . The authority of Yes rules over everything and finally gives rise to their felicity after the wretchedness that had touched them in the measure in which they had made claims. The property of Yes never leaves them from its own moment ad infinitum—in this world, in the interworld, and in the last world. (II 213.6)

The *fiṭra*, then, is the original human disposition that stays with people forever. In Ibn al-ʿArabī's view, God will never change the *fiṭra*. He finds support for this idea in the Qurʾānic verse "God's words possess no changing" (10:64), which is usually understood to mean that God does not change his scriptural promises. But, as Ibn al-ʿArabī points out, God's "words" may also be the created things, which are articulated within the all-merciful breath. God uses the term in this sense in reference to Jesus, when he calls him "His word that He cast to Mary" (4:171). From this point of view, the verse means that the existent things, which are God's words, never change. The verse of the *fiṭra* reads: "Set thy face to the religion, a man of pure faith—God's *fiṭra* upon which He originated [*faṭara*] people. There is no changing God's creation (30:30). "Thus He negated that people have any changing in that; rather, to God belongs the changing" (II 534.32). Ibn al-ʿArabī reads this verse as another instance of God's giving good news to his servants. Their original disposition never changes, even when they associate others with God (*shirk*), which is the worst of all sins in Muslim eyes.

> Since He does not ascribe changing to them, this is good news in their case that their final issue will be at mercy. Even if they take up residence in the Fire, they will be there by virtue of the fact that it is an abode, not because it is an abode of chastisement and pains. On the contrary, God will give them a constitution through which they will take enjoyment in the Fire such that, were they to enter the Garden with that constitution, they would suffer pain, because of the lack of the agreement of their constitution with the equilibrium possessed by the Garden. (II 534.34)

One of Ibn al-ʿArabī's bolder assertions of the ruling authority of the *fiṭra* is offered in the context of the constant Qurʾānic criticism of the *mushrikūn*, those who associate others with God. In some verses, the *mushrikūn* give the excuse that they only worshiped the others as a means to gain nearness to God, as in 39:3: "We only worship them so that they may bring us nigh in nearness to God." It was in answer to this sort of excuse that God tells Muhammad to ask them to name their associates (Qurʾān 13:33). In Ibn al-ʿArabī's reading, "Once they named their associates, it became clear that they worshiped none but God, for no worshiper worships any but God in the place to which he ascribes divinity to Him." Hence, despite associating others with God, such people are standing firm in the *tawḥīd* that belongs to him, "because they acknowledged Him at the covenant," and so they remain in their *fiṭra*. "Through the strength of remaining in their *fiṭra* they did not in reality worship Him in the forms. Rather, they worshiped the forms because they imagined that within them was the level of bringing about nearness, as if they were intercessors," and this also will open them up to God's forgiveness and pardon (III 24.34).

Pleasure in the Fire

One of the strongest arguments against universal mercy is the Qurʾānic assertion of hell's everlastingness. Ibn al-ʿArabī does not deny that those who belong in hell will remain there forever. What he does deny is that their suffering will be permanent. His basic argument is simply the precedence of mercy: "How could there be everlasting wretchedness? Far be it from God that His wrath should take precedence over His mercy—for He is the truthful—or that He should make the embrace of His mercy specific after He had called it general!" (III 466.20).

The Qurʾānic verse that supports Ibn al-ʿArabī's position most explicitly is probably 39:53: "O My servants who have been immoderate against yourselves, despair not of God's mercy! Surely God forgives all sins." The Qurʾān often says that the sins of those who repent and do good deeds will be forgiven, but here it suggests that the sins of everyone will be forgiven. Concerning this verse, Ibn al-ʿArabī says, "He brought forgiveness and mercy for the repenter and those who perform wholesome deeds, just as He has brought it for those who are immoderate, those who do not repent. The latter He forbids to despair, and He confirms the point through His word *all.* Nothing could be greater in divine eloquence concerning the final issue of the servants at mercy" (III 353.1).

One might object by citing the many Qurʾānic verses that explicitly cite the sinners as objects of divine wrath and punishment. Ibn al-ʿArabī answers that God only becomes wrathful in this world. In the next world, everything follows his command exactly. Hence he will be pleased with his creatures, whether they dwell in paradise or hell, because they can do nothing but obey him through their own *fiṭra*. Both the folk of the Garden and the folk of the Fire will act in keeping with God's good pleasure (*riḍā*), "for this is required by the homestead, in contrast to the homestead of this world." In this world, they were addressed by the prophets, and they were able to act "both in that which pleases God and that which angers Him." God created the situation in this way "because He made the Fire the abode of those with whom He is angry, so, in this world, its folk have no escape from acting in that which angers God." Once they enter the Fire, however, it becomes impossible for them to act, save in God's good pleasure. "That is why the final issue of its folk will be at the ruling property of the mercy that 'embraces all things' [7:156], even if the Fire is an abode of wretchedness" (III 495.22).

The Qurʾān says, "God is well-pleased with them, and they are well-pleased with Him" (5:119, 58:22, 98:8). One should not be misled by the fact that these verses refer explicitly to paradise: "The Real does not make good-pleasure manifest until the folk of the Fire have taken up their domiciles and the folk of the Garden have taken up their domiciles. Then everyone will be pleased with that in which they are by the Real's making them pleased. None will desire to leave his domicile, and each will be happy with it" (II 244.1). Ibn al-ʿArabī continues this passage by referring to the unpopularity of this sort of good opinion of God. No one, as far as he knows, has explained that good pleasure pertains specifically to the next world in *both* paradise and hell. He supposes that some people have been aware of this fact, but that they have concealed it, to ward off criticism from themselves and to protect others from the harm of rejecting the truth. In his own case, he points out that mercy itself drives him to speak of such things.

> This is a marvelous mystery. I have seen none of God's creatures calling attention to it, even though some have known it, without doubt. They have safeguarded it—and God knows best—only to safeguard themselves and as a mercy to the creatures, because the listeners would hurry to deny it. And, by God, I have called attention to it here only because mercy has overcome me at this moment. Those who understand will be felicitous,

> and those who do not understand will not become wretched by their lack of understanding, even if they are deprived. (II 244.3)

One of God's names that has become manifest in the present world is Patient (*ṣabūr*). God is patient with the disobedience of his servants, and the Qur'ān repeatedly says that despite their wrongdoing, he will put off taking them to task until the next world. He is patient despite the fact that he is "annoyed" (*īdhā'*). In commenting on the Qur'ānic verse "Those who annoy God and His Messenger—them God has cursed in this world and the next (33:57), Ibn al-ʿArabī points out that when this world comes to an end, so also does God's annoyance and, along with it, the property of the divine names that answer to this annoyance, such as avenger and severe in punishment.

> Thus the wisdom in the disappearance of this world is the disappearance of annoyance from God, since there can be annoyance only within it. So, give good news to God's servants of the all-inclusiveness of mercy, of its spaciousness, and of its application to every created thing other than God, even if after a while. For, with the disappearance of this world, annoyance disappears from everyone who is annoyed, and through the disappearance of annoyance, patience disappears. One of the causes of punishment is annoyance, but annoyance has disappeared, so there is no escape from mercy and the lifting of wrath. Inescapably, mercy will include everything, through God's bounty, God willing. This is our opinion concerning God. After all, God says—and He speaks the truth—"I am with My servant's opinion of Me, so let his opinion of Me be good." Thus has He reported and commanded. (II 206.31)

Ibn al-ʿArabī finds a divine allusion to the final issue at mercy in the Qur'ānic word for chastisement, which is *ʿadhāb*. The basic sense of this word's root is to be sweet and agreeable. An apparently unrelated meaning is found in the noun form *ʿadhab*, which means "bits and pieces, strips, the extremity of a thing, the end of a whip." The word *ʿadhāb* seems to have originally meant the "pain of being whipped." In the Qur'ān, it is the generic term for the punishment that is inflicted upon the folk of the Fire. But the Qur'ān could have used other Arabic words to make the same point. Why did God choose this particular word? For Ibn al-ʿArabī, the reason can only be that in the end, the chastisement will become "sweet" (*ʿadhib*) for those who suffer it: "That which causes pain is named *ʿadhāb* as a good news from God. Inescapably, you will find that everything through which you suffer pain is sweet when mercy envelops you and you are in the Fire" (II 207.1).

One of Ibn al-ʿArabī's more common arguments in proof of the end of hell's chastisement is that people go where they belong. Once they arrive, they find that the domain is appropriate to their own natures. After all, "bliss" and "chastisement" are determined by the nature of the person who experiences them, not by the location in which they are experienced. The angels of chastisement enjoy hell, and the sinners will, too. The general principle is that "bliss is nothing but what is accepted by the constitution and the individual desire of the souls—places have no effect in that. Wherever are found agreeableness of nature and achievement of individual desire, that is bliss for the person" (III 387.22). The same line of reasoning helps explain why the Qur'ān refers not only to the "fire" of hell, but also to its "bitter cold" (*zamharīr*). Those who go to hell do so because their individual divine images—their "constitutions"—are imbalanced and therefore inappropriate for the equilibrium of the Garden:

> The person of a cold constitution will find the heat of the Fire pleasant, and the person of a hot constitution will find the Bitter Cold pleasant. Thus Gehenna brings together the Fire and the Bitter Cold—because of the diversity of constitutions. What causes pain in a specific constitution will cause bliss in another constitution that is its opposite. So wisdom is not inoperative, for God keeps the Bitter Cold of Gehenna for those with hot constitutions and the Fire for those with cold constitutions. They enjoy themselves in Gehenna, for they have a constitution with which, were they to enter the Garden, they would suffer chastisement, because of the Garden's equilibrium. (II 207.2)

Ibn al-ʿArabī finds another allusion to the pleasures of the Fire in the verse "Whosoever comes unto his Lord a sinner, for him awaits Gehenna, wherein he shall neither die nor live" (20:74). The folk of the Fire "will not die therein, because of the relief they gain through the removal of the pains." When the pain is removed, chastisement turns sweet: "Nor will they live therein, which is to say that they will not have a bliss like the bliss of the folk of the Gardens, a bliss that would be something in addition to the fact that He has relieved them in the abode of wretchedness" (III 245.26).

In several places Ibn al-ʿArabī insists that the pleasure of the Fire is precisely the removal of suffering and pain. But this is not something small, given the Fire's severity: "The enjoyment of the Companions of the Blaze is tremendous, for they witness the abode, while security is one of its properties. There is no surprise if roses are found in rose gardens. The surprise comes when roses grow up in the pit of the Fire" (IV 307.34).[14]

Ibn al-ʿArabī sees the root of wretchedness in the refusal to submit to God's wisdom and to accept one's own nature as his servant. The fire of hell arises, in other words, from mistrusting God and from insisting that the world needs to be reformed according to one's own opinions: "The wretched have chastisement only from themselves, for they are made to stand in the station of protestation and seeking the reasons for God's acts among His servants. 'Why did such and such happen?' 'If such and such had been, it would have been better and more appropriate'" (II 447.8).

By protesting in this manner, people dispute with their Lord and join among those who "broke off from God and His messenger" (8:13). Here Ibn al-ʿArabī explains a meaning of the verse by playing on the similar spelling of *shaqq*, which means "breaking off," and *shiqāʾ*, which is the "wretchedness" that belongs to the people of the Fire: "Their wretchedness is their breaking off. Hell is 'the abode of the wretched' because they enter it in this state." Eventually, however, their state changes and they gradually come to realize that there is no profit in questioning God and refusing to submit to their own natures. "When the period becomes long for the wretched and they come to know that [dispute] has no profit, they say, 'Agreement is better.'" At this point, their situation changes, and their "breaking off" disappears: "Then the chastisement is removed from their inner selves and they achieve ease in their abode. They find in that an enjoyment known by none but God, for they have chosen what God has chosen for them, and at that point they come to know that their chastisement had been only from themselves" (II 447.12).

It is at the point of accepting their own natures that people realize that they will not be removed from the Fire. This makes them secure in their places, and they no longer wonder if they will be among those who, according to a *ḥadīth*, will be taken out of the Fire by the most merciful of the merciful, even though they did "no good whatsoever" in the world:

> They had feared leaving the Fire when they saw that the most merciful of the merciful was taking people out, whereas God had placed in them a constitution that is appropriate for one who settles in that abode. . . . When they give up the thought of leaving it, they become happy, so their bliss is in this measure. This is the first bliss that they find. . . . Thus they find the chastisement sweet, for the pains disappear, though the "chastisement" remains. This is why it is called *ʿadhāb*—the final issue is that those who abide within it find it sweet. (III 463.6)

Among the Qurʾānic verses that criticize the *mushrikūn* is the following: "Be not among those who associate others with God, those who have divided up their religion and become sects, each party rejoicing in what is theirs" (30:31–32). Ibn al-ʿArabī, as usual, finds good news lurking in the text, even for sectarians. He is in the process of explaining how the Qurʾān encourages its readers to seek the deepest meanings of its verses, which are the signs that God appointed "for a people who use intelligence" (2:164) and "for a people who reflect" (10:24). These are the people that the Qurʾān calls *ulu'l-albāb*, which Qurʾān translators normally render with expressions such as "possessors of minds" or "people of understanding." Literally, the term means "owners of the kernels," and Ibn al-ʿArabī contrasts them with "owners of the shell," though the latter is not a Qurʾānic expression. He points out that those who penetrate to the kernels of things enjoy their knowledge, but those who remain with the shells are happy in their ignorance. Each group has its own idea of what happiness is, and none of them is wrong, because each idea corresponds with the nature of the group that holds it. This is God's mercy, but in this world it filters in somewhat haphazardly. All are not happy with what they have. Things only become sorted out in the next world. There the true meaning of every party's "rejoicing in what is theirs" becomes manifest:

> The kernel is veiled by the form of the shell. No one knows the kernel save those who know that there is a kernel. Were it not for this, they would not break the shell. . . . The knower of the kernel enjoys his knowledge of it, while the person ignorant of it is given joy through his ignorance, though he does not know that he is ignorant. After all, he does not know that the situation, which is other than what he knows, is indeed other than what he knows. On the contrary, he says, "There is nothing but this." Were he to know that there is other than what he knows and that he has not perceived it, he would be troubled, just as everyone in this world is troubled when he lacks what is demanded by his station, such as the merchant in his trading, the jurist in his jurisprudence, and every scholar in his own domain.
>
> The verification of His words, "each party rejoicing in what is theirs" [30:32], occurs only in the next world, in contrast to this world. It is not known in this world, or rather, it occurs for many people but not everyone. . . . The final issue of all in the next world, after the expiration of the term of taking to task, will be at rejoicing in what they have and what they are busy with. (III 471.4)

A final passage can serve to summarize Ibn al-ʿArabī's good opinion of God. Again, he points to the Qurʾān and insists that God never explicitly links the return to God with wretchedness and ugliness. What the Qurʾān does say along these lines should be understood as threats, and no person of true nobility and generosity would carry out his threats. In one of these more threatening passages, the Qurʾān says, "The clatterer! What is the clatterer! And what shall teach you what is the clatterer? The day that men shall be like scattered moths, and the mountains shall be like plucked wool-tufts" (101:1–5). This indeed sounds like a terrible situation, and it is typically taken as a dire warning of the calamities of the day of resurrection. But Ibn al-ʿArabī's good opinion allows him to read it in terms of God's precedent and all-embracing mercy:

> The ultimate end of the affair will be that "with God is the most beautiful place of return" [3:14]. God does not explicitly link any ugliness whatsoever to the place of returning to Him. Things of that sort that have come to us play the role of threats in the first understanding.
>
> "Those who do wrong shall surely know by what overturning they shall be overturned" [26:227]. Concerning God's generosity they shall surely know "what they had never reckoned with" [39:47]. In the case of those who are forgiven, this happens before being taken to task, and [for others, it happens] after being taken to task, when this is cut off from them. For His mercy is all-embracing, and His blessing is abundant and all-comprehensive. The souls of the cosmos wish for His mercy, since He is generous without restriction and nondelimited in munificence, without any limitation.
>
> This explains why all the world will be mustered on the day of resurrection "like scattered moths" [101:4]. Mercy will be scattered in all the homesteads, so the world will scatter in search of it, for the world has diverse states and variegated forms. Through the scattering they will seek from God the mercy that will remove from them the form that leads to wretchedness. This is the cause of their being scattered on that day. (III 390.35)[15]

NOTES

1. On the visionary life of Ibn al-ʿArabī in the context of the personalities and events of his times, see the unsurpassed study by Claude Addas, *Quest for the Red Sulphur: The Life of Ibn ʿArabī* (Cambridge, 1993). On Ibn al-ʿArabī's intellectual perspective, see William C. Chittick, *The Sufi Path of Knowledge: Ibn al-ʿArabī's Metaphysics of Imagination* (Albany, 1989); idem, *The Self-Disclosure of God: Principles of Ibn al-ʿArabī's Cosmology* (Albany, 1998).
2. Citations from the Qurʾān are indicated by the number of the *sūra* and the verse. Quotations from Ibn al-ʿArabī are indicated by Roman numerals, which refer to the volume number of his *al-Futūḥāt al-makkiyya* (Cairo, 1911), followed by the page and line number.
3. See especially, Michel Chodkiewicz, *An Ocean without Shore: Ibn Arabi, the Book, and the Law* (Albany, 1993).
4. On the "one look," see Chittick, *Sufi Path*, p. xiv; Addas, *Quest*, chap. 2. On his dwelling in "God's vast earth," see Addas, *Quest*, chap. 5.
5. For these and other passages on this theme, see Chittick, *Sufi Path*, p. 242–244.
6. See M. Chodkiewicz, *The Seal of the Saints: Prophethood and Sainthood in the Doctrine of Ibn ʿArabī* (Cambridge, 1993).
7. For another passage that makes the same general point, see III 370.15, translated in William C. Chittick, *Imaginal Worlds: Ibn al-ʿArabī and the Problem of Religious Diversity* (Albany, 1994), pp. 114–115. See also III 120.4, 552.2; and IV 163.6.
8. J. I. Smith and Y. Y. Haddad conclude, "In general it can be said that the non-eternity of the Fire has prevailed in the understanding of the Muslim community" (*The Islamic Understanding of Death and Resurrection* [Albany, 1981], p. 95). However, other specialists disagree. W. Madelung writes, "There is . . . no sound basis for disputing the common Qurʾānic and Islamic doctrine . . . that the punishment for infidels in hell-fire is everlasting" (*Journal of the Royal Asiatic Society* [1994], p. 101).

9. See Chittick, *Imaginal Worlds*, chap. 7.
10. For the passage in its context, see Chittick, *Self-Disclosure of God*, p. 188.
11. For another example of Ibn al-ʿArabī's use of the imagery of horse racing in this context, see II 673.30.
12. Ibn al-ʿArabī identifies those who maintain that God will implement his threat as the Mu'tazilite theologians (II 478.14; II. 533.24).
13. See Chittick, *Self-Disclosure*, pp. 186–189.
14. For the passage in its context, see ibid., p. 81.
15. For the passage in its context, see ibid., p. 367.

8

Sacred Scriptures and the Mysticism of Advaita Vedānta

ARVIND SHARMA

This chapter illustrates the relationship between mysticism and sacred scripture in the philosophical tradition within Hinduism that is known as Advaita Vedānta. In this essay I use the word *mysticism* to mean "the doctrine or belief that direct knowledge of God, of spiritual truth, of ultimate reality, or comparable matters is attainable through immediate intuition, insight, or illumination and in a way differing from ordinary sense perception or ratiocination."[1] Similarly, I use the word *sacred* to mean "worthy of religious veneration"; I leave the word *religion* undefined and use the word *scripture* to mean "a body of writings considered authoritative";[2] and hence I take the expression "sacred scripture" to mean religiously authoritative texts. As the relationship between mysticism and sacred scripture is explored here in relation to Advaita Vedānta, I use that term in consonance with its general employment.[3] In the course of this disquisition, I may often employ the expression "mystical experience" in preference to "mysticism," in keeping with the preference of the tradition of Advaita Vedānta itself, for the question of the formulation of this experience and of its assessment lies at the core of the tradition and also constitutes the issue to be explored. The point, however, requires some elaboration.

The preceding definition of mysticism referred to it as a "doctrine" that is, "attainable through immediate intuition." This naturally disposes one to ask: How do the two relate? At the moment, however, one must make a more preliminary observation. Although the general semantic landscape covered by a word may be indicated by a definition, if a word is to be fully meaningful when applied to a specific case, it must properly account for the actual contours of the particular landscape of meaning represented by the specific case, such as that represented by Advaita Vedānta in the present instance. This attempt to make the definition fit the case requires two major shifts of nuance in the case of Advaita Vedānta. The first of these is the ultimacy we accord to experience over doctrine in the form of the mysticism we associate with it. What precise implication this has for their relative status remains to be determined, but the important point is that even if the experience has to be judged in light of the doctrine, the experiential component remains the primary (though not the sole) referent. When one prefers the term *mystical experience* over *mysticism*, one is only conforming to this bent of the tradition.

The second notable point is that ordinary sense perception and ratiocination are definitionally blocked as means of attaining an immediate illumination of ultimate reality. But while these two doors are closed, two others are opened—those of faith and intuition—along with undoubtedly a few other portals. But I specify these two as they constitute the two main mystical avenues that have gained wide mystical currency in general in Hinduism and they conform, respectively, to the well-known paths or yogas known as *bhakti* and *jñāna*. Of the two, the philosophical school of Advaita Vedānta accords primacy, if not ultimacy, to *jñāna*. This has a bearing on the "attainability" component of the definition. Advaita Vedānta asserts the premortem attainability of this immediate mystical insight in a way not matched by many of the other philosophical schools of Hinduism.

A more general observation on the nature of mystical experience and sacred scripture may also be in order, before we delve further into this relationship in the context of Advaita Vedānta. It is obvious that not all that is said or written is scripture. In fact, most of what is said or written is mundane and ordinary. Some of this qualifies as being out of the ordinary, and within that, some statements aspire for the even higher status of moral and spiritual discourse. Some parts of this moral and spiritual discourse, again, attain a measure of sanctity that enables the status of sacred scripture to be conferred on them. Finally, within this body of sacred scripture certain parts come to be considered as more significant than the rest. In a similar way, most of our experience of life is ordinary, even banal. Some of it, however, becomes memorable due to its extraordinary character. Out of this generally higher order of experience as compared to the ordinary, some portion stands apart due to its moral and spiritual component. Finally, within these higher reaches, some experiences attain the status of "peak" experiences due to their superb quality. In this sense "sacred scripture" and "mystical experience" possess an isomorphic nature. It seems fair to put these points in place at the very outset as they have a vital bearing on the rest of this analysis.

The Nature of Advaitic Mystical Experience

Having said this, I now point out that the nature of the relationship between the Advaitic mystical experience and its sacred texts has been a focus of much recent debate. To participate in that debate, it will be useful (1) to indicate the nature of Advaitic mystical experience and (2) to identify the sacred texts that come into play in this context. The Advaitic plenary mystical experience is called *jīvanmukti*, "living liberation," and the sacred text involved here is *śruti*, or revelation as conceived in Hinduism. The two famous *śruti* texts cite the same verse on the issue of *jīvanmukti* (Bṛhadāraṇyaka Upaniṣad 4.4.7 and Kaṭha Upaniṣad 6.14): "When all desires that dwell in the heart are cast away, then does the mortal become immortal, then he attains *brahman* here (in this very body)."[4]

Brahman in Advaitic thought, as in Hinduism, denotes the ultimate reality. In Advaitic thought, consequent to realization, a person's *empirical existence* does not cease—that is, he does not disappear from view—but his or her *empirical experience* ceases, especially in the form of potentiality for rebirth. During the rest of his or her earthly existence, he or she is in the world but not of it. According to Advaita Vedānta, this realization consists of the experiential knowledge that "the principle underlying the world as a whole" (*brahman*) and "that which forms the essence of man" (*ātman*) "are ultimately the same." As to what happens to the liberated being after death, nothing can be said, except that he or she is liberated (*mukta*); indeed even in life, in a sense little can be said since the absolute is indescribable.[5]

Now, the crucial question we ask at this stage is; How is this nondual experience to be related to the sacred scriptures of the school of nondualism that is called Advaita Vedānta?

This question can be broken down into a series of questions as we probe the various hermeneutical issues and strategies generated by this interface of mystical experience and sacred scripture:

1. Do sacred texts derive their authority from mystical experience, or vice versa? This may be called the question of authority.
2. Are sacred texts necessary and/or sufficient for mystical experience, or vice versa? This may be called the question of adequacy.
3. Is the relationship between the two more complex if our analysis includes such questions as *which* texts, *whose* interpretation, *whose* experience, and *which* experience? This may be called the question of selectivity.

The Question of Authority

It is perhaps best to begin the exploration of the question of authority by contrasting the two divergent views that are encountered on this point in the current literature on the subject. According to one school of scholars, the authority of the scriptures derives from experience. Its collective position has been summarized by one of its critics as consisting of the following seven points: (1) the scriptures—that is to say, the Vedas (or *śruti*)—are a record of the transcendental experience of the mystics; (2) such experience possesses a self-certifying character; (3) the Vedas, being an expression of reality rather than really itself (which is itself experienced mystically), are secondary to it; (4) however, they point to it and point the way to it, by following which of their statements about it could be verified; (5) the reality can be known independently of the Vedas; (6) but they are the normal way of knowing it, by resorting to the three steps indicated within the Vedas: those of hearing the truth (*śravaṇa*), reflecting on the truth (*manana*), and (c) meditating on the truth (*nididhyāsana*); (7) experience as a means of knowing reality constitutes a class by itself.[6]

The other school, which accords primacy to scripture over experience, presents its case as follows: (1) the ultimate reality, like one's self, is self-evident; (2) the fact that it exists is clear, but *what* it is, is not clear because its true nature is obscured by ignorance; (3) this ignorance is corrected by scriptural knowledge; (4) only the scriptures can tell us what that reality is and how to reach it, and therefore (5) they alone can lead to its experience and adjudge our experience of it as valid or invalid.[7]

Thus, according to one school, *anubhava* (experience) leads and *śruti* (scripture) follows its lead, while according to the other school, *śruti* (scripture) leads and *anubhava* (experience) follows. To this larger philosophical issue is often appended a historical issue: What was the view held on this point by Śaṅkara (the celebrated exponent of the system usually placed in the eighth century), especially as both the schools claim his support?[8] This point is further complicated by the fact that Śaṅkara's famous predecessor, Gauḍapāda, on whose work he comments, plausibly even conceded that the Advaitic insight could be gained by reason *alone*[9] and is still further convoluted by the fact that later Advaitins were perhaps arguably less equivocal than Śaṅkara in accepting that the Advaitic insight could be gained by experience (*anubhava*).[10] In other words, the issue is both philosophically and historically a hot potato. Let us see if we can make it into a baked one.

On the basis of my studies, I have come round to the view (which of course remains open to correction) that it might be possible to distinguish between two views espoused by Śaṅkara on this point, without implying duality. Thus two views of Śaṅkara's attitude toward scripture and experience can be identified as being thermostatic[11] and homeostatic.

According to the thermostatic model, the search for reality commences with inquiry into brahman, which is initiated by scripture. One gradually advances toward it through scriptural procedures, but as soon as brahman is realized, the scriptures drop out of sight—for the ultimate reality is beyond duality of any kind. The example of a thermostat works as follows: once it is set at a certain temperature, it sets the process of heating in motion, raises the temperature to the desired point, but *shuts itself off automatically* as soon as the desired temperature is reached.

According to the homeostatic model, the universe (and the Vedas, which are part and parcel of the universe) and brahman have existed from beginningless time, although the eternality they possess is different in nature. Brahman is eternal in the sense of being *outside* time and the Vedas are eternal *within* time, as part of the universe in eternal flux. The Vedas appear with the universe and dissolve with it. The various creatures are also caught in this process from beginningless time, and so the Vedas, too (or the Veda, if referred to in the singular), are part and parcel of their existence in the empirical sense, as well as in the cosmic sense. So the scene keeps ceaselessly unfolding as follows: *brahman* is always there and so are the universe and the Vedas, in the state of cosmic manifestation. This is a stable scenario. Because of their constant presence, one could experience *brahman* either directly or through the Veda in the course of a life, or because in some life one was already exposed to the Veda, or even to any kind of literature that conveyed the Advaitic insight, at any time in the past, apart from the Veda.

It is clear that in both these versions of Śaṅkara's views the relationship between sacred scripture and experience is a close one. They remain soteriologically either necessary or sufficient—or both.

The Question of Adequacy

Three points thus emerge into clear view. The first is that at least parity, and even priority, has been accorded to elements other than scripture in the context of mystical experience by many of its modern exponents. Some have indeed accorded clear primacy to experience, as when M. Hiriyanna writes:

> But it may be thought that the doctrine, however important the place it assigns to reason may be, is essentially dogmatic, because its truth is primarily to be known through revelation. That such a conclusion, however, does not follow will be seen when we remember the exact function of revelation. The aim here, as in the case of other Indian doctrines, is not merely to grasp the ultimate truth intellectually but to realize it in one's own experience. The scripture as such, being a form of verbal testimony, can however convey only mediate knowledge. To attain the ideal therefore means to advance farther than merely comprehending the scriptural truth. Scriptural knowledge, accordingly, is not sufficient, though necessary; and like reason, it also therefore becomes only a subsidiary aid to the attainment of the goal. The Upanishads themselves declare that when a person has seen this truth for himself, he outgrows the need for the scriptures: "There a father becomes no father; a mother, no mother; the world, no world; the gods, no gods; the Vedas, no Vedas." Thus we finally get beyond both reason and revelation, and rest on direct experience (*anubhava*). Hence if Advaita is dogmatic, the dogma is there only to be transcended. Further, we should not forget that revelation itself, as stated in an earlier chapter, goes back to the intuitive experience of the great seers of the past. It is that experience which is to be personally corroborated by the disciple.[12]

The second point is that, although it may be arguably claimed that Śaṅkara accorded supremacy to scripture over experience, the experiential dimension is often invoked by Śaṅkara and later Advaitins. Apart from the well-known references,[13] Lance Nelson has drawn attention to his comment on Chāndogya Upaniṣad 6.14.2.[14] Therein, while defining *jīvanmukti*, Śaṅkara refers to the need for a *living* teacher—who has himself experienced brahman—to *instruct* one in Advaita Vedānta in order that its truth may be realized. Hence, while a synchronic view of *śruti* tends to downplay the role of experience vis-à-vis scripture, a diachronic view of Advaita as a living tradition handed down from teacher to pupil—coupled with the desirability of a *realized* teacher—brings experience back into the picture. Here the two tracks of *acquisition* and *transmission* of Advaitic knowledge seem to merge.

Finally, what about the sacred scriptures themselves? We do find instances of individual teachers, such as Yājñavalkya, expounding their experiences. "Thus in a general way Brahman may be inferred from the world or learnt from the texts or experienced by the individual."[15] However, what are the exact dynamics of this relationship? Are the dynamics only *internal* to the scripture or can they also be *external* to the scripture—that is, can the other two operate only within the scripture or alongside it in their own right if necessary? These are philosophically disputed points within the tradition. In the latter case, the significance of sacred scripture vis-à-vis mystical experience will tend to become reduced and, in a more radical interpretation, may even be eliminated.

However, while the role of experience thus comes to the fore in the soteriology espoused within the system, it recedes to the background when the school is dialectically engaged in defending itself against other systems. Then its chief weapon is the scriptural authority used in dealing with other Hindu systems that accept Vedic authority, and reason and polemics in dealing with other Indian systems that do not accept Vedic authority. Experience must take the back seat in such situations because an intersubjective criterion for resolution is required; otherwise, the two parties could continue to appeal unilaterally to their own experience without hope of resolution. The point is also complicated by the essential subjectivity of the Advaitic experience, for the proof of *anubhava* (experience) is in one's own heart, just as a person who is attached to wealth will grieve when it is stolen but will not grieve once he has given up such attachment, and only he or she will know the difference.

Śruti texts—the Advaitic sacred texts par excellence—are intersubjective in another sense distinct from the one alluded to above. While non-Vedic systems of thought point to an individual as their ultimate source of authority, such as to a Buddha or a Mahāvīra, the Hindu tradition points to the Vedas as its ultimate source of authority, which is traced back not to an individual but to a plurality of persons called seers, so that here the standard becomes eventually a society of men, and not an individual; and, by virtue of the objective status it thus acquires, its deliverances are taken to possess an authority that cannot belong to those of anybody's private intuition.

Advaita Vedānta seems fairly committed to the view that mere *formal* familiarity with the sacred text cannot bring about mystical experience. However, the Advaitic tradition becomes divided into two subschools on the question of whether merely the audition of the quintessential sayings called *mahāvākya*s is sufficient to bring about realization, as the Vivaraṇa school seems to hold, or whether reflection and meditation on them are also necessary to achieve liberation,[16] as held by the Bhāmatī school. This issue should be distinguished from the larger issue of whether the *śruti*—the sacred scripture—is a sine qua non for attaining enlightenment. The *mahāvākya*s, which are listed further on in this discussion, are seminal sentences said to be capable of triggering realization directly or at least serving as a catalyst for the process.

Hindu cosmology bestows a kind of eternality on the Vedas or the *śruti*, but historically speaking, the *mahāvākya*s, or (great utterances), were presumably uttered by teachers who had achieved realization *before* they framed them. Similarly, despite considerable intellectual investment in the view that Advaitic realization cannot be achieved except through the Vedas and the attempt to associate this view with Śaṅkara, exceptions to this rule can be identiried in Śaṅkara himself. However, the most telling example of how one may have the Advaitic realization without taking the Vedic route is provided by a modern Advaitin, Ramaṇa Maharṣi, who is referred to as Bhagavān in the ensuing dialogue:

DEVOTEE: Is Bhagavan's teaching the same as Shankara's?

BHAGAVĀN: Bhagavan's teaching is an expression of his own experience and realization. Others find that it tallies with Sri Shankara's.

DEVOTEE: When the Upanishads say that all is Brahman, how can we agree with Shankara that this world is illusory?

BHAGAVĀN: Shankara also said that this world is Brahman or the Self. What he objected to is one's imagining that the Self is limited by the names and forms that constitute the world. He only said that the world has no reality apart from Brahman. Brahman or the Self is like a cinema screen and the world like the pictures on it. You can see the picture only so long as there is a screen. But when the observer himself becomes the screen only the Self remains.[17]

As Arthur Osborne explains in the preface, although the teachings of Ramaṇa confirmed that of Śaṅkara, "The agreement does not, however, mean that Bhagavan was, as a philosopher would put it, 'influenced by' Shankara, merely that he recognized Shankara's teaching as a true exposition of what he had realized and knew by direct knowledge."[18]

The presence of the sacred texts, like that of a textbook, is no doubt a great convenience in the larger context of Advaitic experience, but the question of its actual necessity continues to be a moot point.

The question of the requirement of the scripture and of its exact operation also seems to rest on the readiness of the seeker. Thus, according to *modern* Advaita, a guru and the associated scripture are not indispensable, while the *classical* position veered more toward the idea that

according to Śaṅkara, *anubhava* is the assured conviction, the clear undoubted awareness that one is Brahman, which is *generated* by *Vedānta Vākyas*. A man who has realised this is unaffected by agency, pleasure and pain; he continues to live, but for him his body and the world are dead, as a slough is for a snake. His way of life and behaviour have been described in the *Gītā bhāṣya*. Śaṅkara also says that such a man will have no change of condition after death; he will only be not connected with another body.[19]

A Question of Selectivity

The issue of mystical experience and sacred scriptures now needs to be further problematized by raising another set of issues, involving such questions as *which* text, *whose* interpretation, *whose* experience, and *which* experience.[20]

Which Text?

The Vedas are the foundational scriptures of Hinduism, and Advaita Vedānta performs three maneuvers in relation to them to adapt them to its purposes. The first maneuver is textual: it distinguishes between the earlier and the later sections of the Vedas, the way Christianity distinguishes between the Old and the New Testaments in the Bible.[21] Next, apart from claiming, again like Christianity, that the later texts supersede the earlier, it also claims that the nature of the subject matter in the two sections is distinct, that while the statements in the earlier section are injunctive in nature, those in the later one are assertative[22]—this is the hermeneutical claim. Then it claims further that this body of literature is to be understood in the light of certain key utterances, called *mahāvākyas*—this is the exegetical claim: that the Vedānta, or the Upaniṣads, as the later sections are called, have to be read in light of the following overarching insights:

That thou art (*tattvamasi*). (Chāndogya Upaniṣad 6.8.7)

I am Brahman (*ahaṃ Brahmāsmi*). (Bṛhadāraṇyaka Upaniṣad) 1.4.10)

This Self is Brahman (*ayamātmā Brahma*). (Bṛhadāraṇyaka Upaniṣad 2.5.19)

All this, verily, is Brahman (*sarvam khalvidam Brahma*) (Chāndogya Upaniṣad 3.14.1)

This conclusion is supported by a sophisticated exegetical apparatus.[23]

Whose Interpretation?

The interpretation under discussion is primarily that of Śaṅkara. It is interesting that other systems that came *after* Śaṅkara did not so much discard the *mahāvākya*s as interpret them in their won way. The point is highly significant, although it cannot be pursued in detail here. Given the *mahāvākya*s, it is clear that the exact sense in which they are to be understood has depended on who is interpreting them, within both Śaṅkara's school of Vedānta and those schools that differ from it. Thus the statement "That thou art" is interpreted differently. Within Advaita it is interpreted as indicating the literal identity either of *ātman* and *brahman* or of the "conditioned *jīva*" and God; outside Advaita it is interpreted by Rāmānuja as representing not pure identity but that of "God having the entire universe as his body" and as "having the individual soul as his body" and by Madhva as denoting a resemblance, rather than identity, between *ātman* and God.[24] Each of the interpreters has understood the text in such a way as to bring his own special mystical interpretation to life.

Whose Experience?

Although these statements are drawn from the sacred scriptures and therefore on the surface reflect the experience of the figures contained therein, Advaita Vedānta, like the allied tradition of Mīmāṁsā, conferred on the Vedas the status of impersonal texts, even to the extent of denying any authorship to them, human or divine. How this result was achieved need not detain us, but the fact that it was achieved is of prime importance. Thus, in regard to the question of whose experience is involved, the answer is, nobody's experience. The experience of the communication to, and the reception by, the seers of these propositions is experience of a different order and is not to be confused with the text itself.

Which Experience?

The Vedic texts contain references to experiences of many kinds: nondualistic, dualistic, or pluralistic. Advaita Vedānta selected the nondualistic type for special emphasis. Why this was done can only be answered in a conjectural way. Such an answer is attempted in the next section.

In Nondualistic and Dualistic Schools

Each school claims, equally indubitably, that the experience enshrined at the core of its own system is indisputably self-evident and provides the key for unlocking the true meaning of scripture, which it interprets accordingly. To illustrate this point, let us select the following four statements from the Upaniṣads: (1) *tattvamasi*, (2) *māyayā mohitaṃ jagat*, (3) *neha nānāsti kiñcana*, and (4) *ekamevādvitīyam*. Each statement has been understood in its own way, within each system of Vedānta, whose interpretation of the sacred text was presumably influenced by the mystical experience of the founder of that system; the experience was subsequently elaborated into a philosophical school based on the tradition founded by him. To be sure, this is not how the tradition presents the development. Formally, these mystical founders of the tradition are represented as correctly interpreting of the revelation. Thus one might say that, according to tradition, it is the scripture that is defining the experience, and qua traditionists we may accept it as such. However, if we approach the issue as historians, then the perspective is reversed, or at least is capable of being reversed.

Let us first examine the case of Śaṅkara (788–820?) and his school of Advaita (or nondualistic) Vedānta. He is normally depicted as interpreting the vast body of Vedantic literature in light of the four *mahāvākyas* (the great utterances). This is the formal position. A historical perspective, however, may be developed with the help of a hint contained in his commentary on Vedāntasūtra 4.1.15, "which tradition views as an allusion to his own direct experience of the ultimate truth."[25] It runs as follows:

> *kathaṁ hyekasya sva-hṛdayapratyayaṁ brahma-vedanaṁ deha-dhāraṇaṃ ca apareṇa pratikṣeptuṁ śakyeta?*
>
> How can one contest the heart-felt cognition of another as possessing *brahman*-knowledge, even though bearing a body?[26]

If we now start with this experience, then it is quite clear that Śaṅkara will gravitate toward those passages of the scriptures that resonate with this experience and will select them as the key with which to open previously closed, even forbidden, doors.

We turn next to Rāmānuja (1017–1137) and his school of Viśiṣṭādvaita (nondualism of the qualified)[27] form of Vedānta. Again, the traditional view is that he offered the correct interpretation of the scripture—a kind of theistic interpretation as against Śaṅkara's transtheistic interpretation. Once again, formally, the mystical founder is represented as correctly interpreting the revelation. Thus one could say again that according to tradition scripture is defining the mystical experience, and qua traditionists we may be disposed to go along with this. If I approach the issue as a historian, however, the perspective can again be reversed. This perspective can be further developed with the help of a hint contained in the introductory verses to his work called *Gadyatraya*, where Rāmānuja alludes directly to having been reduced to a devotionally servile status as a result of his experience of God (*tavānubhūtisaṃbhūtaprītikāritadāsatām*). If we now start with this experience, then again, as in the case of Śaṅkara, one would expect Rāmānuja to gravitate toward those sections of the scriptures that resonate positively with his experience. There is a curious bit of evidence to support this. One of the Upaniṣads, the *Bṛhadāraṇyaka*, is predominantly Advaitic or absolutistic, yet Rāmānuja uses it as one of his major proof texts. It is revealing, however, that he presses into repeated service one of the few sections of this Upaniṣad (3.5) that can be interpreted theistically as simultaneously celebrating God's immanence and transcendence: "He who, dwelling in the fire, is yet other than fire, whom fire does not know, whose body the fire is, who controls the fire from within—he is your soul, the inner controller, the immortal."[28]

Our last example is provided by the case of Madhva (1238–1317). Madhva originally belonged to the nondualistic school of Śaṅkara but then turned against him, using epithets sometimes too gross to admit of being stated. One would assume that such a sharp, indeed a hostile, break would have been prompted by some overwhelming personal experience of the road-to-Damascus type in reverse. In his case the putatively autobiographical clues are difficult to retrieve, but it seems very likely that the experience of the overwhelming grace of Viṣṇu played a major role in determining Madhva's orientation.[29] Such an experience is bound to evoke a realization of the gulf set between God and humans, thereby leading one philosophically in the direction of dualism. Once again, formally, Madhva would only claim that he was interpreting the text correctly. This seems to be the implication of the tradition that says that, while in the Himalayas, he was directed by the seer Vyāsa to write a commentary on the *Vedānta Sūtra* to clarify its meaning, which had been obscured by earlier commentators.

We turn to the examination of some other instances in which the same scriptural statement is interpreted differently, presumably reflecting the different mystical orientations through which their meaning is being refracted.

tattvamasi (Chāndogya Upaniṣad 6.8.7)
"That thou art."

According to Advaita, this means that you are the same as the ultimate reality, when both are respectively viewed without their limiting adjuncts (*upādhi*s). In other words, man – limitations = God – superimpositions.

According to the Viśiṣṭādvaita school, "that thou art" means that God embodied in the universe is the same as God embodied in the individual (as the soul).

According to the Dvaita school, one of the meanings of this saying is that "you are God's," that is, you belong to God.

*māyayā mohitaṃ jagat (*Kṛṣṇa Upaniṣad 12)
"The universe is entranced by *māyā*."

According to the Advaita school, *brahman* is the only reality and the universe is less than ultimately real, although it is experienced as real. This is the result of *māyā*.

According to the Viśiṣṭādvaita school, which interprets *māyā* not as illusion but as the magician's power to create an illusion, the universe is a magical manifestation of God's power, as it were.

According to the Dvaita school, which interprets *māyā* as the divine knowledge of God, the universe is created by that knowledge of God (thus imparting a new spin to the aphorism about knowledge being power).

neha nānāsti kiñcana (Bṛhadāraṇyaka Upaniṣad 4.4.19)
"There is no diversity within it whatsoever."

According to Advaita Vedānta, this confirms its basic position that Brahman is devoid of all kinds of distinctions, internal or external.

According to Viśiṣṭādvaita Vedānta, the statement means that there is nothing outside Brahman—it is the sole and whole reality.

According to the Dvaita school, the statement means that the qualities of Brahman are in no way different from Brahman—and to see such difference is to fall in the clutches of delusion.

idam agra āsīd ekam evādvitīyam (Chāndogya Upaniṣad 6.2.1)
"This, in the beginning, was one without a second."

According to Advaita Vedānta, this means that prior to creation, there was one undifferentiated homogeneous mass of consciousness, with nothing beside it.

According to Viśiṣṭādvaita Vedānta, prior to creation, it [God] was internally differentiated but there was nothing outside it in the sense of an externally differentiated cause or substance.

According to Dvaita Vedānta, this means that in the beginning there was only one independent Lord or God.

This detour through other schools, along with that of Advaita Vedānta, and through their various interpretations brings us to an interesting question. It is a question that would arise in the context of each school, but as this chapter claims to focus on Advaita Vedānta, let me raise it in that context. Given the various options, why did Advaita Vedānta choose to take the nondualistic route?

Śaṅkara might have done so under the influence of some overpowering nondualistic experience (although this is virtually impossible to confirm or deny). Could it not also now be suggested, given the impersonalization of the Vedic text, that the decision to emphasize the nondual experience was an outcome of the same impersonal thrust? In principle, a plenary experience that sweeps both subject and object into a unitary vortex is of a kind that is not only the most impersonal but also, on that account, the least open to challenge on philosophical grounds because it cannot be subrated. Eliot Deutsch has made the point well:

> The only experience, or state of being, whose content cannot be subrated in fact and in principle by any other experience—which no other experience can conceivably contradict—is the experience of pure spiritual identity; the experience wherein the separation of self and non-self, of ego and world, is transcended, and pure oneness alone remains. This is the experience celebrated by the Advaitin as one of perfect insight, bliss, and power; as one of infinite joy and understanding. In spiritual identity (*nirvikalpa samādhi*) the pretensions to ultimacy of anything else are shattered, and a complete self-realization and self-knowledge are said to be obtained. What kind of experience could conceivably subrate unqualified identity—the experience of absolute value wherein the unique oneness of being stands forth as the sole content of consciousness? Sureśvara, a ninth-century Advaitin, puts it thus: Wheresoever there is doubt, there, the wise should know, the Self [the Real] is not. For no doubts can arise in relation to the Self, since its nature is pure immediate consciousness.[30]

Special Features of Advaita Vedānta

In this section some special features of the scriptural and experiential dimensions of Advaita Vedānta and their relationship are explored.

According to Advaita Vedānta, Brahman or the reality alone is real; all else is *māyā* or less than ultimately real. The universe as we experience it is *māyā* and so are the scriptures, namely, the Vedas. They are not reality, they are *about* reality. This naturally raises the question of whether the less than real can lead to the real. This scriptural point also has an experiential parallel: Can the metaphysically less-than-real empirical human being attain the real? The Advaitin answers both these questions in the affirmative. The first question "signifies that a false means can lead to a true end—a position that may appear untenable; but there are many instances in life when this happens. The image of a person reflected in the mirror is not real, but it does not therefore fail to serve as a means of showing to him so many facts about his appearance. The roaring of a lion in a dream is not real, but it may wake the dreamer to actual life."[31] The other question signifies that the false subject can realize the real subject. This position may also initially appear untenable, until it is realized that in Advaitic realization the false subject, by realizing its own falsity, realizes itself as the real subject, just as an adopted child, on realizing that it is adopted, realizes its true identity.

Thus this dimension of the relationship between scripture and experience is not merely soteriological but also more general in nature. It might be described as existential—blurring the distinction between essence, experience, and existence, as it were. As M. Hiriyanna points out:

> All philosophy starts from experience. But it is usually assumed that the data of experience, if they are to lead to right conclusions, should stand for actual facts or be valid. This is not admitted by the Advaitin as necessary; and he illustrates his position by examples like the false image of a person, reflected in a mirror, being the means of showing to him what is true about his appearance. That is, the Advaitin attaches no necessary ontological significance to the data that serve as the bases of reasoning. He begins his inquiry, taking them at their face value, and leaves their validity or invalidity to reveal itself in the course of the inquiry or as its result. This is the meaning of the distinction of *prasiddha* and *pramāṇa-siddha* among them, which is sometimes made in Advaitic works. The former are mere reiterations (*anuvāda*) of common beliefs, and are not demonstrated truths like the latter. They are psychologically given, but are not logically established. In other words, *kalpita* factors may, according to Advaita, be as fruitful in philosophic inquiry as actual ones. Or, as it is somewhat differently stated, empirical facts, though they are not finally true, may be the means of leading us to transcendental truth.[32]

This concession that Advaita Vedānta makes to both scriptures and human beings, due to their location in *māyā*, does not compromise its attitude toward Brahman. Contrary to the tenets of radical constructivism, Brahman is not a construct. It is a reality in itself (*vastutantra*) and not an object of human fancy (*puruṣatantra*), however philosophically refined. Śaṅkara states:

> All option depends on the notion of man; but the knowledge of the real nature of a thing does not depend on the notion of man, but only on the thing itself. For to think with regard to a post, "This is a post or a man, or something else," is not knowledge of truth; the two ideas, "It is a man or something else," being false, and only the third idea, "It is a post," which depends on the thing itself, falling under the head of true knowledge. Thus true knowledge of all things depends on the things themselves, and hence the knowledge of Brahman also depends altogether on the thing, i.e., Brahman itself.[33]

It is equally worth noting that, according to Advaita Vedānta, all may experience the same reality but not in the same way—that is, they may not express the experience in the same way.

This point is made explicit by a modern Advaitin, Ramaṇa Maharṣi:

DEVOTEE: Is the experience of the highest state the same to all, or is there any difference?

BHAGAVĀN: The highest state is the same and the experience is the same.

DEVOTEE: But I find some difference in the interpretation given of the highest truth.

BHAGAVĀN: The interpretations are made with the mind. The minds are different, so the interpretations also differ.[34]

Summary

The general point that emerges from this discussion is that the relationship between experience and scripture (and the doctrines as embodied in them) could be transcriptive or transformative at both ends. When it is transcriptive, the relationship between experience and scripture could be merely repetitive or regulative. When it is transformative, the relationship could be progressively innovative, inventive, or creative—or regressively restrictive. If all the views that have been expressed, from both the experiential and scriptural standpoints, on the question of the relationship between the two are surveyed in Advaita Vedānta, the chips will not fall where they may—they are likely to fall somewhere on this grid.

NOTES

1. *Webster's Third International Dictionary of the English Language*, 1961 edition.
2. Ibid., p. 1996.
3. See Eliot Deutsch and J.A.B. van Buitenen, *A Source Book of Advaita Vedānta* (Honolulu, 1971).
4. S. Radhakrishnan, ed., *The Principal Upaniṣads* (London, 1953), pp. 273, 646.
5. S. Radhakrishnan, trans., *The Brahma Sūtra: The Philosophy of Spiritual Life* (London, 1960), p. 207. On the indescribability of Brahman, see M. Hiriyanna, *Indian Philosophical Studies* (Mysore, 1957), pp. 98–103. Some attempts to describe the state of being of the *jīvanmukta* are cited below. Thus M. Hiriyanna writes (in *Outlines of Indian Philosophy* [London, 1932] pp. 381–382): "The jīvan-mukta's life has two phases: It is either *samādhi* or mystic trance when he turns inwards and loses himself in Brahman; or the condition known as *vyutthāna* or reversion to common life when the spectacle of the world returns but does not delude him since he has once for all realized its metaphysical falsity. Diversity continues to appear then as the sun, we may say, continues to appear as moving even after we are convinced that it is stationary. A jīvan-mukta experiences pain and pleasure, but neither really matters to him. He does not necessarily give up all activity as is abundantly illustrated by the strenuous life which Śaṅkara himself led, but it does not proceed from any selfish impulse or even from a sense of obligation to others. Blind love for the narrow self which ordinarily characterizes man and the consequent clinging to the mere particular are in his case replaced by enlightened and therefore equal love for all. The basis for this universal love is furnished by the Upaniṣadic teaching 'That thou art.' We should do unto others as we do to ourselves, because they are ourselves—a view which places the golden rule of morality on the surest of foundations. 'Who sees all beings in himself and himself in all beings—he will dislike none,' as the Upaniṣad says; or as the Gītā puts it, 'He harms not self by self.' The common laws of social morality and ritual

which are significant only in reference to one that is striving for perfection are meaningless for him. The jīvan-mukta, having transcended the stage of strife, is spontaneously virtuous, Impulse and desire become one in him. He is not then realizing virtue but is revealing it. 'In one that has awakened to a knowledge of the self, virtues like kindness imply no conscious effort whatsoever. They are second nature with him.' When at last he is dissociated from the physical accompaniments, he is not reborn, but remains as Brahman. That is videha-mukti."

Karl H. Potter [pp. 33–34; see n. 8] offers the following description: "What, specifically, happens to a man when he becomes liberated? As we have seen, bondage arises because actions automatically—or with God's help—produce karmic residues, which in turn produce *vāsanās* and experiences. The condition under which this happens is *avidyā*. When *avidyā* is removed, two of the three kinds of action (karma) are rendered inoperative. The residues that have been stored up but have not started to reach fruition in this life lose their potency; they are 'burned,' suggests the etymology of the common verb used here, and like burned seed they no longer have the power to produce sprouts. As for the actions still to be performed in this life, they will no longer bind. Behavior after liberation is not action at all, since for a bit of behavior to be an action it must be done with desire for something distinguished as different from oneself, a something that one desires to obtain or avoid; when one realizes through the perfect knowledge that constitutes liberation that there are no other things, the necessary condition for action is annulled, and so no future actions can take place.

"That leaves the question of the karmic residues that determine the birth, length of life, and experiences of this very lifetime during which liberation is achieved. The Advaita doctrine here is that this *prārabdhakarman* had to work itself out—it cannot be destroyed by Self-knowledge as the other two kinds of karma can; it cannot be 'burned' for it has already begun to bear fruit. Thus the liberated person normally continues in bodily existence, working out his *prārabdhakarman*, and this state is known as 'liberation while living,' *jīvanmukti*.

The *jīvanmukti* state seems paradoxical. The liberated self has achieved Self-knowledge and thus no longer recognizes any distinctions; yet he moves among us, performs the necessary activities of eating, drinking, etc., that suffice to keep him alive through his allotted years. Having no desires he does not act, but he nevertheless does act insofar as he is impelled by the *vāsanās* produced by those karmic residues that are still working themselves out. Not recognizing anything as a possible object to be experienced, and not recognizing any organs through which he might experience anything, it follows that he has no experiences; yet because of the operation of *prārabdhakarman* and the *vāsanās* he is visited with objects experienced through the organs of sense.

"Indeed, the *jīvanmukti* or liberated person can be viewed from two perspectives: from the 'higher standpoint' (*pāramārthika*) he is liberated and thus incapable of ordinary knowledge, action, and experiences, but from the 'lower standpoint' (*vyāvahārika*) he is a *samnyāsin* or renunciate, capable of all such things. The Advaitin tends to switch back and forth between the two standpoints in describing one and the same individual."

6. I have drawn these points (but presented them less starkly) from Anantanand Rambachan, *Accomplishing the Accomplished: The Vedas as a Source of Valid Knowledge in Śaṅkara* (Honolulu, 1991), pp. 13–14.
7. Ibid., pp. 119–120.
8. Karl H. Potter, ed., *Encyclopedia of Indian Philosophies: Advaita Vedānta up to Śaṁkara and His Pupils* (Delhi, 1981) pp. 97–98, and Radhakrishnan trans., *The*

Brahma Sūtra, p. 104, present Śaṅkara as placing more weight on experience. K. Satachidananda Murty, *Revelation and Reason in Advaita Vedānta* (New York, 1959), and Rambachan, *Accomplishing the Accomplished*, present Śaṅkara as placing more weight on scripture.

9. Murty, *Revelation and Reason*, pp. 158–159.
10. See Lance E. Nelson's review of Anantanand Rambachan, *The Limits of Scripture: Vivekananda's Reinterpretation of the Vedas* (Honolulu, 1994), in *Religious Studies Review* 21:3 (July 1995), p. 250.
11. The first metaphor was suggested to me by Francis Brassard, a doctoral candidate in our faculty at McGill University.
12. M. Hiriyanna, *The Essentials of Indian Philosophy* (London, 1948), p. 173. For a striking parallel to the statement that one needs to go beyond both reason and revelation in Śaṅkara, see his gloss on Bṛhadāraṇyaka Upaniṣad III.1.1. Interestingly enough, Hiriyanna, in his other book (*Outlines of Indian Philosophy*, pp. 370, 376) distinguishes between the roles of empirical and mystical experience in this context.
13. See *Philosophy East and West* 43:4 (1993), pp. 737–744 and 45:1 (1995), pp. 105–113.
14. Lance E. Nelson, "Living Liberation in Śaṅkara and Classical Advaita: Sharing the Holy Waiting of God," in Andrew O. Fort and Patricia Y. Mumme, eds., *Living Liberation in Hindu Thought* (Albany, 1996), p. 25.
15. Radhakrishnan, *The Principal Upaniṣads*, p. 243.
16. Murty, *Revelation and Reason*, pp. 106–107.
17. Arthur Osborne, ed., *The Teachings of Bhagavan Sri Ramana Maharshi in His Own Words* (Triuvannamalai, 1971), p. 11.
18. Ibid., p. 10.
19. Murty, *Revelation and Reason*, p. 114. *Vedānta Vākya*s = *Mahāvākya*s.
20. I raised similar issues earlier at a presentation before the annual meeting of the American Academy of Religion in New York in 1982 in the Philosophy of Religion section.
21. T. M. P. Mahadevan, *Outlines of Hinduism* (Bombay, 1971), pp. 139–140.
22. Rambachan, *The Limits of Scripture*, pp. 79–80; also see George Thibaut, trans., *The Vedānta-Sūtras with the Commentary of Śaṅkarācārya* (Oxford, 1890), part 1, pp. 22–47.
23. Murty, *Revelation and Reason*, chap. 5.
24. I am particularly indebted to Professor N. Veezhinathan of the University of Madras for this section. However, I alone am responsible for any errors it might contain.
25. Hiriyanna, *Outlines of Indian Philosophy*, p. 381.
26. Mahadevan, *Outlines of Hinduism* (Bombay, 1971), p. 43.
27. The term is regularly *mis*translated as "qualified monism"; see Hiriyanna, *The Essentials of Indian Philosophy*, p. 178.
28. Robert Ernest Hume, trans., *The Thirteen Principal Upanishads* (London, 1968), p. 115.
29. B. N. K. Sharma, *Philosophy of Śrī Madhvācārya* (Bombay, 1962), p. 307.
30. Eliot Deutsch, *Advaita Vedānta: A Philosophical Reconstruction* (Honolulu, 1969), pp. 18–19.
31. Hiriyanna, *Outline of Indian Philosophy*, p. 359.
32. Hiriyanna, *Indian Philosophical Studies*, p. 100.
33. George Thibaut, trans., *The Vedānta Sūtras of Bādarāyaṇa with the Commentary by Śaṅkara* (New York, 1962 [first published, 1890]), part 1, pp. 18–19.
34. Osborne, *The Teachings*, pp. 71–72. For the formal Advaitic explanation for this, see Arvind Sharma, *The Philosophy of Religion and Advaita Vedānta: A Comparative Study in Religion and Reason* (University Park, Pa., 1995), pp. 221–222.

9

Mystical Cognition and Canonical Authority

The Devotional Mysticism of the Bhāgavata Purāṇa

BARBARA A. HOLDREGE

The Bhāgavata Purāṇa, one of the most important textual monuments to Hindu devotional (bhakti) mysticism, claims as its source and goal ecstatic union with Lord Kṛṣṇa. This paradigmatic devotional text, which originated in South India in the ninth or early tenth century,[1] attempts to invest its mystical teachings with canonical authority by securing for itself a place within the brahmanical Hindu canon. The Bhāgavata establishes its canonical status through assimilating itself to two principal categories of brahmanical scripture: Purāṇa and Veda. This essay will attempt to elucidate the various strategies used by the Bhāgavata Purāṇa—in terms of its form, language, content, and self-representations—to establish its dual status as the "Purāṇa-Veda" that is the culminating scripture of the brahmanical canon.

The Bhāgavata Purāṇa establishes itself as an authoritative, encompassing scripture by integrating the religiocultural traditions of South and North India and reconciling the claims of Vaiṣṇava bhakti with brahmanical orthodoxy. More specifically, it adopts the canonical form of a Purāṇa and incorporates the South Indian devotional traditions of the Āḻvārs—Tamil Vaiṣṇava poet-saints—within a brahmanical Sanskritic framework that reflects North Indian ideologies.[2] The Bhāgavata Purāṇa, as an "*opus universale* attempting to encompass everything,"[3] was ultimately successful in securing for itself canonical status within both orthodox brahmanical traditions and Vaiṣṇava devotional traditions—as the most popular and influential of the eighteen Purāṇas in the brahmanical canon, and as one of the most important scriptures in the Vaiṣṇava canon. Through its Sanskritization of Kṛṣṇa bhakti, the Bhāgavata Purāṇa provided the foundation for the development of Kṛṣṇa devotional movements in North India. The five classical Vaiṣṇava schools (*sampradāyas*) recognize the authority of this devotional text, and each school has accordingly produced commentaries to demonstrate the Bhāgavata's support of its particular views—the Viśiṣṭādvaita school of

Rāmānuja (eleventh century), the Dvaita school of Madhva (thirteenth century), the Dvaitādvaita school of Nimbārka (twelfth–thirteenth century), the Śuddhādvaita school of Vallabha (sixteenth century), and the Gauḍīya Vaiṣṇava school of the Gosvāmins (sixteenth century).[4]

The Bhāgavata Purāṇa thus participates on a number of levels in the category of "sacred scripture," one of the two categories that is the focus of this volume. However, before turning to an analysis of the Bhāgavata's multivalent participation in the category of scripture, we must consider the text's relationship to the category of "mysticism"—the other category that is the focus of this volume—and determine the sense in which it may be termed a "mystical" text.

The Bhāgavata Purāṇa and Devotional Mysticism

The Bhāgavata Purāṇa is generally characterized as a preeminent bhakti text,[5] and therefore, in order to assess the Bhāgavata's role as a mystical text, we must first consider the more fundamental question of whether Hindu bhakti constitutes a form of mysticism. John B. Carman has given an insightful, nuanced analysis of the issues involved in responding to this latter question. In the end, he concludes that the Hindu category of bhakti can be appropriately correlated with the category of "theistic mysticism."[6] This hybrid category "theistic mysticism" is itself somewhat problematic, however, and, as Carman notes, scholars of mysticism have presented contending perspectives concerning the validity and significance of such a category.

> "Theistic mysticism" is a more restricted term [than mysticism], which some students of mysticism would consider a contradiction in terms, since for them theism implies a fundamental distinction between creator and creature which mysticism denies or overcomes. At most they would view theistic mysticism as a mixed type or impure variety of mysticism, a practical compromise concealing a metaphysical contradiction. A quite different view of mysticism sees theistic mysticism as a fully legitimate type, possibly even the most legitimate type of mysticism, exemplified repeatedly in the tradition from which the concept derives, the mystical theology or *via contemplativa* of Christian tradition, both Eastern and Western.[7]

As Carman points out,[8] those scholars whose work focuses primarily on Christian, Jewish, or Islamic mystical traditions, such as Evelyn Underhill,[9] Rufus Jones,[10] Gershom Scholem,[11] and Annemarie Schimmel,[12] have tended to allot an integral place to theistic mysticism.

With respect to scholars who have proposed cross-cultural typologies of mystical experience, R. C. Zaehner and W. T. Stace represent opposite ends of the spectrum in their evaluations of theistic mysticism. Zaehner posits three types of mysticism—pantheistic, or pan-en-henic; monistic; and theistic—and, in accordance with his Roman Catholic biases, assigns primacy of place to theistic mysticism.[13] Stace, by contrast, establishes a twofold typological distinction between introvertive and extrovertive forms of mystical experience and gives primary emphasis to monistic, introvertive experience as the highest form, with theistic mysticism relegated to a secondary place.[14] Both Zaehner's and Stace's phenomenological typologies have been rightfully criticized as overly simplistic and inadequate, for, like most attempts at cross-cultural typologies, they fail to account for the manifold varieties of mystical phenomena and do not give sufficient attention to the specific religious, cultural, and historical contexts that shape these phenomena.[15]

If we turn from cross-cultural typologies to a consideration of studies of Indian or Hindu mysticism more specifically, we find that bhakti is generally included as a central category by both Western and Indian scholars. S. N. Dasgupta, for example, includes bhakti, or devotional mysticism, as one of the four major types of Indian mysticism, along with the Upaniṣadic, the Yogic, and the Buddhistic.[16] Zaehner, in his study of Hindu and Muslim mysticism, builds on Dasgupta's fourfold typology and arrives at three types of Hindu mysticism: "The types are (i) the pantheistic or pan-en-henic, . . . the 'I am this All' of the Upaniṣads; (ii) the realization of undifferentiated unity, however philosophically interpreted; and (iii) the loving dialogue with God which results in transforming union."[17]

Zaehner's threefold Hindu typology is simply an adaptation of his threefold cross-cultural typology mentioned earlier, with the three Hindu types corresponding, respectively, to the pantheistic, monistic, and theistic forms of mysticism. In this context, bhakti mysticism, as "the loving dialogue with God which results in transforming union," corresponds to theistic mysticism. Once again betraying his Christian bias toward theism, Zaehner proclaims theistic mysticism a "higher form of religious life" for Hindus than monistic mysticism.[18] A. Govindāchārya and P. N. Srinivasachari, two modern Hindu scholars who are adherents of the bhakti tradition, go even farther and assert that devotional mysticism—the quest for union with a personal God—alone qualifies as "true" mysticism.[19] Such characterizations of bhakti as an important—or indeed, the most important—form of Hindu mysticism, are, as Carman points out, in striking contrast to "the view that many in India and the West have come to take for granted: that Śankara's monistic interpretation of the Upanishads is the primary type of Hindu mysticism."[20]

A more balanced, differentiated treatment of Indian mystical traditions is presented by Gerald J. Larson, who proposes a fourfold typology of Indian mystical experience: unitive, exemplified by the Upaniṣads and Vedānta traditions; isolative, represented by Jain traditions, classical Sāṃkhya, and classical Yoga; copulative, exemplified by theistic traditions and late tantric traditions; and nihilative, represented by early Buddhist traditions.[21] Bhakti traditions, according to Larson's taxonomy, are representative of "copulative mystical experience," in which "the relationship of the devotee to the Lord is described in relational and interpersonal terms. . . . The devotee longs for God or the Lord as the lover longs for the beloved."[22]

In accordance with the scholarly consensus of both Western and Indian interpreters, we can thus affirm that Hindu bhakti constitutes a form of mysticism and can be more specifically correlated with the category of "theistic mysticism." However, bhakti itself assumes many forms, as does theistic mysticism. Therefore, to be able to define more precisely the Bhāgavata Purāṇa's role as a bhakti-cum-mystical text, we need to differentiate among types of bhakti.

A number of eminent Indologists have emphasized the importance of distinguishing among the different forms of bhakti that are expressed in different texts and in different periods. In particular, several scholars have noted that the type of bhakti expressed in the Bhāgavata Purāṇa constitutes a distinctive new form of devotion that is intensely "emotional," passionate, and ecstatic, in contrast to the more "intellectual," contemplative, and serviceful forms of bhakti expressed in the Bhagavad Gītā, in the Viṣṇu Purāṇa, and in the Śrī Vaiṣṇava tradition of Rāmānuja. Before we turn to an analysis of scholarly opinions on this subject, it would be helpful to examine a sample of the Bhāgavata's own characterization of bhakti: "Without the hair of the body standing on end, without the heart melting, without being inarticulate due to tears of joy—without bhakti how can the heart be purified? He whose speech is stammering, whose heart melts, who weeps repeatedly and sometimes laughs, who unabashedly sings and dances—such a person, united by bhakti with Me, purifies the world."[23]

J. N. Farquhar was one of the first scholars to suggest that the Bhāgavata Purāṇa presents a "new theory of *bhakti*," which he characterizes in terms that are reminiscent of the passage just cited:

> What distinguishes it [the Bhāgavata Purāṇa] from all earlier literature is its new theory of *bhakti*; and therein lies its true greatness. Some of its utterances on this subject are worthy of a place in the best literature of mysticism and devotion. . . . Bhakti in this work is a surging emotion which chokes the speech, makes the tears flow and the hair thrill with pleasureable excitement, and often leads to hysterical laughing and weeping by turns, to sudden fainting fits and to long trances of unconsciousness. . . . Thus the whole theory and practice of bhakti in this purāṇa is very different from the bhakti of the *Bhagavadgītā* and of Rāmānuja.[24]

Jan Gonda similarly suggests that the "passion and emotionalism" of devotion in the Bhāgavata Purāṇa constitutes a "new stage" of bhakti that differs from the "more speculative description of the earlier texts":

> Bhakti has entered here a *new stage, or perhaps better*, displays here aspects which in the older texts *did not, or less so*, become manifest, and these aspects were illustrated and stressed with a fervour and a conviction which can amaze the unprepared Western reader. Particularly in the life of the young herdsman god Kṛṣṇa a theory and practice of bhakti is developed in very emotional and sensual poetry, which *differs* in its passion and emotionalism from the more speculative description of the earlier texts. Bhakti is here an overpowering, even suffocating emotion, which causes tears to flow and the voice to falter, and even, stimulates hysterical laughter, loss of consciousness, and trance.[25]

Dasgupta, in his discussion of the category of devotional mysticism, distinguishes three stages of development, from (1) the self-abnegation, self-surrender to God, and contemplative union with God, as taught in the Bhagavad Gītā and reflected in the teachings of Rāmānuja, to (2) the desire for contemplative union combined with the longing to taste God's love, as expressed by the devotee Prahlāda in the Viṣṇu Purāṇa, to (3) the intoxicating, sensual, blissful, and ecstatic love of God that is celebrated in the Bhāgavata Purāṇa. Dasgupta notes:

> This bhakti . . . is no longer the old contemplative meditation of God, stirred by a deep-seated love. It is the ebullition of feelings and emotions of attachment to God. It manifests itself in the soft melting of the heart and expresses itself in tears, inarticulate utterances of speech, laughter, songs and dances, such as can only be possible through a mad intoxication of love. This kind of bhakti is entirely different from the calm contemplative life of complete self-abnegation and self-surrender to God and a mind wholly immersed in God and the thought of God. . . . They [the bhaktas] come to experience such

> intense happiness that all their limbs and senses become saturated therewith and their minds swim, as it were, in a lake of such supreme bliss that even the bliss of ultimate liberation loses its charm. . . . The bhakta who is filled with such a passion does not experience it merely as an undercurrent of joy which waters the depths of his heart in his own privacy, but as a torrent that overflows the caverns of his heart into all his senses. Through all his senses he realizes it as if it were a sensuous delight; with his heart and soul he feels it as a spiritual intoxication of joy. Such a person is beside himself with this love of God. He sings, laughs, dances and weeps. He is no longer a person of this world.[26]

Paul Hacker, through a comparison of the portrayals of the devotee Prahlāda in the Viṣṇu Purāṇa and the Bhāgavata Purāṇa, has demonstrated the differences between the representations of bhakti in the two Purāṇas. The more "intellectual" bhakti of the Viṣṇu Purāṇa is characterized by Prahlāda's remembering, thinking about, or contemplating Viṣṇu, while the more "emotional" bhakti of the Bhāgavata Puraṇa is characterized by Prahlāda's ecstatic weeping, laughing, singing, and dancing while immersed in the bliss of Kṛṣṇa's love.[27]

Friedhelm Hardy, in his extended study of the early history of Kṛṣṇa devotion in South India, emphasizes that the Bhāgavata Purāṇa is the first work in Sanskrit that expressed this new type of "emotional Kṛṣṇa bhakti," which he characterizes more specifically as an "aesthetic-erotic-ecstatic mysticism of separation."[28] The Bhāgavata is the first text that provided a brahmanical Sanskritic framework for this mysticism of love-in-separation, *viraha-bhakti*, which has its roots in the Tamil devotion of the Āḷvārs.[29] This *viraha-bhakti*, as expressed in the Bhāgavata Purāṇa as well as in the poetry of the Āḷvārs, involves a dialectic of union and separation that is never fully resolved. Charlotte Vaudeville remarks:

> The theoricians of Bhakti entertained, from the time of the Āḻvārs, a *dynamic* conception of Bhakti, whose highest state is less a repose than a tension, an unquenchable thirst even in the possession of God, a continual yearning and stretching for a fuller apprehension of the divine Lover, who unceasingly draws all souls to Himself. There can be no satiety in divine Love; and so it was the pathetic character of the *virahiṇī*, the faithful wife forever tormented by the pangs of separation from her Lord and longing for Him even when she enjoys the bliss of His presence, which remained for the Āḻvārs, as well as for their spiritual descendents, the most adequate symbol of Love divine.[30]

The Bhāgavata Purāṇa and Canonical Authority

The Bhāgavata Purāṇa thus gives expression to a new type of Kṛṣṇa bhakti, an ecstatic mysticism of union-in-separation, rooted in South Indian devotional traditions. The Bhāgavata is at the same time concerned with domesticating and legitimating its innovative devotional teachings by incorporating them within a Sanskritic framework that accords with the norms of brahmanical orthodoxy. The devotional mysticism of the Bhāgavata Purāṇa thus provides a striking example of what Steven T. Katz has characterized as the dialectic of mysticism, which "oscillates between the innovative and traditional poles of the religious life."[31] Katz argues that while mystics may at times introduce "radical" teachings, at the same time they exhibit a "conservative" tendency in which they seek to locate their teachings within the broader normative framework of their respective religious traditions. The mystic's experience is, moreover, "preconditioned" by his or her embeddedness in a particular religious tradition, in that both the distinctive character and the subsequent interpretation of the experience are shaped and informed by the inherited images, symbols, and categories that the mystic brings to the experience from the larger tradition. Katz emphasizes in this context the important role that scriptures have assumed as sources of authority and legitimation for mystical traditions.[32] The formative role of scriptures in shaping and authorizing mystical teachings is vividly exemplified by the devotional mysticism of the Bhāgavata Purāṇa, which not only invokes brahmanical scriptural traditions but, even further, seeks to establish its own scriptural status as an authoritative text within the brahmanical canon.

The Bhāgavata Purāṇa's concern in "scripturalizing" its devotional mysticism derives in part from the nature of the brahmanical tradition, which self-consciously defines itself in relationship to a canon of authoritative scriptures. The brahmanical tradition constitutes an elite "textual community"[33] that has sought to shape and articulate the central norms of the tradition by codifying symbol systems and practices in the form of a scriptural canon of which it is the custodian. The brahmanical canon includes two categories of sacred texts: *śruti* (that which was heard) and *smṛti* (that which was remembered). The core *śruti* texts are the four Vedic Saṃhitās—Ṛg-Veda, Yajur-Veda, Sāma-Veda, and Atharva-Veda[34]—the versified portions of which are termed *mantras*.[35] The domain of *śruti* was subsequently extended to include not only the Saṃhitās but also the Brāhmaṇas, Āraṇyakas, and Upaniṣads.[36] While the domain of *śruti* is in principle circumscribed, *smṛti* is a dynamic, open-ended category, which includes the Dharma-Śāstras, the Itihāsas (the Sanskrit epics—the Mahābhārata and the Rāmāyaṇa of Vālmīki), and the Purāṇas, as well as a variety of other texts that have been incorporated within this ever-expanding category in accordance with the needs of different periods and groups.[37] The primary criterion for distinguishing between *śruti* and *smṛti* texts is generally characterized by both Indian and Western scholars as an ontological distinction between "revelation" and "tradition."[38] *Śruti* texts—Saṃhitās, Brāhmaṇas, Āraṇyakas, and Upaniṣads—are traditionally understood to have been directly cognized, or "seen" and "heard," by inspired "seers" (*ṛṣis*) at the beginning of each cycle of creation. The formal schools of Vedic exegesis, Pūrva-Mīmāṃsā and Vedānta, maintain that the *śruti*, or Vedic, texts are eternal (*nitya*), infinite, and *apauruṣeya*, not derived from any personal—human or divine—agent, while the Nyāya, Vaiśeṣika, and Yoga schools of Indian philosophy view the Vedic texts as the work of God.[39] All other sacred texts are relegated to a secondary status as *smṛti*, for they are held to have been composed by personal authors and are therefore designated as "that which was remembered" rather than "that which was heard." On the basis of this criterion, the Purāṇas are classified in the brahmanical canon as *smṛti* texts, even though, as we shall see, the Purāṇas seek to identify themselves with *śruti* by claiming the status of the "fifth Veda."

The Bhāgavata Purāṇa attempts to invest its mystical teachings with canonical authority through assimilating itself to two principal categories of scripture within the corpus of *śruti* and *smṛti* texts: Purāṇa and Veda. The Bhāgavata's dual status as a Purāṇa-Veda is evident in terms of its *form*, in which it adopts the Purāṇic literary form and, more specifically, models itself after the Viṣṇu Purāṇa; its *language*, which employs Vedic grammatical forms and vocabulary; its *content*, which incorporates numerous references to Vedic deities, myths, and rituals; and its *self-representations*, which celebrate its role as the preeminent Purāṇa that is equal to the Veda.

The Bhāgavata as Purāṇa

One of the primary mechanisms through which the Bhāgavata secures its place in the brahmanical canon is by adopting the literary form of a Purāṇa, one of the categories of *smṛti* texts. Giorgio Bonazzoli has argued that the Purāṇas themselves constitute a "canon" within the larger brahmanical corpus of sacred texts. He suggests, moreover, that a number of mechanisms have been used by the Purāṇas to delimit the Purāṇic canon and to establish the authenticity and authority of those texts that are included in the canon.[40] The Bhāgavata Purāṇa, as one of the latest of the Purāṇas, follows the example of the earlier Purāṇas and uses each of these mechanisms in order to secure its canonical status as a Purāṇa.

First, the Purāṇas attempt to delimit the Purāṇic canon by including, in their own texts, lists of the eighteen authoritative Mahāpurāṇas (major Purāṇas), as distinct from the eighteen Upapurāṇas (minor Purāṇas).[41] The lists of eighteen Mahāpurāṇas given in the various Purāṇas all include the Bhāgavata Purāṇa.[42] The Bhāgavata itself mentions the distinction between major (*mahat*) and minor (*alpa* or *kṣullaka*) Purāṇas[43] and makes reference twice to the standard list of eighteen Mahāpurāṇas in which it has a place.[44]

A second mechanism used by a number of the Purāṇas to standardize the Purāṇic canon involves the inclusion, in their enumerations of the eighteen Mahāpurāṇas, of idealized representations of the number of *śloka*s (verses) contained in each Purāṇa, which do not correspond to the actual number of *śloka*s in the extant printed editions of the Purāṇas. The total number of *śloka*s in all the Purāṇas taken together is said to be 400,000 (four lakhs)—a number that figures prominently in Purāṇic theories of their own origins. Among these idealized representations, the Bhāgavata is consistently said to contain 18,000 *śloka*s.[45] The Bhāgavata itself includes such a list, in which it ascribes to itself and to the other seventeen Purāṇas the standard number of *śloka*s.[46]

A third strategy used by the Purāṇas to establish their canonical authority is to invoke the classical definition of a Purāṇa, which is said to be distinguished by five characteristics (*pañca-lakṣaṇa*): descriptions of the creation (*sarga*) and of the re-creation (*pratisarga*) of the universe after its periodic dissolutions; genealogies of gods, sages, and kings (*vaṃśa*); accounts of the ages of Manu (*manvantara*); and histories of the royal dynasties (*vaṃśānucarita*).[47] However, as scholars have frequently noted, the extant Purāṇas contain much more than this definition suggests, and some give only minimal attention to these five topics.[48] The *pañca-lakṣaṇa* definition nevertheless remains a sign of authenticity, and hence even those Purāṇas that do not conform to the definition make reference to the *pañca-lakṣaṇa* as the distinguishing marks of a Purāṇa.[49] The Bhāgavata Purāṇa fulfills this criterion of authenticity in that it deals with all five topics. In addition, it makes explicit reference to the *pañca-lakṣaṇa*, while at the same time expanding upon the normative tradition by incorporating the five topics into an extended list of ten characteristics (*daśa-lakṣaṇa*) that distinguish a Purāṇa.[50]

A fourth mechanism used to establish the authority of the Purāṇas is to ascribe their authorship to Vyāsa, one of the most renowned sages of the brahmanical tradition. This great sage is traditionally said to have accomplished three formidable literary feats: he divided the one Veda into four distinct Saṃhitās; he composed the epic, the Mahābhārata; and he subsequently compiled and disseminated the eighteen Purāṇas. The Purāṇas contain a number of traditions concerning the role of Vyāsa in forming the Purāṇic canon, which I discuss farther on in this chapter. The Bhāgavata Purāṇa builds on these traditions and attempts to surpass them, as I delineate in the following discussion, by establishing its own preeminent status as the last of the eighteen Purāṇas compiled by Vyāsa, which constituted the culmination and fruition of his long career.

The Bhāgavata Purāṇa thus accords with Purāṇic standards of authenticity in order to secure its place in the Purāṇic canon. In adopting the Purāṇic literary form, the Bhāgavata appears to have used the Viṣṇu Purāṇa, in particular, as its model. It follows the general scheme of topics found in the Viṣṇu Purāṇa, while at the same time expanding upon and reconfiguring the scheme.[51] More specifically, the life of Kṛṣṇa and his love-play with the cowmaidens (*gopīs*) of Vṛndāvana, which are celebrated in Book 10 of the Bhāgavata, appear to have been modeled after the *gopī* episodes in the Viṣṇu Purāṇa.[52] The Prahlāda episode in Book 7 of the Bhāgavata similarly appears to have been modeled after the Viṣṇu Purāṇa's accounts of Prahlāda.[53] However, the Bhāgavata Purāṇa, in its portrayals of the devotional mysticism of the *gopīs* and of Prahlāda, introduces important innovations—in particular, as discussed earlier, in its representations of bhakti as a passionate, sensual, ecstatic love of the Lord, in contrast to the more intellectual, contemplative bhakti expressed in the Viṣṇu Purāṇa.

While the Bhāgavata thus conforms with the Purāṇic model, particularly as represented by the Viṣṇu Purāṇa, it at the same time distinguishes itself from the other Purāṇas in significant ways. First, it is the most unified and homogeneous of all the Purāṇas. M. Winternitz remarks that "it is the one Purāṇa which, more than any other of the others, bears the stamp of a unified composition, and deserves to be appreciated as a literary production on account of its language, style and metre."[54] Second, the homogeneity of the Bhāgavata is characterized by a consistent focus throughout the text on bhakti—and, moreover, a distinctive type of devotional mysticism—in contrast to the more sporadic treatment of devotional concerns in the other Purāṇas. Third, the language and style of the Bhāgavata Purāṇa are different from those of the other Purāṇas. In contrast to the epic-Purāṇic vernacular Sanskrit that is generally employed in the Purāṇas,[55] the Bhāgavata regularly uses Vedic grammatical forms and vocabulary.[56] J.A.B. van Buitenen interprets the Bhāgavata's use of Vedic archaisms as an attempt to Sanskritize and legitimate Kṛṣṇa bhakti by establishing itself as an orthodox scripture suffused with the power of the Vedic *mantras*: "I am not only orthodox in the Vedic tradition, I even sound like the Veda."[57]

The Bhāgavata as Veda

To invest its mystical teachings that celebrate devotion to Lord Kṛṣṇa with the authority of brahmanical orthodoxy, the Bhāgavata Purāṇa not only adopts the canonical form of a *smṛti* text, a Purāṇa, but also attempts to appropriate the status of the core *śruti* texts at the center of the brahmanical canon, the Vedic Saṃhitās, or *mantras*.

While adopting the form of a Purāṇa, the Bhāgavata, in its language, content, and self-representations, seeks to relate itself to the Veda, which is the most authoritative symbol of brahmanical orthodoxy. In attempting to assimilate itself to the Veda, the Bhāgavata Purāṇa exemplifies a well-documented phenomenon in Indian history whereby any Hindu text or teaching seeking to legitimate its authority had to do so with reference to the Veda. As J. C. Heesterman emphasizes, "The crux of the matter is that the Vedas hold the key to ultimate legitimation. Therefore, even if the Vedas are in no way related to the ways of human life and society, one is still forced to come to terms with them."[58]

The legitimating function of the Veda within Hindu traditions derives from its role as a *transcendent* source of authority. The core *śruti* texts, the Vedic *mantra*s, are represented in the mythological speculations of Vedic and post-Vedic texts as eternal, transcendent knowledge that exists perpetually as the source and blueprint of the universe. The Vedic *ṛṣi*s are portrayed as able to station their awareness on that subtle level where they could "see" and "hear" the impulses of knowledge reverberating from the Transcendent as the fundamental rhythms of creation. They subsequently "recorded," on the gross level of speech, that which they cognized on the subtle level, and in this way the *mantra*s assumed a concrete form on earth as recited texts.[59] The Vedic *mantra*s are thus granted the status of transcendent knowledge. Any subsequent text or *śāstric* discourse can participate in that status only by assimilating itself to the Vedic *mantra*s through a variety of strategies, including (1) claiming to form part of *śruti*, the original cognitions of the *ṛṣi*s, in the case of the Brāhmaṇas, Āraṇyakas, and Upaniṣads; (2) claiming the status of the fifth Veda, in the case of the Itihāsas and Purāṇas;[60] (3) establishing a genealogy that directly links the text's teachings to the Veda or to some form of divine revelation, in the case of the Manu-Smṛti; (4) claiming that the text's teachings derive from lost Vedic texts, a claim that could apply to all *smṛti* texts;[61] or (5) otherwise conforming to the model of the Veda.[62] Through such strategies, the term *Veda* is extended beyond the circumscribed boundaries of the Vedic *mantra*s and, through a process of "vedacization," comes to include within its purview not only an expanded array of *śruti* texts but also potentially all *smṛti* texts and teachings that are promulgated by brahmanical authorities.[63]

Such strategies, including a variety of other modes of assimilation, have been used not only by exponents of the brahmanical hierarchy but also by nonbrahmanical Hindu groups to invest their sacred texts with the transcendent authority of the Veda.[64] The domain of Veda is thereby expanded beyond the brahmanical Sanskritic canon of *śruti* and *smṛti* texts to include a variety of vernacular texts derived from nonbrahmanical origins. For example, the *Tiruvāymoḷi* of Nammāḷvār (c. ninth century)—the Tamil hymns composed by one of the most acclaimed of the South Indian Āḷvārs—are said to represent the four Vedic Saṃhitās and are designated as the "Dravidian Veda" or "Tamil Veda."[65] The *Rāmcaritmānas* of the poet Tulsīdās (c. sixteenth century), a Hindi version of the Rāmāyaṇa popular throughout North India, has been ascribed a similar status as the "fifth Veda" or "Hindi Veda."[66] Even scriptures derived from non-Hindu traditions have at times been identified with Veda. For example, in South India certain Tamil Christians deem the Bible to be the "true Veda,"[67] while Tamil Muslims invest the Qur'ān with a comparable status.[68] Whether the Veda is revered or rejected, appropriated or subverted, it remains a symbol invested with authoritative power that must be contended with by all those who wish to position themselves in relation to the brahmanical hierarchy.[69]

The Purāṇas, although technically classified as *smṛti* texts in the brahmanical canon, are nevertheless concerned with connecting themselves with *śruti*, the Veda. The relationship of the Purāṇas with the Veda has been debated by both Indian and Western scholars, with some scholars arguing that there is a close connection between the two classes of scripture and others arguing that there is little or no connection.[70] The Purāṇas themselves claim direct continuity with the Veda and emphasize their role in interpreting and elaborating the Vedic teachings for the general populace. Thus, while the Vedic Saṃhitās are socially circumscribed scriptures, restricted to male members of the three higher social classes (*varṇas*), the Purāṇas are socially inclusive scriptures, intended for people of all social classes, including *śūdra*s (servants) and women. The Purāṇas represent themselves as the Veda of the general populace, complementing and supplementing the Vedic Saṃhitās by incorporating popular devotional teachings alongside traditional Vedic teachings. Let us briefly examine three of the strategies used by the Purāṇas to assimilate themselves to the Veda before turning to an analysis of the ways in which the Bhāgavata Purāṇa appropriates, adapts, and extends these strategies in order to invest itself with the transcendent authority of *śruti*.

First, the Purāṇas simply assert their identity or their equality with the Veda. They claim the status of the fifth Veda for both the Itihāsas and Purāṇas[71] and at times refer to themselves as the Purāṇa-Veda.[72] They also declare themselves to be equal to the Vedas[73] and a necessary complement to them. The Vāyu Purāṇa, for example, emphasizes that knowledge of the Vedas is not sufficient but must be supplemented by knowledge of the Purāṇas.[74] Moreover, the Purāṇas declare themselves the repositories of efficacious *mantra*s, comparable in power to the Vedic *mantra*s, and regularly proclaim the fruits of hearing (*phala-śruti*) the recitation of a particular Purāṇa or sections thereof.[75]

A second mechanism through which the Purāṇas emulate the paradigmatic Veda involves providing accounts of their origins that parallel Vedic accounts, both in their emphasis on primordial origins and in their focus on the sage Vyāsa's role in the process of transmission. One tradition, which is found in the Matsya, Vāyu, Brahmāṇḍa, Padma, and Nārada Purāṇas, claims that at the beginning of each cycle of creation a single primordial Purāṇa emerges from the creator Brahmā as the first of all the *śāstra*s, even prior to the Vedas. This Purāṇa, consisting of one hundred crores (one billion) of *śloka*s, is first recalled by Brahmā, after which the four Vedas issue forth from his mouths.[76] According to an extended account given in the Matsya Purāṇa, it is through the agency of Vyāsa—who is acclaimed as the partial incarnation of Viṣṇu—that the one primordial Purāṇa, which was "the source of all the *śāstra*s," came to assume its present earthly form as eighteen Purāṇas. Vyāsa, the sage responsible for dividing the one Veda into four Saṃhitās in every Dvāpara Yuga,[77] is credited with condensing the original Purāṇa of one hundred crores of *śloka*s into an abridged edition of four lakhs (400,000) of *śloka*s, which he subsequently divided into eighteen Purāṇas. Although it thus assumed a modified earthly form, the original Purāṇa of one hundred crores of *śloka*s continues to exist in the world of the gods (*deva-loka*).[78] Variants of this account are found in the Padma, Nārada, and Liṅga Purāṇas.[79]

An alternative tradition concerning the origins of the Purāṇas, which is found in the Brahmāṇḍa, Vāyu, and Viṣṇu Purāṇas, ascribes to Vyāsa the role of compiling the Purāṇa Saṃhitā from tales, episodes, verses, and accounts of the ages.[80] When Vyāsa taught the four Vedic Saṃhitās to four of his disciples, respectively, he taught this Purāṇa Saṃhitā to his fifth disciple, Sūta Lomaharṣaṇa (or Romaharṣaṇa). Lomaharṣaṇa in turn taught it to his six disciples, three of whom compiled their own Saṃhitās. These three Saṃhitās, together with that of Lomaharṣaṇa, constitute the original (*mūla* or *pūrva*) Saṃhitās from which the eighteen Purāṇas were derived.[81] The Vedic paradigm is clearly evident in these accounts of Vyāsa's role in compiling, dividing, and disseminating the Purāṇa Saṃhitā as the fifth Veda alongside the four Vedic Saṃhitās.

A third strategy used by the Purāṇas to connect themselves with the Veda involves asserting the identity of the Veda with that supreme deity who—in accordance with the sectarian emphasis of the particular Purāṇa—is celebrated as Brahman, the ultimate reality. The identification of the personal God who is the object of devotion—whether Viṣṇu, Śiva, or Devī (the Goddess)—with the Upaniṣadic Brahman and with the eternal reality of Veda represents one of the essential mechanisms through which the popular devotional teachings of the Purāṇas attained legitimacy as part of the normative brahmanical tradition. The Purāṇas emphasize that the nature of the supreme deity, in his identity with Brahman, is knowledge, and the Veda constitutes both the inner essence and the outer form of this reality. The Viṣṇu Purāṇa, for example, celebrates Viṣṇu as the supreme Brahman, whose nature is knowledge (*jñāna-svarūpa*),[82] who is knowledge incarnate (*jñāna-mūrti*),[83] and who is one with the Vedas,[84] his form being composed of the Vedic *mantras*.[85] Viṣṇu-Nārāyaṇa is extolled as the embodiment of knowledge, whose form is constituted by the Vedas not only in Vaiṣṇava Purāṇas such as the Viṣṇu Purāṇa, but also in nonsectarian Purāṇas such as the Mārkaṇḍeya Purāṇa and in cross-sectarian Purāṇas such as the Matsya and Kūrma Purāṇas that contain both Vaiṣṇava and Śaiva material.[86] For example, the Matsya Purāṇa, in its account of creation, eulogizes Viṣṇu-Nārāyaṇa, who is identified with Brahman, as the secret essence of the Vedas (*vedānām rahasya*)[87] whose very substance is Veda (*veda-maya*).[88] In Śaiva Purāṇas such as the Śiva Purāṇa, it is Śiva who is extolled as the supreme Brahman whose Self is knowledge (*jñānātman*) and who is composed of the three Vedas (*trayī-maya*).[89]

The Bhāgavata Purāṇa, like other Purāṇas, is concerned with establishing its canonical authority in relation to the Veda. However, even more than the other Purāṇas, the Bhāgavata is confronted with a significant problem in connecting itself with the Veda: Kṛṣṇa, the supreme Godhead who is the focus of the text's devotional teachings, is not mentioned in the Vedic Saṃhitās. Although in the Bhagavāta Purāṇa Kṛṣṇa is identified with Viṣṇu—who does appear as a minor deity in the Vedic Saṃhitās—it is as Kṛṣṇa, not Viṣṇu, that he is above all celebrated as Bhagavān, the Lord. The Bhāgavata proclaims that "Kṛṣṇa is Bhagavān himself"[90]—and yet nowhere in the Vedic Saṃhitās is a deity named Kṛṣṇa mentioned.[91] Frederick Smith remarks: "Rarely is any single Purāṇic deity so estimably beyond the boundaries of Vedic discourse than is Kṛṣṇa. . . . It is well known that Śiva, as Rudra, as well as the Goddess reside at the peripheries of Vedic mythology and ritual; more central is Viṣṇu. But nowhere in the Vedas is Kṛṣṇa mentioned, at least in any form that could predict his future course on the subcontinent."[92]

The authors of the Bhāgavata Purāṇa seek to overcome this problem by vedacizing the text and its teachings in a number of ways. In terms of language, as discussed earlier, the Bhāgavata makes use of Vedic archaisms in its imitation of the language of the Vedas. In terms of content, Vedic material is incorporated throughout the text, with the exception of Book 10, which celebrates the life of Kṛṣṇa. Smith notes that "the Purāṇa, taken as a whole, is saturated with references to Vedic deities, sages, rituals, and myths."[93] In terms of self-representations, in order to invest itself with Vedic authority, the Bhagavata Purāṇa adapts and extends the three types of Purāṇic strategies discussed earlier: it directly asserts its identity and equality with the Veda; it gives accounts of the Purāṇas' origins that emulate the Vedic paradigm; and it affirms the Vedic status of its devotional mysticism by asserting the identity of Kṛṣṇa—the supreme Godhead who is the focus of its teachings—with the Veda. In making use of each of these mechanisms, the Bhāgavata Purāṇa, as I discuss in the following analysis, is concerned not only to connect itself with the Veda but, even further, to establish its paramount status as the greatest of all the Purāṇas and as the culminating scripture of the entire brahmanical canon.

First, like other Purāṇas, the Bhāgavata Purāṇa ascribes to the Puraṇas as a whole, along with the Itihāsas, the status of the fifth Veda.[94] However, beyond making claims regarding the Vedic status of the Purāṇas generally, it is also concerned to set itself apart as the preeminent Purāṇa that most perfectly embodies Veda.[95] As the *śruti* pertaining to Lord Kṛṣṇa,[96] the Bhāgavata proclaims itself equal with the Veda (*brahma-sammita*, *veda-sammita*),[97] the fruit (*phala*) of the wish-yielding tree of Veda (*nigama-kalpa-taru*),[98] the essence of the entire *śruti* (*akhila-śruti-sāra*),[99] and the essence of all the Upaniṣads (*sarva-vedānta-sāra*).[100] Moreover, the Bhāgavata goes further and declares itself the quintessential scripture that represents the concentrated essence of all the sacred texts—not only *śruti* but also *smṛti*.[101]

Second, the Bhāgavata Purāṇa, following the example of earlier Purāṇas, invokes the Vedic model in its accounts of the primordial origins of the Purāṇas and of Vyāsa's role in transmitting the texts. It does not, however, mention the Purāṇic tradition concerning the primordial Purāṇa that first emerges from the creator Brahmā, after which the four Vedas issue forth from his mouths. Instead, the Bhāgavata provides an alternative account in which the order of precedence is reversed: the four Vedas issue forth, respectively, from the four mouths of Brahmā, after which the Purāṇas, together with the Itihāsas, emerge from all four mouths together.[102] While chronological precedence is thus ascribed to the Vedas, the ontological precedence of the Purāṇas is implied by the image of Brahmā sending forth the fifth Veda from all four of his mouths simultaneously, in contrast to the emergence of each of the four Vedas from only one of his mouths.

The Bhāgavata Purāṇa also includes a number of traditions that emphasize the role of Vyāsa in dividing the one Veda into four Saṃhitās in every Dvāpara Yuga and in transmitting the four Vedas along with the fifth Veda—the Itihāsas and the Purāṇas—to his disciples.[103] Veda-Vyāsa, the "divider of the Veda," who is also credited with composing the Mahābhārata and with compiling the eighteen Purāṇas, is celebrated in the Bhāgavata Purāṇa as a partial incarnation of Bhagavān, Kṛṣṇa.[104] He is, moreover, represented as a great *ṛṣi*, who, like the ancient *ṛṣi*s who cognized the Vedic *mantra*s, is endowed with the faculty of divine sight (*divya cakṣus*) and unerring vision (*amogha-dṛś*), through which he knows the past, present, and future.[105] One account in the Bhāgavata Purāṇa emphasizes the parallels in the process of transmission of the Vedas and the Purāṇas and in this context includes a variant of the Purāṇic tradition concerning the Purāṇa Saṃhitās. Just as Vyāsa divided the one Veda into four Saṃhitās, which he transmitted to his four main disciples and their respective lineages, so too did he teach the Purāṇas, as the fifth Veda, to his fifth disciple, Romaharṣaṇa, who in turn transmitted four original (*mūla*) Purāṇa Saṃhitās to his disciples.[106] The account concludes with a discussion of the ten characteristics (*daśa-lakṣaṇa*) that distinguish a Purāṇa, followed by an enumeration of the eighteen Purāṇas that display these characteristics.[107]

In a second account, the Bhāgavata Purāṇa represents itself as the culminating achievement of Vyāsa's life and thereby claims for itself a special place not only in the Purāṇic canon but also in the broader canon of brahmanical scriptures. The account emphasizes how Vyāsa, after dividing the one Veda into four, composing the Mahābhārata, and compiling the Purāṇas, was not satisfied. Even though he had accomplished these great literary feats, had mastered the Vedas, and had attained realization of Brahman, he did not feel fulfilled. While Vyāsa was lamenting his lack of fulfillment, the divine *ṛṣi* Nārada approached him and explained to him that although he had attained mastery of all knowledge and had realized the truth of existence, his heart was not satisfied because he had not yet sung the praises of Lord Kṛṣṇa and extolled the glories of devotion to Bhagavān.[108] Thus inspired by Nārada, Vyāsa returned to his hermitage and sat down and meditated, and "in his mind, freed of impurity by *bhakti-yoga* and completely collected, he saw (root *dṛś*) the primordial Puruṣa."[109] He then composed the Bhāgavata Purāṇa as a record of his mystical cognitions of Lord Kṛṣṇa, in which his heart overflowed in blissful celebration of the play, or *līlā*, of the Lord of creation and of the path of devotion through which he is realized.[110]

To invest its mystical insights concerning Lord Kṛṣṇa with the transcendent authority of the Veda, the Bhāgavata Purāṇa adapts a third Purāṇic strategy to its own sectarian ends: it celebrates Kṛṣṇa as the supreme Godhead who is identical with Brahman and Veda incarnate. By identifying Kṛṣṇa with the Veda, the Bhāgavata overcomes the problem posed by the lack of reference to Kṛṣṇa in the Vedic Saṃhitās: Kṛṣṇa is not mentioned in the Vedas because he himself *is* the Veda. He is that ultimate reality who is celebrated in the Upaniṣads as Brahman, whose inner essence is Veda, knowledge, and whose outer form is constituted by the Vedic *mantras*. Ecstatic union with Lord Kṛṣṇa, which is the goal of the Bhāgavata Purāṇa's devotional mysticism, is understood in this context to be tantamount to realization of the eternal Veda.

Kṛṣṇa—who is variously designated in the Bhāgavata as Viṣṇu, Nārāyaṇa, Vāsudeva, and Hari—is extolled as that supreme Bhagavān whose Self is the threefold Veda (*trayī-vidyātman*)[111] and whose very substance is Veda (*sarva-veda-maya*).[112] The Bhāgavata emphasizes that the Veda constitutes both the Lord's inner nature and his outer form. The cosmic body (*tanu*) of the Lord is identified with the Veda as Śabdabrahman—Brahman embodied in the Word[113]—and is said to be composed of the Vedic *mantras*.[114] The Lord is celebrated more specifically as the embodiment of Veda when he assumes the form of a sacrificial boar (*yajña-varāha*), his body constituted by the Vedic *mantras* and the elements of the sacrifice, so that he may rescue the earth from the cosmic waters in which it is submerged.[115]

Lord Kṛṣṇa is extolled in the Bhāgavata Purāṇa not only as the embodiment of Veda but also as the means through which the Vedic *mantras* are manifested on earth in every cycle of creation. He is celebrated as the ultimate source of the tradition of Vedic transmission and is also identified with each of the three major agents in the transmission process: the creator Brahmā, the Vedic *ṛṣi*s, and Vyāsa. Brahmā, as we have seen, is the primary agent in the process of transmission, who brings forth the four Vedas from his four mouths at the beginning of each cycle of creation.[116] The second link in the process of transmission consists of the Vedic *ṛṣi*s, who "see" (root *dṛś*) and preserve the primordial impulses of divine speech.[117] Brahmā is described as teaching the Vedas to his sons, the *brahmarṣi*s (brahmin seers), who preserve the Vedic *mantra*s through recitation and subsequently teach the *mantra*s to their own sons, initiating a tradition of oral transmission through which the Vedas would be passed down to each succeeding generation.[118] The third principal agent in the process of Vedic transmission is the great *ṛṣi* Vyāsa, who, at the beginning of each Dvāpara Yuga, divides the Veda into four distinct collections, or Saṃhitās, to facilitate its preservation and understanding, as well as to promote the performance of the Vedic sacrifices.[119]

The opening verse of the Bhāgavata Purāṇa proclaims that it is the Lord himself who, by his mere intention, reveals the Vedas to Brahmā, the first seer (*ādi-kavi*).[120] After the Veda disappears during the cosmic dissolution at the end of each cycle of creation, it is the Lord who transmits it to Brahmā at the beginning of the next creation. Kṛṣṇa himself declares: "In the course of time this Word (*vāṇī*) designated as Veda disappeared during the dissolution (*pralaya*). In the beginning [of the next creation] I imparted to Brahmā this [Word, Veda], in which resides the dharma of devoting oneself to Me."[121] Lord Kṛṣṇa's transmission of the Veda to Brahmā is represented by the Bhāgavata as a process of self-disclosure, for the Lord himself is the eternal reality of Veda. The Veda finds differentiated expression in the Vedic *mantra*s, which issue forth as the impulses of divine speech from Brahmā's mouths and are preserved by the *ṛṣi*s and their lineages as recited texts. The Vedic texts preserved through recitative transmission are the precipitated expressions of the eternal Veda, the Lord himself, and thus their true purpose is to reveal the manifest and unmanifest forms of the supreme Bhagavān and to teach the dharma of devotion to him.[122]

The creator Brahmā is himself described in the Bhāgavata Purāṇa as the manifest form that Lord Kṛṣṇa assumes for the purpose of fashioning the forms of creation. He thus participates in the Lord's nature as Veda incarnate and is correspondingly said to be composed of Veda (*veda-maya*)[123] and the abode of Veda (*veda-garbha*).[124] When he embarks on his role as demiurge, Brahmā brings forth the four Vedas from his four mouths, and it is through his utterance of the Vedic words that the manifold phenomena of creation are projected into concrete manifestation. As he proceeds with his cosmogonic activities, Brahmā extols the glories of the supreme Lord, whose creative powers he embodies, and beseeches him not to allow his utterance of the Vedic words to fail.[125]

Lord Kṛṣṇa, the embodiment of Veda, is thus represented in the Bhāgavata Purāṇa as assuming the form of Brahmā in order to bring forth the Vedic *mantra*s and to manifest the phenomenal world. In the second phase of the process of Vedic transmission, he is represented as assuming the form of the *ṛṣi*s (*ṛṣi-rūpa-dhara*) to cognize and preserve the Vedic *mantra*s and thereby inaugurate the recitative and sacrificial traditions.[126] Finally, in the third phase of the transmission process, he assumes the form of the *ṛṣi* Vyāsa in every Dvāpara Yuga to divide the one Veda into four Saṃhitās.[127]

The Bhāgavata Purāṇa thus represents Kṛṣṇa as assuming a series of manifest forms in order to bring forth the Vedic *mantra*s, cognize and preserve them as recited texts, and divide them into distinct collections. The entire process is ultimately understood as a process of self-referral, for the Vedic *mantra*s that the Lord thus brings forth, cognizes, and divides are simply the differentiated expressions of his own eternal nature as Veda.

This self-referral process culminates in the Bhāgavata Purāṇa itself, which the Lord himself reveals to the creator Brahmā[128] and which he himself composes through the agency of his partial incarnation, the *ṛṣi* Vyāsa.[129] The Bhāgavata proclaims itself equal to the Veda,[130] because Lord Kṛṣṇa, who is the eternal Veda, discloses himself most perfectly and completely in this text, which is extolled as the embodiment of the Lord (*bhagavad-rūpa*).[131] Kṛṣṇa is thus both the *ṛṣi* Vyāsa and the object of this great *ṛṣi*'s mystical cognitions. Through the agency of Vyāsa, his partial incarnation, the Lord reveals himself to himself in the form of the Bhāgavata Purāṇa, in which he revels in the bliss of his own divine nature and celebrates the rapturous delights of his own divine play, or *līlā*. While from the perspective of the Lord, the Bhāgavata's narration of the *līlā* (*līlā-kathā*) is self-revelation, from the perspective of the enlightened sage Vyāsa, it is a record of his mystical cognitions of the Lord of creation. Vyāsa's cognitions of Kṛṣṇa's *līlā* are represented as the culminating stage of spiritual realization, for even though he had attained Brahman he did not feel completely fulfilled until he realized the supreme reality of Kṛṣṇa and began to extol the glories of ecstatic union with Bhagavān. In this highest state of realization, with his consciousness united with Kṛṣṇa, he cognized the hidden dynamics of the Godhead and witnessed the unfoldment of the Lord's cosmic dance. Like the Vedic *ṛṣi*s, who cognized the activities of the gods in their celestial realms and gave expression to their cognitions in the form of recited hymns, the *ṛṣi* Vyāsa cognized the play and display of the supreme Godhead and gave expression to his cognition in the form of recited narratives. The recitation of the Lord's *līlā* is thus understood to be tantamount to the recitation of the Vedic *mantras*.[132]

The Bhāgavata Purāṇa, moreover, emphasizes the fruits of reciting this *śruti* pertaining to Lord Kṛṣṇa,[133] as well as the fruits of hearing (*phala-śruti*) the recitation.[134] A brahmin who recites the Bhāgavata Purāṇa is said to attain fruits comparable to those attained through reciting the Vedic *mantra*s.[135] However, the Bhāgavata also distinguishes itself from the Vedic paradigm in that, while the Vedic *mantra*s may be recited and heard only by male members of the three higher social classes, this Purāṇa-Veda may be recited and heard by people at all levels of the social hierarchy, including *śūdra*s and women.[136] The Bhāgavata, the fruit of the wish-yielding tree of Veda, declares itself to be full of bliss-bestowing ambrosia (*amṛta*, *rasa*) in the form of stories of Kṛṣṇa's *līlā* (*līlā-kathā*), which are savored and enjoyed by all who hear them and which captivate the hearts of gods and humans alike.[137] Reciting the Bhāgavata Purāṇa and listening to its recitation are celebrated as a means through which the devotee may purify his or her heart and mind of all sin,[138] attain freedom from suffering and ignorance,[139] and cross over the ocean of *saṃsāra*, the cycle of birth and death, to a state of liberation.[140] Through recounting the glorious deeds of Lord Kṛṣṇa and describing, in vivid, sensuous detail, his love-play with the *gopī*s, recitation of the Bhāgavata Purāṇa is intended, above all, to inspire devotion in the hearts of the listeners[141] and to culminate in the attainment of the highest goal of human existence: realization of the supreme reality of Kṛṣṇa.[142]

Ecstatic union with Lord Kṛṣṇa is thus represented as the source and the goal of the Bhāgavata Purāṇa's devotional mysticism. Vyāsa, having realized the supreme reality of Bhagavān, recorded his mystical cognitions of Kṛṣṇa's *līlā* and extolled the glories of devotion as the means to attain that sublime state of realization in which one directly witnesses the Lord's cosmic dance. The Bhāgavata Purāṇa insists, moreover, that devotion to Kṛṣṇa is the means of realizing the true import of the Vedas, for the Lord himself is the eternal Veda, who manifests himself in the differentiated expressions of the Vedic *mantra*s. The entire canon of *śruti* and *smṛti* texts celebrates this supreme reality, the Bhāgavata declares. The four Vedas, together with the Itihāsas and Purāṇas as the fifth Veda, bow down at the feet of the Lord of creation.[143] The Bhāgavata Purāṇa, as the embodiment of Bhagavān, thus claims for itself the status of the quintessential scripture that is the culmination and fulfillment of the entire brahmanical canon.

NOTES

These abbreviations are used in the notes to this chapter.

Agni	Agni Purāṇa	Mbh.	Mahābhārata
AV	Atharva-Veda Saṃhitā	MP	Matsya Purāṇa
BĀU	Bṛhadāraṇyaka Upaniṣad	Nār.	Nārada Purāṇa
BP	Bhāgavata Purāṇa	Padma	Padma Purāṇa
Brahm.	Brahmāṇḍa Purāṇa	Rām.	Rāmāyaṇa
CU	Chāndogya Upaniṣad	ŚB	Śatapatha Brāhmaṇa
KP	Kūrma Purāṇa	Skanda	Skanda Purāṇa
LP	Liṅga Purāṇa	ŚP	Śiva Purāṇa
Maitri	Maitri Upaniṣad	Vāyu	Vāyu Purāṇa
Mārk.	Mārkaṇḍeya Purāṇa	VP	Viṣṇu Purāṇa

1. For a summary of scholarly opinions concerning the date of the Bhāgavata Purāṇa, see Friedhelm Hardy, *Viraha-Bhakti: The Early History of Kṛṣṇa Devotion in South India* (Delhi, 1983), pp. 486–488, including n.10; and Ludo Rocher, *The Purāṇas*, A History of Indian Literature, vol. 2, pt. 3 (Wiesbaden, 1986), pp. 148–149. With respect to the Bhāgavata Purāṇa's place of origin, the scholarly consensus is that it originated in the Tamil region of South India. For a summary of the evidence for the text's South Indian origin, see Hardy, *Viraha-Bhakti*, pp. 488, 637–646. See also Rocher, *The Purāṇas*, p. 148; Radhakamal Mukerjee, *The Lord of the Autumn Moons* (Bombay, 1957), pp. 72–74; Thomas J. Hopkins, "The Social Teaching of the *Bhāgavata Purāṇa*," in Milton Singer, ed., *Krishna: Myths, Rites, and Attitudes* (Chicago, 1966), pp. 4–6; T. S. Rukmani, *A Critical Study of the Bhāgavata-Purāṇa (with Special Reference to Bhakti)*, Chowkhamba Sanskrit Studies, vol. 77 (Varanasi, 1970), pp. 9–11; and Ganesh Vasudeo Tagare, trans., *The Bhāgavata-Purāṇa*, pt. 1, Ancient Indian Tradition and Mythology Series, vol. 7 (Delhi, 1976), p. xl.
2. In his extended study of Kṛṣṇa devotion in South India, Hardy emphasizes the importance of the Bhāgavata Purāṇa's role in Sanskritizing the Tamil bhakti of the Āḷvārs and in attempting to integrate North and South Indian traditions. He remarks:

"Northern culture orientated itself by a social system (the brahmins as the foremost *varṇa* [social class]) and an ideology (the Vedānta, viz. the systematization of the teaching of the *Upaniṣads*), while Southern culture was characterized by an emotional religion (of the Āḻvārs) and by great aesthetic sensibility (the old *caṅkam* poetry, and the *akattiṇai*). The BhP tries to integrate all four complexes, and it uses the symbol of the Vedas to achieve this, while adopting the purāṇic literary form" (Hardy, *Viraha-Bhakti*, p. 489).

3. Ibid.
4. For an enumeration of representative commentaries on the Bhāgavata Purāṇa, see Tagare, *The Bhāgavata-Purāṇa*, pt. 1, pp. lxvi–lxix; Rocher, *The Purāṇas*, p. 149.
5. For extended studies of the role of bhakti in the Bhāgavata Purāṇa, see Hardy, *Viraha-Bhakti*; Rukmani, *A Critical Study of the Bhāgavata-Puraṇa* (*with Special Reference to Bhakti*); Adalbert Gail, *Bhakti im Bhāgavatapurāṇa. Religionsgeschichtliche Studie zur Idee der Gottesliebe in Kult und Mystik des Viṣṇuismus*, Münchener Indologische Studien, vol. 6 (Wiesbaden, 1969).
6. John B. Carman, "Conceiving Hindu 'Bhakti' as Theistic Mysticism," in Steven T. Katz, ed., *Mysticism and Religious Traditions* (Oxford, 1983), pp. 191–225.
7. Ibid., p. 191.
8. Ibid., pp. 192–193.
9. Evelyn Underhill, *Mysticism: A Study in the Nature and Development of Man's Spiritual Consciousness* (1910; rpt., New York, 1955).
10. Rufus M. Jones, *Studies in Mystical Religion* (London, 1909).
11. Among Gershom Scholem's numerous studies of Jewish mysticism, see, in particular, his *Major Trends in Jewish Mysticism*, 3rd rev. ed. (1954; rpt., New York, 1961).
12. Annemarie Schimmel, *Mystical Dimensions of Islam* (Chapel Hill, 1975).
13. See, in particular, R. C. Zaehner, *Mysticism Sacred and Profane: An Inquiry into Some Varieties of Praeternatural Experience* (London, 1957); and Zaehner, *Hindu and Muslim Mysticism*, School of Oriental and African Studies, University of London, Jordan Lectures in Comparative Religion, no. 5 (London, 1960).
14. See, in particular, W. T. Stace, *Mysticism and Philosophy* (Philadelphia, 1960).
15. See, for example, Steven Katz's critiques of Zaehner and Stace in his "Language, Epistemology, and Mysticism," in Steven T. Katz, ed., *Mysticism and Philosophical Analysis* (New York, 1978), pp. 25–32. Katz emphasizes that "the phenomenological typologies of Stace and Zaehner are too reductive and inflexible, forcing multifarious and extremely variegated forms of mystical experience into improper interpretative categories which lose sight of the fundamentally important differences between the data studied" (p. 25). Katz's "contextualist" approach to the study of mysticism will be discussed later in this chapter.
16. S. N. Dasgupta, *Hindu Mysticism* (1927; rpt., New York, 1959).
17 Zaehner, *Hindu and Muslim Mysticism*, p. 19.
18. Ibid., p. 11. In his treatment of bhakti mysticism, Zaehner focuses on the Bhagavad Gītā together with Rāmānuja's commentary on the Gītā. See ibid., pp. 64–85. For a critique of Zaehner's "dogmatic approach to the study of mysticism," see Frits Staal, *Exploring Mysticism: A Methodological Essay* (Berkeley, 1975), pp. 67–69.
19. A. Govindāchārya, *A Metaphysique of Mysticism* (*Vedically Viewed*) (Mysore [Adyar], 1923), pp. 7–9; P. N. Srinivasachari, *Mystics and Mysticism* (Madras, 1951), pp. 1–43. As Carman notes, both scholars' treatments of mysticism betray their bias toward bhakti as members of the Śrī Vaiṣṇava community that derives from Rāmānuja. See Carman, "Conceiving Hindu 'Bhakti'," pp. 195, 202–203.
20. Carman, "Conceiving Hindu 'Bhakti'," pp. 201–202. The tendency to privilege the

monistic mysticism of identity as the central form of Hindu mysticism is reflected, for example, in Rudolf Otto's classic study *Mysticism East and West: A Comparative Analysis of the Nature of Mysticism*, trans. Bertha L. Bracey and Richenda C. Payne (London, 1932), in which he takes Śaṃkara as the paradigmatic exemplar of "Eastern" mysticism.

21. Gerald James Larson, "Mystical Man in India," *Journal for the Scientific Study of Religion* 12, no. 1 (1973): 1–16. One of the innovative contributions of Larson's typology, which is reminiscent of Dasgupta's fourfold schema (albeit more highly nuanced and differentiated), is his attempt to correlate the four types of Indian mystical experience with four stages in human development: infancy and early childhood, adolescence, marriage and adult sexuality, and old age and death, respectively.
22. Ibid., p. 11.
23. BP 11.14.23–24; cf. BP 1.6.16–19. All translations of Sanskrit texts are my own.
24. J. N. Farquhar, *An Outline of the Religious Literature of India* (London, 1920), pp. 229–230.
25. J. Gonda, "Het begrip bhakti," in *Tijdschrift voor Philosophie* 10 (1948): 640; translation cited in Hardy, *Viraha-Bhakti*, p. 38.
26. Dasgupta, *Hindu Mysticism*, pp. 124–126. See also Hopkins, "The Social Teaching of the *Bhāgavata Purāṇa*," p. 9, which notes the "significant change" from the "quiet contemplation" of the bhakti of the Bhagavad Gītā to the "emotional fervor" of the bhakti of the Bhāgavata Purāṇa.
27. Paul Hacker, *Prahlāda. Werden und Wandlungen einer Idealgestalt. Beiträge zur Geschichte des Hinduismus*, 2 vols., Akademie der Wissenschaften und der Literatur, Abhandlungen der Geistes- und Sozialwissenschaftlichen Klasse, nos. 9, 13 (1959), esp. vol. 1, pp. 93–147. Cf. Otto, *Mysticism East and West*, pp. 160–162, where the mystical experience of Prahlāda in the Viṣṇu Purāṇa, for whom bhakti is "the stilling of the soul before God, a trustful, believing devotion," is contrasted with the experience of Caitanya (sixteenth century), for whom bhakti is "'Prema,' a fevered, glowing Krishna-eroticism, colored throughout by love passion." The Kṛṣṇa bhakti of Caitanya and of the Gauḍīya Vaiṣṇava movement that he founded is closely allied with the bhakti of the Bhāgavata Purāṇa, which provided the authoritative scriptural basis for Gauḍīya Vaiṣṇava theology.
28. Hardy, *Viraha-Bhakti*, esp. pp. 36–43, 573.
29. See ibid., pp. 41–43, for a brief overview of scholarly opinions concerning the connections between the Bhāgavata Purāṇa and the Āḻvārs. Hardy himself asserts that the Bhāgavata Purāṇa is "an attempt to render in Sanskrit (and that means *inter alia* to make available for the whole of India) the religion of the Āḻvārs" (p. 44).
30. Charlotte Vaudeville, "Evolution of Love-Symbolism in Bhagavatism," *Journal of the American Oriental Society* 82, no. 1 (1962): 40.
31. Steven T. Katz, "The 'Conservative' Character of Mystical Experience," in Katz, *Mysticism and Religious Traditions*, pp. 3–4.
32. Katz, "The 'Conservative' Character of Mystical Experience," esp. pp. 3–32. For Katz's arguments concerning the preconditioned nature of mystical experience, see "Language, Epistemology, and Mysticism." See also Robert M. Gimello's discussion of the "essential contextuality" of mystical experience in "Mysticism in Its Contexts," in Katz, *Mysticism and Religious Traditions*, pp. 61–88.
33. This term derives from Brian Stock, *The Implications of Literacy: Written Language and Models of Interpretation in the Eleventh and Twelfth Centuries* (Princeton, 1983).
34. These four Vedic Saṃhitās constitute collections of verses (*ṛc*s), sacrificial formulae (*yajus*es), chants (*sāman*s), and incantations and imprecations (*atharvāṅgiras*es or

atharvans), respectively. The earliest references to the Veda(s) in Vedic texts generally focus on the triad *ṛcs*, *yajus*es, and *sāmans*, which are designated as the "threefold knowledge" (*trayī vidyā*) or the "threefold Veda" (*traya veda*). This emphasis on the "threefold knowledge" of the Ṛg-Veda, Yajur-Veda, and Sāma-Veda suggests that it took some time before the *atharvans* of the Atharva-Veda were accorded an equivalent status as forming part of the "four Vedas" (*catur veda*).

35. The term *mantra* is used in the present context to refer to the *ṛcs*, *yajus*es, *sāmans*, and *atharvans* collected in the four Saṃhitās, as distinct from the Brāhmaṇa and Upaniṣadic portions of the Veda. It should be noted, however, that although the terms *mantra* and *Saṃhitā* are often used interchangeably, they are not entirely synonymous, as the Taittirīya Saṃhitā (Black Yajur-Veda) contains, in addition to *mantras*, some Brāhmaṇa material discussing the sacrificial ceremonies.
36. Although the canon of *śruti* is technically closed, the category of Upaniṣads has remained somewhat permeable, with new Upaniṣads being added to the traditionally accepted 108 Upaniṣads until as late as the medieval period. Many of the later Upaniṣads are highly sectarian, and thus this phenomenon represents one of the strategies used by sectarian movements to legitimate their own texts through granting them the nominal status of *śruti*.
37. See Thomas Coburn's illuminating discussion of the relationship between *śruti* and *smṛti* in Hindu conceptions of scripture in "'Scripture' in India: Towards a Typology of the Word in Hindu Life," *Journal of the American Academy of Religion* 52, no. 3 (1984): 435–459; rpt. in Miriam Levering, ed., *Rethinking Scripture: Essays from a Comparative Perspective* (Albany, 1989), pp. 102–128.
38. See, for example, Louis Renou and Jean Filliozat, *L'Inde classique. Manuel des études indiennes*, vol. 1 (Paris, 1947–1949), pp. 381, 270; Sarvepalli Radhakrishnan and Charles A. Moore, eds., *A Source Book in Indian Philosophy* (Princeton, 1957), p. xix; R. N. Dandekar, "Dharma, The First End of Man," in Wm. Theodore de Bary et al., eds., *Sources of Indian Tradition*, Records of Civilization: Sources and Studies, no. 56 (New York, 1958), p. 217; Jan Gonda, *Die Religionen Indiens*, vol. 1, *Veda und älterer Hinduismus*, Die Religionen der Menschheit, vol. 11 (Stuttgart, 1960), p. 107; A. L. Basham, *The Wonder That Was India: A Survey of the History and Culture of the Indian Sub-continent before the Coming of the Muslims*, 3rd rev. ed. (London, 1967), pp. 112–113; and Oscar Botto, "Letterature antiche dell'India," in Oscar Botto, ed., *Storia delle Letterature d'Oriente*, vol. 3 (Milan, 1969), p. 294. For a discussion and critique of such characterizations of *śruti* and *smṛti* as a distinction between "revelation" and "tradition," see Sheldon Pollock, "'Tradition' as 'Revelation': *Śruti*, *Smṛti*, and the Sanskrit Discourse of Power," in Siegfried Lienhard and Irma Piovano, eds., *Lex et Litterae: Essays on Ancient Indian Law and Literature in Honour of Oscar Botto* (Turin, forthcoming). Pollock's views are discussed in n. 61 in this chapter.
39. In opposition to the view of the Mīmāṃsakas and Vedāntins that the Vedas are eternal and *apauruṣeya*, the exponents of the Nyāya, Vaiśeṣika, and Yoga schools use a variety of arguments to establish that the Vedas are noneternal (*anitya*) and *pauruṣeya*, created by the agency of a personal God, Īśvara.
40. See Giorgio Bonazzoli, "The Dynamic Canon of the Purāṇa-s," *Purāṇa* 21, no. 2 (1979): 116–166. For a discussion of central issues in the scholarly debates concerning the nature and origin of the genre of texts known as "Purāṇas," see Thomas B. Coburn, "The Study of the Purāṇas and the Study of Religion," *Religious Studies* 16, no. 3 (1980): 341–352. For extended analyses of the problems involved in the study and dating of the individual Purāṇas, along with descriptions of the character and

contents of individual Purāṇas, see Rocher, *The Purāṇas*; and R. C. Hazra, *Studies in the Purāṇic Records on Hindu Rites and Customs*, 2nd ed. (Delhi, 1975).

41. In his examination of twenty Purāṇas, Bonazzoli notes that twenty-seven lists of Purāṇas are given in seventeen of the Purāṇas, with only the Brahma, Brahmāṇda, and Vāmana Purāṇas containing no lists. All of the lists, with the exception of two cases, contain eighteen Purāṇas. See Bonazzoli, "The Dynamic Canon of the Purāṇa-s," pp. 132–134; table 1, pp. 144–149. See also Anand Swarup Gupta, "Purāṇas and Their Referencing," *Purāṇa* 7, no. 2 (1965): 334–340.
42. The standard list gives the Bhāgavata Purāṇa as the fifth of the eighteen Mahāpurāṇas: Brahma, Padma, Viṣṇu, Śiva, Bhāgavata, Nārada, Mārkaṇḍeya, Agni, Bhaviṣya, Brahmavaivarta, Liṅga, Varāha, Skanda, Vāmana, Kūrma, Matsya, Garuḍa, Brahmāṇḍa. For variants of this list, see Bonazzoli, "The Dynamic Canon of the Purāṇa-s," table 1, pp. 144–149; and Gupta, "Purāṇas and Their Referencing," pp. 336–338.
43. BP 12.7.10,22.
44. BP 12.13.4–8 lists the eighteen Maḥāpurāṇas in the standard order noted earlier in n. 42. BP 12.7.23–24 lists the same eighteen texts in a different order.
45. The actual number of *ślokas* in the Gītā Press edition of the Bhāgavata Purāṇa is 14,579. See Bonazzoli, "The Dynamic Canon of the Purāṇa-s," pp. 134–137; table 2, p. 150; and Gupta, "Purāṇas and Their Referencing," pp. 348–351.
46. BP 12.13.4–9.
47. One of the earliest formulations of this definition is found in the *Amarakośa* (c. fifth century), which defines "Purāṇa" as "that which has five characteristics (*pañca-lakṣaṇa*)" (Śabdādivarga 5). For a collation of relevant Purāṇic passages concerning *pañca-lakṣaṇa*, see Pandurang Vaman Kane, *History of Dharmaśāstra (Ancient and Mediaeval Religious and Civil Law in India)*, vol. 5, pt. 2, Government Oriental Series (Poona, 1962), pp. 838–839, including n.1365. For an extended study, see Willibald Kirfel, *Das Purāṇa Pañcalakṣaṇa. Versuch einer Textgeschichte* (Bonn, 1927).
48. P. V. Kane, for example, remarks: "The extant Purāṇas contain far more subjects than the five. Some Purāṇas barely touch these five and deal at great length with altogether different topics. Only a few of the extant Purāṇas can be said to deal with all the five topics at some length. The five characteristic topics occupy less than three percent of the extent of the extant Mahāpurāṇas" (Kane, *History of Dharmaśāstra*, vol. 5, pt. 2, p. 841).
49. Bonazzoli, "The Dynamic Canon of the Purāṇa-s," p. 131.
50. See BP 12.7.8–20. An alternative enumeration of the ten characteristics is given in BP 2.10.1–7.
51. See Bonazzoli's comparison of the Bhāgavata Purāṇa and the Viṣṇu Purāṇa in his "Schemes in the Purāṇas (A First Approach)," *Purāṇa* 24, no. 1 (1982): 160–162, 182–183.
52. For a comparative analysis of the *gopī* narratives in the Bhāgavata Purāṇa and in the Viṣṇu Purāṇa, see Hardy, *Viraha-Bhakti*, pp. 497–510. As Hacker (in *Prahlāda*) has noted, the Prahlāda episode in Book 7 of the Bhāgavata similarly appears to have been modeled after the Viṣṇu Purāṇa's accounts of Prahlāda.
53. See Hacker, *Prahlāda*, pp. 98, 111 n.1, 224.
54. M. Winternitz, *A History of Indian Literature*, vol. 1, pt. 2, trans. S. Ketkar, 2nd ed. (Calcutta, 1963), p. 488. Among other scholars who have noted the homogeneous character of the Bhāgavata, see Hardy, *Viraha-Bhakti*, p. 486; Hopkins, "The Social Teaching of the *Bhāgavata Purāṇa*," p. 4; and Sheo Shanker Prasad, *The Bhāgavata Purāṇa: A Literary Study* (Delhi, 1984), p. 66.

55. See Richard Salomon, "The Viṣṇu Purāṇa as a Specimen of Vernacular Sanskrit," *Wiener Zeitschrift für die Kunde Südasiens* 30 (1986): 39–56.
56. See F. J. Meier, "Der Archaismus in der Sprache des Bhāgavata-Purāṇa," *Zeitschrift für Indologie und Iranistik* 8 (1931): 33–79; Louis Renou, *Histoire de la langue sanskrite* (Lyon, 1956), pp. 120–121; J.A.B. van Buitenen, "On the Archaism of the *Bhāgavata Purāṇa*," in Singer, *Krishna: Myths, Rites, and Attitudes*, pp. 23–40; Hardy, *Viraha-Bhakti*, pp. 489–490; and Rocher, *The Purāṇas*, pp. 145–146. For a formal analysis of the linguistic peculiarities of the Bhāgavata Purāṇa, see Ashutosh Sarma Biswas, *Bhāgavata Purāṇa: A Linguistic Study, Particularly from the Vedic Background* (Dibrugarh [Hoshiarpur], 1968). For a general study of the language, style, and meter of the Bhāgavata, see Prasad, *The Bhāgavata Purāṇa*, pp. 65–97.
57. Van Buitenen, "On the Archaism of the *Bhāgavata Purāṇa*," pp. 31, 33.
58. J. C. Heesterman, "Veda and Dharma," in Wendy Doniger O'Flaherty and J. Duncan M. Derrett, eds., *The Concept of Duty in South Asia* (New Delhi, 1978), pp. 92–93. For a survey of the different attitudes, beliefs, and practices that the major texts, philosophical schools, and sects of the Indian tradition have adopted with respect to the Veda in the course of its history, see Louis Renou, *The Destiny of the Veda in India*, trans. Dev Raj Chanana (Delhi, 1965). See also Wilhelm Halbfass's discussion of the role and significance of the Veda in traditional Hindu self-understanding in his *Tradition and Reflection: Explorations in Indian Thought* (Albany, 1991), esp. pp. 1–22. For a recent collection of essays on the role of Vedic authority in various Indian religious traditions, which challenges a number of Renou's conclusions, see Laurie L. Patton, ed., *Authority, Anxiety, and Canon: Essays in Vedic Interpretation*, SUNY Series in Hindu Studies (Albany, 1994).
59. For a detailed analysis of the cosmogonic and epistemological paradigms associated with the Veda in the mythological speculations of Vedic and post-Vedic texts, see Barbara A. Holdrege, *Veda and Torah: Transcending the Textuality of Scripture* (Albany, 1996).
60. See, for example, Mbh. 1.57.74; Mbh. 12.327.18; Rām. 1.1.77; BP 1.4.20; BP 3.12.39; Skanda 5.3.1.18. For a discussion of the Mahābhārata's representations of itself as the fifth Veda, see James L. Fitzgerald, "India's Fifth Veda: The *Mahābhārata*'s Presentation of Itself," *Journal of South Asian Literature* 20, no. 1 (1985): 125–140; and Fitzgerald, "The Veda in the 'Fifth Veda' of Vyāsa's *Mahābhārata*" (paper presented at the Annual Meeting of the American Academy of Religion, New Orleans, 1996). For an analysis of how the Mahābhārata's depiction of the sage Vyāsa legitimates its claim to be the fifth Veda, see Bruce M. Sullivan, *Kṛṣṇa Dvaipāyana Vyāsa and the Mahābhārata: A New Interpretation* (Leiden, 1990), esp. pp. 29–31, 81–101, 112–117. The strategies used by the Bhāgavata Purāṇa and other Purāṇas to establish their Vedic status is discussed farther on in this chapter. The Vedic antecedents of the concept of the fifth Veda are found in the Upaniṣads in the notion that the Itihāsa and Purāṇa are "the fifth" among sacred brahmanical texts and sciences, although they are not explicitly referred to as the fifth Veda. See CU 7.1.2,4; CU 7.2.1; and CU 7.7.1; these passages enumerate "the Ṛg-Veda, the Yajur-Veda, the Sāma-Veda, the Atharvaṇa as the fourth (*caturtha*), Itihāsa-Purāṇa as the fifth (*pañcama*). . . ."
61. Sheldon Pollock has brought to light an essential mechanism whereby the domain of the Veda was extended to include not only *śruti* but also *smṛti*. He locates this mechanism in the definition of the terms *śruti* and *smṛti* themselves, which, he argues, have been incorrectly construed as representing a dichotomy between "revelation" and "tradition." He maintains rather that, according to the etymology derived from the Pūrva-Mīmāṃsā school, which is still prevalent among certain traditional brahmanical

teachers, *śruti* refers to the extant Vedic texts that can be "heard" in recitation, whereas *smṛti* is an open-ended category that encompasses any teachings or practices pertaining to dharma that have been "remembered" from lost Vedic texts. The term *Veda* is thus extended through a process of "vedacization" and comes to include not only *śruti* but also *smṛti* texts. See Pollock, "'Tradition' as 'Revelation'"; and Pollock, "From Discourse of Ritual to Discourse of Power in Sanskrit Culture," in *Ritual and Power*, ed. Barbara A. Holdrege, *Journal of Ritual Studies* 4, no. 2 (1990): 322–328. David Carpenter has argued that the extension of the purview of Veda—beyond the ritual practices delineated in the *śruti* texts to the broader domain of sociocultural practices laid out in *smṛti* texts—was accomplished primarily by shifting the locus of Vedic authority from a circumscribed set of "texts" to the brahmanical custodians who were responsible for the "ritualized reproduction of the 'divine speech' of the Vedic tradition." In the Dharma-Sūtras and the Dharma-Śāstras the conduct of the brahmins became synonymous with *śiṣṭācāra*, the "practice of the learned," and was ascribed normative status alongside *śruti* and *smṛti* as an authoritative source of dharma. Thus, even when the teachings of the brahmins went beyond the teachings of the *śruti* texts, they were nevertheless deemed "Vedic," for they were promulgated by those who, by virtue of their privileged role as transmitters of the Vedic recitative tradition, had become "living embodiments of the Veda." See David Carpenter, "Language, Ritual, and Society: Reflections on the Authority of the Veda in India," *Journal of the American Academy of Religion* 60, no. 1 (1992): 57–77, esp. 58–63.

62. A number of these modes of assimilation are discussed by Pollock in "From Discourse of Ritual to Discourse of Power in Sanskrit Culture," p. 332.
63. The mechanisms of vedacization through which specific texts and traditions have sought to invest themselves with Vedic status have been explored in two recent scholarly forums, the symposium "Whose Veda?" held at the University of Florida in Gainesville (1996), and the panel "Whose Veda? Revelation and Authority in South Asian Religions," held at the Annual Meeting of the American Academy of Religion in New Orleans (1996). For references to papers presented at the American Academy of Religion meeting, see nn. 60, 66–68 in this chapter.
64. See Brian K. Smith, *Reflections on Resemblance, Ritual, and Religion* (New York, 1989), pp. 3–29, esp. pp. 20–29. Smith goes so far as to claim that "the Veda functions as a touchstone for Hindu orthodoxy" and that Vedic authority is constitutive of "Hinduism" itself, including not only the brahmanical tradition but also devotional sects and tantric movements: "Hinduism is the religion of those humans who create, perpetuate, and transform traditions with legitimizing reference to the authority of the Veda" (pp. 26, 13–14). Jan Gonda similarly defines Hinduism as "a complex of social-religious phenomena which are based on the authority of the ancient corpora, called Veda" (Gonda, *Change and Continuity in Indian Religion*, Disputationes Rheno-Trajectinae, vol. 9 [The Hague, 1965], p. 7). For statements by other Indologists concerning the authority of the Veda as the decisive criterion of Hindu orthodoxy, see Smith, *Reflections on Resemblance, Ritual, and Religion*, p. 18 n.45.
65. See N. Subbu Reddiar, "The Nālāyiram as Drāvida Veda," chap. 26 of his *Religion and Philosophy of Nālāyira Divya Prabandham with Special Reference to Nammāḻvār* (Tirupati, 1977), pp. 680–693.
66. For a discussion of the vedacization of the *Rāmcaritmānas*, and of *Mānas* recitation rituals in particular, see Philip Lutgendorf, "The Power of Sacred Story: *Rāmāyaṇa* Recitation in Contemporary North India," in *Ritual and Power*, ed. Holdrege, *Journal of Ritual Studies* 4, no. 2 (1990): 115–147. See also Lutgendorf's *The Life of a Text: Performing the Rāmcaritmānas of Tulsidas* (Berkeley, 1991). Lutgendorf reflects

more generally on the mechanisms of vedacization in "'Vedacization' Revisited" (paper presented at the Annual Meeting of the American Academy of Religion, New Orleans, 1996).

67. M. Thomas Thangaraj, "The Veda-Āgama in Tamil Christianity" (paper presented at the Annual Meeting of the American Academy of Religion, New Orleans, 1996).
68. Vasudha Narayanan, "The Veda in Tamil Islamic Literature" (paper presented at the Annual Meeting of the American Academy of Religion, New Orleans, 1996).
69. While some groups have thus sought to legitimate their texts through assimilating them to the Veda, certain bhakti and tantric movements have responded to the Veda by rejecting or subverting its authority. For example, the *vacana* poets of the Vīraśaiva sect, which originated in the Kannada-speaking region of South India in the tenth century, were leaders of a protest movement that rejected the Vedic texts and rituals because of their association with the caste system and other brahmanical institutions. See A. K. Ramanujan, trans., *Speaking of Śiva* (Harmondsworth, Eng., 1973), pp. 19–55. Certain left-handed tantric sects such as the Kashmir Śaivas have not only rejected Vedic authority, but they have also treated the Veda as a symbol that is to be actively subverted through adherence to teachings and practices that directly transgress orthodox brahmanical traditions. Abhinavagupta (tenth century), the most famous exponent of Kashmir Śaivism, asserts: "The wise *sādhaka* [tantric practitioner] must not choose the word of the Veda as the ultimate authority because it is full of impurities and produces meager, unstable, and limited results. Rather, the *sādhaka* should elect the Śaivite scriptures as his source. Moreover, that which according to the Veda produces sin leads, according to the left-handed doctrine, promptly to perfection. The entire Vedic teaching is in fact tightly held in the grip of *māyā* (delusional power)" (*Tantrāloka* 37.10–12; cf. 15.595–599, cited in Paul E. Muller-Ortega, "The Power of the Secret Ritual: Theoretical Formulations from the Tantra," in *Ritual and Power*, ed. Holdrege, *Journal of Ritual Studies* 4, no. 2 [1990]: 49).
70. For a summary of the scholarly debates, see Rocher, *The Purāṇas*, pp. 13–17. Among more recent discussions, see Frederick M. Smith, "Purāṇaveda," in Patton, *Authority, Anxiety, and Canon*, pp. 97–138.
71. See, for example, Skanda 5.3.1.18. For the Vedic antecedents of this notion, see CU 7.1.2,4; CU 7.2.1; and CU 7.7.1, which list "Itihāsa-Purāṇa" as the "fifth" after the Ṛg-Veda, Yajur-Veda, Sāma-Veda, and Atharvaṇa. A number of other references in Vedic texts associate the term *Purāṇa* (singular) with the Veda(s). For example, AV 11.7.24, in discussing the remnant of the sacrificial offering, speaks of the "*ṛc*s, *sāman*s, meters, Purāṇa, together with the *yajus*." ŚB 13.4.3.13, in describing the procedures for a particular sacrifice, specifies that the Adhvaryu should say, "The Purāṇa is the Veda; this it is," and then should "relate some Purāṇa." A passage that occurs in BĀU 2.4.10; BĀU 4.5.11; and Maitri 6.32 describes the Itihāsa and Purāṇa as being "breathed forth" from the great Being, along with the Ṛg-Veda, Yajur-Veda, Sāma-Veda, and *atharvāṅgiras*es. For a discussion of the meaning of the term *Purāṇa* in the earliest Vedic text, the Ṛg-Veda Saṃhitā, see Ludo Rocher, "The Meaning of *purāṇa* in the Ṛgveda," *Wiener Zeitschrift für die Kunde Südasiens* 21 (1977): 5–24.
72. MP 289.9; Vāyu 1.18.
73. See, for example, Vāyu 1.11.
74. Vāyu 1.200–201 declares: "A brahmin who knows the four Vedas with their subsidiary limbs (*aṅga*s) and Upaniṣads but who does know the Purāṇa is not really learned. With both Itihāsa and Purāṇa one should complement the Veda. The Veda is afraid of one with little knowledgc." Variants of these two *śloka*s appear in separate places in the Mahābhārata, in 1.2.235 and 1.1.204.

75. With respect to their perspectives on recitation, the Purāṇas depart from the Vedic model in significant ways. For example, whereas recitations of the Vedic Saṃhitās may be heard only by male members of the three higher social classes, Purāṇic recitations are intended for the general populace and are therefore open to *śūdras* and women. In addition, the Purāṇas emphasize not only the power of *mantra*, but the power of sacred narrative as well. In contrast to recitations of the Vedic Saṃhitās, which focus almost exclusively on *śabda* (sound), on verbatim reproduction of the Vedic sounds, in Purāṇic recitations both *śabda* and *artha*, "sound" and "meaning," are important, for the content of the texts is intended to convey important teachings to the general populace. See Coburn, "'Scripture' in India," esp. pp. 445–455; and Brown, "Purāṇa as Scripture: From Sound to Image of the Holy Word in the Hindu Tradition," *History of Religions* 26, no. 1 (1986): 74–76. As Brown indicates, this shift in emphasis from sound to meaning in the Purāṇic tradition was accompanied by a shift in modes of scriptural transmission, in which the Purāṇas depart from the Vedic paradigm of exclusively oral transmission by emphasizing the importance of written transmission as well. They declare the fruits not only of hearing a Purāṇa recited but also of writing or copying the text itself and then of giving the book away as a gift. For a discussion of the Purāṇic "cult of the book," see Brown, pp. 76–83. For an analysis of the role and interrelationship of oral and written transmission in the Purāṇas, see Giorgio Bonazzoli, "Composition, Transmission and Recitation of the Purāṇa-s," *Purāṇa* 25, no. 2 (1983): 254–280.
76. See, for example, MP 3.3–4: "Of all the *śāstras* the Purāṇa was first recalled (*smṛti*) by Brahmā—eternal (*nitya*), consisting of the Word (*śabda-maya*), holy, having the extent of a hundred crores [of *ślokas*]. Afterward the Vedas issued forth from his mouths and also Mīmāṃsā and the science of Nyāya together with the eightfold means of valid knowledge (*pramāṇa*)." Variants of this tradition are given in MP 53.3–4; Vāyu 1.60–61; Brahm. 1.1.1.40–41; Padma Sṛṣṭi. 1.45; and Nār. 1.92.22–23.
77. In Purāṇic cosmogonies, creation occurs in endlessly repeating cycles of creation and dissolution. Among the basic units of time that constitute these cycles are the four *yugas*, or ages—Kṛta, Tretā, Dvāpara, and Kali. The Purāṇas emphasize that as the *yugas* progress, the strength, understanding, and morality of human beings progressively decline and their knowledge of the Veda gradually diminishes. For this reason, in every Dvāpara Yuga, Vyāsa divides the Veda into four distinct collections, Saṃhitās, in order to facilitate its understanding and preservation.
78. MP 53.3–11.
79. See, for example, Padma Sṛṣṭi. 1.45–52; Nār. 1.92.22–26; LP 1.1.1–3.
80. Brahm. 1.2.34.21; Vāyu 60.21; VP 3.6.16.
81. Brahm. 1.2.34.12–16; Brahm. 1.2.35.63–69; Vāyu 60.12–16; Vayu 61.55–61; VP 3.4.7–10; VP 3.6.17–20; cf. Agni 271.10–12. These two alternative Purāṇic traditions concerning the origins of the Purāṇas have been noted by a number of scholars, including Coburn, "The Study of the Purāṇas and the Study of Religion," pp. 344–346; Bonazzoli, "Schemes in the Purāṇas," pp. 174–175; Bonazzoli, "The Dynamic Canon of the Purāṇa-s," pp. 139–140; and Gupta, "Purāṇas and Their Referencing," pp. 323–326. For additional discussions of these traditions, see Rocher, *The Purāṇas*, pp. 45–48; Kane, *History of Dharmaśāstra*, vol. 5, pt. 2, pp. 829, including n.1349, 858, including n.1392, 861–862; V. S. Agrawala, "Original Purāṇa Saṃhitā," *Purāṇa* 8, no. 2 (1966): 232–239; R. C. Hazra, "The Purāṇas," In *The Cultural Heritage of India*, vol. 2, 2nd rev. ed. (Calcutta, 1962), p. 244; V. R. Ramchandra Dikshitar, "The Purāṇas: A Study," *Indian Historical Quarterly* 8, no. 4 (1932): 751–755; and F. E. Pargiter, *Ancient Indian Historical Tradition* (London, 1922), pp. 21–23.

82. VP 3.3.30.
83. VP 6.4.42.
84. VP 3.3.22; VP 1.22.81.
85. See, for example, VP 3.3.29–30: "He is composed of the *ṛcs*, of the *sāmans*, of the *yajuses*, and he is the Self (Ātman). He whose Self is the essence of the *ṛcs*, *yajuses*, and *sāmans*, he is the Self of embodied beings. Consisting of the Veda (*veda-maya*), he is divided; he forms the Veda with its branches (*śākhās*) into many divisions. Creator of the *śākhās*, he is the *śākhās* in their totality, the infinite Lord, whose very nature is knowledge (*jñāna-svarūpa*). See also VP 1.22.81–83; VP 2.11.7–11.
86. The Purāṇas particularly extol Viṣṇu-Nārāyaṇa as Veda incarnate when he assumes the form of a sacrificial boar (*yajña-varāha*), his body composed of the Vedas and sacrifices, in order to rescue the earth that lies submerged beneath the cosmic waters. See, for example, KP 1.6.15; VP 1.4.9,21–25,32–34; MP 248.67–73. Cf. Mark. 47.3–9, esp. 8, which depicts the creator Brahmā, not Viṣṇu, as Nārāyaṇa, who assumes the form of a boar composed of the Vedas in order to save the earth.
87. MP 164.20.
88. MP 167.12.
89. See, for example, ŚP Rudra. 2.15.46,52,64. See also ŚP Rudra. 1.8.1–53, which describes Śiva in his manifest form as Śabdabrahman—Brahman embodied in the Word—his body constituted by the forty-eight Sanskrit *varṇas* (phones) and the Vedic *mantras*. The Śaiva sections of the Kūrma Purāṇa similarly celebrate Śiva as the eternal Brahman whose Self is knowledge (*jñānātman*, *vidyātman*) and who, as the secret essence of the Veda (*veda-rahasya*), is the embodiment of the very self of Veda (*vedātma-mūrti*). See KP 2.3.6,20; KP 1.10.46–47,68.
90. BP 1.3.28.
91. The earliest reference to Kṛṣṇa is in Chāndogya Upaniṣad 3.17.6, which represents "Kṛṣṇa, the son of Devakī," as a disciple of Ghora Āṅgirasa.
92. Smith, "Purāṇaveda," p. 98.
93. Ibid. Smith's article analyzes how the Bhāgavata Purāṇa attempts to establish its Vedic identity through reinterpreting and reshaping three central Vedic categories: the infallibility of the Veda, the Vedic deities Agni and Soma, and the institution of sacrifice.
94. BP 1.4.20; BP 3.12.39.
95. See, for example, BP 12.13.14–17.
96. BP 1.4.7.
97. BP 1.3.40; BP 2.1.8; BP 2.8.28; BP 12.4.42.
98. BP 1.1.3.
99. BP 1.2.3.
100. BP 12.13.12,15.
101. See, for example, BP 1.1.11; BP 1.3.42.
102. BP 3.12.37,39.
103. BP 1.4.14–24; BP 12.6.46–12.7.7.
104. BP 1.4.14; BP 1.5.21; BP 12.6.49; BP 1.3.21.
105. BP 1.4.16–18; BP 1.5.21.
106. BP 12.6.46–12.7.7; cf. BP 1.4.19–23.
107. BP 12.7.8–24.
108. BP 1.4.14–1.5.40.
109. BP 1.7.3–4.
110. BP 1.7.3–8.
111. BP 8.16.31.

112. BP 7.11.7.
113. BP 6.16.51. For the relationship between Kṛṣṇa and the Veda as Śabdabrahman, see also BP 11.21.36–43.
114. See, for example, BP 7.3.30; BP 1.5.37; BP 5.22.3.
115. BP 3.13.34–44, esp. 34, 41, 44. Similar descriptions of the sacrificial boar as Veda incarnate are found in earlier Purāṇas, as discussed in n. 86 in this chapter.
116. BP 3.12.34,37; BP 12.6.44.
117. See, for example, BP 8.14.4.
118. BP 12.6.44–46; cf. BP 11.14.3–7.
119. BP 1.4.14–20,24; BP 12.6.46–50.
120. BP 1.1.1.
121. BP 11.14.3.
122. See, for example, BP 7.9.47; BP 1.2.28; BP 5.22.3; BP 11.5.10; BP 11.21.43; BP 11.14.3.
123. BP 3.18.15; BP 3.9.43; cf. BP 2.6.34. See also 3.12.34–35,37–40,44–47, which describes Brahmā as Śabdabrahman, whose form is composed of the Sanskrit *varṇa*s and the Vedic *mantra*s and meters.
124. BP 3.12.1; BP 3.13.6.
125. BP 3.9.24; cf. BP 3.12.34.
126. See, for example, BP 8.14.4,8.
127. BP 12.6.49; BP 1.4.14; BP 1.5.21; BP 1.3.21.
128. BP 2.8.28; BP 12.13.10. See also BP 2.9.43–44 and BP 12.13.19–20, which delineate an extended line of tradition in which the Lord reveals the Bhāgavata Purāṇa to the creator Brahmā, who transmits it to his son Nārada, who in turn imparts it to Vyāsa. Cf. BP 12.4.41.
129. BP 1.3.40; BP 1.4.14; BP 1.5.21; BP 12.6.49; BP 1.3.21.
130. BP 1.3.40; BP 2.1.8; BP 2.8.28; BP 12.4.42.
131. Bhāgavata Māhātmya 1.20.
132. See, for example, BP 1.5.22; BP 12.12.62; cf. BP 12.13.1.
133. BP 1.4.7.
134. See esp. BP 12.12.57–64.
135. BP 12.12.62.
136. BP 1.4.25; BP 12.12.64. As discussed in n. 75, this socially inclusive approach to recitation is characteristic of the Purāṇas in general. For a discussion of the Bhāgavata Purāṇa's attitudes toward the brahmanical social system, see Hopkins, "The Social Teaching of the *Bhāgavata Purāṇa*."
137. BP 1.1.3; BP 12.13.11; BP 12.4.40; BP 12.13.15.
138. See, for example, BP 12.12.58–59,64; BP 1.5.11.
139. See, for example, BP 1.5.40; BP 1.7.6–7; BP 3.8.2; BP 12.4.40; BP 12.12.57.
140. See, for example, BP 12.4.40; BP 1.5.13; BP 12.13.18.
141. See, for example, BP 1.7.6–7; BP 2.1.10.
142. See, for example, BP 1.1.2; BP 12.12.63.
143. BP 8.21.2. See also BP 10.87.12–41, in which the personified Vedas are represented as singing a hymn of praise (*veda-stuti*) to the Lord.

10

Experiencing Scriptural Diversity

Words and Stories in Hindu Traditions

DANIEL GOLD

Both to its adherents and to those who study it, Hinduism can present a bewildering scriptural diversity. Not only across broad Hindu horizons but also within particular Hindu traditions, individuals are regularly confronted with a multitude of authoritative religious texts.[1] Even though individuals might recognize alternative kinds of authority in different texts, they may still feel bound to give serious attention to many of them.[2] What are the ways in which diverse religious texts are approached? Perhaps more intriguing, what are the effects on religious experience of interaction with authoritative texts whose perspectives sometimes complement one another but sometimes seem contradictory, too? The answers to these questions depend not only on the kinds of authority given to different texts but also on the types of religious experience toward which those texts and their adherents are oriented.

Among the broad typologies of experience used across Hindu traditions, one of the most pervasive is the contrast between realization of the divine as either *nirguṇa* or *saguṇa*. *Guṇa* is a word that means "quality," "attribute," or "virtue," so the primary distinction drawn here is one between divinity perceived without attributes, formless and ultimate (*nirguṇa*, *niḥ* = "without"); and divinity embodied in some way—concrete, with some perceptible form (*saguṇa*; *sa* = "with"). Over the millennia different traditions have employed the *nirguṇa/saguṇa* contrast with different intellectual emphases, but for religious consciousness the principal force of the distinction appears largely the same. The *nirguṇa* in the Upaniṣads, for example, seems to refer most of all to the formless Brahman, an ultimate, abstract consciousness; two thousand years later, in Hindi devotion, the *nirguṇa* divinity—while sometimes presenting these characteristics—is also treated as a loving Lord into whom the devotee may be absorbed. In both cases, however, the *nirguṇa* refers to the essential being of the universe, with whom the aspirant seeks finally to identify; the ultimate beginning and end of things, it is perceived as something unformed and still. The *saguṇa*, by contrast, refers to something manifest and moving, with which individual embodied beings can engage through their senses. In Vedantic philosophies, rooted in the Upaniṣads, the *saguṇa brahman* often refers to the manifest universe itself, in which individuals are bound to engage; still sacred in its way, it does not always appear as highly valued as its *nirguṇa* counterpart. A radically more positive valuation of the *saguṇa* divine is found in devotional traditions, where the term normally refers to the embodied mythic deity envisioned in worship: the Goddess in one of her many forms, Śiva, Rama, Kṛṣṇa. Particularly in the image of the youthful Kṛṣṇa—playmate, lover, friend—the *saguṇa* divine becomes an object of blissful mystical interaction.

People seeking experiences of the divine as *nirguṇa* or *saguṇa* not only follow different textual traditions, but also approach these traditions differently as scripture. Following Thomas Coburn and Philip Lutgendorf, we can identify (at least) two dimensions to scripture in Hindu traditions: "word," which nicely translates the term *śabda* from Sanskrit and Hindi; and "story," which presents a variety of narrative and poetic forms.[3] Important traditions oriented toward the *nirguṇa* divine highlight the term *śabda*, although they give it substantially different implications. Consistently in these cases, however, scripture as *śabda*—an abstract and essential "word"—is somehow seen to point to (or reflect or reverberate) a formless reality conceived as some kind of substantial being. Scriptural exegesis, when it occurs, regularly focuses on nouns ("substantives," in grammar): What does this word really mean? How does it present the essential? Devotional traditions, by contrast, focusing on embodied *saguṇa* divinities, emphasize scripture as story, which reveals the ways of mythic deities in human and superhuman worlds. The basic mythic stories are presented in diverse ways, with narrative lines, textual genres, and retellings, all liable to evoke differing experiences of interaction with the divine beloved.

Two different dynamics of experiencing scriptural diversity thus emerge. When followers of *nirguṇa* traditions encounter apparent contradiction in the "words" that intimate an ultimate formless reality, they may "doubt" (a favorite word in philosophical texts), query, and alter their perspective. Even if full knowledge of that reality remains beyond their grasp, perceptions of it can thus become more subtle. By contrast, when followers of *saguṇa* traditions encounter diverse scriptures, they are likely to find them more easily complementary, different scenes of the same endless story. Instead of stretching perceptions more finely, encountering diverse scriptures is likely to layer experience—to enhance it and to deepen it.

For religious consciousness, the idea of scripture seems to denote first of all an *attitude* toward a text, one investing it with an authority able both to provide foundation for experience and to offer resistance to ingrown habits and preconceived ideals. In *nirguṇa* traditions, apparently contradictory foundations revealed by diverse scriptures may loosen preconceptions of a formless truth. In *saguṇa* traditions, diverse scriptures are more likely to add new dimensions to a foundational story that suggests an alternative to mundane ways of life.

To illustrate these differing experiences of scriptural diversity, I will focus on three traditions—two focusing on the *nirguṇa* divinity and one on the *saguṇa*. The two *nirguṇa* traditions fall at opposite ends of the Hindu socioreligious spectrum: the Advaita Vedānta of Śaṅkara (c. 700 C.E.)—abstruse, philosophical, and brahmanic;

and the *nirguṇa* devotion of the Hindi *sants* (c. 1400–)—rough in style, yogic in idiom, and sometimes highly unorthodox. Together, these two traditions present some interesting similarities in their religious attitude toward scripture as *śabda*, while maintaining crucial differences in the metaphysical significance that they attach to the term. To explore the socioreligious import of those differences, I will briefly examine some attitudes toward scripture in twentieth-century neo-Vedānta—which in fact seem to have as much in common with those of *sants* as with those evident in the work of Śaṅkara. The *saguṇa* tradition I treat is the Krishnaite devotion propounded by Vallabha (1480–1533), which is known as the *puṣṭimārg*. Roughly contemporaneous with the devotion of the Hindi *sants*, it has, like that tradition, also nurtured a sizable body of Hindi verse known broadly in North India. Looking at these two traditions together will show us some ways in which people oriented toward either the *nirguṇa* or *saguṇa* divine respond to scriptures revealing the other.

In dealing with the diversity of their scriptures, Hindus employ some common strategies, both theoretical and practical. Among the orthodox, there is a general acknowledgment of the distinction between *śruti*—important foundational texts of the Vedic period—and *smriti*, all the other "remembered" texts of subsequent Hindu tradition. *Śruti*, "heard" by Vedic sages, can ideally provide an absolutely firm foundation; *smriti*, "remembered" by later mortals, is subject to human fallibility. The *śruti*/*smṛti* distinction is of most crucial religious import to traditions close in time and in spirit to the *śruti* themselves; and among the texts considered *śruti*, those whose lasting religious significance was most widespread were the Upaniṣads, whose visionary speculations on the Vedic ritual would continue to have resonance long after the ritual itself had become virtually extinct. Thus, for Śaṅkara, the early orthodox interpreter of the Upaniṣads' *nirguṇa brahman*, the distinction between *śruti* and *smṛti* was of crucial religious import. Devotional traditions that developed after millennia of accumulated textual expansion, however, could treat the *śruti*/*smṛti* distinction with varying degrees of diffidence. For Vallabha, the later orthodox devotee, *śruti* was acknowledged and used as authority, but later scriptures were in fact more important for the religious tradition he propounded. The unorthodox *sants*, in contrast to both, sometimes held the Vedas up to scorn.

In practice, Hindus, as they encounter diverse scriptures, are likely to begin with those taken as authoritative within their own particular traditions, move experientially outward to those in similar types of traditions, and socioreligiously upward toward those classical Hindu texts on which their own traditions draw. Other factors can pull them in alternative directions, as well: a text's regional popularity, its familiarity from an individual's childhood, or a personal predilection for a particular genre. For mystically inclined Hindus, their extended scriptural tradition presents itself as extending layers of texts with which they may or may not feel bound to come to terms. Where the lines between these layers are drawn, and how firmly they are maintained, can vary considerably among individuals and groups.

Eternal Words Provoke Thought

Of the three Hindu traditions to be examined, Śaṅkara's Advaita Vedānta has the best demarcated scriptural terrain. Literally, "the end of the Vedas," the term *Vedānta* can be understood to refer to the Upaniṣads—the last part of the Vedic corpus. Regularly commenting on passages from the Upaniṣads, Vedantins take *śruti* as their primary scripture in practice as well as in theory. But as "the end of the Vedas," the term *Vedānta* also suggests that the extended Vedantic philosophic tradition is a continuing explication of Vedic truth. Thus, serious attention is also paid to the accumulated textual heritage of the Vedantic schools. The basic text taken as the starting point for all the Vedantic schools is known as the Vedānta Sūtras,[4] which give some order to the philosophical insights of the Upaniṣads. For Vedantins, then, the essential scripture is the Upaniṣads as *śruti*; the next most basic is the Vedānta Sūtras; and then the classical commentaries of their own particular schools.

Both the Upaniṣads themselves and the Vedantic schools present scriptural diversity, but they do so in different ways. The classical Upaniṣads, though they together present a bounded scriptural corpus, are visionary and speculative. While they may be characterized as attempts to systematize knowledge and the means to it, the systems they present are not always obviously consistent with one another.[5] Separate Upaniṣads thus present different images of divine realities and offer alternative progressions to truth, while the longer ones can appear internally disjointed, if not inconsistent. The Vedantic schools, by contrast, develop different coherent philosophies that build on particular intuitions gleaned from the Upaniṣads. Through both internal debates and debates among one another, the schools articulate and rearticulate particular insights, helping to bring them into lived experience.

The process of mutual debate is facilitated by the dominant commentarial genre. Sūtras are very terse, easily memorizable "threads" (English *suture* is cognate), on which extensive commentaries are regularly woven. They are preeminently a schoolman's genre: suitable for oral elaboration by a teacher, they were subject to extensive written treatments as well. Different schools of Vedānta—of which Śaṅkara's Advaita is the most famous among about a dozen worth noting[6]—have produced their own commentaries and subcommentaries. The greater Vedantic textual tradition thus appears largely as a number of continuing chains of commentaries on the Vedānta Sūtras. The different Vedantic philosophies that develop then find themselves articulated against the same set of reference points. For in clarifying the meaning of the Upaniṣads, Vedantins can all come back to the same topics of debate.

The Vedānta Sūtras frequently refer to the Upaniṣadic texts as *śabda*, a term with a very wide valence. Its most concrete meaning is "word," that is, an "everyday utterance"; but in Hindu natural philosophy, which correlates the sense perceptions with the elements, *śabda* also refers to the abstract principle of sound that inheres in the unchanging ether pervading everything. The sense of *śabda* as revealed scripture tends to hover between these two poles of meaning. Scripture as *śabda* consists of concrete vocable words that reflect an unchanging pervasive reality.

In Vedantic usage, moreover, the term carries specific philosophical implications. For orthodox Hindu intellectual traditions, *śabda* is also a *pramāṇa*, a "means of knowing," a valid ground for argument. Alongside other *pramāṇa*s like perception, inference, and analogy, *śabda* can serve as a basis for proof in academic debate.[7]

In many philosophical contexts, *śabda* as *pramāṇa* is best translated as "testimony" and can include the word of authoritative teachers; but for Śaṅkara, *śabda* refers primarily to the extended Vedic corpus, which is very specifically superhuman—

a-pauruṣeya, "not deriving from a human being."[8] This emphasis follows from a reading of the Upaniṣads as a continuation of the Vedic ritual injunctions. The more technical name for Vedānta—*uttara mīmāṃsā* "the later interpretation" of the Vedic texts—highlights its continuity *with pūrva mīmāṃsā*, "the earlier interpretation," which focused on ritual. The *pūrva mīmāṃsā* is a different kind of philosophical enterprise—one attempting to make practical sense of a vast, and sometimes apparently conflicting, array of ritual injunctions that would be reasonable to follow only if they were indeed held as somehow superhuman. But unlike the earlier *mīmāṃsāka*s, who were concerned with proper ritual action and its fruits in present and future lives, Śaṅkara was concerned with knowledge of Brahman, presented in the Upaniṣads as the ultimate foundation of all things. The fruit of this realization was liberation from the state of ignorance that bound one to rebirth.[9] For Śaṅkara, the Upaniṣadic scriptures consisted of superhuman words that could be the basis for salvation. As such they were absolutely firm objects on which one could build to ascend the heady salvational path for which Śaṅkara is justly celebrated.

Scripture, then, plays a very central role in Śaṅkara's presentation of Brahman. Logically, it offered sufficient grounds for knowledge of ultimate reality. Advaita justifiably claims that only one *pramāṇa* is necessary for valid cognition. We can recognize sweetness only through our sense of taste, but that is enough for us to accept our cognition as valid; if we trust our sense of taste, we have no reason to doubt our knowledge. Similarly, if hearing scripture gives rise to some cognition of the ultimate, we have no intrinsic reason to doubt our knowledge; since scripture is beyond human origin, it is completely trustworthy.[10] Throughout his long commentary on the Vedānta Sūtras Śaṅkara makes creative use of other *pramāṇa*s, like inference and analogy, but he keeps leading his inferences and analogies back to scriptural utterances. His argumentation is subtle and his vision is grand, but he rests his case on repeated, collected references to the Upaniṣadic texts.

Śaṅkara's problem is that the diverse Upaniṣads deal more in images than systematic philosophy and do not unambiguously support his radical claim: the only true reality, asserts Śaṅkara, is Brahman; everything else is an appearance superimposed on it. Other Vedantins, however, have seen the relationship between Brahman and the world differently. The Vedantic schools have presented the universe of the Upaniṣads variously as a duality of Brahman and the world; as ultimately nondual, with some systems (like Śaṅkara's) giving strong primacy to the ideal, and others emphasizing a continuity of consciousness and matter; or as showing several varieties of identity in difference.[11] How do these all read their different meanings into the same basic texts?

One of the problems that Śaṅkara and other commentators face when reading the Upaniṣads is how to make sense of the many images appearing there that are extolled as the supreme and unequaled: for example, space, light, and life force. Indicating abstract qualities, these images are nicely suggestive of the abstract Brahman, but they have qualities nonetheless and exist in the world of appearances. One could easily argue that something of their more concrete meaning is also meant in the Upaniṣads. Śaṅkara deals with this question at a number of points in his commentary on the first main part of the Vedānta Sūtras, which is devoted to a "reconciliation" of the meaning of diverse Upaniṣadic texts.

In its most general import, Śaṅkara's argument uncontroversially follows the Vedānta Sūtras, which are regularly read as identifying the abstract images of the Upaniṣads with Brahman. But the terseness of the sūtras leaves the import of that identification open to interpretation. The eleventh-century philosopher Ramanuja, for example, probably the next best-known Vedantin after Śaṅkara, gives a more theistic turn to the sūtras than does his predecessor. In discussing the meanings of light and space, he takes up a reference found a little earlier in the sūtras, broken by a digression, to the Kaṭhopaniṣad's "person in the size of the thumb" that dwells in the heart.[12] Ramanuja then makes this person the focal point of the identification of those qualities with Brahman. Yes, Brahman is the absolute, but it is *also* appropriately conceived in a personal way, intimately involved with embodied beings—in accordance with the more devotional thrust of Ramanuja's Vedānta, known as Viśiṣṭādvaita "*modified* nondualism." Śaṅkara, by contrast, consistently talks about Brahman as radically absolute. In the subsequent discussion of the meaning of light in a particular Upaniṣadic passage, Śaṅkara affirms the same basic theoretical point made by Ramanuja: that the abstract images in question refer to Brahman. But he cites different Upaniṣadic passages that offer a very different religious thrust and philosophical perspective. As is conventional in Indian philosophical discussion, he argues against a hypothetical opponent, whose position he states and refutes.

A question arises about the word *light* in this verse from the Chandogya Upaniṣad: "This serene one rises up from this body, attains the highest light, and takes on his own form" (8.12.3). The opponent notes that the context of the verse is the way in which someone desiring liberation attains the sun after death—a process described as following rays through the subtle nerves of the body. In this case, argues the opponent, the reference to the term *light* here is not Brahman, but "the familiar light" of every day.

Śaṅkara says no: "The supreme Brahman itself is meant by the word *light*. Why? Because it is seen as such in the Upaniṣads." This answer makes a reference to the sūtra on which the commentary is based, which is very pithy indeed: "Light, from seeing 1.3.40 (*jyotir darśanāt*)"—and which in context can be uncontroversially expanded to mean, "Light is Brahman, from seeing it as such in the Upaniṣads."

Śaṅkara supports this claim by first establishing that Brahman as the ultimate self is the predominant subject of Chandogya 8, citing three passages from it: "'The self that is free from evil' (8.7.1). . . . 'I shall explain this [that is, the self] to you again' (8.9.3). Further, the self is meant because light is attained to reach a bodiless state, as mentioned in 'Happiness and sorrow do not touch a bodiless one' (8.12.1); and bodilessness only comes through identity with Brahman." Śaṅkara then cites two passages from chapter 8 suggesting that Brahman is called light: one, coming soon after the mention of light in the passage in question, refers to "the highest person" (8.12.3); the other, describing a transformation apparently similar to the one in that passage, refers to the "supreme light" (8.3.4).

Perhaps more crucial for Śaṅkara himself than the weight of the Upaniṣadic texts, however, is his belief that those who interpret the passage as the opponent does have totally misconceived what liberation entails. For Śaṅkara immediately goes on to conclude by dismissing the opponent's concept of liberation entirely: "He said that the aspirant attains liberation through the sun. But that is not absolute liberation because it depends on a course to be followed (after leaving the body). And in absolute liberation, as we shall show, there is nothing like a course to be followed. . . ." For nothing actually occurs in absolute liberation, according to Śaṅkara, but the realization of Brahman as the sole reality.[13]

Although easily said, the Advaitin's belief about absolute reality is not accepted by everyone and admittedly is fully realized only with great difficulty. Śaṅkara's is supremely the path of the intellect, entailing constant reflection and philosophical distancing. Among the many salvational paths—ritual, devotional, yogic—available in Hindu tradition, the Advaitin's is recognized as the path of knowledge par excellence.[14] It has traditionally included an active religious practice that is intellectually oriented to an extreme: a continuing dialectic of text and commentary and subcommentary, of opponents' thrusts and counterarguments, with all cogitation leading back finally to the understanding that Brahman is ultimately the only reality. Whatever practice of meditative contemplation may also occur on Advaitic paths, the experience of ultimate knowledge they traditionally offer is carefully informed by rigorous analytic discrimination.

In the Advaitin's continuing mystical reflection, the Upaniṣads serve not only as a proof text, but also as a foil. The Advaitin is convinced both of his conception of Brahman and of the veracity of his scripture, but the match between these two verities is not neat. The very tension between the two, however, proves to be a central dynamic for Advaitic practice. In clarifying the Upaniṣads, disambiguating them, arguing from them and about them, the Advaitin discriminates ever more finely about appearance and reality.

To offer this kind of experience forcefully, however, the Upaniṣads need the weight of the Vedantic schools. Themselves subtle and multivalent,[15] the Upaniṣads alone offer extremely little resistance to alternative interpretations. To serve as an intellectual foil, they need to be raised by an opponent approaching them from another point of view. The Upaniṣads, in their diversity, can thus effectively reveal the formless divinity, but to those on a path of intellectual effort, they do this most effectively through a secondary layer of seriously received textual tradition.

Gurus' Words and Disciples' Visions

Although *nirguṇa* and *śabda*—the formless divinity, and the "word" or "sound" through which it can be known—have substantially different meanings among Advaitins and *sant*s, for both they are crucial terms. In both cases, too, the practical link between the two terms is, in part, one of default. A formless divinity cannot be easily approached through the senses—seen in an icon, felt in an image, or tasted through leftover food offerings. What remains is to hear about divinity through scripture or, as the *sant*s add, through internal yogic sound. Both socioreligiously and experientially, the force of this conjunction is particularly evident among the *sant*s.

By late medieval India, the vigorous espousal of a *nirguṇa* divinity began to strike a confrontative note. In the popular religious world of the *sant*s, the dominant tenor had become overwhelmingly devotional, focused on the adoration of mythic deities. Images of divinity—Śiva and the Goddess, Rama, and, increasingly, Kṛṣṇa—attracted both devotees' affections and ritual worship according to brahminic norms. The *sants*, in extolling a Lord beyond mythic image and ritual worship, were also extolling a Lord who ignored brahminic sanction and was equally accessible to all strata of society. Early *sants* and their followers characteristically came from low castes, which were excluded from much brahminic ritual. They extolled their formless divinity forcefully and poignantly, and, with it, the *śabda* as the wondrous power of divine manifestation. The Lord beyond all forms was the true divinity within; *śabda* provided a path to Him and an experience of the divine.

The *sants*' senses of *nirguṇa* and *śabda* thus both reflected the devotional tenor of their age. The *sants*' divinity looks much less like Śaṅkara's *nirguṇa brahman* than like Ramanuja's—the ultimate divine "person" in modified nondualism, a being in whom one could merge. But unlike Ramanuja's divinity, the "formless Lord" of the *sants* was not to be imagined in the image of a popular deity, with hands and feet. Instead, the *sants* sang of a personal but aniconic Lord familiar from Sufi traditions, to which important formative *sants*, born in castes recently converted to Islam, were probably exposed.[16] Yet any Sufi impact on *sant* tradition became assimilated into a thoroughly Indic, Hindu-oriented worldview. *Sants* had no qualms about identifying with an absolutely transcendent God: for the *sants* the "qualityless" Lord was someone in whom one could lose one's self totally. Any Sufi auditory practice (*zikṛ*) they may have assimilated became understood through ideas of *śabda*—a term used, during the age of the *sants*, in reference to a wide variety of yogic practices focusing on sound, which themselves had become subject to sophisticated metaphysical elaboration.

The range of meanings commonly given to the term *śabda* by the *sants*, then, drawing on yogic precedent, is much broader than its principal significance in Advaita, but it overlaps with the Vedantic usage in a crucial respect: as in Advaita, *śabda* refers to a scriptural text with metaphysical referents; the scriptures, however, are different and the referents, metaphysical and practical, are much more extensive among the *sants*. Instead of Vedic texts, the scriptures in *sant* tradition are the recorded songs of the *sants*, which served as the basis for canon in continuing *sant* lineages. These songs carried weight because they were uttered by people who had realized the formless divinity, as, in the eyes of disciples, had their own gurus. So *śabda* also comes to mean the guru's word: his instructions, commands, and particularly his words of power—mantras or divine names imparted by the guru to the disciple. The words of power, moreover, are embodiments of the guru's experience of divine sounds within, which are themselves known as *śabda*. *Sants* have developed widespread yogic practices that entail concentrating on particular internal sounds; they speak of them as different "melodies" or liken them to audible natural phenomena, like rumbling thunder.[17] *Śabda* then becomes taken by *sants* as a primal manifestation of divine energy, and it is this aspect of the term that is most often its dominant sense in the *sants*' songs.

For the *sants*, then, *śabda* is a high mystical experience, which is embodied in the words of realized gurus, whose songs, also sometimes called *śabdas*,[18] in turn become canonical among larger and narrower circles of tradition. In contrast to the meaning of *śabda* for Śaṅkara—which as Veda was eternal and transcending the human, beyond any person (*apauruṣeya*)—for *sants* the concept of *śabda* as scripture is firmly grounded in the experience of realized individuals. Thus for the *sants*, a vision of scriptural terrain emerges that is quite different in shape from that of Vedānta—one less well bounded and continually growing, charted differently by individuals and groups according to their particular attitudes toward the bearers of specific "words."

Indeed, the idea that scripture reflects the experience of a realized guru opens the way in theory, if not always in practice, to the idea of continuing revelation—or, more precisely put, to the accumulation of authoritative visionary songs. A number of *sant* lineages have produced creative poets over several generations.[19] The verses of these poets are revered within the lineages and known outside them, commented on by gurus in the extended *sant* tradition with lesser (or no) poetic gifts. Yet even gurus with very little endowment as poets sometimes compose verse, the conventional form of expression among *sant*s. Those verses, which in some cases have been uttered to profusion, are generally preserved only within circumscribed fellowships of devotees. Commenting on the abundance of verse produced in the regional devotional traditions of India, the late scholar and poet A. K. Ramanujan once remarked that much of it has been poetry that "only a disciple could love."[20] But love the verses they do—not, perhaps, as beautiful poetry, but as authoritative vision, holding secrets that devotees initiated into a particular lineage are especially qualified to learn.

Individual adherents to *sant* lineages thus mark their scriptural terrain not only through the perceived greatness of particular sant-poets, but also by their nearness to them. Authority lies first of all in verses of their own lineage, with weight given especially to those of an illustrious founding *sant* and of recent gurus with whom disciples may feel personal ties. Other lineage successors, more or less prolific or poetically gifted, will also be given considerable authority, even if their verses were not as frequently heard. Outside the lineage, people could be more discriminating. There were many *sant*s and many verses. Not all the poets, perhaps, had experienced an ultimate realization, as understood within any one *sant* lineage. Still, many gave expression to interesting experiences, and it was worth paying attention to what they reported.

As a class of scripture for their adherents, the extended corpus of sant texts differs from the classical Upaniṣads, which as *śruti* ideally speak with equal authority for all Vedantins. As verses of devotion to a formless divinity—a literary genre—all the *sant*s' songs present experience of the same broad type, but some speak with more authority to particular groups than others. For those who see the songs primarily as receptacles of an esoteric, mystical vision, the main division was at the boundaries of their own guru's lineage. Disciples would then approach scriptures inside and outside their lineage in different ways.

To describe their experiences, the *sant*s drew on a technical jargon common to North Indian yogic traditions but did not always use it in the same way.[21] Within lineages, technical usage could be reasonably consistent; terms were understood to refer to specific experiences that gurus taught to disciples.[22] Outside particular lineages, however, consistency was much more elusive. Devotees who meditated on visionary songs outside their own lineage might have found familiar terms used in apparently confounding ways. As among Advaitins, the problem of scriptural diversity here is likely to present itself as a problem with the referents of individual words. Moreover, as in Advaita, the problem was often whether or not, or how, a word intimated a higher formless reality.

Songs produced in the Radhasoami lineage, for example—a late *sant* group founded in the mid-nineteenth century and still vital—present a consistent internal landscape, with conventional language used to describe a progression of experiences leading to the highest divine state. Associated with certain points for concentration in the subtle body, they together recall the sort of path described by Śaṅkara's opponent, cited above—a movement through subtle nerves to liberation through the "sun," here taken as a point of concentration on the formless divine. And as on that path, terms are supposed to have particular meanings for sense-experience, subtle if not physical. The following extract from one of the songs of the lineage founder, known as Soamiji, gives a concise presentation of the path. Note the frequent references to the sounds emanating from particular named places, which are capitalized here:

Song 1

I went inside the sky and glimpsed the Flame
then saw the stars and heard the Sound (*śabda*)
Going up the Crooked Tunnel, I called out Three Corners' glory.
The indestructible tune I heard in the Void
Then reached the Great Void and opened the door
to hear the Whirling Cave's ponderous melody (*rāga*).
I went to the True Abode, the immortal palace
and touched the feet of the unseeable, the unapproachable.[23]

The True Abode (*sat pad*) represents the highest experience; it is regularly described as the unseeable (*alakh*) and unapproachable (*agam*). All the rest of the technical terms here—the Flame (*joti*); Three Corners (*trikuṭī*); the Void (*sunna,* from the Sanskrit *śunya*), the Great Void (*mahāsunna*); and the Whirling Cave (*bhaṃvar guphā*)—refer to specific stages along the way. In the Hindu devotional context, these are all experiences of formless divinity, in the sense that they are not embodied mythic images "with arms and legs" but ever more subtle states described as places in the heavens, with their own presiding divinities. But to reach the highest "unapproachable" experience, the intermediate stages must be surpassed. In the songs of Soamiji and of the gurus of his extended lineage, the terms are used consistently and in the same order.

What, then, might devotees with some experience of the inner world described in Radhasoami texts make of this song attributed to the eighteenth-century poet Gulal Sahib? As a sant text it certainly seems to describe some similar experience, in some of the same language. It talks of ascension, and hearing sounds, but appears to use terms in somewhat different ways:

Song 2

Closing the *mūla cakra*, I gathered my consciousness;
The lotuses bloomed and spread in the ten directions.
Half way up, in the middle, *soham* is sung out;
Hearing the melody, the mind pays attention.
There's the cave of knowledge, where the *siddha* doesn't dwell—
In the circle of the sky: dancing and revelry . . .
At the mount of the Void, where fierceness comes forth,
the true guru's Sound (*śabda*) and Words (*vacan*) are in my heart.
The light of love blazes:
When karma's destroyed, you're separate from the world.
Call him a swan then, says Gulal;
Bliss arises and spreads over the unapproachable home.[24]

Although this song would have meaning to a Radhasoami devotee, it would not elicit the same easily familiar recognition that texts from his own lineage elicit. It mentions *mūla cakra*, which is near the bottom of the charts in most Radhasoami maps of the cosmos and not usually mentioned in the songs.[25] The song mentions a "cave," but it is not an exalted place like the Radhasoamis' "Whirling Cave" : the *siddha*, the "perfected yogi," doesn't dwell there; moreover, "the Whirling Cave" would normally come later in Radhasoami texts—although there it is the place where the sound *soham* is heard, as it seems to be here. But once we get beyond these somewhat confusing waystations, we find some familiar territory with the Void, an important intermediate station for Radhasoamis. For Gulal, however, here experience stops. The Void is presented less as an intermediate place than as an ultimate goal.

How might a Radhasoami devotee, approaching this song as scripture, comprehend it? There are a number of alternatives. Perhaps Gulal was describing a somewhat different path along the same general line of experience, while stopping at the Void to enjoy it. This is not something normally done in Radhasoami songs, but it is imaginable. Yet if Gulal was just stopping for a while, why did he call *sunna* "the unapproachable," which for Radhasoamis is usually reserved for the highest state? Maybe, then, the Void was as far as Gulal had gotten, and he was not a fully realized *sant*. Or maybe he was describing *another* Void, somewhere in the highest realm, and perhaps this Void, too, is also truly "unapproachable." Or maybe Gulal was just using language in another way.

With technical usage linked to their own, but differing from it, the diverse verses of *sant*s outside a particular lineage could lead people to reflect more broadly about their own experience—making them question it, perhaps, or leading them to expand it through new experimentation. But in any case they took those verses seriously. They let their more familiar experience be jarred, called into question, or transformed, because they saw the *sant*s' songs as records of an experience of a realized person that they, too, might attain. This, for them, was what defined scripture and gave it power.

Mystical Practice, Scriptural Authority, and the Vision of the Wise

This general attitude toward scripture found among *sant*s—that it reflects the visions of realized sages—also reverberates through the neo-Vedānta that has flourished in India from the mid-nineteenth century. Both Swami Vivekananda and Sarvepalli Radhakrishnan, the most influential of modern exponents of Vedānta, identified most with Advaita, idealizing Śaṅkara.[26] But in establishing the authority of the Upaniṣads, both also seemed to give more weight to perceptions of realized seers than is obviously given by Śaṅkara, who, as we have seen, treats revealed scripture sooner as an objective basis for argument. During the course of his voluminous writings, Śaṅkara seems neither to make explicit reference to any visionary origins of the Upaniṣads[27] nor to suggest them through his commentarial style, which is highly academic and discursive. This apparent divergence in attitudes toward the Upaniṣads between neo-Vendantins and early Vedantins has given rise to a contemporary scholarly debate about the nature of authority in Advaita: Which is prior—internal experience or some externally objective revelation?[28]

In part, the neo-Vedantic approach to scriptural authority reflects the impact of nineteenth- and twentieth-century thought. Neither Western-educated Vedantins nor, especially, their audience were ready simply to take scriptural revelation as a given. But in seeking some kind of internal verification of scripture, they follow an attitude generally characteristic of independent-minded Hindu mystics and explicit in *sant* tradition. The *sant*, we hear,

> . . . tells the secret as he sees it
> Singing couplets and *śabda*s in books.
> Bowing again to the Lord's holy feet he sees and speaks . . .[29]

Scriptures, from this perspective, record direct experience. A comparison of *sant* and different Advaita attitudes toward scripture can thus help us better understand some of the socioreligious factors at stake in the contemporary debate on authority in Advaita. Accepting revisionist conclusions about the primacy of revelation in Śaṅkara, I suggest, in the discussion that follows, how a more experientially oriented neo-Vedānta position may have emerged. This clarifies some implications of the different understandings of scriptural authority in the Hindu world.

In the context of Hindu tradition in general, staunch advocates of a "qualityless" deity stood at the extremes, relative minorities on opposite sides of the socioreligious spectrum: on the one side, early Advaita Brahmins seeing *nirguṇa brahman* at the basis of an eternal social order; on the other side, iconoclastic *sant*s seeing the Formless Lord beyond all traditionally sanctified religion.[30] The neo-Vedantins of modern India, then, share characteristics of both early Advaitins and *sant*s: like their Vedantic predecessors, they attempted to revive the eternal verities of Hindu tradition, but like the *sant*s, they saw a newly desanctified world that called for fresh means of expression.

Any conscious adaptation of tradition like that found among neo-Vedāntins highlights the agency of the religious actor, which seems to be at the crux of the issue of Upaniṣadic authority separating classical and modern Vedantins: Just what was the religious role of the Upaniṣadic seers? Even for Śaṅkara, of course, the eternal Vedic sounds had been transmitted to humanity by holy persons. Hindu tradition speaks of these persons as *ṛṣi*s and *muni*s, (seers and hearers), who perceived and gave utterance to the sounds of the Vedas. Contemporary usage tends to treat them collectively as the great sages of the past. Save for some Upaniṣadic figures, the *ṛṣi*s and *muni*s are not usually referred to by name, but they are generally revered as elevated beings.[31] For Śaṅkara, however, their greatness seems to have lain in their ability to be passive transmitters; their personalities became ciphers through which the sounds understood to be at the root of the brahminic order passed. Neo-Vedānta tends to see the ancient sages sooner as a group of gifted visionaries, individuals with at least the potential for agency. They were, in this way, like medieval *sant*s, fully endowed holy persons whose words and visions could have some effect on individuals, if not on the larger society. The different conceptions of scripture occasioned by these alternative perceptions of the Upaniṣadic seers then play out within different socioreligious agendas.

More so in Śaṅkara's India than in today's, a significant challenge to the Hindu order was posed by Unorthodox Indic philosophies—that is, those not revering the Vedas and brahminic sanction. Jainism was vital, as was Buddhism, whose idealistic Mahāyāna variants were becoming increasingly popular. Both Indian and Western scholars have understood Śaṅkara's radical idealism as a brahminic response to Mahāyāna Buddhism, seen as potentially subversive to the orthodox social fabric.[32] If this is true, then it was crucial for Śaṅkara to ground his synthesis in the one eternal Vedic truth, not in any seer's particular experience of it. Buddhist and Jain visionaries also had experiences; Śaṅkara wanted to highlight a Vedic revelation taken as an objective reality.

Neo-Vedantists faced a different situation. Like the early *sant*s, they saw themselves as individuals able to help foster change at a time of external cultural impact—now Western instead of Muslim. Unlike most *sant*s, however, the neo-Vedantists revered the Vedas, seeing them as a product of creative vision like their own. Early neo-Vedantists wanted to have the visionary sage alongside the Vedas and found they could have them both by adapting already widespread popular notions of scriptural authority shared by the *sant*s: the Upaniṣads are revelation, in this view, *because* they are the utterances of realized seers.

Not always explicit in specific Hindu traditions, notions of scriptural authority seem to depend on factors of intellectual age, socioreligious import, and cosmopolitan sophistication. The early Vedantists, neo-Vedantists, and *sant*s show us how these factors come together in different religiohistorical circumstances. At the same time, since all three were oriented toward the *nirguṇa* divinity, they all present the origins of scripture as somehow impersonal. Scripture was ultimately "the word"—as cosmic revelation, uttered insight, or sound—which could reveal a supremely limitless consciousness. Diversity in scripture could then present apparently contradictory texts with which people were bound to engage, pushing them beyond old limits, and ultimately extending their understandings of a qualityless divinity beyond any concepts whatsoever.

Stories Converge to Evoke the Embodied Lord

The Divinity with qualities, by contrast, in the form of a great mythic deity, stood in the middle of the devotee's universe, not beyond it. It presented a focus for the convergence of diverse scriptures, each able to highlight some particular divine quality. While the *nirguṇa* divine attracts rigorous adherents from the extremes of the Hindu socioreligious continuum, the *saguṇa* divinities collectively hover over the wide middle ground; worshiped by the majority of Hindus, they can be revered through sanctified ritual but are often also seen to embrace all, irrespective of their caste. The texts through which they are approached come in many varieties, in Sanskrit and vernacular languages, suited to different groups of devotees.

Taken in their diversity, these texts present some dynamics of experience different from those seen so far for the Advaitin and *sant*. Both of those, in finding their way to a "qualityless" divinity through scripture, were concerned with the referent of individual words: the former, as we saw, sometimes justifying scriptural words through other scriptural passages; the latter attempting to fathom the meaning of yogic technical terms in unfamiliar contexts. With the advent of the embodied Lord who plays on earth, the weight shifts to comprehending the true meaning of the Lord's story, which is revealed in different literary forms. More important for most devotees than the philosophical texts they had (which included a number of devotional Vedāntas) were mythic narratives in several genres, and delicate lyric poetry. These different framings of sacred story—metaphysically reasoned, magnificently pictured, and intimately encountered—could then all reverberate in the mystical contemplation of the devotee.

The Krishnaite tradition of Vallabha (1480–1533), which flourished among Hindi speakers in about the same era as that of the *sant*s, illustrates the richness of scriptural tradition to which an erudite devotee might have access. Known as the *puṣtimārg*, this tradition has nurtured philosophical and poetic literature in Hindi and Sanskrit and continues to flourish in western India today.[33] Of all the scriptural landscapes discussed so far, it presents the broadest and most layered.

At the most abstract level, the *puṣtimārg* offers a metaphysical story. Since every respectable tradition needed a philosophy, Vallabha, a brahmin with a sense of mission, wrote a commentary on the Vedānta Sūtras, proceeding through the customary verbal dialectics of Vedantic philosophy that we saw in Śaṅkara. Like Śaṅkara, he called his philosophy a nondualism—*śuddhādvaita*, "pure non-dualism"—but his devotional attitude led him to a very different idea of what that concept implied. For Vallabha, nondualism meant not that the visible universe was mere appearance in the face of absolute divinity, but that the physical world itself was integrally connected to the divine; Kṛṣṇa had made himself present here, and he should be worshiped and enjoyed through his concrete manifestation. The orthodox philosophical story behind the manifestation of Kṛṣṇa, then, gave reasoned justification for the highly luxuriant forms of image worship for which the tradition is known.

More important for the devotional life of the tradition than Vallabha's commentary on the Vedānta Sūtras, however, was his commentary on a text familiar to more devotees: the Bhāgavata Purāna, the tenth book of which gives a detailed retelling of the story of Kṛṣṇa. The last of the long Kṛṣṇa narratives in classical Sanskrit literature, the Bhāgavata's is also the most magnificent.[34] It focuses less on Kṛṣṇa's later life as a sagely heroic king than on his childhood in the sylvan paradise of Vraj. There he frolics with the cowherds and milkmaids as an overwhelmingly attractive youth, fully divine and humanly exquisite. Vallabha's many-faceted commentary on the tenth book can lead the learned to absorbing reflection about the moral and aesthetic dimensions of Kṛṣṇa's divine play.[35]

As an orthodox tradition, the *puṣtimārg* sees itself as thoroughly grounded in classical Sanskrit texts. In addition to his commentaries on the Vedānta Sūtras and the Bhāgavata, Vallabha also wrote commentaries on the Bhagavad Gītā and the *pūrva mīmāṃṣā* sūtras. Reasons for Vallabha's deeming these works worthy of commentary are not hard to find. The Gita was a popular synthesis of classical religious ideas that acknowledged the value of the householder's life and ended on a note of devotion. Of appropriate religious import for Vallabha's largely householder devotees, it had already achieved a semicanonical status. Moreover, it was understood to have been delivered by Kṛṣṇa himself as a mature sage. The commentary on the *mīmāṃṣā* sūtras—which deal with the proper performance of Vedic sacrifice—reveals a respect for Vedic authority, if not an interest in the old sacrifice, which was of little practical import to the devotion Vallabha offered. Only a short portion of this work remains extant, which suggests that it was never given much active attention in Vallabhite tradition, being more important as a sign of orthodoxy than as a treatise for study.

The Vedas, the Gītā, the Vedānta Sūtras, and the Bhāgavata Purāṇa—the four classical works given substantial commentaries by Vallabha—are thus understood to be foundational in *puṣṭimārg*.[36] Taken in this order, and read in the light of Vallabha's interpretation, each is said to resolve doubts raised by the one preceding it, the Bhāgavata Purāṇa being "the ripe fruit of the wish-fulfilling tree."[37] Vallabha, a brahmin scholar like Śaṅkara, wanted, like him, to lead his interpretations back to the sacred ground of *śruti*. But coming nearly one thousand years later, he knew an expanded canon, and selected pieces from it to add to *śruti* to present an orthodox, Sanskrit scriptural base for his tradition.

Sanskrit texts and commentary, however, were not easily accessible to most devotees. Those who were of mystical but little scholarly inclination were less likely to become absorbed in stories of Kṛṣṇa through perusing Vallabha's commentary on the Bhāgavata Purāṇa than through the songs of devotional poets, which became incorporated into high Vallabhite liturgy. Thus, as in *sant* tradition, the composition, performance, and hearing of Hindi verse became an important religious activity. Eight Hindi Krishnaite poets in particular were adopted by the Vallabha tradition, their legends becoming part of sectarian history. Among these, the most illustrious is Sur Das, whose name is attached to literally thousands of short verses in praise of Kṛṣṇa. Comprising an extended tradition of Hindi Krishnaite poetry—much of which probably came later than any historical Sur—these verses have been compiled as the Sur Sagar, *The Sea of Sur Das*.[38] The chapter organization of this compilation consciously models the Bhāgavata Purāṇa, with the tenth chapter, which focuses on Kṛṣṇa's childhood, by far the longest. Presenting itself in the image of the great classical scripture of Kṛṣṇa, it offers the sacred story in forms more immediately accessible, intimate, and familiar than does the Sanskrit text.

The lyric verses of the Sur Sagar play on the devotee's sentiments in different ways. Some focus on the singer's devotional feelings,[39] without evoking a picture of Kṛṣṇa, but by far the majority feature some sort of "verbal icon"[40]—presenting an image of Kṛṣṇa as a child or young man in one of many conventional situations. Very often, these are simply childhood scenes described in a way that engages the devotee's human affections: baby Kṛṣṇa learning to walk, stealing butter, or playing with cowherds. Devotees already *know* that Kṛṣṇa is divine and want to appreciate his human aspect.

Many songs, though, frame Kṛṣṇa's divinity more obviously. Occasionally sharp contrasts are employed—Kṛṣṇa, stumbling while learning to walk, is juxtaposed with the creator and destroyer of worlds and then appears again playing with his mother, "Nanda's wife":

Song 3 (fragment)

He trips and he falls, doesn't manage to cross
  Which makes the sages wonder:
Ten millions of worlds he creates in a flash
  And can destroy them just as fast
But he's picked up by Nanda's wife,
  Who sets him down, plays games with him
Then with her hand supports him
  While he steps outside the door.[41]

More often, as in the following song, the framing is more subtle. Here the scene moves from Kṛṣṇa's early childhood to his adolescence as a cowherd: Sporting with his friends, Kṛṣṇa—also called by his epithets Mohan, Shyam, and Ghanshyam—consistently occupies center stage:

Song 4

Here comes Mohan grazing cows—
On his head a peacock crown, a wild-flower garland on his neck:
  Kṛṣṇa—stuck with cow-dust; stick in hand.
At his waist small bells make music,
  He moves his feet and tinkling anklets sound.
In the center of the circle of the cowherd boys—Ghanshyam,
  With yellow clothes to shame the lightning.
Singing of his qualities, his cowherd friends arrive:
  In the middle—Shyam and Balram, spreading splendor.
Sur's Lord's destroyed the demons
  Then came to Vraj, to boost our minds' delight.[42]

Kṛṣṇa is given some humble attributes toward the beginning of this song—dirty, he's grazing the cows with a stick in his hand. But he soon moves into the center of the circle, beautiful in sight and sound, "spreading splendor" with his brother Balram. By the next to the last line, he truly is treated as a divinity: his "qualities" (*gun*, from the Sanskrit *guṇa*) are sung, and in conclusion we are reminded of his previous magical act of destroying the demons. Bringing conventional images together in striking detail, the Sur Sagar presents Kṛṣṇa as the human god of Vraj country.

Sur's scenes evoking Kṛṣṇa as a child, helpless, attractive, and divine; Vallabha's commentary on the Bhāgavata Purāṇa elaborating the implications of the childhood drama; a Vedantic philosophy that gives cosmic dimensions to the story of Kṛṣṇa's incarnation and meaning to his ritual worship—all these diverse scriptures complement one another. Their effect on the sensitivities of the cultured devotee is cumulative—they build one upon the other. Their total effect, further, is enhanced by liturgical practice. Devotional songs are sung against elaborate painted backdrops of Kṛṣṇa. More than in many devotional traditions, images here are treated as physically manifesting the presence of the deity, and they are approached, dressed, and fed with care. Devotees should strive to live always in the presence of Kṛṣṇa—a state, they say, reached by Vallabha, who, together with his chosen disciples, was reliving the divine play of Vraj country.

These different modes of sacred story in Krishnaite tradition, then, present a very different experience of scriptural diversity than that seen in traditions oriented toward formless divinity. There we saw a stretching of mystical consciousness through encounters with puzzling texts. Here we see instead an intensifying of experience through increased layers of scripture—all toward an ideal of living one's daily life richly while at play with the Lord.

Encountering Someone Else's Scripture

By the mid sixteenth century, traditions of both *sant* and Krishnaite verse were flourishing on the northern plains. Still vital today, they are linguistically intelligible across a broad population and provide a basis for different types of religious practice: popular village songfests, liturgical performances in sectarian settings, and solitary mystical contemplation. Across this broad socioreligious spectrum, attitudes vary toward the Hindi devotional repertoire as a whole. While aficionados of village songfests might listen attentively to both types of songs, they remain aware of the distinction between them, and singers specialize in one type or the other. Among those seriously engaged in a specific practice, tastes tend to be more exclusive: the internal devotional yoga of the *sant* and the outward liturgical practice of the Kṛṣṇa devotee pull in different directions. Nevertheless, in the normal course of rural (and urban) life, practitioners are still likely to be exposed, at least, to a broad range of devotional texts. What do they make of those that they do not immediately regard as scripture? Differing types of responses have been characteristically offered by Kṛṣṇa devotees and sants.

Kṛṣṇa devotees, on the whole, ignored scriptures from other traditions. Since the different sectarian Kṛṣṇa traditions often had condescending attitudes even toward one another, their attitude toward worship of the "qualityless" divinity was conventionally dismissive: if they had Kṛṣṇa, what did they need with anything else? Expressing this attitude, a genre of verse has been dedicated to mocking both yogic means and "qualityless" ends as irrelevant for the true devotee. It is framed within a Krishnaite legend: As a young man studying in the city, Kṛṣṇa sends his friend Uddhava to console the milkmaids in his village home. Uddhava, misguided, thinks that the best solace in this situation is a message of renunciation. The milkmaids, however, will hear nothing of this. They want Mohan, the "captivating" Lord, the joy of his father Nanda; yoga is something they simply do not understand:

Song 5

Uddhava what can we do with this yoga?
  Put it on, or spread it out, or drink it down, or eat it?
Is it a pretty toy, perhaps, or something nice to wear?
  Our Kṛṣṇa is the one we want: Nanda's delight, our soul's life—Mohan!
You've told us Hari's endless, "without qualities," what scripture calls "not this."
  But he's become a thing of beauty too enchanting to abandon.
He's just left his place a while to graze the cows; he'll be back soon . . .
  Sur, he's our support, who plays on his sweet flute.[43]

The milkmaids long for the experience of Kṛṣṇa the cowherd as envisioned in song 4, above, not for any formless divinity. The reference in song 5 to the *nirguṇa* is explicit ("without qualities") and is associated with both yoga and Upaniṣadic scripture.[44] The meditative truths contained in those scriptures—even granted their orthodox validity—are not accessible to everyone, certainly not to the milkmaids:

How can we weak women meditate, how can we know that one truth?
  How can you tell us to shut up our eyes, where Hari's image glistens . . .[45]

Those who are truly attached to their vision of Kṛṣṇa, these songs tell us, have no reason to look in any other direction.

*Sant*s engaged in yogic practice tended to be more adventurous. While early *sant*s were characteristically from low castes and scornful of orthodox ways, by the eighteenth century many came from middle castes and were more accepting of their extended Hindu heritage.[46] They understood the mysteries of that heritage, however, in their own ways. With Charandas of Delhi, from an eighteenth-century merchant family, a writer of *sant* verse could present full-blown Krishnaite mythology but then claim that a subtle inner eye was needed to understand it.[47] More often, the treatment was more exclusively subtle, exploring the inner yogic meaning of a traditional image. In the following song, a contemporary *sant*, known as Malik Sahib (1909–1983),[48] explores the inner yogic meaning of Kṛṣṇa from a Radhasoami perspective. Here the inner play of Kṛṣṇa is seen to have its seat at Three Corners, one of the conventional stages seen in Soamiji's song 1, whose triangular shape suggests a mountain. Malik Sahib begins by taking the legendary Mt. Meru, commonly used in Yoga to refer to the "peak" of the body, as Mt. Govardhan, which the youthful Kṛṣṇa miraculously lifted up as an umbrella when Indra poured rain on Vraj country. Like the senses, the cows of Vraj are attracted to Kṛṣṇa, the captivating Lord. This is a play on the word *go*, still used archaically to mean "cow" in Hindi, but which in Sanskrit can also mean "sense organ," "eye," or "ray of light."[49]

Song 6

I saw Three Corners at the top of the sky, where Govardhan stands as Mt. Meru,
  Where all of the senses are settled like cows, gazing at the golden mountain
Where angry Indra thunders,
  The senses tremble at the mind's Kṛṣṇa.
The lightning flashes; the low-cloud resounds.
  They call Him Lord of the three worlds.
This is what the Purana calls Govardhan,
  Which is not known without the guru's grace.
The temple of delight is up ahead
  Where Radha's bridegroom, Kṛṣṇa, resides forever.
Where he plays his flute of light,
  The milkmaids of white consciousness shine forth.
They dance and sing; there's blissfulness.
  Seeing it cuts the soul's ties to the world.
Ten thousands of Brahmās and Viṣṇus and Śivas:
  Each hair on their bodies presents many shapes
I've sung of the eternal home, the Fourth State
  Of which the Vedas said "not this," not finding its secret.
Where there's play, a thousand pleasures—that's the sign of Vraj.
  The guru shows his mercy and the heart's eyes see![50]

The song reveals a mystical sensibility informed by one tradition apprehending an image most crucial in another. Pervasive themes from Krishnaite poetry are used here to describe an experience of a formless Lord. Kṛṣṇa's flute is formed of light; the cows as senses are rays of white consciousness. In the background, the raincloud, lightning, and thunder recall at once (1) the narrative of the story of Kṛṣṇa and Mt. Govardhan; (2) the conventionally romantic rainy season, in which some of the most passionate Kṛṣṇa poetry is set ("the senses tremble"); and (3) the lights and sounds of the *sant*'s inward experience. Particular references found in the Krishnaite songs discussed here recur but with different import. Like the milkmaids of song 5, Malik Sahib dismisses the Vedas' "not this"—a negative reference to the Upaniṣadic *nirguṇa brahman* that is in fact a more frequent refrain in *sants*' songs than in Krishnaite ones, which are frequently preserved in orthodox traditions. Yet despite its orthodox sanction, the milkmaids don't even want to try that "Vedic" experience; Malik Sahib, by contrast, suggests he has gone beyond it. Fantastically large numbers ("ten thousands," "ten millions"), which were used to suggest the magnificence of Kṛṣṇa in song 3, here suggest the infinite forms of divinity that are to be experienced by inner vision. The wondrous story of Kṛṣṇa, as represented in myth, the song suggests, is indeed a spiritual reality; but it is one that is only truly known to an accomplished yogi. In this way, then, Malik Sahib has converted the "story" of Kṛṣṇa into a "word"—that is, *śabda* as the *sant*'s utterance—intimating a particular blissful divine state.

Sant verses on mythic themes—of which Malik Sahib, alongside other later *sant*s, wrote several[51]—thus present a new turn to the dynamic between scripture and mystical experience in Hindu tradition. For in writing verses like this, Malik Sahib effectively rescripturalized pieces of the extended Hindu mythic tradition for devotees who might otherwise not take them seriously.[52] In Malik Sahib's case, this seems to have been deliberate. By the time he had been initiated into the Radhasoami line, some of its sublineages had taken a sharp sectarian turn. Malik Sahib saw his mission, in part, as taking the *sant* experience he had learned from a sectarian perspective and integrating it with the heritage of the broader Hindu tradition that he also valued. He saw this mission as feasible because his attitude toward scriptural authority resonated with that seen in *sant*s and neo-Vedantins—the sages of the past knew deep experience and recorded it in texts. Malik Sahib could then rediscover the inner nature of that experience and rearticulate it for followers of *sant* tradition in general and for his own devotees in particular. To the extent that these devotees, who were oriented toward an aniconic divinity through a somewhat unorthodox *sant* lineage, felt distanced from any more orthodox mythic roots, Malik Sahib's yogic appropriation of scriptural story here gave them back something of their own.

NOTES

1. In recent years, scripture and its interpretation have been subjects of renewed interest among scholars of Indian religions, becoming the focus for several valuable edited volumes: Jeffrey R. Timm, ed., *Texts in Context: Traditional Hermeneutics in South Asia* (Albany, 1992); Wendy Doniger, ed., *Purāṇa Perennis: Reciprocity and Transformation in Hindu and Jaina Texts* (Albany, 1993); and Laurie L. Patton, ed., *Authority, Anxiety, and Scripture: Essays in Vedic Interpretation* (Albany, 1994).
2. The idea that scripture is defined largely by an attitude toward a religious text has been propounded by Wilfred Cantwell Smith in his *What Is Scripture: A Comparative Approach* (Minneapolis, 1993). Similar perspectives inform an important collection of essays written mostly by his students: Miriam Levering, ed., *Rethinking Scripture: Essays from a Comparative Perspective* (Albany, 1989). An interesting comparative study of scripture, with particular relevance to Hindu traditions, is Barbara A. Holdredge, *Veda and Torah: Transcending the Textuality of Scripture* (Albany, 1996). See also Frederick M. Denny and Rodney L. Taylor, eds., *The Holy Book in Comparative Perspective* (Columbia, S.C., 1985).
3. See Thomas B. Coburn, "'Scripture' in India: Towards a Typology of the Word in Hindu Life," in Levering, *Rethinking Scripture*, pp. 102–128; and Philip Lutgendorf, "The Power of Sacred Story: Ramayana Recitiation in Contemporary North India," *Journal of Ritual Studies* 4, no. 2 (1990): 115–147. Note that the distinction between *word* and *story* as elaborated here carries a different force from that propounded by Coburn, who

stressed the difference between "stories" meant to be understood and powerful "words" that may have little referential meaning for most people who hear them.

4. This text is also known as the Uttara Mīmāṃsā Sūtra, and perhaps most commonly as the Brahma Sūtra; I will refer to it consistently as the Vedānta Sūtra, its most transparent name. The text was purportedly written by Bādarāyaṇa and probably dates from about the fourth century.
5. My thanks go to Frank Clooney for this formulation, generously given to me as part of a close reading of this chapter.
6. See S. Radhakrishnan, *The Brahma Sūtra: The Philosophy of Spiritual Life* (London, 1960), p. 27.
7. On *pramāṇa* theorists, see Bimal Krishna Matilal, *Perception: An Essay on Classical Indian Theories of Knowledge* (Oxford, 1986), pp. 21–45. Philosophical schools differ as to just which *pramāṇas* they accept.
8. See, for example, Śaṅkara's commentary on Vedānta Sūtra 1.3.28 in Swami Gambhirananda, *Brahma-Sūtra Bhāṣya of Śri Śaṅkarācārya* (Calcutta, 1965), pp. 208–216.
9. For an insightful discussion of Advaita as a commentarial tradition leading to salvation and its relationship to *pūrva mīmāṃṣā*, see Francis X. Clooney, S.J., *Theology after Vedanta: An Experiment in Comparative Theology*, Towards a Comparative Philosophy of Religions, series ed. Frank Reynolds and David Tracy (Albany, 1993), pp. 14–30.
10. See Murty's discussion of "theory of intrinsic validity" in K. Satchidananda Murty, *Revelation and Reason in Advaita Vedanta* (Waltair, India, 1959), pp. 12–14. Murty draws on a number of later Advaitic sources.
11. For a presentation of the ways the Vedānta Sūtras are read from these different perspectives, see Radhakrishnan, *The Brahma Sūtra.*
12. Ramanuja, *Śrībhāṣyam*, ed. Śrī Uttamūr Vīrarāghavācarya (Madras, 1963), pp. 381–382; for a translation, see M. Rangacharya and M. B. Varadaraja Aiyangar, *The Vedānta Sūtras with the Śrībhāṣya of Rāmānujāchārya* (Madras, 1964) vol. 2, pp. 286–287. The relevant sūtra is numbered 1.3.41 here, not 1.3.40, as in Śaṅkara's commentary. For more on image and experience in Ramanuja's Vedānta, see Francis X. Clooney, S.J., *Seeing through Texts: Doing Theology among the Śrīvaiṣnavas of South India* (Albany, 1996), chap. 3.
13. This is my rendering, following the text of Svāmī Hanumāndās Ji Ṣaṭśāstrī, *Brahmasūtra Śankarabhāṣya* (Varanasi, 1964), pp. 290–291, and the translation of Gambhirananda, *Brahma-Sūtra Bhāṣya*, pp. 236–238.
14. Contemporary Hindu discourse often cites the "three yogas" propounded by Swami Vivekananda in the late nineteenth century: those of "works," "devotion," and "knowledge." Among these, Advaita has been given as the foremost example of the "yoga of knowledge." See Anantananda Rambachan, *The Limits of Scripture: Vivekananda's Reinterpretation of the Vedas* (Honolulu, 1994), chap. 3 and pp. 92–93.
15. For this characterization of the Upaniṣads' ambiguity, my thanks again to Frank Clooney.
16. Muslim-born early *sant*s included two of the best known, Kabir and Dadu. On Kabir, see Charlotte Vaudeville, *A Weaver Named Kabir: Selected Verses with a Detailed Biographical and Historical Introduction*, French Studies in South Asian Culture and Society, no. 6 (Delhi, 1993); on the tradition of Dadu, see Monika Thiel-Horstmann, *Crossing the Ocean of Existence: Braj Bhāṣā Religious Poetry from Rajasthan* (Wiesbaden, 1983). On early *sant*s and the Kabirpanthi tradition, see David Lorenzen, *Praises to a Formless God* (Albany, 1996).
17. Sometimes referred to generically as *śabda* in yogic texts, internal auditory experiences are more frequently referred to there as *anāhata nāda* (the unstruck sound); for examples, see Lilian Silburn, *Kuṇḍalinī, the Energy of the Depths: A Comprehensive Study Based*

on the Scriptures of Nondualistic Kaśmir Śaivism, The SUNY Series in the Shaiva Traditions of Kashmir, (series) ed. Harvey P. Alper (Albany, 1988), pp. 48–49, 94, 131; examples from *sant* texts can be found here in songs 1, 2, and 6.

18. *Sant* verses are also known generically as *bānī* (from the Sanskrit *vāṇī*), "sayings." *Śabda* is a common term for a hymn in *nirguṇa* devotion, particularly in the Sikh tradition (*sabad*), which is directly related to that of the *sants*; see Daniel Gold, *The Lord as Guru: Hindi Sants in North Indian Tradition* (New York, 1987), pp. 20–21. For examples of *śabda* as a genre of *sant* song, see Linda Hess, *The Bîjak of Kabir* (San Francisco, 1983), pp. 42–78.
19. Most notably, the lineages of Dadu and Bauri Sahiba. For examples of the first, see Thiel-Horstmann, *Crossing the Ocean of Existence*; on the second, see Gold, *Lord as Guru*, pp. 137–147.
20. I recall that Professor Ramanujan made the remark in a public forum, probably at a seminar at the University of Chicago in the early 1980s; the phrase stuck in my mind but the exact context did not.
21. The most immediate esoteric predecessors to the *sants* were the Nath yogis, on which the fullest reference remains George Weston Briggs, *Gorakhnāth and the Kānphaṭa Yogīs*, 2nd ed. (Delhi, 1973). A collection of Nath esoteric songs in Hindi—showing many technical terms that would be used by *sants*—has been published in Pitambardatt Barthwal, *Gorakh Bānī* (Prayag, 1971).
22. This phenomenon has been discussed at length in my *Lord as Guru*, chap. 5.
23. Soamiji Maharaj (Shiv Dayal Singh), *Sār Bachan Rādhāsvami* (Beas, Punjab, 1963), p. 65 (ch. 6, song 19, vs. 5–8). This and following translations of poetry are my own.
24. *Mahātmāoṃ kī Bānī* (Bhurkura, Gazipur, 1933), p. 376.
25. Closing the *mūla cakra* here may refer to a particular yogic sitting position.
26. On the Vedānta of each, see Rambachan, *Limits of Scripture*, and Swāmi Agehānanda Bhārati, "Radhakrishnan and the Other Vedānta," in Paul Arthur Schlipp, ed., *The Philosophy of Sarvepalli Radhakrishnan* (New York, 1952), pp. 459–480.
27. Anantananda Rambachan, *Accomplishing the Accomplished: The Vedas as a Source of Valid Knowledge in Śaṅkara*, Monographs of the Society for Asian and Comparative Philosophy, no. 10 (Honolulu, 1991), p. 53.
28. Rambachan, in his introduction to *Accomplishing the Accomplished*, frames the debate, citing a number of well-known Indian philosophers (especially Radhakrishnan) who present a general position on revelation and experience that I am calling "neo-Vedantic." They explain the primacy of experience as grounds for Indian religious thought and attribute a belief in that primacy to Śaṅkara as well. Rambachan then argues against this position. Clooney's reading of Vedānta as theology supports Rambachan's, although he does not explicitly argue the case.
29. Translated from Tulsi Sahib, *Ghaṭ Rāmāyaṇa*, *Sant Bānī Pustakmālā* (Allahabad, 1976–77), p. 59. For the context of the quote and a discussion, see my *Lord as Guru*, pp. 128–131.
30. On the theoretical significance of a formless divinity at the socioreligious extremes in general, see my *Comprehending the Guru: Towards a Grammar of Religious Perception*, American Academy of Religions Academy Series, no. 57, (series) ed. Carl Raschke (Atlanta, 1988), pp. 110–114.
31. The *ṛṣis* as individuals seem to have been given most attention in the *brāhmaṇa* texts. For a full and lucid account of the *ṛṣis* in Hindu tradition, see Holdredge, *Veda and Torah*, pp. 233–243.
32. The scholarship on the relationship between early Advaita and Mahāyāna is most complex. Natalia Isayeva, *Śhaṅkara and Indian Philosophy* (Albany, 1993), reviews

the literature in her introduction and clarifies some of the philosophical differences in chap. 5. Detailed philosophical comparisons of particular topics are given by Richard King, *Early Advaita Vedānta and Buddhism: The Mahāyāna Context of the Gauḍapādīya Kārikā*, SUNY Series in Religious Studies, series ed. Harold Coward (Albany, 1995).

33. On the *puṣṭimārg*, see Richard Barz, *The Bhakti Sect of Vallabhacarya* (Faridabad, Haryana, 1976); and Rajendra Jindel, *Culture of a Sacred Town* (Bombay, 1976).
34. Written by an anonymous author in the Tamil country at around the tenth century, the Bhāgavata Purāṇa finds precedent as a classical narrative of Kṛṣṇa in the Harivamsa (c. third century), a sort of epilogue to the Mahābhārata, and then the Viṣṇu Purāṇa (c. fifth century). In each, Kṛṣṇa is depicted less like a human hero and more like a divine being. For translations, see M. A. Langlois, *Harivansa ou histoire de la famille de Hari: Ouvrage formant un appendice du Mahabharata* (Paris, 1834); H. H. Wilson, *The Vishnu Purana: A System of Hindu Mythology and Tradition* (London, 1840); and Swami Venkatesananda, *The Concise Śrīmad Bhāgavataṁ* (Albany, 1989). On early Kṛṣṇa Bhakti, see Friedhelm Hardy, *Viraha-Bhakti: The Early History of Kṛṣṇa Devotion in South India* (New Delhi, 1983).
35. A section of Vallabha's commentary has been translated in James D. Redington, S.J., *Vallabhācārya on the Love Games of Kṛṣṇa*, (Delhi 1983).
36. See Jeffrey R. Timm, "Scriptural Realism in Pure Nondualistic Vedānta," in Jeffrey R. Timm, ed., *Texts in Context: Traditional Hermeneutics in South Asia* (Albany, 1992), pp. 127–146.
37. Navneet P. Gandhi, "Shri Vallabhacharayaji (His Life and Philosophy)," in C. M. Vaidya, ed., *Puṣṭimārga and Śrī Vallabhacārya* (*A Collection of Four Articles*) (Baroda, 1984), pp. 27–44; the citation is from p. 34.
38. For legends of Sur and the growth of the Sur Sagar, see John Stratton Hawley, *Sur Das: Poet, Singer, Saint* (Delhi, 1984), chaps. 1–2.
39. See ibid., chap. 5.
40. The term is from Kenneth E. Bryant, *Poems to the Child God* (Berkeley, 1978), where a number of examples are presented.
41. The song is translated in full in my *Lord as Guru*, p. 42.
42. From the Hindi text given by Rupert Snell, *The Hindi Classical Tradition: A Braj Bhāṣā Reader*, SOAS South Asian Texts, no. 2 (London, 1991), p. 98.
43. My translation from the Hindi text in ibid., p. 102.
44. *Nigama*, the word for "scripture" in the text, is commonly used for the Vedas, in contrast to *āgamas* understood as later texts.
45. For the full song, see my translation in Wendy Doniger O'Flaherty, ed., *Textual Sources for the Study of Hinduism* (Manchester, 1988), p. 145.
46. See Daniel Gold, "What the Merchant Guru Sold: Social and Literary Types in Hindi Devotional Verse," *Journal of the American Oriental Society* 111, no. 1 (1992): 22–35.
47. Charandas's verses have been published as *Bhakti Sagar*, "The Sea of Devotion" (Lucknow, 1966). On Charandas, see my *Lord as Guru*, pp. 67–77.
48. A Hindi biography of Malik Sahib has been published: Pītāmbar Miśra, *Divya Caritāmrit* (New Delhi, 1973). For a short note, see my *Lord as Guru*, pp. 166–169.
49. Monier Monier-Williams, *A Sanskrit-English Dictionary*, s.v. *go*. Monier-Williams also makes a reference to the rays as the herds of the sky for which Indra fights with Vṛtra.
50. Miśra, *Divya Caritāmrit*, p 198.
51. Malik Sahib called them *rahasyas*, "secrets,"; see ibid., pp. 94–96.
52. For a listing of some different *saguṇa* texts within the *sant* tradition, see Lorenzen, *Praises to a Formless God*, pp. 260–261.

11

Mysticism and Scripture in Theravāda Buddhism

NINIAN SMART

Buddhism—above all, the Theravāda—can be considered the most mystical of religions. If mysticism involves inner meditation, then the way of life preached by the Buddha Gotama's teaching was centrally focused on the mystical path. It centers on *jhāna* (*dhyāna*, in Sanskrit). Of course, ethical behavior and sundry reminders and rites form part of the ambience of the Buddhist life. And, of course, the philosophical side is vital, since the liberated person needs insight into the nature and structure of the world.

There are gods around, for the Buddha did not want to deny people's beliefs, but they are unimportant in the matter of spiritual liberation. There are brahmins, but Gotama's approach was moralizing, meaning that the true brahmin is the person of restraint and virtuous conduct (D.I.115).

The Statues of the Early Canon

In Theravāda Buddhism there can be no *unio mystica*, for the simple reason that there is nothing to be united *with*—no God or Ground of Being. A commonplace of much literature of the West has therefore no application in this tradition. In Western religions, God reveals; hence there must be a connection between mysticism and scripture. But in the Theravāda there is no revelation or *śruti*. That was a brahmin conception. Neither Brahma nor the Vedic revelation were taken seriously by Gotama. The former represented himself as the creator of the universe (D.I.18) when he wasn't, he himself being a victim of illusion. The brahmin might master the Vedas, but the true master of the mantas (mantras) is the Buddha (Sn 997). In the Theravāda, rituals are a means of self-improvement, and sacrifice (condemned especially in the Jatakas as cruel, for example, J.3.518ff.) is reinterpreted as gift-giving or alms (Sn 295). Even offerings to the Buddha are a matter of *puñña*, and the rite is reflected back on the individual. Since, strictly speaking, the Buddha neither exists nor does not exist, there can be neither this-worldly nor cross-worldly interplay with him. The person who offers a flower to him is like the tennis player who practices against the wall: his good play tests himself, not some other person.

All this affects attitudes to scriptures. The Pali canon has typical contrasts to later Hindu concepts of revelatory truth. First in the matter of language, the brahmins held that the Sanskrit tongue was both natural and everlasting: it was the ur-language of the cosmos. It was natural in the sense that it has a built-in affinity to what it describes (though the Mīmāṃṣā interpretation saw the Vedas as a set of injunctions, not of descriptions). By contrast, the Pali tradition considered language a creation of the human mind, which was based on convention (Miln 160; Sn 648). Second, the brahmin ideology treated *śabda* or verbal testimony as one of the *pramāṇa*s or (sources of knowledge), together with perception and inference. Verbal testimony covered scripture (testimony to matters transcendental). Strictly speaking, the term *scripture* is misleading: the Veda was of course transmitted orally—it was oratory. Instead, the Buddha, while taking steps to ensure that his teaching was transmitted with a reasonable amount of accuracy, considered that ultimately the truth has to be personally experienced: the truth in Buddhism is *ephipassiko* (D II.217, A 1.158). In later terms, we would say that the Buddha confined his sources of knowledge to perception and inference. Naturally, perception is here a stretched knowledge, including paranormal experience and yogic perception. Third, the Buddha distrusted the natural fit of language to reality. It misleadingly suggested the substantiality of things and of the ego, for instance. Human language can express and contribute to human ignorance.

If we stick to the attitudes of the Pali cannon and, for that matter, of early Mahāyāna, we would see knowledge in terms mainly of experience, both everyday and contemplative. Importantly, too, the contemplative life was itself a chief source of cosmology, and not just of inner psychology. The spiritual adept—and, obviously, the historical Buddha—was the great hero and the *arhant*s, or saints, were the secondary heroes, since they followed the pattern of his behavior. A saint could remember his or her previous births, could have knowledge of paranormal phenomena, and could voyage to the ends of the cosmos (D.III 131, D.I.85 ff.). Liberated persons and, in particular, the Buddha, have the *dibbacakkhu* (divine eye) enabling them to perceive paranormally (D.II.20). So it was that the Buddha could see the gods (though brahmins talked about them, but not from experience—another ironical critique of their ideology). And the Buddha, for that matter, could see *through* them.

Some scholars will view my account so far as being oversimplified and untrue to the facts as they exist now in Theravādin countries. What I have presented here is part of the philosophy of the fairly early Theravāda, as found in the Pali canon; however, one may add the following observations. First, the Sangha had its own point of view but lived in a symbiosis with various religious movements, customs, and beliefs. Though it considered that the "true brahmin" was a genuinely moral being, it nevertheless had to live with real brahmins, engaged in mantric practices, for example, formulaic magic. It was sometimes important in civil society to harness their ritual expertise; hence, in Southeast Asian Kingdoms, monarchs were installed in brahmin-infused ceremonials.

Moreover, the Sangha lived in a state of amity with various agricultural and other rituals. Basically, the teachings of Buddhism are those designed for the Sangha, including lay disciples. There is an indefinite penumbra of relatively faithful people around the Sangha and, beyond them, the rest of society at large. This has tended to make Buddhism easily symbiotic, though, notably, some forces have been dedicated to breaking up the Sangha (such as Islam, from the eleventh century C.E., in parts of India). Generally, the Sangha has survived in unison with surrounding religions; but it is wrong to identify Buddhism with those peripheral religious forces. There is a tendency in anthropology to do this.

But there is, beyond this, a philosophical point to be made. Throughout most of Indian philosophy the vital distinction between entities focuses on the question whether or not they are timeless. However important the gods might be, they are inferior because they are temporal. But nirvana is timeless (M.I 326; Sn 69, 220), and everything else is impermanent. Living with brahmins is a concession (but not ultimately a serious one) to timed reality. Certainly it does not involve accepting any thought of substance in their ignorant mantric activities (S.IV.28).

The Theravāda we have today has of course been affected by the Mahāyāna, which, in turn, was increasingly affected by brahmin practices and ideas, as witnessed by the fact that the new Buddhist scriptures were written in Sanskrit (admittedly somewhat hybrid). In evolving mantric chantings of selected texts in the rites known as *pirit*, the Theravāda mimicked brahmin and other kinds of magic (Vin.II 110; JI 200; Vism 414). The use of Buddha images and the ritual painting in of the eyes reflect Hindu practices, even if the spirit of Buddha images is most serene and not numinous as in the Hindu style. The Hindu tradition has had its influence within temple complexes, in the *devalayes*, with Viṣṇu and other gods being present and ready for offerings (admittedly for mundane rather than spiritual ends). And the South Indian war god Kataragama plays a notable part in the pilgrimage life of the island, and so, primarily, of Buddhists. Nevertheless, the Theravāda is almost everywhere opposed to the notion that sacramental rituals help to liberate persons—for instance, there is a strong attack on brahmin ablutionary rituals (Th 238). The gods do not get you beyond this world; these numinous beings are only important for material concerns. Strictly speaking, monks should not deal with them. The eightfold path lies in a different direction. And its culmination lies principally in its last three members—namely, right effort, right awareness, and right contemplation—which help transform trust (*saddha*) into insight (*paññā*). The path is traditionally divided into morality, contemplation, and insight (*Mahāparinibbāna Sutta*, I.12); and the Buddhist life, into morality, giving, and contemplation. In brief, mystical training, practice, and experience are crucial to liberation. The rest is secondary.

Of course, we have to take into account here the framework of karma theory. Since the spiritual life is suffused with moral training and action, and since morality creates merit and merit creates advancement, then following the Buddha is prudent in the long run. An important role in creating moral attitudes is Buddhist ritual. This, as we have seen, is one reason Buddhism rejects brahmin ritual. Eventually its attitude to noninjury and the rejection of animal sacrifices came to dominate the brahmin ethos, even if animal sacrifices have not even today vanished from the Indian scene. But apart from animal sacrifices, Theravāda Buddhism was more or less rigorously opposed to sacramental rites (ND2, 493). So when the Sangha or pious laypersons use ritual, it is nearly always given an ethical efficacy and significance.

A critic might note that though I began by saying that the Theravāda is pure mysticism, the religion of the numinous is not without its manifestations in the tradition. More particularly, the huge Buddha images might encourage the thought that the faithful really worship the Buddha, even though he is not "there" to be worshiped. We have already noted that there can be no transaction between the Tathāgata and his followers. He is no creator, either, of course. The Theravāda is generally free from presumptions drawn from the Mahāyāna of the Tantra. The imagery of sexual union, for instance, as a symbol of contemplative communion makes no sense in philosophy which has neither substances nor an other.

Let me discuss the principles that animate the Theravāda doctrine in a little more detail, since they bear on the relation between contemplation and liberation. First, nothing is permanent (S 5.197). Nothing has substance. Language misleads us into thinking that items in the world have continuity; and language is in this and other ways systematically misleading. In describing the gross and unanalyzed world, language suggests that there are things and selves, which, upon reflection, break down into simpler constituents, all of which, in one form or another, are events. Second, Buddhist philosophy sees the whole cosmos as conditioned. That is, every phase of existence is the effect of chain of events, multiply conditioned (S.II.7). This vision of the world, discerned by *aniccavipassanā*, is not merely abstract; it also contains particularities that bear on the makeup of human individuals. In this, Buddhism differs markedly from Western psychology, and also from Indian analyses, such as that of Sankhya, despite the latter's affinities with Jainism and Buddhism; probably it was a sramanic system captured by the brahmin tradition. In any event, Buddhism's theory of the five *khandhas*, "groups of events" (or heaps, *rasi*) (S.111, 101, 47, 86) is characteristic of its analytic vision. It shows the Theravāda's preoccupation with psychology as a science—which forms the background to meditation but also is the basis for framing a cosmology, since each meditative state has a corresponding plane of outer existence.

The vision also places consciousness, or rather the events of consciousness, in a strategic location. Contemplation is aimed at the purification of consciousness. Not for nothing is Buddhaghosa's great classic entitled *The Path of Purification* (*Visuddhimagga*). It is not an inspirational book, but one that is highly technical and logically laid out. It belongs with the apparent aridities of the *Abhidhamma*, rather than with the colorful *Suttas*, or with the songs of the monks and nuns, the Jatakas, and so forth.

As we have already noted, Buddhism in the Theravāda is empiricist, but in a stretched way that differentiates it from most Western empiricism of modern times. This is so, first, because it incorporates paranormal experiences, together with contemplative states—for instance, the most subtle treatment of the stages of *jhāna*—which are not counted typically as informative or important in most Western empiricisms. Second, Buddhism has a place for a state "beyond" the cosmos, namely, nirvana. To be accurate, it is both within and outside the cosmos. A saint experiences or realizes nirvana and enters into a dispositional state of liberation in which his liberation is a continuous and active awareness, while he lives. This is the so-called *saupādisesa* state—that is, nirvana "with a substrate" (It 38; Nett 92). When he is deceased, he is "in" *anupādisesa* nirvana. This implies, of course, among other things, that the saint is no longer reborn. This is an unutterable, indescribable transcendental state.

Incidentally, the Buddha greatly simplified the idea of liberation by freeing it from identification with the location of a soul. Instead of a permanent self, he substituted nirvana or liberation. In effect, the soul became the potentiality for liberation. Later in Mahāyāna Buddhism, this became the Buddhanature. So the Buddha reduced the idea of liberation to its bare essentials: an indescribable and unanalyzable transcendental state, consequent upon treading the path; the summit of the contemplative life consists in the realization or experience of nirvana.

It is true that many occasions are cited where the Buddha's presence and words have a role in bringing on liberation; nevertheless, because there is no divine Being, there seems to be no call for testimony of a scared, liturgical kind. His religion was open (he claimed not to have the *acariyamuṭṭhi*, "closed fist of the teacher" [D.II.100; S.V. 153]). The point, of course, is that an insecure teacher holds something back to avoid becoming superfluous. The Buddha was not like that: if you follow his path, you will end up seeing the truth—having a mystical and articulated vision of nirvana and of its counterposing cosmos. And the Theravāda tradition is not esoteric in inclination; there are no secret truths that need ordained gurus and numinously guaranteed interpretation. Who knows what the Buddha would have thought of the mantras of Tantra and secret instructions? He doubtless would have reckoned it as part of the decline of the faith a thousand years after his decease.

Naturally, because in our age the Buddha is the one teacher (having made his own way to nirvana without immediate assistance from any other person, while later saints made their way thither because of the teaching and inspiration of the Buddha), the words of Gotama and his early disciples had to be preserved. This is why the most important of the three divisions of the *Tipiṭaka* is the *Sutta*, or discourse basket. There is, of course, even here a fluid connection between the words of the Buddha and of his disciples. A vital pair of collections includes the songs of the monks and of the nuns (the *Theragāthā* and the *Therīgāthā*), which are intended to be autobiographical verses (for the most part) describing how the said elders achieved their liberation. Although they are often somewhat formally put together and a bit repetitive, they do incorporate personal experience. They incorporate the scenes of nature, some charming, as part of the setting for the attainment of the peace and the insight of nirvana and of the heroic saintly feats of their putative authors.

The authority of the Buddha and of the saints extends beyond their practical interior expertise in the process of attaining the higher states of consciousness, since liberation involves social and moral qualities. As part of this there are vital things to say about rules, and, of course, this is the justification for the basket known as the *Vinaya* (Vin I.356, II.96; D.I.229). This supplies the framework for the community. An interesting point about Buddhism—that may indeed tell us something about its generally symbiotic character—is that as a faith it centers on its inner band of monks, nuns, and pious lay disciples. It does not strictly identify with the community at large. When you take refuge in the Sangha, it is not like (in some countries) taking refuge in the church, which comprises the whole community. Within the wider society, Buddhism lives with other religions. It does not necessarily merge with society in the larger sense. It might use brahmins for coronations and the like, but it need not pay attention to their theology and values. Of course, it has undergone changes as it moves into differing societies. Ultimately in Pure Land Buddhism, the tradition took over Hindu-type devotionalism—bhakti. Such numinous motifs could be depicted on its wider canvas, and they could become a vital asset in China, Korea, and Japan. But in Sri Lanka and Southeast Asia, the religion of the environment (other than Buddhism) was agricultural, and its adherents lived amicably alongside the Sangha and the Buddhist laity. The main thrust of Buddhism—the contemplative or mystical life—could continue as the dominant partner (insofar as it was practiced by the Sangha).

If the Buddha's message was affected in Sri Lanka, it was more by nationalism as a worldview, even long before modern nationalism came into existence. The Sinhalese were proud of their history, in part because their island status defined them well, and in part because surrounding populations spoke Dravidian languages, while theirs was North Indian in provenance. Further, their neighbors were, for much of their history, Hindu in practice. The preservation of the *dhamma* came to be thought of as both a duty and destiny. Of course, the Buddha had set this in train with his mythic visits to the island, leaving a footprint on Adam's Peak. Though the *vamsa* (chronicles) were not part of the Buddhist canon, they were vital in shaping the consciousness of the Sinhalese, especially in modern times.

The Buddha, then, is the central authority because he blazed the trail to nirvana and experienced the truth in his enlightenment. The latter was indeed the personal experience from which (in this age) the whole religion flows. The Buddha is the exemplar of the true mystic and liberated human being. In some respects he has a superhuman status. It is said in the canon that he is *devātideva*, "god above gods" (Sn 1134; J.IV. 158; VvA 18), and even that he is *brahmaatibrahma*, "Brahma above Brahma." This does not make him God, as Westerners might be tempted to think. He is above the gods because they are ignorant and because he has attained nirvana, which they can never do as long as they remain gods (only humans can attain the highest state). Like nearly everyone else in the universe, the gods are confused, blundering about the cosmos exuding a slight degree of raw power. Enlightenment involves a certain style—the Buddha worked at it over the years, and when it came to him it was highly cerebral, as well as greatly calm. He was not an inspired and turbulent prophet like Isaiah, speaking when possessed by a powerful Other. The Buddha could not have used the formula "Thus spake the Lord." Still, he is centrally authoritative because in our age he discovered the path to nirvana, including the philosophy that underlies the growth in understanding and insight, which is essential if we are to attain our goal. This, then, to repeat the main point, is why it is important to preserve the canon. But it is not as if Buddhists rely on a sacred scripture; rather, the Pali canon is a decent record of the words of our supreme teacher and mystical exemplar. Ultimately, when we achieve insight, the words can be thrown away. It is like the case of Einstein: he forged the path to general relativity, but now that he has gone, we can learn about it through physics textbooks. To do physics we do not need to know the biography of Einstein or his exact testimony.

The next refuge is the Dhamma, "teaching." Here there is a typical ambiguity. Is the Dhamma the teaching or is it what the teaching is about? In the Indian tradition the conflation of meaning and reference is frequent, since the same word *artha* (Pali; Sanskrit = *attha*) is used. Hence the expression *attho ca dhammo ca* (A 169; A.V. 222).

The *dhamma* is the deeper meaning and reference of the text. From one point of view, the Dhamma is the structure of reality as indicated by the teaching of the Buddha, including the unutterable nature of nirvana; from another point of view, it is the teaching itself. Because of the Buddhist theory that language is conventional, there is a certain distance between words and reality. Moreover, there are indications, even in the Theravāda texts, of that *upāyakosalla* (D III. 220), "skill in means," which the Buddha exercised in his teaching methods. He adapted his teaching to the mental and cultural condition of his hearers. Consequently, the words of the canon are often indirect and not to be taken too literally. So we have to take the Dhamma to be the *point* of his teaching, not necessarily the exact words. It is as if the Dhamma is the median between the words and the reality.

Another factor to consider is the existential nature of truth, in this context. To understand the Buddha's teaching, you need to experience what it is about. This is the message in quite a number of the songs of the elders and is attested elsewhere by the following usages: *saccānubodha* (awakening to the truth), *saccābhisameya* (comprehension of the truth), and *saccānupatti* (realization of the truth) M II 171ff.; Sn 758; M II 173ff.). A monk, for instance, goes to a village and sees a woman dancing in the main street (he is not, by the way, supposed to watch such entertainments) and at once sees the misery of her condition. It is this burst of recognition that brings his understanding of the truth of *dukkha*, "suffering" ("ill-fatedness" might be a better translation, though "suffering" has become the norm in English). So the Dhamma is much more than words—evident from the very fact that its goal is nirvana, and that that ultimately has to be realized in experience.

All this means that, given the contemplative heart of the Theravāda, the scriptures are not revelatory in themselves. This is part of the reason Sri Lankans have a relatively relaxed view of the whole business of scholarly probing of the canon. The canon is an indicator of the truth and a testament to the mystical hero Gotama; but it is essentially a means to an end. The scriptures are surely not, like the Veda (according to Mīmāṃṣā), everlasting; nor do they tell you of the mind of God.

With regard to the third refuge, the Sangha, how should we estimate it relative to the path to liberation? It is, importantly, the living vehicle of the Dhamma. It is the vehicle of the teaching since it is entrusted with the transmission of the canon and with scholarly work on it. Special arrangements were made to ensure the accurate recitation of the texts (Vism 74–76). Regarding the entrusting of scholarship on the canon to the Sangha (until modern times, when the better scholars tended to be university educated and English speaking), it is interesting that the third basket, the *Tipiṭaka*, is the analysis of doctrine, *Abhidhamma* (Dpvs V 37). This seems to have begun developing in the first two centuries after the decease of the Buddha. It indicates how a rather austere and abstract exposition of the philosophy and the psychology was deemed important, as the composition of commentaries was later esteemed. The creation of analysis was evidently expected of the order. Significantly, this involved listing the various stages of the spiritual path, including the meditations, the nature of the sense-faculties, and the detailing of the constituents, both physical and psychological, of the human being; the classification of all types of phenomena; and, finally, the description of sequences of causality. The analyses are not to be divorced from contemplation, however, since many of the items were used in meditation—for instance, the constituents of the human being. Although the *Abhidhamma* has been thought of as being scholastic, it nevertheless is continuous with analytic meditation. This is where the juncture between philosophy and the path of liberation is most evident. We have already noted, too, that psychology is the central engine for a Buddhist understanding of the cosmos. The accurate understanding of human psychology is an important ingredient in training, which aims eventually at liberation. More generally, for adepts, the philosophical dimension of the Theravāda (as with most other branches of Buddhism) is of vital importance toward understanding the end that they are seeking and the means to get there. The experiential, philosophical, and ethical dimensions are indeed intertwined. It is on this triangle that the drive of Buddhism is based. So the *Abhidhamma* sets forth in systematic ways the whole realm of forces that the mystic needs to cope with and use.

This leads to a further observation about the Sangha: it should be an organization that facilitates traversing of the path. If we accept that Buddhism considers greed, hatred, and delusion to be the great obstacles to the good life (VnA 31 ff.), we can understand how the order protects its members and pious laypeople from these faults: the rules that govern possessions and eating protect us against greed; the order's community spirit protects against hatred; and its analysis protects against ignorance and delusion. Buddhist meditations begin to tackle the problem of egos, while monks and nuns are encouraged, through imaginative practice, to suffuse the world of living beings with benevolence and compassion and with joy at other's joy (SnA 128; S V 118). It is within this framework of practice that the study of the *Abhidhamma* is important. Its abstract style leads beyond the bright illustrations of mythic stories. Mara dissolves into spiritual forces that hinder the individual from attaining her or his goal. In brief, the analytic philosophy and psychology of the third basket has a practical reference to the contemplative life as it was conceived in the Theravāda two millennia ago.

We may note that the scriptures depict role models for the mystic—above all, the Buddha but, of course, notable arhats as well. This is one of the main jobs of the *Therīgāthā* and the *Theragāthā*: to reveal the values of the faith through the lives of its saints. They are role models, of course, for the pious layperson and for the community as a whole, but also for the Sangha itself as it threads its way through history and geography. There was never absolute agreement about the criteria of sanctity. Thus, the first major schism in the Buddhist tradition concerned such questions. The proponents of the new school of the Great Sangha (the *Mahāsanghikas*) were in favor of slightly relaxing the severity of the tests of arhatship. Notably they allowed that an arhat might have a "wet dream," accounted for as a visit by a *devatā* and hence involuntary on the person's part. Who knows? Maybe the incidence of nighttime lust reduced the number of candidate saints too drastically? Further, they allowed that a saint might be ignorant on some matters, that he might receive instruction from another and that he might enter the path as a result of spoken words only. All this indicates a prior very high standard of sainthood—as though the saint should be omniscient in matters affecting doctrine and the Buddha's teaching. Perhaps the relative laxity of the *Mahāsanghikas* helped to further elevate the Buddha. This, in turn, could lead to the bhakti, which was most obvious in the Pure Land stream of piety, which took on a numinous character, and a different kind of religion from the austere mysticism of the Theravāda.

The high standard of the Theravadin saint was, in the early centuries, an encouragement, and later a cause of a lack of spiritual ambition. At first, it held up an ideal that pointed optimistically to perfectibility—the unblemished life indeed was possible and was expressed in the careers of those who trod a heroic path. But later, given the usually pessimistic Buddhist view of history, perfection came to seem to be unrealizable; nirvana no longer occurs. The backlash to this in recent times is the Vipassana movement, which restores the real possibility of sainthood, and for laypersons, too.

The scriptures also depict ways in which the contemplative life was not just a means to liberation but also a means of knowledge. In the Buddhist tradition, it was always a way of gaining insight into the facts of cosmology and psychology. As we noted apropos of the *jhāna*s, each level of meditation corresponds to a level of cosmic reality. In the famous *Sutta* called the *Brahmajāla*, this is clearest (Vism 30). Here the Buddha rejects no fewer than sixty-two viewpoints, or *diṭṭhi*s. One of the accomplishments of a meditator is to remember prior births, and this can lead to thinking that one is everlasting, occupying an everlasting universe, without end. But the two views—that the universe is endless in time and that it is not—depend on undetermined or unanswerable questions because the question is wrongly put (D II 229). Amusingly, the Buddha attributes false perception to the creator god of the brahmins. Since he, Brahma, is the first being to come into existence at the start of a world epoch, he notes that he would like to have other beings for company. When they come into existence thereafter, he wrongly concludes that he brought them into existence, when in fact they were all part of a karmic sequence that had nothing to do with Brahma. He foolishly thinks that they arose because of his creative powers. So people who trace their lives back to Brahma, as a result of meditation, confusedly believe that there is nothing before him. And so they believe in an eternal Creator.

Of course, not all fallacies derive from false inferences in meditation. But this enhances the importance of logic and reasoning in the Buddha's teaching. Since it was on the bases of logic and experience (or perception) that the Buddha founded his authority, the scriptures essentially play an auxiliary role, and not a primary one. Since experience was chiefly mystical or contemplative in character, this is the crucial practice and appeal of the Buddha's message.

Nevertheless, we have to reckon with echoes of Brahmanism. The Buddha rarely attacked brahmins. He would prefer to undermine brahmin concepts and practices by reinterpreting them in moral terms, as we have seen. If he used the abstract *brahma*, it only referred to the idea of the sacred, notably in a solemn ethical sense; hence the *brahmavihāra*s were "sacred places"—that is, holy virtues that the true follower of the path ought to cultivate. And *brahmacariya* meant simply "sacred conduct"—that is, in regard to sex. In short, and as we have already seen, the Buddha sidestepped brahmin ritual and the actual role of brahmins in society and sought analogues in moral conduct. He gave credit to them where it was due but repudiated their rituals, for the most part. He would not utterly forget the notion of *śruti* (sacred oral tradition), and he seems to have seen merit in retaining his own authority, but ultimately his teachings were verifiable in individual experience. As things developed, his authority was planted most clearly in the Sutta basket of the *Tipiṭaka*. So the start of the Sutta beings with the words *evam me sutaṃ*. The word is heard but not in the same sense as it is in Hindu revelation.

To sum up: First, Brahmanism rested on a kind of sacramental and mantric ritual, but Buddhism did not encourage such rites. Buddhism concentrated mostly on concentration, involving the purification of consciousness. Second, the Buddhist theory of causation was inimical to both mantric causation and the use of ritual other than in a psychological manner. Third, there could not be any strict revelatory transaction between the transcendent and this world. The numinous experience of the Other is more hospitable to truly sacred revelation. This did not significantly figure in the Buddha's worldview.

Thus in this sense, the scriptures are a bit of a disappointment in the Theravadin canon, compared to the "high" views of scripture elsewhere. But because of its strong concern with psychology and analysis, parts of the canon function like handbooks for practical living, including, notably, meditation. Scripture, therefore, has powerful uses in the life of the Sangha. It contains many materials of general relevance to the wider community, beyond the loose frontier of the order. It also reflects the amazing originality of Gotama, while giving a moral prehistory in the wonderful stories of his previous births, which so often take existing material, characteristically, of the Gangetic culture and bend them to Buddhist uses. It also contains a good deal of poetry.

BIBLIOGRAPHY

Pali Texts

A	Anguttara Nikāya	ND2	Cūlaniddesa
D	Dīgha	Nett	Netti-pakarṇa
Dhs	Dhammasangini	S	Saṃyutta
Dpvs	Dīpavaṃsa	Sn	Sutta-nipāta
IT	Itivuttaka	Th1	Theragāthā
J	Jātaka	Th2	Therigāthā
M	Majjhima	Vbh	Vighanga
Mhvs	Mahavamsa	Vin	Vinaya
Miln	Milindapañha	Vism	Visuddhimagga
Nd1	Mahāniddesa	Vv	Vimānavatthu

Katz, Steven T. ed., *Mysticism and Language*. Oxford, 1993.
Smart, Ninian. *Reasons and Faiths*. London, 1958.
Smart, Ninian. *Dimensions of the Sacred*. London, 1996.
Warder, A. K. *Indian Buddhism*. Delhi, 1970.

12

Tao, World, and Mind

Mystical Adaptations of the Taoist Classics

LIVIA KOHN

The two major classics of the Taoist tradition, the *Daode jing* and the *Zhuangzi*, are philosophical writings from about 300 B.C.E. that contain a rich store of ancient wisdom. They are not at all alike. The *Daode jing*, a collection of proverbs, aphorisms, and traditional sayings, is very short and rather mysterious in its often elliptic and enigmatic verses. The *Zhuangzi*, all thirty-three chapters of it, is a compendium of prose that includes stories, fables, and parables in happy imitation of a footloose Taoist lifestyle. Yet combined, the two texts contain the essence of the Taoist mystical tradition and, over the centuries, have stood at the center of Taoist beliefs and practices, adapted and reinterpreted ever anew in light of contemporaneous concerns and sectarian preferences.

This chapter examines the two texts and their development in the Chinese middle ages. I first present a detailed description of the texts; then, proceeding in pairs, I look at two major commentaries from the early centuries C.E. and at the use of the classics in sectarian Taoist practices of the fourth and fifth centuries. Finally, I focus on their reinterpretation under Buddhist impact during the Tang dynasty (618–906). This study shows how the tradition remains true to its original sources without ever giving up its flexibility or strength to serve the needs of later generations. It also documents the continuing importance of ancient sacred texts in the practical efforts of living Taoist mystics.

The Basic Texts

The *Daode jing*, which has been translated numerous times into English,[1] often as the "Scripture of the Tao and the Virtue" or as the "Book of the Way and Its Power,"[2] consists of about 4,500 Chinese characters—which is why it is also called the "Scripture in Five Thousand Words." The text is divided into eighty-one chapters and two major sections; the first section deals with the Tao (chaps. 1–37), while the second focuses on virtue (chaps. 38–81).

The *Daode jing* is closely linked with the ancient philosopher known as Laozi, the Old Master. He was a shadowy figure who allegedly lived around 500 B.C.E. and was a contemporary of Confucius; he has been venerated as a senior sage from an early age and, with his own mystique, contributed greatly to the influence of the text both among religious followers and other readers. The latest research suggests that he was originally a Confucian hero and only later, because the emerging Taoist school was in need of a suitable founder, did he become associated with the text, which had been transmitted orally among its followers.[3] As Taoism grew, both he and the *Daode jing* were divinized to represent the Tao at its purest level—he as a celestial deity (the Highest Venerable Lord); the text as his foremost revelation.[4]

The *Daode jing* has been read in many ways, as "a handbook of prudential mundane life philosophy, a treatise on political strategy, an esoteric treatise on military strategy, a utopian tract, or a text that advocates 'a scientific, naturalistic' attitude toward the cosmos."[5] Within the Taoist tradition, however, the *Daode jing* has always been the key expression of its mystical vision, with the concept of the Tao as its centerpiece.[6] The Tao is the underlying power of creation and cosmic harmony that cannot be named or known, only intuited. It is what makes the world function, what makes beings what they are. While originally beyond sensory grasp, in the visible, concrete world of everyday life, the Tao manifests as change, expressed by the two complementary aspects yin and yang—the giving and the grasping, the resting and the moving.

Governing the natural so-being of the world, the Tao, with these two forces, maintained a pure society in primordial times[7] but was lost through increased cultural sophistication and the higher complexity of consciousness. Since then, the world has not been in harmony and disasters of various types have plagued it. To remedy this situation—this pervasive state of hypocrisy and disorder—the *Daode jing* proposes that we return to a simplicity of life and a tranquility of mind by leaving behind all luxuries and practicing mental concentration.[8] If done successfully, the result of this is nonaction—a state of mental equilibrium and oneness with the Tao—expressed in an attitude of laissez-faire toward the world, when one refrains from actively imposing one's will on things and lets them happen naturally and without force. The person who fully realizes this is the sage, who clearly sees the eternal patterns of the cosmos and acts in proper harmony with them.[9] As, ideally, the ruler of the world, the sage brings peace and contentment to all.

While this vision is at the root of Taoist mysticism—which forever seeks oneness with the Tao in lifestyle and consciousness—its emphasis on simplicity and concentration represents only one aspect of the classical ideal. The *Zhuangzi*, the second major Taoist text—which, in its "inner chapters," goes back to the philosopher Zhuang Zhou (d. 290 B.C.E.) but also contains the views of other early Taoist schools[10]—sees the Tao and its realization in a more internalized way, focusing on the individual's psychological development.[11] Lacking political and social concerns, the text finds the golden age not in some distant past but in the pure unspoiled mind of every living individual. The Tao here is the principle of the universe, the flow of existence as such that is always present and can always be accessed. A return to the Tao therefore does not imply going back to the past and leaving behind the luxuries of the present age, but rather, attaining complete oneness with the rhythm of the world in a state of ecstatic mental freedom or spontaneity[12]—what Zhuangzi calls "free and easy wandering."

Nonaction, still a major ideal, is accordingly redefined as a state of consciousness, an utter freedom of the mind, independent of whatever one may do in the world. It means the complete absence of conscious evaluation, the disappearance of all likes or dislikes, the attitude of "making all things equal." Rather than a prescribed way of (not) acting, it is a way of going along with whatever situation has developed.[13] Because all conscious knowledge is a form of deviation from the Tao, the mystical methods found in the *Zhuangzi* involve not so much concentration and single-pointedness of mind as reunion of the previously split subject and object, the complete dissolution of the conscious mind in a state of chaos, the utter obliviousness to all.[14] Instead of sensory limitation in a state of quietude, there is a sense of ecstatic accordance with the world in a situation of "perfect beauty and perfect happiness."[15]

Critical, rational choice is replaced by formless spontaneity, which appears in the world in innumerable different facets and forms of behavior. Unlike the *Daode jing*, the *Zhuangzi* never defines the proper activities of oneness with the Tao but refuses to prefer one over another. Nor does the text insist on any one way to attain it, but opens Taoist mystical practice to all forms of thinking and acting, illustrating them with numerous colorful stories and showing perfected beings (or true persons) in all walks of life and at all levels of the universe.[16]

Together, the two ancient classics provide basic models of Taoist mystical theory and practice. They share the understanding of the Tao as the underlying power of all existence and concur in their demand for mystical practice and liberation. Their emphases, however, vary between the concrete and the psychological, the political and the individual; they see oneness with the Tao in quietude and simplicity, or in ecstasy and universal freedom. Over the centuries, this fundamental difference has led to differences in interpretation and emphasis among the various Taoist schools.

Two Commentaries

Many commentaries have been written on the two ancient classics, especially on the *Daode jing*.[17] Among the most influential ones, two early works stand out: the commentary by Heshang gong (the Master on the River) on the *Daode jing*, and Guo Xiang's (d. 310 C.E.) exegesis of the *Zhuangzi*. Both have been highly influential in the later mystical tradition, which tended to read the texts largely through their lenses.

The Master on the River is a legendary figure who allegedly lived in the second century B.C.E. Emperor Wen of the Han dynasty (ruled 179–156) heard of him and, after being firmly put in his place as a mere mortal, received an explication of the *Daode jing* from him.[18] The text associated with his name entitled *Daode zhenjing zhu* is contained in the Taoist canon (DZ 682)[19] and has been both translated[20] and studied in English.[21] Its date of compilation is questionable, with some scholars seeing it in a Han-dynasty context[22] and others finding evidence of a much later, fifth-century compilation.[23]

The commentary's ideas center on the immediate relation between cultivating oneself and governing the country, linking *Daode jing* philosophy with the worldview and practices of Chinese medicine and early cosmology.[24] According to the text, the creation of political order is structurally isomorphic with the cultivation of personal longevity. Politics and philosophy, as well as magic and morality, are interconnected; and the cultivation of oneself, one's personal body, leads inevitably to the perfect order of one's family, community, and state, and eventually the world. On the statement, for example, that "one may see the Tao of heaven without looking through the windows" (*Daode jing* chap. 47), the Master of the River says:

> The Tao of heaven is the same as the Tao of humanity. Thus, when the ruler of humanity is pure and tranquil, the energy of Heaven will naturally be upright. When the ruler of humanity is full of desires, the energy of Heaven will be troubled and turbid. For this reason all good and bad fortune, profit and harm, issue only from one's own self.[25]

To attain the desired state, the self or the personal body must therefore be cultivated. To do so, the Master on the River says, he recommends physical practices and breathing exercises as prescribed in Chinese medicine, which understood human life as the accumulation of vital energy (*qi*), as manifested in the spirit-forces of the body's five essential inner organs. Because this cultivation, however, is essentially a bodily one, it has not only spiritual but also physical effects, giving people good health and a long life. Heshang gong thus uses the text to bolster his conviction that the universe is populated by numerous spirits, and that increasing vital energy is the key to maintaining these spirits and thereby reaching a long life and immortality. In this sense, he reinterprets the chapter 6 of the *Daode jing*, which begins, "The spirit of the valley does not die." As Heshang gong explains:

> "Valley" means "nourish." If one can nourish the spirits, one does not die. The "spirits" are the spirits of the five inner organs: the spirit soul in the liver, the material soul in the lungs, the spirit in the heart, the intention in the spleen, and the essence in the kidneys. If the five inner organs are exhausted or harmed, the five spirits will leave [and one dies].[26]

With this interpretation, the very text of the passage has been transformed. Instead of reading, "The spirit of the valley does not die," it now clearly reads, "Nourish the spirits and you will not die."

The same pattern holds true for the next line of the chapter 6, traditionally (and literally) rendered as, "It is called the mysterious female." On this, Heshang gong says:

> This means that the Tao of no-death lies in the mysterious and the female. The mysterious is heaven; in the human body it is the nose. The female is earth; in the human body it is the mouth.
>
> Heaven feeds people with the five energies, which enter the organs through the nose and settle in the heart. The five energies are pure and subtle, they cause people to have sentience and spirituality, intelligence and perception, sound and voice, as well as the five kinds of inner nature. They are represented in the spirit soul, which is male and leaves and enters the human body through the nose in order to interact with heaven. Therefore, the nose is the mysterious.
>
> Earth feeds people with the five tastes, which enter the organs through the mouth and settle in the stomach. The five tastes are turbid and heavy, they cause people to have body and skeleton, bones and flesh, blood and pulses, and the six kinds of emotional passions. They are represented in the material soul, which is female and leaves and enters the human body through the mouth in order to interact with earth. Therefore the mouth is the female.[27]

Again, this completely revises the reading of the ancient classic, rendering the two words "mysterious" and "female" apart and understanding them as two terms, so that the line is now, "This is called the mysterious and the female." Instead of containing a vague and obscure reference to the depth and darkness of the Tao as it underlies all existence—the way the passage is most commonly understood—Heshang gong furnishes it with highly technical implications, specifying the meaning in a correlation with Chinese medical cosmology, so that "mysterious" becomes "heaven and breath," and "female" is read as "earth and taste." He then asserts his particular physical vision of the mystic quest: that, through nourishing themselves on both heaven and earth (breath and taste), people will find oneness with the Tao. This, in turn, he specifically interprets as manifest in vigor and health in this body, in immortality in the spirit realm, and in political stability in the family, state, and world.

Seeing social harmony and personal longevity as parts of the same ideal, and integrating the highly technical thinking of medical cosmology into the Taoist mystical tradition, the Master on the River opens the teachings of the *Daode jing* to include a technical path and a magical element, incorporating the ideals of political philosophers, immortality practitioners, and traditional physicians. The ancient classic, actively cited and used in the new vision, is adapted to a completely different worldview and reinterpreted accordingly. Yet its ultimate worth, its high veneration, is never diminished. On the contrary, the text grows with its continuing transformation.

The major commentary on the *Zhuangzi* that was done by Guo Xiang of the early fourth century C.E. and was also contained in the Taoist canon (DZ 745), moves in the opposite direction.[28] Guo Xiang, who was not only the commentator on the text but also its main editor, reduced the volume from fifty-two to thirty-three chapters and rearranged materials to suit his vision.[29] He had a very clear idea of what *Zhuangzi*'s worldview was about and, unlike the Master on the River, who had opened his classic to new speculations, proceeded to delimit the original fluidity of the work.

Like the *Zhuangzi*, Guo Xiang sees the Tao as the underlying flow of pure existence and finds its foremost characteristic in *Ziran*—that is, spontaneity, or "self-so." Beyond that, however, he describes a specific pattern in its manifestation, a pattern he defines in psychological rather than cosmological terms. Specifically, he introduces the twin concepts of allotment (*fen*) and principle (*li*) to detail the notions of inner nature (*xing*) and fate (*ming*) found in the *Zhuangzi*.

Beginning with the *Zhuangzi*'s notion of inner nature, Guo Xiang establishes his ideal of "order" and says, "Order means relying on and going along with one's inner nature, while disorder means opposing and repressing it."[30] He proceeds to narrow the concept of "inner nature"—a rather vague term in the *Zhuangzi* that just indicates the way people naturally are, by defining it as "allotment," the "share people have in the Tao," which is part of who they are but also limits them in their abilities and potentials.[31] Similarly, he takes the *Zhuangzi* notion of fate—the life and earthly position one is given by heaven—and specifies it through the notion of principle, the "pattern of the Tao" that is inherently present in every human being. As an inescapable characteristic of identity, it determines the particular way beings are in the world. As he says, "What is, as it is, without ever knowing why, we call fate. By giving up any conceptualization of it, by letting it be as it is, fate and, through it, principle are complete."[32] The two together determine the way people are, both genetically and in their character, as well as in the concrete conditions in which they are born, and which determine their status, political environment, and opportunities. Guo Xiang thus links both nature and nurture intimately with the Tao and defines them as equally beyond human control or conscious knowledge.

Attainment of the Tao in Guo Xiang's vision is, accordingly, both a return to spontaneous unconsciousness and an adaptation to the given facts of inner nature and fate. Ideally, people should thus develop an attitude of accordance, harmony, adaptation, and even resignation in regard to the facts of life. The more spontaneously such accordance is achieved, the better, because knowledge and decision making only cause rifts between subject and object and make true inner spontaneity impossible.[33] The mystical process in this context is a reversal of the decline from purity, interpreted radically in psychological terms. Guo Xiang bases his vision specifically on a list of four stages contained in the *Zhuangzi* but not explained there. They are Chaos Complete, Beings, Distinctions, and Right and Wrong. Guo Xiang interprets these:

> Chaos Complete is the state of complete forgetfulness of heaven and earth, of total abandonment of the myriad beings. Outside never examining time and space, inside never conscious of one's own body. Thus people are boundless and free from all fetters, they go along with beings and are in full accordance with all.
>
> Beings means that even though forgetfulness is no longer complete now and beings are recognized as existing, yet there is still the forgetfulness of distinctions between this and that.
>
> Distinctions is the stage when there is first a distinction between this and that. However, there are no evaluations in terms of right and wrong.
>
> Right and Wrong, finally, indicates that the Tao is no longer complete. With the destruction of the Tao, emotions begin to be partial and love develops. As long as one cannot forget love and free oneself from egoism, there is no way mysteriously to become one in oneself and with others.[34]

The pattern of decline, meant in a more cosmological way in the *Zhuangzi*, is interpreted by Guo Xiang entirely in psychological terms. Originally nothing was there that one was conscious of. Later, although things were already being thought of, people were not conscious of their being distinct. Only in the later stages of decline did they develop relations with beings and things, evaluating these as either positive or negative.[35] The mystical quest is the reversal of this process, an attainment of complete forgetfulness, for which the locus classicus is again in the *Zhuangzi*, with Guo Xiang adding a more limiting, psychological interpretation. It centers on the term *zuowang*—literally, "sitting and forgetting [everything]"—which in the later tradition became synonymous with the mystical experience itself. Describing this state, the *Zhuangzi* notes: "I smash up my limbs and body, drive out perception and intellect, cast off form, do away with understanding, and make myself identical with the Great Thoroughfare."[36]

Guo Xiang specifies:

> Sitting and forgetting, how can there be anything not forgotten? First forget the traces, such as benevolence and righteousness; then put that which caused the traces out of the mind. On the inside [be] unaware of one's body, on the outside never know there is a universe. Only then will one be fully open, become one with the process of change and pervade everything.[37]

Further detailing the mystical achievement reached through this stage of complete forgetfulness, Guo Xiang defines the new cosmic self of the accomplished sage—a self no longer limited to the ego or defined by the body but one that is identical with principle, rejoicing in the definitions given to it by the Tao and never trying to be something that it is not. A sense of utter detachment from life and death, a freedom from personal identity, is defined as the key to mystical realization:

> This life of mine, I did not bring it forth. Thus all that occurs throughout my life of perhaps a hundred years, all my sitting, getting up, walking, and staying, all my movements, all my quiet, all hurrying and resting of mine—even all the feelings, characteristics, knowledge, and abilities I have—all that I have, all that I do not have, all that I do, all that I encounter: it is never me, but principle only.[38]

The clear definition of the mystical consciousness, much more specific than that of the *Zhuangzi* (which is often intentionally vague), is typical for Guo Xiang's adaptation of the classic. In addition, given his own position as adviser at the Jin court, and given the accompanying need to survive in the communal world, Guo Xiang presents a much more positive attitude toward political and official involvement, declaring that the world itself, if everyone accepted his allotment and followed his principle of true Taoist forgetfulness, would be in a state of utter perfection, giving rise to a completely harmonious society, to what Isabelle Robinet suitably calls "le monde comme absolu."[39]

Guo Xiang's mysticism, unlike that of the *Zhuangzi* but similar to that of Heshang gong, thus has a political dimension. The ideal life, also based psychologically, takes place not only in the mind of the individual, but also, since everything is part of the Tao and the Tao determines the nature of all through allotment and principle, human society too is basically an organic whole and the political structure is a natural body. If every thing, and every being, finds its true accordance with the Tao, society must become fully perfect. Because every being, however, has its own particular inner nature and fate, this society is not egalitarian or even simple. On the contrary, it is a hierarchical, closely knit, and complex organized structure, which functions perfectly only because every being fulfills his/her/its particular role in utmost harmony with the Tao. This inherently Confucian vision of Guo Xiang, which he adapted largely from Xunzi, is in turn linked with the *Daode jing* understanding of nonaction as a political ideal. Guo Xiang says:

> When the king does not make himself useful in the various offices, the various officials will manage their own affairs. Those with clear vision will see; those with sharp ears will listen; the wise will plan; and the strong will provide protection. Why take any action? Only mysterious silence, that is all![40]

Both Guo Xiang and the Master on the River, therefore, add a political dimension to the original mystical vision of the Tao classics, true to the general characteristics of Chinese mysticism: that the sage is the ideal ruler, and that full mystical realization means the attainment of great peace in the world at large.[41] Beyond that, the two commentators move in different directions—Guo Xiang delimits the openness of the *Zhuangzi*, while the Master on the River widens the focus of the *Daode jing*. They reinterpret the classics in accordance with the concerns and needs of their time but they never for a moment doubt the central authority of the classics or in any way leave them behind.

Religious Practice

A similar relationship to the classics continued as Taoism fully developed into an organized religion and as mystical practice became more specialized and linked more intimately with myth and cosmology. True to their different natures and outlooks, the two classics played different roles in the newly emerging Taoist schools and were applied in various ways. The *Daode jing* was recited as a sacred text among the early Celestial Masters (tianshi) and, in the fifth century, used in a visualization exercise that focused on Laozi as the central god of the universe. The *Zhuangzi*, at the same time, with its lyrical descriptions of ecstasy, served to inspire a group of poets and, through them, influenced the vision of Highest Clarity (Shangqing) Taoism in the late fourth century.

Recitation of important texts was a classical way of memorizing and venerating them, and, together with various Confucian classics, the *Daode jing* was actively recited as early as the second century B.C.E. The practice gained a religious dimension in the first organized Taoist school of the Celestial Masters, founded in 142 C.E. by Zhang Daoling in southwest China. They considered Laozi as a god who personified the Tao and read his text as a revealed scripture and magical document, using its recitation in the healing of diseases and in the attainment of immortality.[42]

Continued in this school, the recitation of the *Daode jing* in the fifth century stood at the center of a ritualized meditation that is spelled out in a preface to the text called *Daode zhenjing xujue* (Introductory explanations to the *Daode jing*). There a deified Laozi gives instructions on how to properly venerate his scripture, including preparatory purifications and the proper layout of the meditation chamber. Once in the chamber, adepts are to burn incense, straighten their robes, bow to the ten directions, and actively visualize Laozi and his two major assistants—Yin Xi (the Guardian of the Pass and the first recipient of the *Daode jing*) and the Master on the River—in their minds. Only when this is done, in the venerable presence of the divine personages, is the text to be opened. Its recitation must be further preceded by a formal prayer to the Tao, in which the adept sees himself "riding on a bright light and ascending into the purple sky, with the sun and the moon on his right and left."[43]

A full member of the celestials, the adept next places himself more firmly in the position of the Tao at the center of the universe. As the text notes:

> Finish this mental recitation, then clap your teeth and swallow the saliva thirty-six times each. Visualize the green dragon to your left, the white tiger to your right, the red bird in front of you, and the dark warrior in your back.
>
> Your feet stand between the eight trigrams, the divine turtle and the thirty-six masters bow to you. In front, you see the seventeen stars, while your five inner organs give forth the five energies and a network pattern streams across your body.
>
> On three sides you are joined by an attendant, each having a retinue of a thousand carriages and ten thousand horsemen. Eight thousand jade maidens and jade lads of heaven and earth stand guard for you.
>
> Then repeat the prayer, this time aloud, and begin to recite the "Scripture in Five Thousand Words." Conclude by three times grinding your teeth and swallowing the saliva.[44]

Clapping one's teeth and swallowing the saliva are part of the standard Taoist meditation ritual. They are symbolic forms of announcing and terminating one's communication with the heavenly deities. Once communication is established, the adept places himself in the center of the universe by seeing himself surrounded by the four mythical animals of the four directions and by placing his feet firmly on the eight trigrams of the *Yijing* (Book of Changes). Everyone bows to him, he is fully established among the stars, and his body has become a pure constellation of light and energy patterns. Then he sees himself supported by attendants who in turn, as in an imperial procession, are joined by thousands of followers and servants. Only when the celestial position of the meditator, at the very center of the cosmos, is firmly established can he recite the *Daode jing* in its truest environment and to its greatest effect.

This recitation of the *Daode jing* as part of an active visualization, and from a position of the center of the universe, is an act of mystical union with the Tao, now understood as a human-form deity in the center of the cosmos and no longer a formless underlying force or even the flux of pure existence. The recitation has an effect not only on the cosmic standing of the adept but on his eventual immortality, especially if practiced ten thousand times. Although a generic term for a very large number, ten thousand is mentioned frequently in instructional and hagiographic texts and in one incident turns out to be the decisive factor. Three members of the Zhou family, the father and two sons, were given proper recitation instructions and followed them to the letter. The father and elder brother succeeded in reciting the *Daode jing* ten thousand times and flew off as celestials. The younger brother, however, only reached 9,733 times and did not attain immortality.[45]

The *Zhuangzi*, though similarly inspirational to practicing mystics, went a different route and was favored by a different group of practitioners. In the Han dynasty, it lent its phrases to poems on ecstatic and wondrous journeys, as in the *Chuci* (Songs of the south) and the *Daren fu* (Rhapsody of the great man). Here we have, for example:

> Below, lofty openness—there was no more earth;
> Above, empty vastness—there was no more heaven.
> He looked, but his vision blurred—nothing to be seen,
> He listened, but his ears were numb—nothing to be heard.
> Striding on emptiness and nonbeing, he ascends even farther,
> Transcending all, he is without friends and alone survives.[46]

Following this, the text was amply used by poets of the third century, who had formed an escapist community called the "Seven Sages of the Bamboo Grove." Here, the ecstatic vision of the *Zhuangzi*, with its ideal of living in free and easy wandering away from society, and devotion only to the pleasures of personal perfection, together with the wondrous transcendence of the Great Man, became the doctrinal center of an apolitical and nihilistic group, seeking to free itself from the constraints of an ever more insecure and cruel world.[47] *Zhuangzi*'s delightful vision of a free life in the world was turned into an escapist refuge away from the world, where ordinary feelings and emotions had no more impact. Thus Ruan Ji (210–263), in his version of the "Great Man," says,

> Heat and cold don't harm me; nothing stirs me up.
> Sadness and worry have no hold on me; pure energy at rest.
> I float on mist, leap into heaven, pass through all with no restraint.[48]

The poet's descriptions of the otherworld, based on the *Zhuangzi's* ideas and spiced with visions of wondrous immortals and lovely jade maidens, remained an active part of upper-class education and made its way, in the fourth century, into the revelations of Highest Clarity Taoism. Like the poet faced with a frustrating political situation, southern aristocrats found consolation in news from the heaven of Highest Clarity that was presented to the medium Yang Xi in the 360s.[49] The revelations describe the geographical layout and administrative structure of the spirit world; they locate local ancestors among its denizens and spell out methods to reach it. Mystical practice in this form of Taoism, which was to become dominant in the following centuries, consisted of ecstatic excursions to the otherworld and the attainment of celestial rank by active practitioners. While it began as a psychological substitute for lacking honors in this world, it was greatly venerated later because of the subtlety of its vision and the high literary quality of its texts.

Taking from the *Zhuangzi* primarily the idea of ecstatic excursions, Highest Clarity Taoism abounds with its terminology, including, as Isabelle Robinet has shown, terms and phrases such as "perfect man," "Great Clarity," "Great One," "freedom from affairs," "fasting the mind," "making all things equal," and "sitting in oblivion."[50] However, Highest Clarity, as part of organized Taoism, also shares with the Celestial Masters the mythicization of the Tao and the emphasis on gods and immortals. Thus it continues, in its particular and more religious way, Guo Xiang's tendency to delineate the relationship between human beings and the Tao, to define the ways of the universe, with the Tao, or the Great One, as its underlying center and the various heavens and immortals as the most accessible expression of its purity.

Mystical union in this vision is found in the close contact with the gods of the otherworld, by transcending all by going beyond the "Heavenly Pass," a star in the Northern Dipper, and the establishment of a celestial record of immortality in the administration above. Thus, a typical Highest Clarity incantation runs:

> Oh, Yang Brightness of Mystery Pivot!
> Spirit Soul and Spirit of the Heavenly Pivot!
> Oh, Nine Lords of Highest Mystery!
> Merge and transform into one single spirit.
>
> Cut off my route to death at the Gate of Demons!
> Open my registers of life in the Southern Office!
> Let my seven souls be free from the three bad rebirths!
> Let me come to life again as an immortal!
> Let me traverse the sevenfold essence to reach mysterious darkness!
> Let me bodily go beyond all through the Heavenly Pass![51]

The ecstatic freedom of the *Zhuangzi* in the Chinese middle ages is thus mythologically expanded, and made technically available in specific methods of ritualized visualization. The basic ideal of soaring away from ordinary life in the purity of the Tao is still the same, but its thrust is more escapist; its expression, more poetic; and its vision, more mythologically and cosmologically detailed. Medieval Taoist mysticism is a fully developed religious practice that incorporates and honors, yet considerably changes, the ancient philosophical classics.

Buddhist Epistemology

In the Tang dynasty (618–906), both classics were reinterpreted yet again, under the influence of Buddhism. The *Daode jing* was reread and studied in a commentary school known as "Twofold Mystery" (Chongxuan), which outlined the path of mystical attainment by following the logic of Buddhist Mādhyamika. The *Zhuangzi*, similarly read by active practitioners, meanwhile became a source for the Taoist understanding of Buddhist *vipaśyanā* techniques of insight meditation, or "observation." In both cases, a more philosophical and less mythological approach again predominates, but both thinking and practice follow Buddhism and are accordingly centered on the mind and its perception.

"Twofold mystery" is an expression taken from the phrase "mysterious and again mysterious," in chapter 1 of the *Daode jing*. Cheng Xuanying, of the mid seventh century, a leading exponent of this school, explains it in his commentary:[52]

> Mysterious means deep and profound. It is also an expression for being without obstructions. The two minds of being and nonbeing, the two visions of outcome and subtlety, all spring from the one Tao. They arise together, but have different names, yet they are part of the one Tao.[53]

The underlying idea of "twofold mystery" is that the mind functions on the two levels of being and nonbeing, which have to be gradually overcome in favor of the realization of the pure Tao in a state of emptiness. This corresponds closely to the Mādhyamika theory of the "two truths," as formulated in Chinese by Jizang (549–623). According to this theory, one develops a perception of real truth by first overcoming the worldly understanding of the ordinary mind (being) in favor of seeing all as empty (nonbeing). In a second step, one moves on to the realization that even this acquired form of nonbeing perception is only a partial truth and overcomes it in favor of "both being and nonbeing, neither being nor nonbeing."[54]

In terms of mystical practice, the process envisioned by followers of Twofold Mystery is one of "twofold forgetfulness." First, one eliminates all ordinary mental states, the illusory visions of the mind normal people erroneously regard as real. Then one abolishes even the power that made one see through the illusion, here described as wisdom, or the nonbeing mind. Doing so, one transforms one's perception to encompass a multiplicity of views, which at the same time means an attitude of neither mind nor no-mind. This is called "reaching the Tao of middle oneness," a state of inner radiance that is fully realized by the sage. As Cheng Xuanying says, in explaining chapter 3 of the *Daode jing*, "The sage always causes people to be without knowledge and without desires."[55]

> On the outside, the sage has no mental states to desire; on the inside, he has no mind to do any desiring. Mind and mental states are both forgotten, thus the mind becomes no-mind. Where there were mental states and illusions before, there is now only the emptiness of the mind. Yet even though the mind is no-mind, it shines forth in numinous radiance.[56]

"Knowledge" and "desiring," the two inhibiting factors of human life mentioned in the original, indicate the basic intellectual and emotional sources of tension and division in human life. They are redefined as "mind and mental states," a Buddhist notion that divides human reactions into an underlying force—the mind, or the basic ongoing activity of consciousness; and its outside manifestation, the mental states or projections, which indicate the apparently concrete (but ultimately illusory) visions and impressions people have of the world. A more subtle psychology and a meditative awareness raise the words of the *Daode jing* to a more intricate level. Religious practice, by now a highly advanced and subtle art of the mind, then renders both knowledge and desires obsolete, leaving only a state of no-mind (the spontaneity of complete forgetfulness) and an emptiness in the freedom from all categorizations and mental projections.

The reading given to the *Daode jing* under such Buddhist influence both deepens the original and alienates it from its roots, placing a higher value on the foreign religion, and serving the needs of a new religious community that uses sophisticated mental exercises to cleanse the doors of perception relevant to the purity of the Tao. The old ideals of simplicity and tranquility have given way to a complex model of mental states and subtle differences in perception; new definitions of truth and wisdom have superseded the old harmony of Tao and world. For example, Li Rong, another of the seventh-century thinkers, has a detailed analysis of different kinds of knowledge, taking off from the *Daode jing* passage "He who knows others is wise; he who knows himself is enlightened."[57]

> Knowing goodness is to come closer to being a superior person; it is like acquiring the fragrance of an orchid. Knowing evil is to distance oneself from being an inferior person; it is like removing the stench of a fish shop. Knowing how to acquire and fulfill goodness, one will develop a sense of loyalty. Knowing how to reject and abandon evil, one will find feelings of repentance. This is enlightened knowledge.
>
> Now, in purity pursue the path of Twofold Mystery; in radiance follow the gate to empty serenity. Then, knowing others, you will realize that the myriad mental states are all empty. Knowing yourself, you embody the nonexistence of the entire self.
>
> If the entire self is nonexistence, how would one covet fate and profit within? If the myriad mental states are all empty, how would one be defiled by sounds and sights without? Thus we speak of enlightenment.[58]

Li Rong, much more subtly than the ancient classic, although employing the same terms, divides knowlege into three stages: knowing good and evil and applying this knowledge correctly; knowing the world outside and understanding that all conceptualizations are constructs without a reality of their own; and knowing oneself to be without a permanent identity, thus "embodying no-self," instead of being someone or something. Moreover, he distinguishes these three forms of knowledge terminologically as *knowledge*, *wisdom*, and *insight*. "Insight reflects emptiness, wisdom illuminates being," as he says in his commentary on another Taoist text, the *Xisheng jing* (Scripture of Western Ascension).[59]

Although more epistemological and more subtle in its analysis of the mind, the Buddhist-inspired reading of the *Daode jing* at this time is also much less political, although the accomplished sage is still expected to be a model for the world and have a beneficent influence on it. Turning away from self-interest, he is to serve the good of all; having attained utter serenity, he returns to society and takes up his duty, urging people toward salvation along the same meditational path. "A superior person, contented and composed, he teaches people to be proper."[60]

Joining Buddhism and Taoism

Both classics are not only linked with Mādhyamika logic in early Tang visions of knowledge, but also play an active role in the understanding of mystical practice and attainment. This is most clearly documented in the eighth-century treatise *Zuowang lun* (On sitting in oblivion, DZ 1036),[61] written by the patriarch Sima Chengzhen (647–735). This text, an outline of the path toward the Tao in seven stages, integrates Buddhist and Taoist practices and mystical visions into a coherent whole, citing and reinterpreting both classics in each of its sections.

Section 1, to begin with, deals with "Respect and Faith." It emphasizes that any mystical quest first requires that one develop a wish to undertake it, a wish that is fostered by words of wisdom and that is inspired by the reports of earlier mystics. The classics play this role of inspiration, their antiquity and fame encouraging faith in the possibility of mystical attainment. More specifically, the text adduces the *Daode jing* statement (chaps. 17, 23) that one must have faith in oneself in order to inspire others and get anywhere in life, thus grounding the quest in a personal attitude. In addition, the *Zuowang lun* describes the vision of mystical union in the words of the *Zhuangzi*, citing the classical passage on "sitting in oblivion" in conjunction with Guo Xiang's interpretation of it. Inspiring people to "cast off their form" and attain oneness with the Tao, the classics, in this introductory passage, furnish both the raison d'être of the mystical quest and a description of the basic attitude people need to undertake it.

Section 2, "Interception of Karma," states that the Tao cannot grow as long as one is still involved in the daily running of affairs. Thus, at least for a period, a withdrawal from social relations and worldly activities is necessary. This will support a fundamental condition of placidity and of detachment from desires, which in turn helps to intercept karmic activities and free the mind for the quest. Here, too, both classics are cited specifically, to give one the encouragement to leave the world—the *Daode jing* is cited with the words "cut off contacts, shut the doors, and to the end of life there will be peace without toil,"[62] and the *Zhuangzi*, with its admonishment, "do not be an embodier of fame, do not be a storehouse of schemes, do not be an undertaker of projects, do not be a proprietor of wisdom."[63] The passages are cited in their original meaning and not verbally reinterpreted, but their position in this context shows the adaptation of their words from a rather general, and even political, context to a highly organized religious setting. This at the same time radicalizes their message, leaving behind vague social admonitions in favor of clear-cut instructions to come to, and meditate in, a monastic environment.

Section 3 is entitled "Taming the Mind." It specifies actual meditation procedures, describing concentration exercises and their effect on the mind. As thoughts are controlled and limited to the matter at hand, the mind is emptied and becomes detached so as to finally reach a state of utter peace, when any sensory imput is "as if one had heard or seen nothing."[64] Still, the process is long and has its dangers. An uncontrolled mind will overgrow with defilements and increase karma; a too rigidly controlled mind of enforced emptiness will give rise to new tensions. A strict delimitation of the sacred life from the profane will result in new dichotomies, while much conceptualization, after little practice, gives rise to philosophy, a mere distraction from the path.

Especially the latter is illustrated with an example from the *Zhuangzi*, whose author variously quotes dialecticians and sophists (such as Huizi) and denies the use of their ideas for mystical attainment. Absurd statements, such as "a lamp does not shine" or "fire is not hot" are not in fact profound mysteries but only keep people from following the right practice and setting their minds in order.[65] It is much better to go with the simple, with the "doctrines that are very easy to understand and very easy to practice," with the "true words that are not beautiful," as the *Daode jing* notes (chaps. 70, 81). Both classics are here credited with access to an approach that is close to the reality of the Tao, thereby keeping things simple and unadorned, and criticizing the ornate language and mental gymnastics of fancy philosophers. The classics are adduced to emphasize that simplicity is of high value, despite the popular fancy for the complex and intricate.

In a different vein, the *Daode jing* in this section appears as the key to understanding mystical realization—the text cites chapter 16:

> All things flourish, but each returns to its root.
> Return to the root means tranquility,
> It is called recovering life.
> Recovering life is called the eternal,
> To know the eternal is called enlightenment.

The *Zuowang lun* interprets:

> Scrubbing away the defilements of the mind, opening up consciousness of the root of the spirit is what we call cultivation of the Tao. No more unsteady floating—but mystical harmony with the Tao. Resting quietly within the Tao is called returning to the root. Guarding the root and never leaving it is called tranquility and concentration.
>
> When these increase daily, diseases are dispersed and life is recovered. Continuous recovery leads to spontaneous knowledge of the eternal. "Knowledge" here means that nothing is left unclear; "eternal" means that nothing changes or perishes anymore. A break of the cycle of birth and death is truly found thus. Following the Tao and calming the mind therefore ultimately depend on freedom from attachment.[66]

This reinterprets the *Daode jing* by first placing the root of each being into the mind as the "root of the spirit," which is reached by opening up consciousness through the practice of concentration exercises. The recovery of this inner mental solidity, then, is fully reached in a state of meditative trance, described as tranquility (Taoist) and as concentration (Buddhist), and equating the terms of both religions. The integration is taken further by the outlining of a twofold result of the practice: the Taoist attainment of health and long life, and the Buddhist achievement of freedom from rebirth. "Eternal" in the original is consciously given the complex connotations of both immortality, as ascension into heaven; and nirvana, as the cessation of life and death. The same holds true for the last word of the passage, "enlightenment," which indicates both a clear intuition of the Tao and the realization of nirvana.

Section 4, entitled "Detachment from Affairs," focuses on the inner separation gained between oneself and one's life. Relying heavily on Guo Xiang's interpretation of the *Zhuangzi*, it emphasizes that "life has allotments" and "affairs have what is appropriate,"[67] encouraging people "not to labor over what life cannot do" (*Zhuangzi*, chap. 19) and to distance themselves increasingly from ordinary values of gain and fame.

Section 5, "True Observation," continues along the same lines, providing instructions for the budding mystic on how to view life from a cosmic perspective. Again, the *Zhuangzi* looms large, cited specifically with the following passage on the cause of poverty:

> Father? Mother? Heaven? Man? . . . I was pondering what is it that has brought me to this extremity but I couldn't find the answer. My father and mother surely wouldn't wish this poverty on me. Heaven covers all without partiality; earth bears up all without partiality—heaven and earth surely wouldn't single me out to make me poor. I try to discover who is doing it, but I can't get the answer. Still, here I am—at the very extreme. It must be fate.[68]

The *Zuowang lun* follows the exact same kind of reasoning, paraphrasing the ancient classic and reaching the same conclusion. It even cites the text but adds a dimension to its vision by including the notion of karma in its understanding of fate. This is done by adding the word for "karma" to the word for "fate" and thus reinterpreting the *Zhuangzi* term *ye*, meaning "effort" or "task," which, in medieval religious texts, has karmic connotations:

> Going back and forth, I cannot find anyone to blame for my poverty. Thus I cannot help realizing that it must be my own karma, my own fate before heaven. I produce my own karma, whereas heaven provides me with a fate for this life. . . . As the *Zhuangzi* says: "Karma/fate enters one and cannot be prevented from becoming one's own karma/fate."[69]

The basic problem of mental attitude toward fate is the same in both documents, the allegory of poverty is still the same, and even the words are still the same—and yet, the conceptual context has undergone a major shift. The key problem is no longer the unconditioned, accidental Tao-given property of inner nature and fate, but the karmically caused realities of this life, for which the individual is fully responsible, and which he can change through the right efforts. Accordingly, the mystical quest is more than a way to survive in a world of accidental realities; it is the cosmic search for cessation and immortality.[70]

Section 6, "Intense Concentration," describes the estatic trance state reached by total immersion in the Tao. Here again, Taoist and Buddhist visions are fused. The text cites the *Zhuangzi* to describe the trance as "the body like dried wood, the mind like dead ashes, there are no more impulses, no more searches" (chap. 2); and then goes on to define it in Buddhist terms as a "state of no-mind settled in deep absorption."[71] The *Zhuangzi* expression "tranquil wisdom," which is to be reached through the trance, is clearly translated as "concentrated insight," linking nonspecified ancient terms with highly technical Buddhist meditation procedures—concentration and insight being the *samatha-vipaśyanā* of Tiantai practice.

The tendency continues all the way to the highest realization, although here, in section 7 on "Realizing the Tao," the physical manifestation of Taoist immortality is valued higher than the mental attainment of Buddhist enlightenment. "The Tao of emptiness and nonbeing can be deep or shallow," the text says. "When it is deep, it reaches as far as mind and body. When it is shallow, it goes only as far as the mind."[72] The *Daode jing* is adduced to emphasize that the Tao is ultimately "invisible and inaudible," that the realized "spirit is like the valley," and that the perfected immortal will come to reside in the Tao itself.[73] The ultimate superiority of the Taoist path is reasserted; the vague descriptions of the Tao in the ancient classic are interpreted in the light of the celestial immortality that is to be attained through the practice. The perfected is at one with the Tao, lives forever, and penetrates all. An ecstatic freedom from all, first described in the *Zhuangzi*, is attained and manifests in a series of magical powers that go back both to immortals of old and to the supernatural abilities of the accomplished arhat. As the *Zuowang lun* says:

> Body unified with the Tao means that one will survive forever.
> Mind unified with the Tao means that one will pervade all dharmas.
> Ears unified with the Tao means that one will hear all sounds.
> Eyes unified with the Tao means that one will see all sights.[74]

The ultimate mystical realization is thus a mixture of the visions found in the *Daode jing* and in the *Zhuangzi* with the ideal of ecstatic immortality and Buddhist enlightenment. The ancient classics continue to be valued sources of authority and sacred images but their vision has been significantly transformed, reinterpreted through the lens of Buddhist theory and practice. The same words are used, yet understood with new connotations and in different dimensions, integrating ideas of karma, rebirth, and retribution; notions of insight, perception, and no-mind; practices of concetration, mental analysis, and trance-absorption. Both the *Daode jing* and the *Zhuangzi* have entered a new dimension of meaning and relevance for practicing Chinese mystics.

Conclusion

Over approximately 1,300 years of Chinese religious history (from 500 B.C.E. to 800 C.E.), the ancient classics *Daode jing* and *Zhuangzi* have stood at the center of Taoist mystical thinking. In their oldest surviving form, philosophical statements about the original purity and recovery of the Tao in the world and in the mind of the individual, they have undergone massive reinterpretation in every new phase of Chinese mysticism. In the early centuries of the Common Era, they were recast in a more political light and linked with physical longevity techniques; they were highly mythologized and were connected with formalized ritual worship in the fifth century, when the schools of religious Taoism organized themselves; and they were transformed yet again during the Tang dynasty, under the influence of Buddhist logic and meditation practice. Despite all these changes, the ancient classics have remained a central source of inspiration for practicing Taoist mystics and, in both words and meaning, have proved invaluable anchors for seekers throughout the ages.

NOTES

1. For a discussion of some major recent translations, see Michael LaFargue and Julian Pas, "On Translating the *Tao-te-ching*, in Livia Kohn and Michael LaFargue, eds., *Lao-tzu and the Tao-te-ching* (Albany, 1998), pp. 277–302.
2. Arthur Waley, *The Way and Its Power: A Study of the Tao Te Ching and Its Place in Chinese Thought* (London, 1934).

3. A. C. Graham, "The Origins of the Legend of Lao Tan," in A. C. Graham, ed., *Studies in Chinese Philosophy and Philosophical Literature*, pp. 111–124 (Albany, 1990).
4. For a detailed study, see Livia Kohn, *God of the Dao* (Ann Arbor, 1998).
5. Benjamin Schwartz, *The World of Thought in Ancient China* (Cambridge, Mass., 1985), p. 194.
6. Livia Kohn, *Early Chinese Mysticism: Philosophy and Soteriology in the Taoist Tradition* (Princeton, 1992), p. 45.
7. Yu-lan Fung and Derk Bodde, *A History of Chinese Philosophy*, 2 vols. (Princeton, 1952), vol. 1, p. 177.
8. Kohn, *Early Chinese Mysticism*, p. 49.
9. Fung and Bodde, *History of Chinese Philosophy*, vol. 1, p. 189.
10. A. C. Graham, "How Much of *Chuang-tzu* Did Chuang-tzu Write?" *Studies in Classical Chinese Thought, Journal of the American Academy of Religions Supplement*, 35 (1980): 459–501; Xiaogan Liu, *Classifying the Zhuangzi Chapters* (Ann Arbor, 1994).
11. Kohn, *Early Chinese Mysticism*, p. 57.
12. A. C. Graham, *Disputers of the Tao: Philosophical Argument in Ancient China* (La Salle, Ill., 1989), p. 186.
13. Xiaogan Liu, "*Wuwei* (Non-Action): From *Laozi* to *Huainanzi*," *Taoist Resources* 3.1 (1991): 46.
14. Kohn, *Early Chinese Mysticism*, p. 58.
15. Burton Watson, *The Complete Works of Chuang-tzu* (New York, 1968), p. 180.
16. Kohn, *Early Chinese Mysticism*, p. 53.
17. See Isabelle Robinet, *Les commentaires du Tao to king jusqu'au VIIe siècle*, Mémoirs de l'Institute des Hautes Etudes Chinoises, 5 (Paris, 1977).
18. Alan Chan, *Two Visions of the Way: A Study of the Wang Pi and the Ho-shang-kung Commentaries on the Laozi* (Albany, 1991), p. 91.
19. Texts in the Taoist canon (*Daozang* [DZ]) are cited according to the numbers in Kristofer Schipper, *Concordance du Tao Tsang: Titres des ouvrages* (Paris, 1975).
20. Eduard Erkes, *Ho-Shang-Kung's Commentary of Lao Tse* (Ascona, Switz., 1958).
21. Chan, *Two Visions of the Way*.
22. Ibid., p. 107.
23. Kusuyama Haruki, *Rōshi densetsu no kenkyū* (Tokyo, 1979).
24. Kohn, *Early Chinese Mysticism*, p. 65.
25. DZ 682. 3. 9a, trans. in Kohn, *Early Chinese Mysticism*, p. 66.
26. DZ 682.1.5a–b.
27. DZ 682.1.5b–6a.
28. Wing-tsit Chau, *A Source Book in Chinese Philosophy* (Princeton, 1963), p. 326.
29. See Livia Knaul, "Lost *Chuang-tzu* Passages," *Journal of Chinese Religions* 10 (1982): 53–79.
30. DZ 682.2.35b; Livia Knaul, "The Winged Life: Kuo Hsiang's Mystical Philosophy," *Journal of Chinese Studies* 2(1) (1985): 22.
31. Fung and Bodde, *History of Chinese Philosophy*, vol. 2, p. 225.
32. DZ 682.4.11a.
33. Kohn, *Early Chinese Mysticism*, p. 73.
34. DZ 682.3.1b-2a; trans. Kohn, *Early Chinese Mysticism*, pp. 73–74.
35. Knaul, "Winged Life," p. 26.
36. Chap. 6; Watson, *Complete Works*, p. 90.
37. DZ 682.8.39a.

38. DZ 682.6.16a.
39. Isabelle Robinet, "Kouo Siang ou le monde comme absulu," *T'oung Pao* 69 (1983): 87–112.
40. DZ 682.5.52a; trans. Kohn, *Early Chinese Mysticism*, p. 72.
41. Kohn, *Early Chinese Mysticism*, p. 172.
42. Masayoshi Kobayashi, "The Celestial Masters under the Eastern Jin and Liu-Song Dynasties," *Taoist Resources* 3.2 (1992): 31.
43. *Xujue*, part 5. The original version of this text was recovered from Dunhuang and appears under numbers S. 75 and P. 2370. For a full translation of the text, see Kohn, *Early Chinese Mysticism*, pp. 173–174.
44. *Xujue*, part 5; trans. in Kohn, *Early Chinese Mysticism*, p. 173.
45. This is based on the *Zhengao* (Declarations of the perfected; DZ 1016) from approximately the year 500 (DZ 682.5.6a; in Yoshioka Yoshitoyo, *Dōkyō to bukkyō, I* (Tokyo, 1959), p. 123.
46. "Daren fu," *Shiji* 117.3062; trans. Kohn, *Early Chinese Mysticism*, p. 99.
47. Etienne Balasz, "Entre revolt nihilistique et évasion mystique," *Asiatische Studien/Etudes Asiatiques* 1.2 (1948): 27–55.
48. Donald Holzman, *Poetry and Politics: The Life and Works of Juan Chi* (Cambridge, 1976), p. 202; Kohn, *Early Chinese Mysticism*, p. 103.
49. See Michel Strickmann, "The Mao-shan Revelations: Taoism and the Aristocracy," *T'oung Pao* 63 (1978): 1–63.
50. Isabelle Robinet, "*Chuang-tzu* et le Taoisme religieux," *Journal of Chinese Religions* 11 (1983): 63.
51. *Tianguan santu*, DZ 1366, 1b-2a; trans. Kohn, *Early Chinese Mysticism,* p. 259.
52. His text has survived as a manuscript in Dunhuang. It has been edited by Yan Lingfeng, *Jingzi congzhu* (Taipei, 1983) and studied by Robinet, *Les commentaires du Tao to king*.
53. Robinet, *Les commentaires du Tao to king*, p. 108; Kohn, *Early Chinese Mysticism*, p. 142.
54. Kohn, *Early Chinese Mysticism*, p. 143.
55. Chan, *Source Book*, p. 141.
56. Chap. 3; trans. Kohn, *Early Chinese Mysticism*, p. 142.
57. Chap. 33; trans. Chan, *Source Book*, p. 156.
58. Yan, *Jingzi congzhu*, p. 831.
59. *Xisheng jing* 9.1; trans. Livia Kohn, *Taoist Mystical Philosophy: The Scripture of Western Ascension* (Albany, 1991), p. 204.
60. *Xisheng jing* 7.1; trans. Kohn, *Taoist Mystical Philosophy*, p. 207.
61. Trans. Livia Kohn, *Seven Steps to the Tao: Sima Chengzhen's Zuowang lun*, Monumenta Serica Monograph, 20 (St. Augustin/Nettetal, 1987).
62. Chaps. 52 and 56; trans. Chan, *Source Book*, p. 164.
63. Chap. 7; trans. Watson, *Complete Works*, p. 97.
64. Kohn, *Seven Steps to the Tao*, p. 33.
65. Ibid., p. 93.
66. *Zuowang lun*, 3.a b; trans. Kohn, *Seven Steps to the Tao*, p. 88.
67. Kohn, *Seven Steps to the Tao*, p. 95.
68. *Zhuangzi*, chap. 6; trans. Watson, *Complete Works*, p. 91.
69. *Zuowang lun*, sec. 5; trans. Kohn, *Seven Steps to the Tao*, p. 100.
70. There is an equivalent change in the notion of the transformation of the personal body, or self-identity. The *Zuowang lun* cites the *Daode jing* to the effect that "if I had no

personal body, what vexations would I have?" (chap. 13); explains it through a passage in the *Zhuangzi*—"there is no true lord" among all the various parts of the body (chap. 2); then goes on to emphasize its impermanence and no-self quality in Buddhist terms. See Kohn, *Seven Steps to the Tao*, p. 102.

71. Kohn, *Seven Steps to the Tao*, p. 104.
72. Ibid., p. 108.
73. *Daode jing*, chap. 14, chap. 6, and chap. 23, respectively.
74. *Zuowang lun*, 7; trans. Kohn, *Seven Steps to the Tao*, p. 110.